The Limits of Hitler's Power

The Limits of Hitler's Power

EDWARD N. PETERSON

Princeton University Press

Princeton, New Jersey, 1969

L.C. Card: 69-18066
Standard Book Number: 691-05175-5

Printed in
the United States of America
by Princeton University Press,
Princeton, New Jersey

This book
has been composed
in 10 point Linotype
Times Roman

Contents

Abbreviations

PARTY ORGANIZATIONS

DAF: Deutsche Arbeits Front—national workers' organization

HJ: Hitler Jugend—Hitler Youth

SA: Sturm Abteilung—original party militia

SS: Schutzstaffel—bodyguard elite which became a police and army

KEY TO DOCUMENTATION

BA: Bundes Archiv, Koblenz, (nearly always the records of Lammers, R43II)

HA: Hauptarchiv, Berlin, (nearly always the records of Pfundtner, Rep. 320)

BSA: Bayerische Staats Archiv, Munich, usually Bavarian Interior Ministry records

GSA: Bayerische Geheim Staats Archiv, Munich

NSA: Nuremberg Stadt Archiv

ASA: Augsburg Stadt Archiv

IMT: International Military Tribunal, Trial of Major War Criminals

TWC: Trial of War Criminals in Nuremberg

SK: Spruchkammerakten (found either in home community or "Strafregister," Munich)

CGD: Captured German Documents, T=Series, R=Roll, F=Frame. National Archives, Washington

IZG: Institut fuer Zeitgeschichte, Munich

References to dates in notes only follow the German practice —day, month, year, e.g., 25.12.36

Organizational Chart

To assist the reader through the maze of state and party offices, the following double listing is offered, with the German titles and English equivalents:

THE DUAL ORGANIZATIONS

THE STATE	THE PARTY
	NSDAP—NS—"Nazi"
Reich—Nation	
Reichspraesident	*Der Fuehrer*—the leader
Reichskanzler—chancellor	
Reichskanzlei —chancellory	*Parteikanzlei*
Reichsminister	*Reichsleiter*—Reichsleader
Staatssekretaer—state secretary, top-ranking official, usually with political assignment	Staff officers
Ministerialdirektor — second-ranking official with nonpolitical function	
Ministerialrat—Ministerial councillor	

Land (plural *Laender*)—provinces or states

Reichsstatthalter—NS creation to represent the national interest and theoretically supreme regionally

THE STATE	THE PARTY
Minister President—comparable to a U.S. state governor	*Gauleiter* (pronounced as Gowlighter)
	Gau (if a small state)
Staatsminister	Staff officers
Staatssekretaer	
Ministerialdirektor	
Ministerialrat	

Organizational Chart

Regierungsbezirk—district

Regierungs Praesident—district president *Regierungs Direktor* *Regierungsrat*	*Gauleiter*—Gau (if state is large)

Kreis—County

Landrat (pronounced Lahndraht) plural: *Landraete* —the county executive	*Kreisleiter* (pronounced Kricelighter)

Stadt—city

Oberbuergermeister—mayor of large city	*Kreisleiter*
Buergermeister—second mayor of large city or first mayor of smaller city	*Ortsgruppenleiter*

Beamten—civil servants (pronounced Bay-ahm-ten)
Beamter—civil servant

An Acknowledgment

A TRUISM of scholarship is that behind every author stands an auxiliary army of persons who have been of vital assistance. Without a myriad of people who have been willing to help, the writing of this book, in particular, would have been impossible. It is equally obvious that despite the efforts of so many, the author's limitations have probably permitted errors of fact or interpretation to creep stealthily into the text.

The stimulation to such a study could be traced back to the doctoral supervision of the estimable Professor C. V. Easum, Wisconsin, more recently to Professor Harold Deutsch, Minnesota, and my eternally optimistic colleagues, Professors J. T. King and George Garlid, who also assumed departmental duties in my absence.

The many interviewed are noted in the bibliography; their willingness to give of time and memory was a constant source of enjoyment. Officials not mentioned as sources, but vital to the research, include: Dr. Fritz Baer, Leiter der Bayrischen Staatskanzlei in Munich, who with his kindness facilitated the trans-Atlantic leap into Bavaria. Professor Waldemar Besson (Konstanz) acted as the efficient liaison with the sometimes mysterious academic bureaucracy and was a constant support with his confidence. The awe-inspiring experts on Bavarian history include Professor Karl Bosl (Munich) and Professor Ernst Deuerlein (Dillingen). Equally inexhaustible are the superb experts on the National Socialist period, Dr. Martin Broszat, Institut fuer Zeitgeschichte, and Professor Hans Mommsen (Bochum).

The tireless and resourceful keepers of the records include: Dr. Hoch, Institut fuer Zeitgeschichte-Munich; Dr. Bernhard Zittel, Bayerisches Staatsarchiv-Munich; Dr. Weis, Bayerisches Geheimstaatsarchiv-Munich; Dr. Heinz Deininger, Stadtarchiv-Augsburg; Dr. Heyder, Schwaebisches Archiv-Neuburg; Dr. Werner Schultheiss, Stadtarchiv-Nuremberg;

Acknowledgment

Dr. Fritz Schnelboegl, Bayerisches-Staatsarchiv-Nuremberg; Fraeulein Truchsess, Registratur "S" der Amtsgerichts, Munich; Miss Lucille Petterson, Document Center-Berlin. Further acknowledgment is due to the staff of the Bundesarchiv-Coblenz and the Geheim Staatsarchiv-Berlin.

High on the list of those to whom a debt of gratitude is owed is the Alexander von Humboldt Foundation, Bad Godesberg, which was willing to help finance two trips of research and do so with the grace and generosity demonstrated by Professor Heinrich Pfeiffer. The Board of Regents, Wisconsin State Universities, offered further support for both trips.

Among those who were forced to make constant sacrifices of time and effort would be the secretarial paragon of efficiency and patience, Mrs. Annie Robbins. Mr. Roy Grisham, Jr., exemplified similar patience in making countless suggestions for improvement of style.

Those who suffer most are the members of the author's family, whose husband and father evolve into a typing monster snarling for peace and quiet. My wife, in particular, is the one without whom the book could not have been written, in part because of the constant intellectual stimulation and suggestion, more overtly by accepting the thousands of husbandly chores about the house for which an author cannot find the time.

Introduction

EVERY history book has a history. This began when an army private entered Germany in the early spring of 1945 and began to learn something of the German language and the German past. This encounter with cities and a dictatorship in rubble began a permanent fascination with the happenings of the "totalitarian state", with "the other kind" of political activity. From countless conversations with numberless Germans, some of whom after 1945 were quite able to make first-hand comparisons of two kinds of totalitarian systems, it became obvious that for all of the machine-like appearance of absolutist states, even these are multi-dimensional institutions created and operated by humans.

What some of these humans did to other humans was "inhuman", at least what we would hope to make unhuman-like behavior, the enormity of an Auschwitz, a crime so horrible as yet to be beyond comprehension. The mountainous black shadow of Auschwitz not only haunts man's view of himself—how can one agree with Anne Frank that man is basically good?—but it has obscured the workings of the totalitarian state which produced it.[1] One imagines that everywhere there were wolf-robots killing lamb-robots.

The mechanical-obedient killing and the mechanical-obedient dying is one source of the popular concept of the dictorial state as a kind of *1984*. Another is the picture of absolute obedience cultivated by the Nazis in their propaganda, particularly in "newsreel" films, which show apparently mindless humans screaming like machines "Heil Hitler", or "Sieg Heil". The image, therefore, is of everyone swearing loyalty

[1] The literature emphasizing the totalitarian aspects would include: Franz L. Neumann, *Behemoth: The Structure and Practice of National Socialism*, New York, 1944; Hannah Arendt, *The Origins of Totalitarianism*, Cleveland, 1958; Carl J. Friedrich and Zbigniew K. Brzesinski, *Totalitarian Dictatorship and Autocracy*, Cambridge, Mass., 1956; Jacob L. Talmon, *The Origins of Totalitarian Democracy*, London, 1952.

to obey the Leader until death, if not beyond. One easily assumes that this was the reality, forgetting perhaps that these mass demonstrations were staged with precisely that end in view: to convince the world, foreign and domestic, that indeed everyone did obey, even when "off camera". As Hitler said, the bigger the lie and the more often it was told, the more it was believed; thus perhaps the concept of the people obeying the state obeying the party obeying the Fuehrer, forever and ever, has come to be believed.

The picture is encouraged by intellectual laziness, a preference for the simple myth to the complex truth. One prefers the world blocked off into neat patterns: this was democracy and that was a dictatorship; this was politics and that was a machine; we were free and they were slaves; we did things humanly and they did things robot-like. The myth is a mechanism of self-defense; if one considered that *their* behavior *there* was in any way related to *our* behavior *here*, one would have to look for Hitler in ourselves".

Histories of Nazi Germany, like those of other dictators, past and present, concentrate on the areas of open conflict such as foreign policy, which is fascinating, important, and documented, or they emphasize the public record of words said and written, self-documentation, assuming that "W"= "A", that Words equal Action, that what people say is what they do. Words are much easier to study than what the words lead to, if anything. Therefore, history presents a more solid documentation of what people said than what they did—except when they killed.

Studies of what really transpire within the governing process of an "absolutism" are rare.[2] Hans Rosenberg's brilliant study of Prussian bureaucracy, aristocracy, and autocracy is an example of probing beneath the external reality, part of a recent reexamination of our assumptions about kings. Merle Fainsod's remarkable study of Soviet Smolensk stands nearly alone, an exception made possible by the chance capture by

[2] For the best recent discussion of the theory of Fascism see Wolfgang Sauer, "National Socialism: Totalitarianism or Fascism," *AHR*, December 1967, 404-24.

the German army of local Soviet documents, the kind that dictators usually destroy so that their true history can never be written.[3]

How can a historian hope to study a system which permits no evidence of the behind-the-scenes struggle being documented to scientific satisfaction, in which the political reality is observed like a dog-fight under a blanket? No one is allowed to speak or write what is not welcome to the state. With evidence systematically withheld or distorted, it may be that histories of totalitarian states must compromise between the half-truths told by its defenders within, who know better, and the half-truths told by enemies without, who can only guess when those within are lying.

Ah, but there is hope! Perhaps, just perhaps, the enormity of Hitler's defeat and the resulting capture, not only of his country but much of his documentary evidence, may make the difference. Among these heaps of liberated documents may lie enough of the truth to make a relatively scientific judgment. The victors displayed some of the documentation at war crimes trials such as Nuremberg, but much more was recovered and has been opened to the scholar by the Washington and Bonn governments. As the emphasis on guilt recedes just a bit, one can approach truth less as a lawyer and more as a scientist, not so much to prove who did what wrong, but rather to find out who did what and why and how.

What motivated this study was, therefore, the curiosity about how dictators—in this case Hitler—actually functioned, whether the power structure was as simple as it seemed, whether its supposed efficiency of operation makes it even in that quality preferable to the quarrelsome democratic process, or whether, as so many remembrances have implied, that the Hitler regime operated with much more chaos than control, with as much conflict as obedience. It poses the question, whether Hitler's Reich operated secretly on similar bases

[3] More recent and empirical literature implying a less "totalitarian" state would include William S. Allen, *The Nazi Seizure of Power,* Chicago, 1965; Alan Milward, *The German Economy at War*, London, 1965; and Arthur Schweitzer, *Big Business in the Third Reich,* Bloomington, 1964.

of force and counterforce, conflict, and compromise as in the more public power struggle in democratic societies, i.e., that *the political process is similar.* This assumption is based on the hypothesis that humans behave much more similarly than our dichotomies imply, however the form of their reaction is warped by the structures of contrasting systems; in short, *the human reaction is similar.*

The basic question here asked is to what extent was the will of Hitler actually implemented within Germany, to what extent did he need but command and it was done? Obviously some of his wishes were implemented; German troops crossed frontiers and won battles, although they did not win the war as commanded, and they did not burn Paris. Obviously Hitler commanded millions of Jews to be killed; most of them were, but others outlived him. Hitler ordered a total war with a total mobilization and never got it. If anything, he got less of a mobilization than his democratic counterparts in England and America. Some things he said he wanted, like the end of Christianity in Germany, he never really tried to implement. Why?

The basic assumption to be tested is that Hitler's power was not complete but limited in some way by most of the people with whom he had to deal directly or indirectly, that the human reaction was much too complicated to classify as either belief or disbelief, obedient or disobedient, support or resistance. A second assumption is that Hitler was partially aware of some of the limitations on his power, at least until Allied success in the war, and therefore did not attempt certain actions, that some of his decisions reflected his lack of confidence in the obedience of his followers.

Question one: To what extent was Hitler's total power limited by Hitler himself, in the sense that he did not know what he wanted, could not decide between contradictory desires, or did not know what he could do and feared to try? His contemporaries came to assume a master planner who, while watching the Berchtesgaden dawn or sunset, planned everything step by step, such as taking advantage of ordinary mortals like Chamberlain. This is the picture Goebbels sold of his "man of destiny" and the one Hitler's enemies have largely bought; an exception is A.J.P. Taylor's Hitler stumbling into a war he had not expected. This question increased in importance as this book progressed.

Question two: To what extent did the party divert rather than implement the will of the Fuehrer? This question became more significant as it was discovered that the party member was by no means satisfied with the status quo and was in the best position by virtue of Hitler's trust in him to implement a personal policy in Hitler's name. Diversion within the party could have occurred at any of the three major levels of its organization: (1) the central party organization, led first by Hess, himself a symbol in 1941 of total flight and disobedience; his successor Bormann is frequently described as the evil spirit who took Hitler prisoner in the last years and totally corrupted him; (2) the regional party princes, the *Gauleiter,* given the power to represent Hitler in their conquered provinces; and (3) the lowest level of the *Kreisleiter*, or *Ortsgruppenleiter*, who had to deal with the people face to face, to persuade or coerce their neighbors. Policy diversion could have come as well from any of the myriad of "party" organizations, the most famous of which was Himmler's SS, operating independently of the party and perhaps even of Hitler's will.

Question three: To what extent did the state organization, the masses of civil servants (*Beamten*), become faithful servants of Hitler and/or his party. Hitler boasted that the party commanded the state, but how could his ragtag mob of street fighters deal with an experienced and intricate apparatus of their intellectual "betters"? Policy diversion could, in theory, occur in the central government, whose Beamten enjoyed the greatest anonymity. It could occur at the intermediate level of the provinces, Laender, accustomed to resist Berlin's will; they survived Hitler's Reich, despite their prematurely reported death in 1934. At the bottom-of-the-state-heap, and forced to deal with the bottom-of-the-party-heap and with the people, were the local officials, the mayors of the towns. Did the mayors truly implement orders, truly passed on to them through the other levels, or did they try to play the role of group defender or exploiter?

In short and regarding all three of the above questions, what was *the policy diversion*, the alteration of policy from within the power structure?

What is implied in policy diversion is a different kind of "Resistance" to that commonly described, a more typically human resistance to power. History reports only the stereotype revolution against a stereotyped absolutism; it calls for a courageous band of men to overthrow the state by revolution or assassination and thereby to change policy. This was The Resistance of brave men such as Mayor Goerdeler, who first tried to divert policy as a "loyal" Beamter, and Colonel Stauffenberg, at first a loyal military Beamter. It was the kind of resistance, rebellion, which the Western world glorifies in the French or American revolutions, and which seemed to recur in 1917 and 1918. This resistance is unthinkable in a modern state which has been identified with nationalism, which has not been defeated in war and which has any wits about it. The monopoly of secret police terror and mass media propaganda give the modern state such overwhelming power one should not wonder that the German resistance did not do more; the real wonder is that it did so much. Against what other modern dictatorial state did so many idealists sacrifice their lives and patriotism in so desperate a romantic venture?

This basic truth emerged with their catastrophic failure: without working from within the state, notably within the army, there is little hope of successful resistance or power. Those who thus share power can conspire for a rapid and bloody change; but such plotting is highly dangerous, as the German resistors knew. Since this risk is not a real choice for most people, not for the modern middle class of an industrial society, the real alternatives are: (a) flight from your country, to become a wanderer in a strange land and without power; (b) flight into your private world, to tend flowers in a garden or private ideas in a study; (c) waiting until an outside force blows up your country, and possibly you along with it, to liberate you; (d) working from within the power structure to achieve a gradual policy change, to slow down disaster by dragging your feet; (e) just doing what you are told.

In theory, therefore, persons within the power structure had the option to attempt to effect a change in personnel or policy and thus to divert social action into channels they preferred. Such diversion was achieved, and possibly planned, by "revisionists" in Russia, by Khrushchev and his successors, but it required a fearful obeisance, a fearful bloodletting, and a fearful 25 years. These revisionists chose the political alternative open to ambitious men in a one-party state, but one which exists only to men who are ostensibly loyal. They share power in proportion to their loyalty, and must pretend and lie to a major or minor extent. They must cooperate or collaborate either in the absence or sacrifice of principle. Unless they succeed in effecting the policy change, one can never know what they really wanted, whether they were lying to the dictator, or should he be defeated, as in Germany, whether they later lie to the victors. The post-1945 suspicion of "collaborators" with fascists, such as Pétain, is the inevitable fate of persons who have to lie either before or after. There is the further doubt whether they did more harm than good by collaborating. No one knows, either before or after.

The assumption during my research was that most men will resist power to some extent and for many varied reasons. Human reaction is complex, rarely a full support or full rejection of any group action; it is rather a wavering between support and rejection, an acceptance of one part, a rejection of another. This reaction to a complex and changing reality is the result of a complex and changing human motivation. Whether a person is largely "pro" or "anti," his action, contrary to the prevailing public pattern, is inhibited by an *insecurity of knowledge*, by a *fear* of punishment often no worse than a diminished respect from his peers, and also by a *hope* that things will get better of themselves, without his risking his place in society, not to mention his life.

I assumed the following possible causes of "loyal disobedience" as counter forces to the great pressures for conformity:

A. Reasons of Idealism

1. *Democratic*: Americans would like to believe that modern man is by nature democratic, with an inalienable wish, when properly informed, to be "free" and to share in government. Nazism made no secret of the fact that it hated democracy, although it said almost as loudly that it expressed the true voice of the people, *Volk*. The formal creed was "the *Fuehrer* principle," that one should command and obey. Would not some men who loved liberty disobey?

2. *Socialism*: Socialists ostensibly controlled Germany during 1918-19; for 15 years it garnered millions of votes and made many true believers. Although Hitler's party, albeit a National "Socialist" party, feared the Marxian socialists, or communists, the most, because they had been willing to fight. With victory in 1933 the party's socialism was ignored. Would not the poor want justice?

3. *Conservatism*: Those who had a liking for "the good old days" (before 1914) were a most significant group of the middle class and aristocracy, representing most of the non-NS middle class and peasantry. They were dissatisfied with the Weimar Republic, and hoped in 1933 for something different. They got something radically different. Would not conservatives resist radicalism?

4. *Christian belief*: Hitler appealed to the Christian to join in a crusade against "red atheists" and the Jews. Many did. Most sooner or later recognized that Hitler's claim to loyalty asserted a priority over their loyalty to Christ and/or the Pope. They had to choose. Would not some choose Christ?

5. *Legalism*: Whatever their belief about the form of government many Germans, particularly those within the state, believed in the rule of law. Many came to see in NS emotion-

alism a threat to legal reason. Would reason not resist emotion?

6. *Humanitarianism*: The man of patriotic duty and loyalty can be a man of other human feelings; even a loyal NS might have some sympathy for the suffering of others, even Jews. How quick and complete was the dehumanization? Would not some choose to remain human?

B. Reasons of Egoism

In this diffusion of ideals, existing in and out of the power structure, one should expect some policy diversion, but motivation is much more complex. People are also selfish. The National Socialist appeal was for the individual to put "the common good above personal good". Many obviously did, at least long enough to die for "the common good". The great majority saved themselves, although Hitler wanted Germany to die if he died. And selfishness survived.

1. *Personal economic gain*: In NS theory everyone was to live Spartan-like lives of sacrifice, as Hitler publicly did and Goering publicly did not. The human drive for personal profit is one the NS should have encountered everywhere. Who got what for himself?

2. *Personal power*: Everyone was supposed to obey, but some must also command, albeit "in obedience" to Hitler. Many humans enjoy power. One would expect policy diversion from the hope of the ambitious for power, though described, of course, as "the power to effect Hitler's will". Who had power?

3. *Group egoism*: Nearly everyone identifies with some group, or groups, and identifies his well-being or the national well-being with that group, as in "What is good for General Motors is good for the country". One would expect loyal ties to family, to a business, or to a local unit of government such as a village, city, or province. One would expect that simply living and associating with a family, business, or any local group would corrupt the loyal Reich subject to think first of something like "General Motors" or his children. Which loyalty came first?

4. *Bureaucratic egoism*: The civil servants themselves constituted a special group with long-standing special interest of personal gain or power. These were asked to subordinate themselves and interests, not only to their bureaucratic chiefs, but to the alien NS who were installed as their political commissars. Can a dictator force the bureaucrat to change?

5. *Miscellaneous humanness*: Should we ignore laziness and sheer "cussedness", there remains human envy, human hatreds and human loves, sublime and petty; these would seem inevitably to be a part of any association, no matter how heavy the patriotic indoctrination. Will not humanness survive? It is human to hope so.

The study of a totalitarian state poses certain, possibly insoluble, problems. The 19th-century Rankean method of finding the documents and validating and interpreting them has its 20th-century limitations. Assuming that the necessary documents were not falsified or destroyed by the NS, the question of their validity is difficult, because telling the truth, even privately, might have meant a death sentence. Therefore, everyone would document his loyalty and avoid a documentation of any disloyalty. Anyone diverting policy would have to record it as an implementation of policy. Contemporary documents alone will not suffice.

Twentieth-century quantitative methodology is of limited value. For one thing, private behavior is scarcely subject to statistical analysis. The useful social science device is the interview—"oral history", asking people what the documents mean. But who can be believed when accused of complicity in genocide? Just as one must publicly swear to complete loyalty up to 1945, it became after 1945 obligatory publicly to swear to some past disloyalty. (Cynics have wondered how the NS accomplished anything at all, if everyone were as opposed in 1939 as they asserted in 1945.) Not only is there a heavy pressure to falsify, but the weakness of the interview technique is the impermanence of the material: people forget and people die. What is not asked soon may never be known again. The best solution appears to be the combination of a maximum number of documents and interviews, and therefrom to painstakingly winnow the truth.

An advantage to the solitary historian is the special kind of available historical research involving both techniques—the postwar trials of the major war criminals in 1946 at Nuremberg, and from 1946 to the present of the more ordinary war criminals. Widely researched, the trials presented massively documented prosecutions to the defendants for rebuttal. Although trials have an incomplete historical purpose, they provided the kind of police detective and clerical assistance for massive documentation historians usually lack.

For purposes of local history, one has the records of the special kind of local trials, "the denazification trials", their records preserved in millions of *Spruchkammerakten.* In all communities in the American sector hundreds of thousands of persons who had been "loyal" enough to join the NS party were asked to prove that they had been actively or passively disloyal to Hitler. Millions more were asked to testify for or against the accused, that is, to recall millions of incidents which indicated that the hundreds of thousands of accused had not been really loyal. These affidavits, called "*Persilscheine*" or soap certificates, make up a unique effort to reconstitute the pasts of vast numbers of people, including nearly everyone of political influence, who survived the war and postwar imprisonment. There exists, therefore, an impressive documentation of "disobedience" in a period when governmental policy was so radical that "normal" men would have had to disobey.

The result of such evidence, of that of the major trials, of minor trials, of interviews, and of the surviving official correspondence, has resulted in a four-dimensional puzzle with many pieces missing but with an apparent pattern. To demonstrate some of this dimensional complexity of the power structure, this book describes a "chain of command" from top to bottom, from the Fuehrer to the Reich, to the Land, to the district, to the city and village. It attempts to describe the struggle in each layer of government, and between the layers, involving diversion and passive resistance.

Largely because of the availability of documents, relatively untouched by war, the Land of Bavaria was selected. It was further assumed that Bavaria would demonstrate, as it had before 1933 and after 1945, the greatest inclination to resist Berlin. What happened in Bavaria may not be typical, but this is precisely the point—the reaction of one group to dictatorial government need not be the reaction of another group.

As a subdivision or district in Bavaria, the first choice was of the relatively small and remote district of Schwaben (Swabia) because the preliminary evidence from microfilm indicated that it was not typical in its moderation. In contrast to the relatively quiet Schwaben, I chose the neighboring, noisy, "more typical", Franken (Franconia), whose Streicher was the Gauleiter tried at Nuremberg as a major war criminal. As major cities, Augsburg and Nuremberg were chosen as the only possibilities in these districts.

For the small towns, as a different kind of case study, there were many choices that could have been made. Friedberg was selected for Schwaben because references to it were common in the microfilm first consulted. The results were surprising. The original choice of Eichstaett was made on the basis of information that this small town had had the most radical leadership in Franken, ergo it would provide a greater contrast to Schwaben. What was discovered was astounding.

Local documentation scarcely existed for the villages, so that the villages described depend largely on the chance discovery of informative and reliable witnesses; as documentation, an overall impression was supported by government reports in Munich on the peasants in general.

I had hoped the selection of various types of communities would permit comparison and contrast, so that I could discover the variety of impact of the central command, the environment, and the personalities. Variety could then support and give spice to the thesis.

Despite the 20-year concern with the problem and the frantic scurrying about Bavaria and Germany to find evidence and despite the sincere effort to be objective and to understand an alien world, there remains the fear that my anti-Nazi bias is too strong. It may be that one must wait a hundred years to be fairly objective about a system so monstrous in its climactic horror. Yet some of the living evidence is disappearing, never to return, and we dare not wait a hundred years to understand the workings of dictatorship.

A further problem exists in dealing with such material, some of which is utterly revolting and stupid by any rational standards. This book cannot leave the implication that Hitler's state, with its banality, pettiness, and absurdity, with the described majority of people leading "normal" lives, did not kill millions of people for "reason" of war hysteria and racial madness. Despite the efforts of most of these humans to find normal pleasures in normal pursuits, a war-born illness pervaded the society. For some, love of country changed by imperceptible stages into an insane hatred of "the enemy".

One cannot stamp on each page "yes, but these normal people killed millions of Jews". This description of the semi-normal world they actually experienced should remind the reader that there is only a thin line between group sanity and group insanity, between self-defense and murder. It is but the other side of the coin; this is the side most Germans experienced, the side human enough to idealize or tolerate. The closeness of the human comedy to the human tragedy is something that a few Germans were able to learn along with defeat. Perhaps history will teach some men this fact before it experiences again the ruin of modern war.

E.N.P.

July 1969

The Limits of Hitler's Power

1 THE REICH GOVERNMENT

THE natural tendency of historians has been to shine their flashlights of knowledge at the figure of the "leader", perforce ignoring the vast gray world of the "followers". In this book I have, therefore, deliberately aimed my tiny light as much at the bottom as at the top of the power pyramid. Competent Hitlerologists exist to analyze and psychoanalyze the "great man" or the "demon".[1] My primary purpose here is not to study the person of Hitler, but rather the governmental structure of which he was the head. What follows, then, is but a simple sketch of Hitler's role as administrator.

Also fragmentary and tentative in this chapter is my subsequent analysis of his top administrators, leaders of the party and the state. Relatively little research is available on more than two or three, yet each of the ministries, so briefly mentioned here could well receive book-length scholarly treatment, like Schweitzer's[2] or Milward's[3] assimilation of the mountains of Economics Ministry documents. The purpose of this sketch is to begin to put these august ministers into some perspective by indicating: (1) their power-ful relationship to Hitler and to their colleagues; (2) their struggles with other leaders of party and state; and (3) their personality conflict and confusion, which helps explain the conflict and confusion at the lower levels of power. Like the proverbial blind men's analysis of an elephant, historical analysis reflects the vantage point of the observer; hopefully it fits each

[1] The most impressive study thus far is Alan Bullock's *Hitler, A Study in Tyranny*, rev. ed., New York, 1962, but the interpretation is being constantly refined by such studies as R.G.L. Waite, ed., *Hitler and Nazi Germany*, New York, 1965.

[2] Arthur Schweitzer, *Big Business in the Third Reich*, Bloomington, Ind., 1964.

[3] Alan Milward, *The German Economy at War*, London, 1965. John Conway has recently published such a documentary analysis of the "church ministry."

report here together into a meaningful mosaic. What follows is a worm's eye view, how it seemed to someone looking up the ladder of administration.

Hitler as Administrator

The first thing to note is how little Hitler was seen. The most startling thing was the relative absence of the dictator in his government. Although there were no apparent barriers to his playing an active role in internal affairs, it is remarkable how seldom he visited any geographical area or appeared as a participant in any administrative area. To be sure, the ultimate appeal of any power-player was to say, "I'll take the matter to the Fuehrer," and this, if done, either settled the argument on the surface or shifted its terrain. But to be able to say that Hitler initiated this change or effected that reform is a rarity.

Usually Hitler appears to have delayed change. He was a remote umpire, handing down decisions from on high when his underlings could not agree, or, almost as frequently, not giving a decision, but delaying it until a more propitious occasion, which rarely came. Joseph Nyomarkay has noted that Hitler's reluctance to make decisions was widely recognized by his subordinates: " 'Hitler hesitates to make a decision no matter how small", writes Otto Strasser (1948, p. 70); 'In my conflict with Esser and Company, Hitler avoided any decision', writes Rosenberg (1955, p. 327). SA leader Stennes complained at the time of the SA crisis in 1930 that Hitler would not make any decision for weeks; 'he always shirked making a decision' (Drage, 1958, p. 73). Goebbels' diary illustrates the exasperation of his co-workers with his indecisiveness".[4] Nyomarkay thought this added to Hitler's power and might well have been deliberate. However, it might have been genuine, a real unwillingness to make the effort for a decision.

Alan Bullock wrote of Hitler that he "hated systematic work, hated to submit to any discipline, even self-imposed.

[4] Nyomarkay, *Charismas and Factionalism in the Nazi Party*, Minneapolis, 1967, 42.

Administration bored him and he habitually left as much as he could to others, an important fact in explaining the power of men like Hess and Martin Bormann, who relieved him of much of his paperwork."[5] Hitler's self-image was that he was an artist. Others see him as a "Bohemian." This is the theme of Helmut Heiber, who regards the early Hitler as a lazy middle class son, who sponged off his family and avoided work at all cost. He finds the same Hitler in the Reich Chancellory. The personality of the cafe-Bohemian was now behind the facade of Prussian discipline and duty.[6] Or perhaps Hermann Rauschning was right in his description of Hitler the Bohemian—a man incapable of working steadily, but who could spend whole days lazing and dozing; "Hitler seems a man of tremendous will power, but the appearance is deceptive; he is languid and apathetic by nature, and needs the stimulus of nervous excitement to rouse him out of chronic lethargy to a spasmodic activity".[7]

Only in the beginning when Hindenburg was close enough to observe and when the work was new and interesting, did Hitler get to his desk at 10 a.m. But the long-despised office work and routine soon bored him.[8] He would appear from his bedroom around noon to receive the adulation of visitors and to spend the afternoon in talk with those inferiors he felt like talking with over food and drink, a life like his previous life in the cafes of Vienna and Munich. He came alive only in the evening, staying up until early morning with a congenial, adoring group, usually occupied with his monologue on whatever interested him.

Hitler's official business was done quickly, Heiber reports, while sitting or walking, whenever he could be cornered. The government, such as it was, operated with the Fuehrer and a cloud of favorities about him, noting every word and making of a spontaneous remark one of his "unalterable decisions": "Whoever wanted something from Hitler, had to

[5] Bullock, 386.
[6] Heiber, *Adolf Hitler*, Berlin, 1960, 92f.
[7] Rauschning, *The Voice of Destruction*, New York, 1940, 216.
[8] Heiber, 92.

cool his heels often for weeks and stand around in his antechamber in order finally, as his own foreign minister complained, to get to talk to him for two minutes alone."[9] For this reason there was what critics called "the rule by private secretaries".

The apparatus was further crippled because Hitler spent so little time in Berlin. "A hectic inner restlessness forced him to change his location constantly."[10] Moving back and forth from Berlin to Munich and Berchtesgaden, he was everywhere and nowhere. Robert O'Neill reported the similar conclusion of the military administrators that Hitler's hours were chaotic and that he was usually gone on weekends.[11] Yet his laziness had an advantage (for others); he was bored by paper work, which meant he usually signed papers on administrative and personnel matters without reading them. Heiber concluded that the system worked as well as it did by virtue of the force of gravity of the bureaucracy, and by Hitler's intuitive feeling for practicable paths, what Economics Minister Schacht called a genius of ingenuity (*Genie der Findigkeit*).

Rauschning agreed with Hitler's February 1934 description of himself: "I am no dictator, and never will be a dictator."[12] Hitler regarded himself as the leader of The Party with whose judgment he must remain in agreement. "There is no such thing as unlimited power, and I should never dream of pretending it to myself. The word dictatorship is misleading; there is no such thing as dictatorship in the accepted sense. . . ."[13] Any autocrat, Hitler said, would have to correct his will by existing conditions. His own greatest problem was never to find himself in opposition to the party. "The party is an incorruptible judge." He must either implement its will or change it. Hitler answered to a Rauschning proposal, "You want to operate in a vacuum, instead of reaching some agree-

[9] *Ibid.*, 93.

[10] *Ibid.*

[11] O'Neill, *The German Army and the Nazi Party*, London, 1966, 14f.

[12] Rauschning, 198.

[13] *Ibid.*

ment between the opposing forces—forces without which there can be no life" (a very perceptive remark).

David Schoenbaum has noted the two revisions Hitler was attempting—to counter Versailles and industrialism's threat to the cherished 19th-century world of small business, small farmers, and small-towners. To destroy Versailles he needed industry: "The result was an inevitable rapprochement, at first with the industrialists, the generals, the diplomats, and the civil servants, whom the Nazi movement was expected to destroy; not, as should be obvious, because they were admired, but because they were necessary. Then came the inevitable rapprochement with labor, without which there is no industrial society, a rapprochement born of industrial recovery and full employment and sustained with both concessions and ideology."[14]

Rauschning thought Hitler timid and sensitive, able only after long preparation to put up a bold front.[15] He always marched with "the big battalions," always choosing the weaker side for an opponent.[16] "One thing, especially, Hitler never did—he never ran counter to the opinion of his Gauleiter, his district commissioners. Each of these men was in his power, but together they held him in theirs. . . . The secret of his leadership lay in knowing in advance what course the majority of his Gauleiter would decide on, and in being the first to declare for that course. . . . They resisted with robust unanimity every attempt to set limits to their rights of sovereignty. Hitler was at all times dependent on them—and not on them alone."[17] If Rauschning is correct, Hitler found himself pushed by these forces which kept him to the fore; "the result was that his policy continually developed along wholly different lines to those which he had envisaged. He maintained his position of supremacy, but he lost his freedom of decision."[18] Rauschning is probably describing the early Hitler, but some of this clearly continued. In generalizing about Hitler one should remember that the Hitler Rauschning saw in 1934 is

[14] Schoenbaum, *Hitler's Social Revolution*, New York, 1967, 276.
[15] Rauschning, 260.
[16] *Ibid.*, 216-17. [17] *Ibid.*, 217. [18] *Ibid.*

not the same Hitler 10 years later. Yet Ernst von Weizsaecker, who knew Hitler at the end, noted: "Dictators are often more sensitive to public opinion than monarchs or the presidents of republics."[19]

Hitler enjoyed, or tolerated, the anarchy. His one firm principle was that the anarchy be kept secret, that the public image be one of universal agreement and calm, an image so deadening to his newspapers and so untrue to the reality of the power struggle constantly going on.

That the "leader" so often did not lead could be interpreted as a lack of ability. At least in 1933 many of his social betters assumed that the "Bohemian Corporal," the low class or outcaste foreigner, could not possibly compete with the traditional upper class holders of power. This fatal underestimation of a man from the masses, a snobbish blunder of incalculable proportions, swung like a pendulum to a fatal overestimation of Hitler, the indestructible world conquerer.

Although postmortems on Hitler have emphasized his mental instability which became gradually a mania, few have regarded him as intellectually incapable of leading the state. One might regard his success as not so much evidence of his abnormal powers as evidence that those who lead governments are not nearly so superhuman as the man in the street assumes. It may have been not so much his strength as the relative weakness of his opposition, a power vacuum, which gave him "power"; perhaps he slipped into "greatness" by the default of "the establishment," weighed in the balance and found wanting. (That power vacuum was maintained by the secret police.)

The ability of Hitler was most evident in his getting people to believe in him, a power based largely on his ecstatic belief in himself, on his conviction that his mission was to save Germany. To the great majority of the German people, naturally and rationally unsure of their own judgment, it was intoxicating to have someone willing to assume the burden of responsibility, someone confident of the success they doubted. In his speeches, which seem endless, simple, and repetitive,

[19] Weizsaecker, *Memoirs*, Chicago, 1951, 136.

he conveyed to millions a self-assurance that was hypnotic. In the private conferences this self-belief could envelop the crafty and powerful, as well as the simpleminded and weak. Millions of people believed in him because they wanted to believe in him and observed that he believed in himself. This is the power of the demagogue.

What ability Hitler possessed other than political is less evident and in a sense irrelevant. There are many witnesses to his remarkable memory. He could overwhelm listeners with his "superhuman" ability to recall details concerning the major ships of the world or operetta librettos. Yet his general store of knowledge seems not to have compared; he had a fatal ignorance of science and industrial economics, and only a fragmentary and highly biased view of history. The singular ability to remember ships and librettos is significant in that it indicates what interested him: power-war and art-music, an adolescent predilection for battleships—which, since the advent of the airplane, were of romantic interest—and romantic operettas.

It is precisely these interests which dominate Hitler's role as government head—the fostering of war preparations (notably construction) and of art; in each case bigness was the object. It is symbolic that his major achievement, or that of hundreds of thousands of nameless laborers, is the Autobahn, at one stroke a preparation for the needs of war, a gigantic artistic conception, and a monument to power. It is for war and for art that Hitler took an active interest in his government, beyond the essentials of keeping himself in power. The rest seems to have bored him, ergo confusion.

A good case could be made for the argument that National Socialism was a movement without an ideology, a "mystique for action," that its program was merely something to ignore.[20] (Robert Koehl finds feudalism, not absolutism, Hitler's model.)[21] Other than the firm belief in the necessity of his personal power and the power of Germany, there seem to be

[20] Nyomarkay, 17ff.

[21] Koehl, "Feudal Aspects of National Socialism," *American Political Science Review*, LIV (December 1960), 921-33.

few principles he would not sacrifice. This is one reason why the majority of the supposed party beliefs were largely ignored after 1933, to the intense dissatisfaction of much of the party's rank and file (a satisfied party member is a remarkable rarity under Hitler's rule). The best analysis, by Schoenbaum, concludes:

> Objective social reality, the measurable statistical consequences of National Socialism, was the very opposite of what Hitler had presumably promised and what the majority of his followers had expected him to fulfill. In 1939 the cities were larger, not smaller; the concentration of capital greater than before; the rural population reduced, not increased; women not at the fireside but in the office and the factory; the inequality of income and property distribution more, not less conspicuous; industry's share of the gross national product up and agriculture's down, while industrial labor had it relatively good and small business increasingly bad. The East Elbian estates continued to be run by the gentry, the civil service by the doctors, and the Army by generals whose name began with "von." Not surprisingly, the history of the Third Reich is a story of frustration, cynicism, and resignation, the history of an apparently betrayed revolution whose one-time supporters . . . denounced it as vehemently as [did] its opponents.[22]

Social reform of poor over the rich, justifying the title of National Socialist, was not forthcoming; Germany remained almost as classbound as before. Economic reform for the small businessman, the NS prototype, was forbidden local idealists by Hitler's government.[23]

Hitler's belief in anything other than power is difficult to discover in governmental operations. Anti-Semitism would be the exception. Yet even here, so strange as it seems, no clear course is apparent from 1933 to Auschwitz. Instead, there were a series of maneuvers for and against violence to

[22] Schoenbaum, 285.

[23] Heinrich Uhlig, *Die Warenhaeuser im Dritten Reich*, Cologne, 1956. Schweitzer, *Big Business in The Third Reich.*

the Jews, in which Hitler restrained anti-Semites who could endanger his power objectives. There seems to have been no clear Hitlerean plan to solve "the Jewish question"; instead, there was a hatred which created problems, then a series of reactions to the created problems, then reactions creating ever more impossible problems. This is the implication of Raul Hilberg's monumental recitation of Nazi horrors.[24]

More uncertain was Hitler's anti-church position, although his hatred of these opponents had risen by the middle of the war to a determination to root out Christianity. As late as 1937 he admitted in a secret speech that he had after a long inner struggle freed himself from his childish religious conceptions.[25] It may well have been his lack of firm convictions that enabled Hitler to appear all things to all people, all minor variants being overshadowed by a massive loyalty to Germany.

More important than ideological, or intellectual, considerations were values traceable to his experiences as a soldier, values that may have played a greater role in his reaction than German philosophy which intellectual historians love to dwell on as the alleged intellectual precursor to National Socialism. Although Hitler was considered a voracious reader, what he read left less perceptible imprint on his actions than what he experienced; so much of his pattern of thought, like that of most of his followers, is better traced to the death-misery-glory of 1914-18 than what had happened before or since. Veterans returned with a "front socialism," the ideal of which was an anti-class, egalitarian community; these ex-soldiers have been described as "the new masses."[26] Proper behavior meant obedience and activism. In practice this meant that Hitler rarely fired anyone, even if they proved incompetent, or even if he did not like what they said or did. His habit was simply to appoint someone else to a similar position who, however briefly, had his attention, leaving the

[24] Hilberg, *The Destruction of the European Jews*, Chicago, 1961.
[25] Percy Schramm, *Der Spiegel*, 5/1964, 58.
[26] Nyomarkay, 59ff.

old comrade with the chance to retain his honor and by fighting perhaps to regain some authority.

This emphasis on fighting, *Mein Kampf*, is another trench-born value, which could be philosophically traced back to Charles Darwin and Social Darwinism, but it seems more historically accurate to find the origin in a trench, not in a book. Hitler believed the strong would survive and the stronger should have the authority. Yet instead of deciding who was stronger, he simply gave similar authority to various persons, leaving their powers vague and letting them "fight it out."[27]

Although a wide variety of people followed Hitler, he was comfortable in the presence of relatively few, which was another reason for his conservative attitude toward his associates; he hated to change.[28] There is a remarkable permanence of associates in civil administration; for a revolutionary regime he made very few changes, including the non-NS ministers first accepted as a compromise simply to get power. He prided himself on his ability to evaluate people quickly and accurately; but other than sensing perhaps who agreed with him and who did not, he chose a remarkably large number of duds, gave them high position, and refused to release them when their incompetence was flagrant. As is evident in the subsequent listing of his closest associates, there is scarcely one who could be regarded as first-rate. Those who survived had survival ability, which meant the ability to convince Hitler.

That so much incompetence at the top did not sink the ship is a tribute to the machinery of government Hitler inherited. It is also a tribute to the society of men which, like man himself, is inordinately able to adjust to a changed environment. Governments must be stupid or unlucky before their citizens forget their own problems long enough to act.

People with whom Hitler felt comfortable had the chance for power. They were good listeners, those who could flatter

[27] Schwerin von Krosigk, *Es Geschah in Deutschland*, Tuebingen, 1951, 209; Dr. Otto Dietrich, *Zwolf Jahre mit Hitler*, Muenchen, 1955, 129-32; Dr. Hans Globke.

[28] Schramm, 44ff.

with their loyalty, and the old-fighters with memories to share. They could also be the artistic people, in the commonly noted empathy between artists, actors, and politicians. Hitler was uncomfortable in the presence of intellectuals; his special hatred was directed toward jurists, persons with legal training who dominated the upper bureaucracy. Although he had the normal respect for the legendary "good old Prussian state," he had a contempt for the bureaucrats. His distrust was a vital factor in his state; he despised and suspected the administrative machine which served to keep him in power.

His dislike of the civil servant can be traced back to the fact that his father was a minor civil servant; some Freud-like interpretations of Hitler insist that his "Oedipus complex" was predominant. Further to be noted, he was never active in government before he became head of the state. Instead he had battled a hostile state to power. As he stated to his party Gauleiter in 1934, he fully expected the officials to oppose his policies, that it would take 10 years to break that resistance by bringing in younger men who had been properly indoctrinated before entering state service.[29]

After seven years of contact with his civil service, he was even more convinced of their idiocy: "I'm not surprised that the country is full of hatred towards Berlin. . . . The Civil Service has reached the point of being a blind machine. . . . There is no possibility of ruling this huge empire from Berlin, and by the methods that have been used hitherto. . . . The civil service is the refuge of mediocre talents, for the State does not apply the criterion of superiority in the recruitment and use of its personnel. . . . In this reorganization the first thing to do will be to chase the lawyers out of the ministries. . . . We can easily get rid of two thirds of them. . . . Every jurist must be regarded as a man deficient by nature, or else deformed by usage."[30] His blind prejudice against those who would in fact keep a machine going despite his best efforts to ruin it, reflected the contempt of the romantic revolution-

[29] BA R43II/1392.

[30] *Hitler's Secret Conversations, 1941-44*, New York, 1953, 85, 106, 306.

ary for the reasonable or cautious academician. The process of bureaucrat-selection was based on the university and the requisite doctorate degree.

The Hitler contempt for Beamten was part of his general low regard for law, evident in part through the increasing reliance on decrees (*Erlasse*) or ordinances (*Verordnungen*) instead of laws (*Gesetze*). Here was his refusal to publish the new NS penal law finished in 1936, and the refusal to accept Ley's request to make his DAF a legal entity, to which he answered, "Someday there will be a DAF law, but I hope not while I live."[31] Instead came the "will of the Fuehrer," for as Goering announced, "Law [Recht] and the will of the *Fuehrer are one*," or as Frank declared, "Our constitution is the will of the Fuehrer." Hitler regarded laws—even his own—as limitations on his freedom of decision and movement. As Buchheim concluded: "[There] is the remarkable discovery that in the absolute total Fuehrer-state, precisely because the will of the Fuehrer replaced all other norms, there was not an apparatus carefully thought out and ordered into the utmost detail, but rather a confusion of privileges and political contacts, competences and plenipotentiaries which became finally a fight of everyone against everyone. . . ." When the war had diverted Hitler's interest almost completely from the internal sphere, "the public administration became so confused that in the last phase one can only speak of a process of self-destruction. . . ."[32]

The startling claim made by some surviving adherents (Gauleiter, F. Florian and K. Wahl) is that Hitler did not behave "dictatorially" toward them, that he requested rather than commanded compliance. Although the view is prejudiced and exaggerated, Hitler did not behave in the civilian sector like the self-assured commander-in-chief one would assume from his public bombasts. Rather than issuing crisp orders, he delivered long and vague harangues. When dealing face to face with skilled associates he was likely to avoid conflict, postpone unpleasant decisions, and delay solutions.

[31] Hans Buchheim, *SS und Polizei im N.S. Staat*, Duisdorf, 1964, 15.
[32] *Ibid.*, 16.

With his cronies he was prone to oral orders based on impulse, ordering those who happened to be about to pass on the order to whatever minister was responsible.[33] These imprecise oral orders lead to unending confusion, because what Hitler said last was supposedly "the last word".

In these chance clique gatherings Hitler was vulnerable to being overrun by a subordinate who had come primed to get his approval to a pet scheme; Hitler would impulsively agree, even to proposals contrary to previous policy, leaving further confusion for his bureaucratic servants to straighten out. The historical evolution was for set meetings with set officials, to give way to chance meetings with chance officials, to no meetings, and finally not even to written orders. In reading through thousands of documents I was startled at how rarely there was any direct written statement by Hitler; instead, someone in the inner circle emerged with the word from Sinai; Hitler had allegedly said such and such. These pronouncements are contradictory enough for one to conclude either that Hitler simply agreed with the last person to see him, or that he was deliberately spreading confusion.

The latter view is supported by Hitler's constant practice of having a variety of individuals, groups, and organizations all working on the same project.[34] This duplication or triplication meant he could choose from among them for someone to implement any whim or plan. Heiber concludes that this confusion, whether by design or indolence, made it possible for Hitler to become the necessary referee in the constant fighting for power[35]—by not defining anyone's authority, he was able to degrade them all.

It may have been "Divide and Conquer", but he had already conquered. What was Hitler afraid of? No institution except Himmler's secret police toward the end, posed a threat to Hitler's position. In a sense, the technique was successful, yet it meant unending strife, vast amounts of wasted energy, and perhaps sufficient confusion to have cost Hitler his victory. At least this is the opinion of more disciplined

[33] Dietrich, 153. [34] *Ibid.*, 129-32. [35] Heiber, 92.

subordinates who did not achieve his power but who did survive him.

The top links in the chain of command were four chancellories through which Hitler funneled his decisions. Two of them were in the party hierarchy and two in the state hierarchy, two functioning and two nominal. As Hitler began as a party leader and remained even after 1933 emotionally closer to his party organization, we should begin with a short sketch of the role played by the party organization in and on the state.[36] It was Hitler's public boast that, "The Party Commands the State", which, like so many of his claims, reflected half-truths or wish-fulfillment.[37]

In one sense, the party was the millions of members, a hundred thousand having joined before the rapid climb from 1930, a few hundred thousand between 1930 and 1933, and several millions climbing on the crowded bandwagon in May 1933. The gate was closed then until May 1937, although there were exceptions. The older the party membership, the more likely the membership reflected a matter of original conviction; the more recent, the likelier it was a matter of opportunism. A perceptive Gauleiter, Roever, noted in 1942 that only a few of the latecomers were dependable NS: "In the coming struggle of *Weltanschauungen* [ideologies] one must be able to depend on the party members. One should not be deceived into thinking that one can do so now".[38] Many of those early believers were also those who were disillusioned early; the turnover was high in party local leadership—40,153 "political leaders" who entered the party before 1933 lost their jobs; 59.6% of the party leaders entered after 1933.[39] The struggle between the old fighters and the newcomers was never settled.

There were simply not enough old party members with

[36] A preliminary examination of the subject appeared in "The Bureaucracy and the Nazi Party", *Review of Politics*, April 1966.

[37] Gottfried Neesse, *Staatsdienst und Staatschicksal*, Hamburg, 1955, 47, denies that even a good start was made.

[38] CGD, T81, R7, F4529.

[39] Wolfgang Schaefer, *NSDAP, Entwicklung und Struktur*, Hannover, 1957, 41-44.

the ability to enable the party to take over the state. In eastern Bavaria 85% of the Landraete had not belonged to the party in 1933; 35% did not join then;[40] in Schwaben, of 21 Landraete, only two were members and both had joined in 1933. The basic party weakness throughout was that persons with evidence of ability in education, in government, in industry, had been too successful or too intelligent to fall prey to Hitler's propaganda until the party's success from mass voting suggested that Hitler was worthy of their attention for their continued success. They were properly distrusted.[41]

The party was further divided, as it grew, by social differences. The original core was the lower middle class, who remained the staunchest members despite the late incursion of large numbers of workers, white or blue-collar, noticeably in the SA, and the late conversion of the wealthy and the noble. The party could find a tissue-paper unity only in an unthinking "loyalty" to Germany and Hitler; beyond that one could find every sort of reaction, conservatism or radicalism, atheists and devout Christians, even a few Jews and more half-Jews who somehow had overlooked the anti-Semitism of the party.

Once in power the party was further divided between those rewarded by a "place at the feeding trough" and those who got nothing but the chance to cheer the Fuehrer. The number getting government jobs was relatively small and most of them were in the lowest of ranks, such as streetcar conductors, so that party members on the outside regarded with distrust those on the inside. Those who became agents of the state as party members became in short order agents of the state first and party members second.

Actually the party suffered just as much from its uselessness. Before the machinery of the state was captured in 1933, the party member was needed for his money, his vote, his willingness to persuade a neighbor to Hitler. Although fine de-

[40] *Ibid.*, 27.

[41] Bracher-Sauer-Schulz, *Die Nationalsozialistische Machtergreifung*, Köln, 1960, 504.

lineations were made of the party's function as "leading the people", and "indoctrination", there was nothing for the organization to do after 1933 that the state could not do better, for example, propaganda from Goebbel's state ministry. In a few cases those with party influence obtained well-paid party jobs, out of others' dues, or more often the honor of a nonpaying party job or the chance to denounce an enemy to the secret *state* police, the Gestapo. Party theory came to give it a kind of democratic function, to restrain the state for the welfare of the people.

The Party Organization

The supposed representation of the nation, albeit appointed from above, by the party organization theoretically connected the people to the Fuehrer, as the state could not do, through a chain from the Block leader to Group leader to County leader to Gau leader to Reichs leader and the party chancellory of Hess and Bormann. This party bureaucracy was supposed to convey party wishes to the top, a process increasingly difficult as first one level and then the next was eliminated from direct contact with Hitler by the party chancellory.

The party organization was to convey party commands down to the party faithful, but it did so in a remarkably loose fashion. The most effective rebellion against Berlin came so much from within the party that many regard the NS period as a renewed feudalism of the party lords; the Gauleiter became princes defying central authority in their areas. A Gauleiter could oppose in an important matter the policy of the foreign ministry because only a short time before he had seen Hitler and thus could claim his support. "The same Gauleiter could arrest as spies on his 'border' the officials of the Interior Minister. . . ."[42] Even Himmler in 1943 could be answered by a Gauleiter: "Himmler cannot tell me anything; if something is to be ordered, Hitler will have to do it and it will be followed".[43]

[42] Walter Petwaidic, *Die Autoritaere Anarchie*, Hamburg, 1946, 12.
[43] Kaltenbrunner to Himmler, 23.9.43, CGD, T175, R31.

The Gauleiter, about 40 in number, with 40 variations of a brawler theme, were idealized by Hitler as his type of loyal party fighters; as most of them were undistinguished in background and therefore owed everything to him, they were "loyal" to him but no one else. Their major enemies were in time Bormann and Himmler. Duesseldorf's Florian was typical in his pride that he had never invited Himmler into his Gau and had forbidden his party men to cooperate with the Gestapo.

The nominal head of the organization was Robert Ley, who early shifted his interest to the *Deutsche Arbeits Front,* the DAF, the captured unions which he set up as a national organization and which became an unwelcome competitor with the party for power. Ley, whose drinking made him an early disgrace but who supposedly reformed after a Hitler ultimatum, was an avid foe of Bormann, Himmler, and Rosenberg.[44]

Roever presented the 1942 party point of view: had the party not headed off four new DAF laws in 1938, the DAF would have had the power to dissolve the party altogether; they had made a clear effort to be independent of the party; the personal union of Ley as party Organization Leader and DAF leader was bad for the party; "The street-cells and block organization of the DAF is false, worthless, and could endanger the entire party"; they should be abolished, their only function was to collect money; the DAF should get out of its various businesses; it should disband its party-competing offices for indoctrination, youth, women, propaganda, and the press.[45] An industrial chamber of commerce complaint about the DAF reportedly achieved Hitler's recognition of the DAF as a serious problem when it noted that neither the state nor the party had any influence over it, that it had become a gigantic apparatus with sovereignty and totalitarian demands.[46]

There were other Reich leaders and other party organizations, all of which, except the SA and SS, were without po-

44 Dietrich, 131.
45 CGD, T81, R7, F4722-41.
46 BA R43II/548b, "Denkschrift A. Pietzsch," 22.6.38.

litical significance, despite their competitive energies. They angered Roever because many of them paid their officers, while the party remained largely unpaid.[47] The first dangerous competitor had been the SA, the part-time party barroom-militia. Its leader, Roehm, wanted a violent revolution in 1933 to destroy the old order, including the officer corps. In February 1934 Roehm had agreed to army precedence as the armed force, but was dissatisfied with the conservative reaction Hitler imposed.[48] Hofer noted further Roehm criticism not only of the lack of a social revolution, but of Hitler's church policy, Jewish policy, union policy, even the police state and the NS suppression of differences of opinion; Hofer thought Roehm even preferred a more reasonable foreign policy. The SA was opposed by the party organization and betrayed by its daughter, Himmler's SS in the notorious "night of the long knives", June 30, 1934. What might have become an anarchic SA state became an SS police-state. The SA remained a docile fossil, its lack of function even more obvious than that of the party and no longer blessed by a Hitler smile.[49] The one exception was its attack on the helpless Jews, possibly to surprise Hitler, in November 1938.

The supposed leader of the party was Rudolf Hess, who had the unique title of "Deputy to the Fuehrer", and was granted the further title of Reich Minister with the right to assist in making the laws for any ministry. The right granted by Hitler was not immediately a factual participation, as Hess complained three months later that the ministries were sending him the required materials so late that participation was illusory. Through Hess the party seems to have played a minor role in law-making, to have settled instead for the right to intervene in appointments to high office.[50]

Hess was regarded highly by the Gauleiter, which implies that he interfered very little. Meissner thought him more a

[47] Roever, CGD, T81, R7, F4648.
[48] Walter Hofer, *Die Diktatur Hitlers*, Konstanz, 1960, 30-34.
[49] Roever, CGD, T81, R7 F4660.
[50] BA R43II/694.

messenger boy for Hitler than a deputy.[51] Krosigk considered Hess not a force for disorder but not a force for order either—he simply lacked the ability for the job, and did not have the strength to stop the party excesses, which he often regretted.

Born in Alexandria, Hess, a kind of refugee, came to Germany for schooling at the age of 12. In 1914, when 18, he volunteered for the army and served for a time in Hitler's company without ever meeting him. Later in the Air Force he rose to lieutenant. After the war, at the University of Munich, Hess was greatly influenced by the geopolitician Karl Haushofer and his belief in a need for *Lebensraum* in the east.

Hess was essentially a passive man, glad to be instructed in his duties and to place himself without question under Hitler's orders.[52] He served with Hitler in prison and took down Hitler's dictation of *Mein Kampf*. By assisting Hitler in spelling and grammar and by believing Hitler the savior of the country, he remained as secretary and adjutant; he even gained a certain fame with his brief but ecstatic introductions of Hitler to the party conventions: "Hitler is the Party! The Party is Germany! Sieg Heil!"

Memoranda piled up in his office while he brooded over the state of Aryan mankind.[53] A kind of mystic, a believer in astrology and with few relations with other people, Hess lived simply and modestly. (Dietrich's story is that the simple lack of taste in Hess's apartment cost him the appointment as second-in-command, given to Goering instead because it offended Hitler.[54]) Hess the puritan was offended by the corruption and pettiness of the party faithful with whom he was supposed to deal: "The more tasks given the party to command the state, the more Hess felt the responsibility, but he had neither the ability nor the energy demanded by his office, and therefore the increased friction in the machine. All suggestions bogged down in his office and it was a difficult

[51] Otto Meissner, *Staatsekretaer unter Ebert, Hindenburg, Hitler*, Hamburg, 1950, 625.

[52] Davidson, 110.

[53] *Ibid.*, 112.

[54] Dietrich, 204.

job to get them cleared. His reserve brought him to a dependence on more self-assertive members of his staff and thus Bormann began to play a role".[55] Krosigk had the impression that when one spoke to Hess, it was often as though he were returning from another world, finding his way back to earth with difficulty.

Hans Frank believed Hess's weakness was fateful for the party, permitting the rise of Bormann, as the weakness of Frick was fateful for the government, which permitted the rise of Himmler.[56] Frank observed that Hess found the meetings of the *Reichleiter* as unwelcome as Hitler found those of the Cabinet, that therefore the *Reichsleiter* ceased to meet after 1934. Hess made so little of his office that when he flew to England, allegedly to gain a Germanic alliance against the Russians, he was scarcely missed. (Davidson believes Hess hoped to negotiate peace with England, which lends substance to the common judgment that he had by then lost contact with reality.[57])

If Himmler has any competitor for the title of the devil behind the throne, it is Bormann, who took over the party leadership after Hess's flight to England in May 1941. Bormann was a "grey eminence" with nondescript face, medium height, thinning hair, bulky shoulders, scarcely known to the country, but he became one of its three most powerful men during the war. It was Bormann who placed his stamp on the second half of the Third Reich as he worked to eradicate the Jews, Christianity, opposition, and criticism. He decided who would see Hitler, and only those who were respectful to himself.

Bormann was born in Halberstadt, the son of a sergeant-trumpeter in a cavalry regiment. He advanced socially when his widowed mother married a bank director. Yet the look of a sergeant survived. Dropping out of school he worked on farms and served as a soldier in the last months of World War I. Then in an anti-Semite group and a Free Corps organ-

[55] Krosigk, 240.
[56] Dr. Hans Frank, *Im Angesicht des Galgens*, Muenchen, 1953, 168.
[57] Davidson, 115ff.

ization, he joined the later commandant at Auschwitz, Rudolf Hoess, in the private murder of a "traitor". The one-year prison term he received made him an "old-fighter" hero to Hitler, although he joined the party only in 1927. Bormann made a political marriage to the daughter of an old NS honored by Hitler. His wife was as fanatic as he; she agreed that the Jew was "the Absolute Evil", and suggested that Hitler deserved not only her 10 Germanic children but proposed that her husband give a good Aryan baby to his actress mistress.[58]

As Krosigk explains Bormann's success: "In Bormann there was no Hess-like dreaminess. He possessed a robust earthy quality, a pleasure in intrigues, uncommon even for those circles, an action-drive like only that of Himmler, with the latter's low regard for human life, with a disregard for the truth that even Goebbels had to envy. He was cut of coarser wood than Hess; he no longer let the party reins drag on the ground. . . ."[59] The most important source of power was his enormous energy and a comprehensive knowledge of all aspects of the party. He worked like a demon, often at trivial assignments he had given himself, such as recording Hitler's table talk.

Bormann simply made himself indispensable and made brief but useful alliances with Hess, Rosenberg, Himmler, Keitel, and Eva Braun. If anyone asked Bormann about a party man, he would find the next day on his desk a complete report which Bormann had gathered through innumerable calls during the night. If Hitler mentioned a book, he would find several airmailed copies the next morning. "Bormann was the tireless clerk who got material together and prepared it so the Fuehrer could deal with it quickly."[60] Right up to the last days in the bunker, he was methodically making notes of Hitler's fantasy commands.

Dr. Frank has emphasized the sinister. After several years as a party cashier, Bormann had become staff leader for Hess who foolishly believed that when Bormann crushed other party organizations in the name of unity, Hess would profit:

[58] *Ibid.*, 102. [59] Krosigk, 243. [60] Davidson, 103.

"Since 1937 Bormann was truly 'around Hitler', a creeping, hypocritical, power-hungry figure, who inhibited everything good and developed everything bad in a calculated exploitation. What Himmler did in developing systematically and hysterically the police and tyrant state, Bormann did for the party. [By so doing] Himmler and Bormann were first the destroyers of Hitler as a human being and later of the entire Reich."[61] By 1942 the two arch-conspirators were also arch-competitors, as Berger, a Himmler assistant, testified after the war that Hitler's isolation was used by Bormann to destroy the Fuehrer's self-confidence. "Then in 1942 this terrific distrust of Hitler's started. . . . Bormann was carrying on an unheard-of-policy. Some people called it clever, but I say [it was] an absolutely disgraceful policy. He managed everything so cleverly by feeding things to Hitler around many back ways. Before that time, Hitler had felt himself to be a very strong man and now, suddenly, he felt that this wasn't true at all."[62]

Yet Bormann was subject as well as the others to the rules of Hitler's game. Clearly on the defensive, he wrote on May 15, 1941 special delivery to all party leaders:

> Since I belong to the closest staff of the Fuehrer, I will continue to accompany him everywhere. . . . If someone says, as recently happened, that they do not want to deal with subordinates [his Berlin office] then I must make a very personal observation to obtain more justice for me and my men. I have worked like a horse since 1933. *Ja*, more than a horse, because a horse has his Sunday and night rest and I have had in the past years scarcely a Sunday and very little night rest. . . . I am of the opinion that we have done a very respectable and useful work. Whoever has a different opinion, should so report to the Fuehrer whom he would think better qualified for my job.[63]

In a less insecure defense of his position, Bormann explained in April 1942, the area of competence of the party

[61] Frank, 167.
[62] Gottlob Berger in *TWC*, XIII, 462.
[63] HA—Rep. 320, 22, p. 66.

chancellory as notably that of always representing the wishes of the party, emphasizing that the Fuehrer wanted the party to speak with one voice—Bormann's voice.[64] That voice was stridently for more pressure on the church (he is commonly regarded as Christianity's worst enemy among the Hitler entourage), more pressure on the civil service and on the Wehrmacht to conform to party wishes. His major foes were Goebbels and Goering,[65] but all leaders were hated as potential rivals.

Bormann could brush aside the other party chancellory, "Chancellory of the Fuehrer", and relegate Bouhler to the role of handling pleas for clemency;[66] and he could take unto himself the title of "Secretary to the Fuehrer", which he did on May 1, 1943.[67] Yet Bormann was not master of the party; some *Gauleiter* had the courage to stand up to him. Most of them had the strength to continue governing their *Gaue* with much the same insolent presumption that Bormann ran the party chancellory.

The party in 1942 remained much the same conglomeration it had been under Hess, so Roever describes it: There was a great need for the definition of responsibilities in the party; in many areas several offices were doing the same work. "Two or more throw themselves on the same task, without any authority restraining them. If there is a superior intelligence among these men, he may be able through his ability to bring the matter entirely into his hands, if he has not been brought to his fall first by intrigues."[68] This remarkably candid analysis continues: "If no one has superior abilities, they either vegetate in a constant jurisdictional struggle or the one who knows best how to use his elbows causes damage. As a result lower officials do not know which authority to follow. It is no secret that the higher the office, the more confused and unclear are the definitions of competence".[69]

The problem was to achieve a definition of authority without bureaucratizing the party. But Roever also saw the party

[64] HA—Rep. 320, 318, p. 131.
[65] Krosigk, 245.
[66] BA R43II/1213a, 1036.
[67] *Ibid.*, 1154.
[68] Roever, 4519.
[69] *Ibid.*, 4520.

as over-bureaucratized—one example, the 104 pages of instructions to the local party cashiers.[70] "Almost every leadership task of the party is dealt with in at least two different party offices, sometimes three".[71] Ley's organization office duplicated step by step the work of the party chancellory. To this, Roever dared add that he did not think that the party chancellory itself was necessary. Worse, the top leaders should accept discipline and not take their fight out on their inferiors.[72]

Nor does Roever shrink from criticizing his peers, from asking the question, what is to prevent a Gauleiter from becoming a despot surrounded by intriguers?[73] (The model he suggested to have central control without bureaucratization was the Roman Catholic church.) He noted quite accurately that the difficulty with the Fuehrer-principle was that if a leader was incompetent, he surrounded himself with other incompetents, and all tried to hide their stupidity and stop any change through masterful intrigue.[74] This Roever description is a classic; it deserves wider notoriety.

The State Chancellories

As with the party, so the state had two organizations about Hitler, one for his office as President, from Hindenburg's death in 1934, and the other the office of Reich Chancellor from his appointment in January 1933. The title Hitler preferred was "Der Fuehrer"; he used for a time the title of Reich Chancellor, but the office of President was a nearly forgotten formality. This is the reason for the weakness of the executive of the presidial chancellory, Dr. Otto Meissner, despite his honored seat at a postwar "Trial of War Criminals".

Although Meissner had been clever and determined enough in 1925 to make the leap from Ebert to Hindenburg, despite Hindenburg's decision to appoint someone else, he had not been clever or determined enough in 1933 to bolster Hindenburg's original refusal to appoint Hitler. A fatal weakness at a fateful moment. Although he kept his title,

[70] *Ibid.*, 4639. [71] *Ibid.*, 4599. [72] *Ibid.*, 4600.
[73] *Ibid.*, 4557. [74] *Ibid.*, 4524.

Meissner had no chance to outwit Hitler as he had outwitted the aged Hindenburg, and the office was relegated largely to processing appeals for clemency, much like Bouhler's party office.

The Nuremberg verdict accepted the defense argument. The verdict stated that Meissner had never joined the party and never enjoyed its favor, that he had opposed Hitler in every way possible, but that his office had very little power. "It is clearly established that insofar and as often as he could, he used his position to prevent or to soften the harsh measures of the man he served, sometimes at considerable risk to himself. He may have remained in office under Hitler because of vanity, weakness and for financial security. There is no evidence that he originated or implemented any crimes against humanity . . . his part was hardly more than that of a messenger . . . not guilty."[75] The scholar need not accept the court's verdict, but it will take some infrared vision to observe a man operating so much in the shadows. It may also need some time-sequence photography to interpret his otherwise imperceptible movements. Other than his unassessed role between January 1933 and the death of Hindenburg in August 1934, the position would appear mired in pettiness.

The significant link between Hitler and his state machinery was the office of the Reich Chancellory and Dr. Hans Lammers. The best Bundesarchiv documents are the staggering amounts of "Lammers papers". Years devoted to a close analysis of these documents could indicate the fantastic ramifications of his continual intervention, its motivation and results. If any bureaucrat modified the general policy of the Reich, it was Lammers, yet this was done so subtly, in so many thousands of affairs, that until someone undertakes the painstaking retracing of bureaucratic footnotes on the pages of time, one can judge him mainly as Hitler's alter ego, to be tarred with the same brush. Until such an intensive investigation, there are only impressions. His war crimes trial, like that of many other men, was lacking in serious evidence. Lammers argued that he was but a secretary like Meissner, a

[75] *TWC*, xv, 609.

claim which both Meissner and the court rejected. Meissner recalled that Lammers had even tried to abolish his competing presidential chancellory as superfluous, but then had decided to use it as an ally to keep Hitler within some legality.[76]

The Lammers' power lay in the fact that the normal correspondence to Hitler on matters of state went through his hands. By 1936 this constituted some 600 communications a day handled by a staff of 10-12 Beamten.[77] Because Lammers prepared state matters to be brought to Hitler's attention and added a written or oral evaluation for Hitler's benefit, and because he became therewith an unofficial coordinator among the ministries and between the ministries and the party chancellory, he held a position approximating a vice-chancellor. In a sense, he achieved more importance than the other ministers. He, not they, had the Fuehrer's ear, unless they were also important as party colleagues like Goebbels and Goering. Lammers and not the ministers had constant knowledge of what was happening throughout the top levels of the German government. It was often left to him to carry out an order and to select the means and the personnel. Meissner regarded him as very ambitious and for that reason Lammers had not used his position to oppose the party or the SS; he had instead maintained close ties with Bormann.

Lammers' party credentials were only fair. He emerged from World War I as captain and possessor of the Iron Cross, first and second class. As an extreme conservative he had been one of two high officials in 1920 to refuse to take the oath to the Weimar Constitution. He was a party member only after 1930, and never considered a valid NS by its leaders.[78] His administrative credentials were better. He was the author of treatises in the field of public law, and after 1933 the coauthor of a successful *Handbook for Beamten.* As a *Beamter* he was necessary to Hitler, but nonetheless suspect.

[76] IZG, NG1541.

[77] Wienstein report, 15.12.36, in BA R43II/1036.

[78] Frick, IZG, NG166. Also Shlomo Aronson, *Heydrich und die Anfaenge des SD und der Gestapo,* dissertation, Berlin, 1966, 290.

Brought to Hitler's attention by Frick, Lammers was the *Beamter* par excellence, energetic and capable in the reading, summation, and writing of reports. Yet he lacked the personal dynamism that might have made of his key position a key power. Such dynamism might have held the state together by compelling the ministers to cooperate, or further, to have held the party and state together. Yet his master Hitler, to whom he was wholly committed, seems also to have been unequal to these two formidable tasks.

Lammers' personality was reflected in his pictures—wizened, bald, restrained, and somewhat cross-eyed, not the type of person to convince Hitler of important policies, although by tenacity able to influence in minor ways, in phrasing and emphasis, the tenor of pronouncements. This influence receded after 1938 as did the importance of civil administration; Lammers testified that already by August 1934 he was permitted infrequent oral reports.[79] He was pushed aside by Bormann in the last years of the war.[80]

Yet Lammers' role was pervasive in that he kept the machinery of government going, however inefficiently, because of Hitler's disorderly procedures. But his influence was cautiously used; it tended toward the legal, that is, restrained direction, as when he tried to convince Hitler that the euthanasia program should be legally arranged.[81] A Himmler agent who eavesdropped on a Lammers-Meissner conversation in 1942 thought it necessary to inform Himmler of their conspiracy to restore law. They had lamented a recent intervention of Hitler to reverse a judge's decision which he thought too mild; the two agreed that there must be an orderly process for all of Hitler's decisions; Lammers was to coordinate information reaching Hitler, "so that he would not take a position based on a newspaper report. The Gauleiter should not be permitted to fire a judge at will. Hitler would agree; one must present the matter to him at the right moment."[82]

The ultimate question concerning Lammers is his complicity in the extermination of the Jews. Early in the regime

79 *TWC*, XII, 305. 80 Frick, IZG, NG166. 81 *Ibid.*
82 Scheel to Himmler, 29.4.42, IZG, NG1623.

he had urged Frick to deport Eastern Jews of foreign nationality.[83] He is on record (Oct. 13, 1941) supporting the sterilization of half-Jews.[84] He wrote Bormann on June 7, 1941 that Hitler had rejected the idea of making German Jews "stateless", because Hitler said there would be no Jews in Germany after the war.[85] Although he did not attend the famous Wannsee conference, Jan. 20, 1942, he was well informed by his delegate.[86]

Lammers gave his version of his noninvolvement in his trial testimony: he had asked Hitler in early 1942 what the "Final Solution" was; Hitler refused to discuss it, except to say he had given Himmler the order for the evacuation of the Jews. After a March 1942 meeting attended by one of his staff, Lammers prepared a long report, hoping to provoke a discussion, but Hitler refused to talk about the matter and insisted there be no more reports about Jewish matters during the war. After the war he would make a decision about where the Jews would go. Lammers, assuming the evacuation order had been stopped, approached Himmler to ask why it had been continued "despite Hitler's orders"; Himmler was very hesitant and evasive and said that he alone was responsible for the evacuations. The only question concerned those partly Jewish and Jews married to Aryans. When Lammers suggested conferences on the matter, Hitler said he had no objection, but there must be no more reports; Himmler would report directly to him. When later in 1942 Lammers noticed the evacuations were continuing, he saw Himmler who told him to mind his own business. In 1943 Lammers had received complaints and sent them to Himmler who usually exempted persons for whom Lammers had interceded. Throughout, Himmler had denied vehemently that killings were taking place; the Jews were simply doing labor in the east and Himmler had thick albums showing their shops.[87]

The court did not find it credible that Lammers was so ignorant of a Hitler policy, but it is possible Hitler and Himmler preferred that he remain ignorant. When the court

[83] IMT NG 902. [84] Hilberg, 268. [85] IMT NG-1123.
[86] Hilberg, 264. [87] *TWC*, XIII, 415-28.

asked Lammers whether he shared Hitler's view that the Jews were to blame for the war, he was undecided. "I do, however, realize that the Jews bear considerable part of the guilt in all the wars of the world." When the court asked whether he had heard Hitler's threat that he would destroy the Jews if they forced a war on Germany, although present on the occasion of the statement, Lammers did not remember.[88] The court was able to prove that in the matter of Himmler's "hard" or Frank's "soft" policy toward Poland, Lammers had sided with Himmler.[89] Lammers was given a 20-year sentence.

The Cabinet was an institution that simply did not fit into the Fuehrer state, although it met for the first four years at ever-widening intervals, and the assembled ministers treated Hitler's prerogatives with the utmost reverence. The meetings were so enlarged with attending assistants that they became mass meetings with no chance for discussion. Important events in 1935-37—the introduction of conscription, the treaty with England, the formation of the "Axis" and "The Anti-Comintern Pact"—were not discussed in cabinet; its members learned of them in the newspapers.[90]

Each minister was permitted to discuss only his own field.

> The cabinet was forbidden to observe a divergence of opinion. Lammers conveyed the desire of Hitler that the Ministers were to bring matters to the cabinet only after all points of conflict had been removed. If this was not possible, a conference of the involved ministers would be called with Lammers as chairman, in an extreme case under Hitler. Hitler reserved the right to decide when a difference of opinion could be mentioned in the cabinet. . . . Each minister presented his draft, on which everyone had already agreed, and Lammers recorded that all were agreed. From time to time Hitler delivered a monologue on some question which interested him at the moment.[91]

In lieu of meetings the procedure became for each minister simply to circulate drafts of his proposed laws and then,

[88] *Ibid.*, 428. [89] *Ibid.*, xv, 591. [90] Krosigk, 202.
[91] *Ibid.*

more simply, to release laws or decrees without informing his colleagues in advance.

To maintain some cooperation, the inner circle of Goering, Goebbels, Ribbentrop, Hess, Himmler, Blomberg, and Keitel was permitted to meet, a group without a Beamter. As Krosigk noted: "Some of the suppressed ministers tried to revive the cabinet at least as an organ of cooperation. . . .This was prevented by the envy of the personalities who were possible chairmen. When Goering made the invitation, Goebbels, Ribbentrop and Hess would not come and vice versa".[92] Something like a war cabinet was created in the Ministerial Council for Reich Defense. Goering called it together during the fall of 1939, but by the following winter it had become incapacitated.[93]

Lammers testified that Hitler forbade his ministers to assemble informally, even socially, such as at a beer party, where serious conversation might develop.[94] Yet in 1944 several ministers agreed to stimulate necessary cooperation through more frequent meetings during the evening in private homes. "These meetings did not remain hidden from Bormann's reconnaissance and these were forbidden in the name of Hitler as 'defeatist Club-evenings.' "[95] The Reich ministers reportedly took greater precautions and met as before, thereby discovering from Speer how the war was really going.

But because of Hitler's attitude toward meetings, cooperation between ministries became nearly impossible. Lammers' office provided a mere appearance of coordination. O'Neill reported no contact between departments; "the administration of Germany was coordinated only by coincidence."[96] No evidence has been discovered of any significant groupings among ministers, even close friendships which might have diminished the competition. Each ministry "ran its own show," so far as it was able. When one "show" conflicted with another, it was a question of power. If one did not acknowledge defeat, it was a battle over the years for one's "rights". Min-

[92] *Ibid.*, 203. [93] *Ibid.* [94] IMT, XI, 127.
[95] Krosigk, 302; also Lammers, IMT, XI, 12.
[96] O'Neill, 15.

isters would order their Beamten to defeat the Beamten of other ministries; papers would be kept waiting as long as possible to sabotage the other's operation. Each minister would compete feverishly for some evidence of Hitler's backing; most impressive was a picture taken with Hitler in a friendly pose.[97]

Perhaps the most confusing tactic was Hitler's creation of new plenipotentiaries to do work already assigned a ministry. A notorious example was Goering's "Four Year Plan" that submerged the Ministry of Economics, or Ley's DAF, which far outweighed the Ministry of Labor.

The Technical Ministries: Post and Transport

Any cataloging of ministries as technical, semi-political, and political has the disadvantage of obscuring their similarities, but it has the advantage of distinguishing between those ministries where there was constant Hitler and/or party pressure for a doctrinaire policy and those which could continue their normal operations, almost as if a revolution had not occurred.

Before the postal and transportation systems were split into two ministries, they were the domain of Freiherr Eltz von Ruebenach, one of the conservatives retained in the original 1933 coalition cabinet. The mail went through and the trains ran on time as before. Eltz has been the one frequently described as the cabinet member who as a good Catholic refused to join the party and resigned in 1940. If one is to believe Goering's testimony at Nuremberg, Eltz had been offered the golden party badge by Hitler in a generous mood. Eltz had hesitated, incorrectly assuming that one had to be a party member to have the party's highest decoration. Hitler was so insulted at the hesitance that he had Goering force the resignation.[98]

That the retired Eltz von Ruebenach was out of step is evident in a long 1940 report of Bormann to Lammers,[99] which began with the refusal of Eltz's wife to accept an NS mother's medal. Her refusal was accompanied by sharp criticism of

97 Petwaidic, 12. 98 IMT, IX, 398. 99 BA R43II/1146a.

Hitler's government. After Bormann's report, Hitler ordered an end to his minister's pension and his passes on the railroad. After Hitler asked for a Beamter to investigate, the district president reported that Eltz stated he had broken with Hitler when he saw the NS wish that the party be regarded as a religion. The Gestapo reported that Eltz's anti-NS position was obvious, in that most of his guests were priests, that his return had stimulated the local church to more hostile activity, that Frau Eltz von Ruebenach had refused to salute the NS flag and had even left the Red Cross after an NS speech. When the President called personally to ask whether she might reconsider and accept the medal, Eltz at first refused to bother her, as she was "busy", but on repeated urging went up to her room; but she had continued her refusal. Finally after evidence of the family's duress, Hitler permitted them a small pension.

With two successors, Julius Dorpmueller for Transport and Wilhelm Ohnesorge for Post, the split brought endless conflicts. Both were party men, Ohnesorge from the early 1920s; both were guilty of anti-Semitic decisions. In November 1939 Ohnesorge protested the granting of pensions to Jews,[100] and Dorpmueller barred Jews from sleepers and dining cars, although not from compartments, waiting rooms, or restaurants—and more than a year after Goering and Goebbels made it an issue.[101]

Any unity between them consisted of opposition to party demands, as in Dorpmueller's objection on the party's evaluation of Beamten, replying that Hitler had stated he wanted only skilled men in the administration.[102] His ministry was particularly out of step with party appointments; a 1941 report noted that there were no NS in a significant office in that ministry and that the Minister simply said that none could be found. Although some postwar patriots have wondered whether the alleged railroad misshipments of wartime munitions was more traitorous than inefficient, none can doubt the cruel efficiency of the railroad deportation of Jews to Poland.

[100] IMT NG-358. [101] Hilberg, 113.
[102] To Lammers, 5.4.39, BA R43II/421a.

As Minister of Labor, Franz Seldte is an example of the fully committed party member, commonly regarded as radical, but who became so caught up in the administrative machinery that he became suspect by the party and was finally bypassed. As the former commander of the conservative Stahlhelm, he had hoped to take his troop of veterans into the party ranks as his power basis, but some refused to follow and many who did became "more than NS" to assuage the serious doubts of their authenticity. He had further expected some influence over Hitler who was, after all, an old war comrade.[103]

Although he could speak radically, Seldte acted in a milder fashion, fully aware that he lacked the capacity to operate a ministry. He had, however, inherited some excellent Beamten, including the former minister, Dr. Syrup. "He left these men, whom he could trust, the freedom of their decisions, and saw his task to defend them from the attacks and resistance of the party."[104] On the rare occasions when the minister had to make the decision himself, he could bring his staff to the deepest dismay. For example, at the beginning of the war a conference was called to consider a wage freeze. Seldte irrelevantly delivered a speech on the *Vaterland*, then left abruptly, telling them to work something out.[105]

Seldte was openly critical of the regime and tried repeatedly to resign. He referred to Hitler only as "Adolf" and spoke openly of Adolf's stupidities[106]—in fact, he seemed to have a "fool's freedom". Seldte hoped to bring some reason to Hitler who did occasionally concede a minor point.

Interesting Seldte-Hitler correspondence of 1936-1938 begins with Seldte's request to Lammers for information concerning the news story that the worker council elections in factories had been postponed, adding that he saw no reason for any delay.[107] Lammers replied that Hitler wanted them delayed a year. The following year, the Interior Ministry

[103] Krosigk, 180.

[104] *Ibid.* See also Herbert Jacob, *German Administration Since Bismarck*, New Haven, 102.

[105] Krosigk, 181. [106] *Ibid.* [107] BA R43II/547b.

agreed with Seldte that it would look much better if the elections were held; the proposed law to end them gave the communists a chance to say that the party was afraid. No elections. Seldte politely asked Lammers again in January 1938, and was as peremptorily informed that Hitler wanted them postponed. The postponement became indefinite with the law (April 1, 1938) to which Seldte addressed a sort of protest to Lammers, quoting both Frick and Himmler: "I would be grateful if Hitler would accept a personal presentation from me." He received instead a short note that Hitler wanted no elections and had no time to see his Labor Minister.

Seldte's officials were able early in the regime, during a push for centralization, to capture previously independent agencies such as the Unemployment Insurance Authority, and to subordinate the various land agencies. The Social Democrats, heavily represented locally, were replaced with party members. Yet, as Jacobs noted, this centralization brought difficulty with the local party. "The Reich Ministry of Labor, while under the direction of an ardent Nazi, remained staffed by professional civil servants who apparently resisted Nazi pressures to implement party policies."[108]

The party was openly disappointed with Seldte's Ministry; as Bormann wrote to Lammers on Feb. 1, 1938, personnel conditions had long been a problem. Of 38 ministerial councillors, only 5 were party members and all since 1933.[109] The vital personnel office had no party members at all, a situation Bormann had tried repeatedly to change, but without success. Even in the matter of "non-Aryans", Seldte had been uncooperative; Bormann's pleas to have two "half-Jews" with politically unfavorable evaluations released were to no avail.

The usual result in Hitler's Reich was not that Seldte would be permitted to resign; that would be poor public relations; instead, there was a private demolition of the ministry. The national union, the DAF, the control of which had been given to Ley, a party figure, became an autonomous group cursed by government, party, and worker alike. Then when labor

[108] Jacobs, 113.

[109] BA R43II/1138.

became a wartime problem, a new agency was created—"The General Plenipotentiary for Work Mobilization"—which was given to a Gauleiter, Sauckel. "At last the only thing left the Labor Ministry was social legislation. But even here it faced the competition of the DAF; Ley brought out a 'Supply plan', through which he hoped to replace the state's social insurance."[110]

The technical ministry that brought the most lasting distinction to Hitler was that of Fritz Todt and his Autobahn, which everyone remembers first as the good Hitler left behind. As analyzed by his colleague Krosigk, Todt was a thoroughly competent technician who understood road-building magnificently.[111] Although obsessed with Hitler, Todt was otherwise a reasonable and independent minister. He was a rarity among the NS leaders: "one could believe what he said". Though courageous in the defense of his ministry, Todt compromised where possible. His one crusade was against the jurist-bureaucrat, who competed with his technicians. The Milward study of the German wartime economy has added to Todt's stature.[112] It asserts that the slow mobilization until 1942 was not because of Todt, but because of Hitler's deliberate decision for only "lightning wars". (This reverses Klein's emphasis that Speer's innovations provided the miraculous increase in production during the increasing bombardment in 1943-44.[113])

Todt's success led to his undoing, as more and more jobs were piled onto his road-building function, until he was given a munitions ministry. The extra assignments overburdened his managerial skills. In Krosigk's opinion, "he did not organize his ministry so that it was a smoothly operating machine. The frictions were too large and the gears no longer meshed."[114]

Todt's trust of Hitler's judgment reached the breaking point

[110] Krosigk, 181.
[111] *Ibid.*, 297-99.
[112] Milward, *The German Economy at War.*
[113] Burton Klein, *The German Economic Preparation for War,* Cambridge, 1959.
[114] Krosigk, 298.

when in the winter of 1941-42 he attempted to get Hitler to reverse the order which shifted army armament, supposedly no longer necessary for a defeated Russia, to air armament against England. "The technician became aware of the limits of the German productivity and felt that it was not sufficient for a war with several fronts. He was too straight-forward a man not to express his concern and criticism directly to Hitler. In the last conference on February 2, 1942 the opposing viewpoints collided. On the next day Todt died in an aircrash just after leaving the Fuehrer's headquarters."[115] Preliminary investigation failed to explain the crash and Hitler forbade any further inquiry. He liked to say later that had Todt lived, "he would have provided everything".

Todt's successor was Albert Speer, who had gained Hitler's respect as the architect of the giant structures for the Nuremberg party day. He appealed so much to the artist in Hitler that he could in time challenge Bormann for power. As Krosigk observed, where Todt was the technician, Speer was the artist; where Todt was the engineer, Speer was the architect; where Todt operated with level-headed reason, Speer relied on rash impulse and compulsive fantasy.[116] These qualities made it impossible for him to organize his ministry in a functional fashion. "Instead of departments with definite powers, he had men with certain assignments, which often conflicted." As the artist, he rejected bureaucratic order.

Speer did not have the temperament for integrated adminis-tration, but with Hitler's backing he could hold his own. Labor Commissar Sauckel, in the chain of command formally under Speer, tried constantly to expand and strengthen his own organization at Speer's expense. Himmler tried to do the same thing with his SS factories; the Gauleiters under Bormann were always pressing for increased authority over the plant managers and Speer's businessmen "honorary co-workers," whom they regarded as well-heeled saboteurs. Goering gave up his authority as plenipotentiary for the four-year plan reluctantly, retreating step by step.[117] Speer had tried to limit

[115] *Ibid.* [116] *Ibid.*, 300. [117] Davidson, 504.

the use of concentration camp workers, but mostly, Davidson thinks, because he wished to avoid asking Himmler for their services.

As long as Speer enjoyed Hitler's special grace, it made possible his challenging the established powers, notably Bormann, in 1943-44.[118] As an example of the struggle: Lammers politely but firmly informed Speer on July 2, 1943 that the rules of the game were that all Fuehrer edicts were to be issued through himself, so that all involved ministries could be consulted. "Dear Speer, you are the only one who ignores these rules. These are not formalities but rules to protect the Fuehrer." Speer replied July 27, 1943 to "Dear Herr Doktor Lammers", that he recognized the correctness of these views, but that he could not promise always to follow the procedures, because they were "extremely inhibitive and cause a loss of time which in particular cases is indefensible". The Fuehrer's orders would permit no delays, therefore Speer could not wait to hear others' views. Lammers answered quickly, thanking Speer for his understanding, but noted that there could be more delays if the other ministers were not consulted. Speer would please inform the Fuehrer when he planned to bypass the ministries.

Bormann added later that month that, "Hitler with every decisiveness was against such a procedure; all orders and degrees must be given to all involved before their declaration; the Fuehrer is to be approached only after *all* involved have taken a clear position. . . . In no case can the Fuehrer be taken by surprise. . . . It would be an impossible situation if every minister would try to push his view through with the Fuehrer without consideration for his fellow ministers".[119] Speer instead worked out agreements with other plenipotentiaries that his plenipotentiary would come first.[120] He added that he took over the most important task at a particularly difficult time and simply could not be crippled by administrative rules. Bormann again quoted Hitler, that everyone must be consulted. Then local authorities began to pressure Speer's

[118] BA R43II/695a. [119] *Ibid.*
[120] *Ibid.*, Speer to Bormann, 18.8.43.

centralization and the whole problem of which provincial agents would carry out whose orders remained unsolved.

Speer battled again in 1944 against the various ministries, seeking power as "Commissar for Instant Measures" to implement any action after bombing attacks.[121] In a special midnight conference on May 31, 1944, it was noted that Hitler had agreed to Speer's request, although Lammers observed that not all ministries had been consulted. Hitler saw the danger that the work of other ministries could be crippled by Speer's commando actions, but resolved it typically by signing the law but requesting Speer "to be careful". The law was further to be kept secret except to the ministries.

Tirelessly Speer intensified the mobilization of the German economy, yet was too late to save the war. Only in the fall of 1944 did his faith in Hitler collapse before the inevitability of defeat; until then, he had been less critical of Hitler than had Todt. But when Speer tried to convince Hitler that the war was lost and failed, he probably became the most effective resistance force in the last months of the war, while Bormann regained lost prestige by turning Hitler against the once-favored protégé. The struggle reached its climax in the last weeks of the war when Hitler ordered that everything be destroyed which might be of help to the enemy. "Speer worked against this order with all possible means. He opposed it passionately to Hitler's face; he was constantly underway to make sure that the order was not carried out; he sabotaged it by making sure that the explosives were placed out of reach. . . . In a moment of weariness as frequently occurred during the last weeks of his life, Hitler decided after one excited session with Speer that the order of destruction remain but that Speer was the one responsible for its implementation."[122] As Krosigk observed, such a solution was not uncommon. A law would declare Hitler's desire, but the implementation order would in effect prevent enforcement—reason balanced fanaticism. Speer planned an assassination of Hitler, using gas through the ventilation pipes, only to find special protective covers, another example of Hitler's sup-

[121] BA R43II/1157a.

[122] Krosigk, 303.

posed sixth sense for danger. At the Nuremberg trials Speer was among the very few to admit regret; he served 20 years in prison.

Semi-political Ministries: Ministry of War—Blomberg

In contrast to the manifold analyses of military campaigns, the activity of the War Ministry per se has been relatively unstudied. Telford Taylor and Wheeler-Bennett[123] followed the Nuremberg trial prosecution of the generals as junior conspirators. Liddell-Hart[124] relied on interviews with generals to picture Blomberg and Fritsch as able and upright, preserving a sanctuary of reason within the NS state until foully attacked by the unscrupulous Himmler and Goering in early 1938.

A beginning of scholarly documentation is provided by Arthur Schweitzer,[125] who affirms that Blomberg (Army) was one of the four power centers in 1933-1938, the other three being "big business" (Schmitt and Schacht), the SS police, and the party. Schweitzer, with the advantage of more research in postwar archives, thought anyone who examined the documents would be "forced to the conclusion that the Nazi Party did not determine military and economic policies in the first phase of the regime."[126] This phase he described as "a partial fascism in which big business and the generals functioned as equal partners in power."

As an example, Blomberg refused at first to permit any of his Beamten to join the party, then was forced back into a compromise which simply forbade them to be active in party work. The ministry, with its particular need for loyalty and secrecy, had little difficulty in maintaining ministerial priority. That Blomberg's Beamten possessed certain immunities from party jurisdiction came to Hitler's attention in August of 1935, and the question was referred to Lammers, why they

[123] Telford Taylor, *Sword and Swastika*, New York, 1952; John Bennett, *The Nemesis of Power*, New York, 1953.

[124] B. H. Liddell-Hart, *The German Generals Talk*, New York, 1948.

[125] Schweitzer, *Big Business in the Third Reich*, Bloomington, 1964.

[126] *Ibid.*, 6.

should be different.[127] He was informed that Blomberg had forbidden SA membership at the time of the Roehm murder, to prevent any command conflict.

Blomberg bent somewhat in December 1935 and permitted membership in the party, but in none of its para-military affiliates, not even the SS or Hitler Youth. Although he "welcomed" the idea of membership, he could not permit his Beamten to hold party office; time did not permit. Any complaint could be only through channels; secrecy must be maintained even toward the party.

The relative independence was reaffirmed by Keitel who noted Nov. 7, 1935 that the recent law about Hess's rights vs. Beamten would not be applied to the army's domain.[128] Hitler refrained from interference in internal army affairs; the selection of officers, O'Neill regarded as nonpolitical. There was no interference in courts-martial. Hitler played no part in the planning of operations until January 1938.[129]

The coalition of generals and big business maintained a serious check on Hitler's power, Schweitzer says, until that coalition broke down from within. The military and the economy became divided—perhaps Hitler divided them deliberately—and were "conquered".[130] The crisis came over the foreign exchange shortage in 1936; the issue was whether to return to international trade, as Schacht and big business favored, or to push for synthetics, i.e., "autarky". Some elements of big business, notably iron and coal, supported Schacht in his argument against the high prices and the low quality of the substitutes, as in Goering's exploitation of low-grade iron ore. But big business was not a monolith. Some industry such as I. G. Farben saw greater profits in synthetics. Those industries—chemical, aluminum, aircraft, and synthetic textiles—had an economic reason for closer collaboration with Goering and the party; thus occurred the dangerous split in business between those profiting from subsidized internal production and those profiting from increased exports.[131]

[127] BA R43II/426. [128] *Ibid.* [129] O'Neill, 15.
[130] Schweitzer, 504f. [131] *Ibid.*, 539.

The army came to fear that foreign trade sources would be insufficient for rearmament. Thus the business-army coalition split further, as Schacht, by insisting too strongly on the right to control the military budget, annoyed the generals and created the doubt that he was serious in collaborating with their military goals. Among Schacht's major tactical errors, Schweitzer emphasizes the miscalculation in his gambit with Blomberg when Schacht proposed that they offer Goering the "nominal" leadership of the committee concerned with the exchange problem, assuming that Goering would be too ignorant of economic matters to challenge the Schacht policy.[132] This underestimation of Goering gave the party "the privilege of taking an active role in selecting policies of economic mobilization for war."[133]

Blomberg failed to support Schacht's efforts in 1936 to use the requirements of rearmament to cut down on the funds and power of the party. Instead followed Goering's four-year plan which, in Schweitzer's judgment, represented an alliance between the party (Goering), the generals, and I. G. Farben. This alliance, which excluded Schacht, most of the bankers, and the Ruhr industrialists, lasted about 15 months. Then in November 1937, when at the "Hossbach Conference" Hitler presented the idea of blitzkrieg, the generals presented his concept with a fairly united opposition. The famous Blomberg dismissal followed the generals' resistance, but it was not so much the party pitted against the army as it was the army pitted against itself; Hitler used the honor code of the traditionalists against their leader. Schweitzer underlines the failure of Chief of Staff Fritsch to follow Beck's advice to use the army to disarm the SS and then to prove the charges of homosexuality against himself as fabricated. This was an incident of fatal inability to use the real power of the army. Fritsch could at least have forced the party back to the 1933 coalition and the original equality of power.

The Schweitzer analysis will require further research. For example, Kielmansegg does not regard the Hossbach inci-

[132] *Ibid.*, 545. [133] *Ibid.*, 545.

dent as a cause for the dismissal of Blomberg, whom he regards as quite cooperative even with the aggressive war plans. He does agree that Fritsch was a successful resistor to Hitler who had never interfered in the personnel policies but began to do so only with Fritsch's disgrace. Jodl had said, "The Fuehrer had always wanted these changes. Blomberg had always promised to report the desires to Fritsch, but nothing had happened".[134]

O'Neill is probably close to the truth about the situation when he wrote that Blomberg could keep the party out of his domain because he had left no doubt of his loyalty to Hitler.[135] Despite the austere appearance of Prussian officers, Blomberg was impulsive and romantic; his experience in Soviet Russia had so impressed him with the simplicity of the place of her soldiers that he had briefly considered becoming a communist. It was therefore easy for Hitler to play on his idealism. Blomberg was able to compromise with Hitler, as his Chief of Staff Fritsch could not. Although they both fell from power in January 1938 their relationship had been tense; Fritsch was much more skeptical of Nazism, and closer to Beck, the later head of the resistance.[136]

Schweitzer's conclusion is persuasive: With Schacht's inability to maintain the unity of big business, and Blomberg's inability to maintain the unity of the army, the imperialist elements of both were won to the side of the party, which tipped the balance toward its radical solutions. The party did not have to fight either; rather, they made each group leaderless by changing the organizations and destroying the reputation of their respective leaders. It was not the inherent weakness of the army or of business but this ineffective leadership of both, along with the absence of rules for succession.[137]

In summarizing the relation of economic policy to Hitler, one has the advantage of significant research in the Eco-

[134] Peter Graf Kielmansegg, "Die Militaerische-Politische Tragweite der Hossbach Besprechung", *Vierteljahresheft fuer Zeitgeschichte*, 1960, 271-73.

[135] O'Neill, 17.

[136] *Ibid.*, 28.

[137] Schweitzer, 552.

nomic Ministry documents. For the period 1933-38 Schweitzer has richly documented the struggle of Schmitt, then Schacht, as leaders of big business against the party.[138] Contrary to the mythology of the harmony of interest between the NSDAP and big business, the documents give evidence of a running battle between the NS leaders, who were sympathetic to the interests of the romanticized small shopkeeper and handworker, and the modern efficient industrial establishment symbolized by the Ruhr.

The struggle began in the spring of 1933, with Alfried Krupp coming forward as the spokesman for industrialist power against the party-state.[139] Kurt Schmitt, an insurance executive, was made Economics Minister, representing a revival of that power. His compromises with the NS theory to protect small business, his opposition to cartels, his delay of subsidies for synthetic oil, and his inability to promise sufficient resources for rearmament, brought on his June 1934 replacement by the more clever Schacht. Pressure also came from the army. On May 20, 1934 Blomberg had protested the Schmitt measures as insufficient; a month later General Thomas argued for an economic dictator.[140]

Schacht thus could lead a full-scale attack on the influence of the party in the economy. Aided by Blomberg's negotiations with Hitler to end SA radicalism,[141] he defeated the 1934 NS effort to control the banks. Schacht's centralized ministry then gained the power—not the party. Two examples were his domination of the "Handicraft Estate", which reduced the power of the NS (HAGO) organization, and his removing intractable NS members from key positions in economic power centers.[142] In 1935-36 Schacht defeated the counterattack by Robert Ley's (DAF) Labor Front, an effort to reverse again the big business-oriented policy. Ley had formed the National Chamber of Labor, which a boycott by business groups defeated. Then Schacht overcame a Ley effort to re-

[138] See also my earlier *Hjalmar Schacht, For and Against Hitler*, Boston, 1954.

[139] Schweitzer, 246ff.

[140] *Ibid.*, 250. [141] *Ibid.*, 133. [142] *Ibid.*, 143.

vive his handicraft organization by suggesting to Hitler that it would create the danger of strikes.[143]

Ley tried to mobilize the Gauleiter and generals to defeat Schacht, but overplayed his hand by falsifying a speech by General Thomas so as to impress business leaders with the generals' support. The exposed lie reunited Schacht and the generals. Then the Ley-Gauleiter coalition failed. Schacht worked to force the Gauleiter out of local economic chambers. This was finally successful, when Goering, as Schacht's successor at the Economics Ministry, backed the ministry against the Gauleiter, who gave up their alliance with Ley's Labor Front. The victory of big business was shown further in November 1936 with the acceptance of the NS-denounced cartels and the right of big business to fix prices and regulate markets.[144] Supported by the business community, the Economics Ministry effectively battled the party on its home ground, until submerged by Goering's bulk and Funk's weightlessness.

The NS goals had been: (a) renewed prosperity, a common objective which was achieved; (b) the elimination of the Jews from the economy, which was delayed until Goebbels' *fait accompli* of November 1938; (c) the destruction of department stores as competitors to the small retailer, which was stifled throughout; and (d) the total commitment of the economy to war mobilization, which was delayed, at least until 1942, although Hitler may share the blame.

The Economics Ministry clearly resisted the anti-Semitic goal of the party. The argument that attacks on the Jews would endanger the nation was used effectively with Hitler, if not with all local anti-Semites. Actions against Jews would threaten not only the delicate national recovery program, i.e., the vital battle against unemployment, but would lead to very difficult foreign trade problems, which would make more difficult rearmament, Hitler's other objective. In the tug-of-war between radicals and moderates the Economics Ministry tried to protect Jewish business, rightly suspecting that party radicalism could eventually be turned against big business. A

[143] *Ibid.*, 149. [144] *Ibid.*, 287.

special bureau was created in the Ministry to stop NS attacks on Jews, the "interference section" (*Eingreifreferat*), "through every possible inconspicuous measure to protect Jewish concerns against NS attacks".[145]

A more open attack on anti-Semitism was the conference of Aug. 20, 1935 which Schacht called to denounce the unlawful activity against Jews as crippling German exports. Schacht played his trump card: the anti-Semitic attacks were a danger to rearmament. This sharp denunciation occurred in front of key cabinet members and a rabid party delegate, Adolf Wagner. Its effect was modified by Schacht's acceptance of "Jews not wanted" signs, which he said could also be found in the United States. But he insisted there must be no more local party "single actions".[146] (Hilberg concluded from this that Schacht was not opposed to anti-Jewish action as such, only the illegal, disorderly, "wild" actions.[147])

Until Goering took effective charge of the ministry in 1938, not even permitting the appointed Minister Funk to enter his office for three months,[148] the "Aryanization" process had been greatly slowed, particularly in the larger firms and in the cities. After the greatest of the party violence against the Jews in November 1938, Goering ordered the Economics Ministry to get the Jews out of the economy. Success had undermined Schacht's economic arguments for human decency; unemployment had disappeared, and Goering's autarky promised to end rearmament's dependence on foreign trade. In short, Hitler's hatred of the Jews proved more lasting than Schacht's economic necessity.

The avoidance of destroying the department stores, as described by Uhlig,[149] is a clearer example of how party objectives were foiled. The NS had begun as the party of the lower-middle-class, suspicious of both big labor and big business. The NS program demanded legislation to save small business. Local party men took the promise seriously, but

[145] Friedrich Facius, *Wirtschaft und Staat, Schriften des Bundesarchivs*, Coblenz, 1959, 147.

[146] IMT NG-4067. [147] Hilberg, 22. [148] Facius, 165.

[149] Heinrich Uhlig, *Die Warenhaeuser im Dritten Reich*, Cologne, 1956.

Hitler, concerned about the support of big business and recovery, did not. Acting in May and June 1933 on the assumption that Hitler privately wanted them to do what the government could not do officially, many local party leaders acted to suppress department stores on their own initiative, even threatening machine-gun violence to customers.

The order from Hess on July 7, 1933, forbidding any action against department stores, hit the local radicals like a bombshell.[150] The local party press either printed the order in the shortest possible form or refused to mention it altogether. Hess's restraining order represented the effective arguments of the Economics Ministry: 90,000 jobs would be lost if the stores were closed; there would be unemployment insurance to pay; production would be depressed; the creditors of 800 million marks would lose. Such good sense won.

A key action was the saving of the second largest department store company, the Hermann Tietz Concern. Schmitt used it as a precedent, arguing that the Reich should save it by a loan. Hitler refused because the firm was "Jewish". After two hours of argument Hitler gave up; the renamed "Hertie" was saved. "Therewith occurred the paradox that only a few months after the total seizure of power, the Fuehrer of the party which had promised the middle-class votes the immediate liquidation of the large department stores, personally saved one of the largest, one which further was under Jewish management".[151]

Minor actions continued despite the party order, but with the disappearance in 1936 of the major enemy, the party's HAGO, the worst was over. The state was fully committed to saving the department stores, though some local Gauleiter used every pretext to boycott them, to burn a few in November 1938, then after 1939 to close some 14%, using the war as an excuse—but this was local rebellion. As Uhlig observed, "The Third Reich had only the superficial attributes of an authoritarian state. Its actual essence was the anarchic-impulsive dictatorship".[152]

[150] *Ibid.*, 111. [151] *Ibid.*, 112. [152] *Ibid.*, 187.

The Ministry played an ambivalent role in war preparation. Schacht, provided with a lending policy, tried hard to avoid any impression of inflation, the wherewithal for a moderate rearmament. When he refused to extend this to a more dangerous credit expansion in 1937, he was fired. By 1936, Goering, more willing to promise the goods for war, had been made, as plenipotentiary for the four-year plan, a more powerful ersatz Economics Minister. Although in 1939-41 Goering's power rested behind both rival organizations, the Ministry and the staff of the four-year plan, economic mobilization lagged behind that of all Germany's wartime competitors. By 1942 the ministry lost areas of jurisdiction to newer agencies such as to Speer, and symbolically the whole ministry burned to the ground November 1943.

Sufficient mystery surrounded the intricate tax and budget system that the Finance Ministry remained relatively free of party influence in its internal workings. The abolition of parliamentary or even cabinet restraint on the ministry, and the ineffectiveness of dictatorial restraint, gave the finance Beamten unusual free rein. "The German finance minister had under Hitler the highest authority that a chief of finances ever achieved. He established (completely alone) every part of the Reich budget. . . . Also in the levying of taxes, which reached unprecedented heights under Hitler, the Reich Finance Minister was scarcely restricted in any fashion."[153]

Count Schwerin von Krosigk was a capable conservative retained by Hitler from the previous cabinet and kept in office throughout. He was described at his postwar trial by the French Ambassador Poncet as "the symbol of a truly modest, noble German aristocrat, and at the same time the embodiment of a reliable, correct and decent German official who could serve as a model to many other men".[154] Bruening, the former chancellor, described Krosigk as being in the best German Beamten tradition of the outstanding expert with the strongest sense of duty, but lacking in political judg-

[153] Friedrich Vialon, "Die Stellung des Finanzministers", *Vierteljahresheft fuer Zeitgeschichte*, 1954, 136.

[154] *TWC*, XII, 364.

ment.[155] The court's verdict agreed; his position was derived from high ability, his private life was above reproach, he was wholly free of any ambition to use his office to enrich himself, he had not been a part of the inner circle, but had suffered many conflicts of conscience in remaining in Hitler's service. Yet he was found guilty of "war crimes" because his private rejection had not found the kind of protest that even Schacht mustered, and that he had signed orders for financing concentration camps and for the confiscation of Jewish property.[156]

Nominal party control within the ministry was through the old NS theorist Fritz Reinhardt who was given the position of state secretary. As with so many party men taken into office, Reinhardt was absorbed into his state position. Instead of pushing party influence into the ministry, he consistently defended the ministry from party attacks, so that Krosigk was rarely disturbed.[157] He learned his job quickly, became quite skillful and offered excellent ideas. He defended the long-standing complicated selection of promotion procedures of the ministry, which most carefully sifted out the most able, a system unchanged during the NS regime.

Krosigk, whose deep religious and moral conviction was accepted by the court, affirmed at the trial that he had hoped to alleviate suffering by remaining in office, that he recognized better after the war that honest service under a dictator must in time succumb before extreme demands, but he would act the same again. Krosigk testified that in some individual cases he had helped Jews first to avoid persecution by leaving and later to avoid extermination by staying.

The official record would support a claim that he acted as a money brake on some party demands, while at the same time finding the money for expenditures dearest to Hitler's heart. His officials had a veto power over budget requests from all agencies; this was used rigorously to halt local proj-

155 *Ibid.*

156 *TWC*, xv, Schwerin von Krosigk verdict.

157 The judgment of the Bundesarchiv expert on the Finance Ministry, Dr. Kahlenberg.

ects or local civil service expansions dear to Gauleiter hearts. It was the kind of central restraint that constantly irked the local powers. A Hitler reversal of a Krosigk decision was possible but difficult; one hesitated to bring every piddling sum vetoed to the Fuehrer's attention, so the finance officials could more often than not maintain a veto during tenacious negotiations.[158]

Further trial testimony reported Krosigk's efforts to restrain military spending, particularly of the secret pre-1933 rearmament, with the interesting assertion that the military reports distrusted by Krosigk were so inaccurate that the British were better informed about German army developments than the German Finance Ministry.[159] Even Himmler's police found their work hampered by finance bureaucrats, as Daluege complained in July 1936.[160] He saw an effort by the Prussian Finance Minister, Popitz, later executed as participant in the Resistance, to thwart the plan for a centralized police, with Krosigk's support. Popitz's motives: "The creation of a Reich police he could never support, because this would mean a separation of police from administration, which he thought had already proceeded much too far through its always aggressive independence of the Executive".[161] With a background similar to Krosigk's, Popitz drew increasingly the logical consequences of this unrestrained executive and moved from support to passive resistance to active resistance and a hero;[162] Krosigk remained passive and was found guilty of war crimes.

Walter Darré was a party "radical" full of romantic intentions of creating a new yeomanry which would save both the racial blood and soil of Germany. As an economic theorist for the party, Darré became Minister of Agriculture with none of the organized corporation power of the industrialists to oppose him, rather the inertia of millions of disorganized

[158] For example, see BA Reich Finance Ministry File R2, 10860 and 10881.

[159] *TWC*, XII, 558, affidavit of Dr. Hans Schaeffer.

[160] CGD, T175, R3, Daluege-Himmler correspondence.

[161] *Ibid.*, 17.7.36.

[162] Annalore Leber, *Das Gewissen Entscheidet*, Berlin, 1960.

peasants. As a "racial specialist" for the SS he should have been on good terms with the party radicals. Further, the enabling act of July 15, 1933 transferred formal authority in agriculture from the states to his Reich Ministry.

Darré's program was quickly introduced.[163] It reversed Hugenberg's principle of aid to the peasants through farm credit agencies and returned to the debt moratorium of 1932. It introduced in September 1933 the principle of corporative organization with an "Estate of Agriculture", lead by party men and encompassing all peasants and processors. The same act established a marketing organization and regulated the various prices, to manipulate the supply and demand for agricultural produce. The hereditary law (Sept. 29, 1933) made it impossible for the peasant family to lose the land or even to sell it; it had to remain in the family. The program further ended the threat to the Junker estates by limiting any resettlement to land bought on the market or reclaimed. These changes Schweitzer has termed "rural middle-class socialism."[164]

Schacht attempted to reverse this backward step which he blamed for the decline in production and increased farm imports. But Darré's effort at anti-capitalism was doomed not so much by capitalist efforts but by the shift to rearmament and the need for efficiency. These theories were not popular or implemented among the peasants Darré hoped to save, nor was his independent mode of operation popular among his party colleagues. As another central minister trying to assert national control, he ran afoul of Gauleiter jealous of power and probably cognizant of the folly of his dream. He ordered on June 13, 1934 the Hanover Gauleiter "Stop interfering with my Peasant Leaders, I appoint them and I have ordered them to ignore such intervention".[165] A similar complaint to another Gauleiter forced Darré to call on Hess and Himmler for support. In the next month he ran afoul of Krosigk when he planned to levy a special farm tax to finance his operations; Krosigk suggested that he could

[163] Schweitzer, 198.
[164] *Ibid.*, 199.
[165] BA R43II/203.

easily cut expenses, and he did.[166] Through 1933-34 he indulged in a long battle with the Reich leader of the party charity, defending himself against the charge that he was sabotaging the collections.[167] In 1938 he was battling the DAF on the charge that he was sabotaging their effort to get more labor for the city.[168] Darré protested that he was simply trying to stop the flight from the land by improving the existing horrible conditions, but that the DAF would not help and instead was constantly violating the farm law although Hess had ordered them to stop.

Although Darré qualified ideologically, an anti-Semite of rank, he lost in February 1938, the backing of Himmler and was eventually pushed out by Backe, Himmler, and Bormann.[169] In no other area were NS goals less successful than were Darré's plans for the peasants.

The Political Ministries: Science, Education, and Popular Education

This new ministry formed on May 1, 1934 under Bernhard Rust theoretically had massive powers over the school system. In actual operation education remained largely a matter of the various Laender; Wagner in Bavaria told Rust to mind his own business. It occupied most of the minister's time trying to defend his ministry from the plentitude of competitors—Goebbel's Propaganda Ministry, Waechtler's NS Teacher Federation, and the Reich Youth Leaders, Axmann and Schirach.

Rust had further difficulties in keeping his subordinates loyal. In 1934 he was challenged by an ambitious State Secretary, Wilhelm Stuckart, who wrote Hitler of the mismanagement of the Ministry, mentioning a top Beamter who compared NS *Kultur* policies with those of the Bolsheviks.[170] The rebel Stuckart was released, but after Hitler's personal intervention was given a comparable position in the Ministry of Interior.

Rust remained in office without Hitler's full support; for

166 *Ibid.* 167 BA R43II/1143. 168 BA R43II/194.
169 *TWC*, XII, 334. 170 BA R43II/1154.

example, he had difficulty getting his personnel appointments approved. In November 1938 Heydrich, acting on a complaint by Wacker, intervened openly to insist that Wacker a subordinate of Rust, be given plenipotentiary power and the position of State Secretary.[171] The substance of Wacker's complaint was that Rust was so incompetent that matters could not continue as they were. The major difficulty was that in the field of *Kultur-politik* there were various forces competing; "a central power is lacking. This fact is most clear in the operation of the ministry that the top of the ministry does not have a constructive relationship to the party, or to its various branches, in contrast to other Reich agencies." The crux of the matter was that everyone knew, "the political position of the Reich Education Minister in fact is very weak, a phenomenon, which makes every work . . . difficult every day. . . . Here rests the sources of the many misunderstandings which have occurred in recent years between the Ministry and other authorities, particularly those of the party".[172] Wacker's solution was "personal union", that someone (Wacker) be at once endowed with SS and ministerial rank. This was the only possibility he had told Rust, because, as Rust had mentioned, "the possibility of an audience with the Fuehrer and Reich chancellor is very limited because of the Fuehrer's burdens of office". This sly reminder was joined to another, that Wacker had already seen Hess and had his support, and then a third threat, "I feel bound to inform Himmler".[173]

Wacker's hopes foundered on Hitler's unwillingness to make a change. Lammers wrote on Dec. 23, 1938 that Hitler had left it up to Rust. Wacker went home; Rust remained, but isolated and insecure. In March 1944 he complained to Lammers that at the Gauleiter meeting on Feb. 22, 1944, his being fired had been discussed as though it had already been decided and that the impetus had come from Goebbels.[174] The answering Gauleiter, Waechtler, observed that for years the party had been seriously dissatisfied with Rust.

[171] BA R43II/1154a. [172] *Ibid.* [173] *Ibid.*
[174] BA R43II/1153a.

The situation of Hans Kerrl was even more precarious, since there was serious doubt whether such a ministry had ever been created. Kerrl, former Prussian Minister of Justice, made himself "Church Minister" after a conversation with Hitler, and the latter accepted the *fait accompli* rather than cause a fuss. As a Lammers aide, Wienstein, drily explained it: "Originally there was no intention to create a particular ministry for church affairs".[175] Hitler's edict of July 16, 1935 had simply stated that the Reich Minister without Portfolio, Kerrl, would administer the sections of the Reich and Prussian Interior Ministries which concerned church affairs. Yet Kerrl had signed a law later that month as "Reichminister for Church Affairs". "One must therefore speak of a Reich Church Minister."

Although the overt NS effort to seize the Protestant church had been lost for the most part by 1935, campaigns would continue, but primarily from Goebbels who arranged the campaign to discredit priests as smugglers and homosexuals, and from Bormann who worked to close church schools and other church activities. Reichbishop Mueller was ignored by Hitler after 1935, and Kerrl nearly so. Kerrl did not even see Hitler after 1938.[176]

Against the powerful of the party, who had Hitler's tacit agreement to persecute religion, Kerrl, who called himself a Christian, could do little or nothing. He approached Weizsaecker for support of a decree for the protection of religious freedom in Germany.[177] "Kerrl spoke of the NS system in terms that one could hardly have expected from the lips of one of the oldest followers of Hitler, such as he was." Kerrl's major foe was Rosenberg, himself having difficulty seeing Hitler between 1938 and 1941.

Kerrl, with a minuscule ministry, a handful of officials, remained largely a minister without portfolio. He died in 1941 and his post was not filled.

The new Ministry of Propaganda, created almost immedi-

175 BA R43II/1036, 15.12.36.

176 Prof. John Conway's study of Reich church policy.

177 Weizsaecker, 282.

ately upon Hitler's accession to power on March 13, 1933, remained the powerful domain of Josef Goebbels who became internationally famous as Hitler's master liar. Goebbels was almost an "old fighter", having joined the party in the mid-twenties through the agency of the socialist wing of the NSDAP of Gregor Strasser, then deserting him for a lifelong loyalty to Hitler. Goebbels' strength rested on his virulent pen and persuasive voice, plus a reputation as Hitler's best listener. He also had a doctor's degree, which added a valued prestige, with Hitler's scorn-admiration nexus toward the academic world.

Goebbels' position was among the most secure, yet even he was at times abjectly fearful of losing Hitler's grace. "His closest colleague, Fritsche, testified that the slightest criticism from the Party Chancellory alarmed Goebbels and brought the entire Ministry into feverish activity."[178] One remembers Goebbels' fearful clinging to Hitler all during the Roehm crisis to be sure that he would not be shot, as was Strasser.

The Ministry was particularly beset with struggles, more so than other ministries, where skill could be measured. Hitler had given Goebbels "control of all publications", but had also appointed a "Reichleader for the Press", Amann, and a "Reich Press Chief", Dietrich. Goebbels fought Rosenberg for the area of culture, Goering in the area of art, Rosenberg and Buehler in literature. Not only the entire party organization felt itself called upon to propagandize, but so did other ministries, particularly Rust's, and even the Foreign Ministry.

The feud with Ribbentrop was particularly bitter as described by a third competitor, Dietrich.[179] "Ribbentrop talked Hitler one day into giving him in writing the entire propaganda outside Germany—without Goebbels being told one word about it." The next morning Ribbentrop's men came to seize all the equipment. Goebbels' men barricaded themselves in their offices and appealed for help. Hitler simply ordered the two to sit together until they had come to an agreement. Three hours later they came out, red-faced that no agreement was possible. Hitler angrily dictated a compromise

[178] Krosigk, 234.

[179] Dietrich, 130ff.

which largely reversed his written promise to Ribbentrop. "Ribbentrop in practice ignored the latter statement, instead used the first 'Command' to work against Goebbels' propaganda efforts all over the world." Hitler was fully informed. "He had often ridiculed Ribbentrop's sick ambition but refused to intervene despite constant complaints about this impossible condition."[180]

Goebbels created a grand system of 41 "Reichs Propaganda Offices". Yet they were hybrids, since they were also the Gau propaganda leaders and therewith subject to the Gauleiter. "So developed a tug-of-war, in which Goebbels usually lost, between the Berlin Minister and the local party bosses, who despite the centralistic ballyhoo of the Third Reich represent the continued princely powers, now with brown shades."[181]

Heiber doubted Goebbels' skills as a propagandist—the master was Hitler not Goebbels—and regarded the NS press as pitiful. The pre-1933 votes were out of all proportion to the press circulation. After 1933 it was primarily dull; even Goebbels knew that able men preferred not to work for the party and that the younger men continued the liberal, not the NS, spirit.[182]

Heiber further observed that Goebbels' brilliance suffered during 1934 to 1938, once the real fight was over; his position was further weakened by his wildly pursued two-year romance with the Czech actress Baarova, for whom he was prepared to renounce his position and wife, which would have pleased his second in command, who wanted them both.[183] In 1938 Hitler stepped in to force the idealized Goebbels' family back together. This reconciliation by fiat occurred just before Goebbels' most famous bid for recognition, the calling out of the SA mobs for the attack on the Jews, November 9, 1938. It also reflected his inferior status at the party meet-

[180] *Ibid.* See also Erich Kordt, *Nicht aus den Akten*, Stuttgart, 1950, 320-21. Seabury, 77, sees this as a defeat for Goebbels.

[181] Helmut Heiber, *Josef Goebbels*, Berlin, 1962, 144.

[182] *Ibid.*, 159. For high praise of Goebbels as propagandist see E. K. Bramsted, *Goebbels and National Socialist Propaganda*, Lansing, 1965.

[183] *Ibid.*, 278ff.

ing in Munich. The infamous attack was a great mistake; it horrified foreigners, many Germans, even many NS. Goering objected to its uneconomic destruction. Bramsted thinks Hitler casually ordered the action. (Bramsted also quotes Himmler's blaming Goebbels' unending pressure for the 1942-44 annihilation of the Jews, which Himmler did not want to do.[184]) Heiber doubted that Goebbels was really anti-Semitic, rather that he saw the move as a way to win back Hitler's favor. Yet already by January 1939 a new campaign was under way against him, led by his old enemies Rosenberg and Himmler.

The greater threat was the infiltration of Dr. Otto Dietrich into Goebbels' office; Dietrich replaced Funk on Jan 15, 1938, over Goebbels' strong protests and a battle ensued between the two for prestige. A local flunky was fired for "misplacing" a Goebbels' speech in the paper, although he had acted on Dietrich's specific order.[185] With contradictory orders, implementation went according to a local agent's awareness of the relative power of the two men. The farther from the capital, the easier it was for the minister to get compliance; but in Berlin Dietrich won 9 to 1. By mid-1942 Goebbels lost officially every right to intervene in the press and was fully dependent on the goodwill of his State Secretary.[186] Dietrich's power rested on the fact that he had a daily conference at Hitler's headquarters while Goebbels remained in Berlin. Dietrich was able to gradually replace nearly all of the Goebbels men in the Ministry with his own clique from the party.

The famous January and February 1943 speeches calling for total war, are best interpreted as a power play. Goebbels, who unlike Hitler, remained close enough to the people to deliver speeches and appear occasionally to inspect bomb damage, hoped for a palace revolt. A shake-up did occur, but the "total-war profiteers", Heiber thinks, were Bormann,

[184] *Ibid.*, 282. Also Bramsted, 384, 392.

[185] *Ibid.*, 170.

[186] *Ibid.* Bramsted places Dietrich behind Goebbels in the power struggle, 111-14.

Lammers, and Keitel. By March 1943 Goebbels tried for an alliance with Goering, but found him much too lethargic. Goebbels then organized a group of Ley, Funk, Speer, later Backe, Stuckart, Milch, and Sauckel, but all were too unimportant. He undertook relations with Himmler and a pact was formed in November 1943 against Ribbentrop.[187] Goebbels then tried to organize the Gauleiter whom he ordinarily regarded as primitive; but their longstanding distrust and hatred were much too great. He would write and speak of the total war, but the only future was total destruction, Germany's suicide and his own.

NS Germany's foreign policy has been studied so thoroughly that a few remarks about Baron Konstantin von Neurath and von Ribbentrop as ministers and von Weizsaecker as State Secretary should suffice. Almost all Beamter remained in the ministry, although Hitler referred to his foreign office as an "intellectual garbage heap". For the handful released, the posts were filled with men of similar background. If anything changed, the aristocratic monopoly was stronger than before.[188] The few NS temporarily sent abroad in 1933, like Ribbentrop, flopped badly. (While drunk at an ILO Conference Ley had publicly compared Latin Americans to monkeys.) As the NS were singularly ill-prepared to be diplomats, Hitler contented himself with setting up competing party organizations. Alfred Rosenberg's flubbed so badly in 1933 that it was shunted off, but Ribbentrop's was less obviously inept and survived.

Neurath was the top Beamter inherited from the pre-1933 cabinet. He came from a long line of state officials, army officers, and nobility. Raised among the small nobility of Wuerttemberg, he was also a staunch Protestant. The French ambassador, François-Poncet, described him as an unassertive, correct, urbane gentleman who had undoubtedly opposed the war. Neurath's credentials included the usual legal training, 30 years' experience in the Foreign Service, and the Iron Cross

[187] *Ibid.*, 333.

[188] Paul Seabury, *The Wilhelmstrasse: A Study of German Diplomats under the Nazi Regime*, Berkeley, 1954.

from World War I. Having risen to Ambassador to England, he was appointed Foreign Minister by Papen in 1932 and so continued until 1938. He testified that Hindenburg wished him to stay to tame the NS revolutionaries; his remaining in office was a Hindenburg condition for the appointment of Hitler as Chancellor. As Davidson concluded: "he said—and his testimony was corroborated by the Swiss Minister, the Papal Nuncio, and the French and Belgian Ambassadors, among others—that he had wanted to change it (The Treaty of Versailles) by negotiation, and the records of his proposals and diplomatic conversations bear this out."[189] As Neurath put it, the question for him had been whether to remain "the rock on the side of the bank or the rock in the stream". He preferred to believe Hitler when the latter told his advisors that he wanted peace. When at the Hossbach Conference in November 1937 the Fuehrer disclosed his intention to go to war, Neurath had a heart attack.[190]

His position seems more the result of good conservative connections, notably with Papen, than his own excellence. (Neurath had hoped by using as State Secretary his son-in-law, Mackensen, son of a World War I field marshal, to bolster his position.) The observers, like Poncet, who thought him sincere also thought him lazy.[191] Another major weakness was "his inability to express himself, particularly in a large circle of people".[192] Physically unimposing, good in conversation but poor with a speech, Neurath lacked energy or bravado to do more than hope Hitler would change. Weizsaecker described Neurath as anything but dynamic personality, "a man who likes shooting game from a stand, but [who] will not go out into the fields after it".[193] This was one reason why he saw much too little of Hitler. Though possessing common sense, and a master of routine, Neurath lacked political imagination. He tried to keep Hitler on the paths of caution. As he failed, he accepted the NS foreign policy barbarisms.

Neurath was asked to resign in late January 1938, during

[189] Davidson, 168. [190] *Ibid.* [191] Seabury, 27.
[192] Weizsaecker, 110. [193] *Ibid.*, 109.

the Blomberg crisis, in the little coup which dropped the three significant "moderates"—Neurath, Blomberg, and Schacht. His caution counted for nothing when he accepted the position as protector of Bohemia-Moravia in 1939, where he was vulnerable to being held accountable for brutal policies he could scarcely alter. His assistant, Karl Frank, implemented Himmler's policies, nearly ignoring Neurath. Although the Czechs later wanted to hang him, Hitler had found Neurath too lenient.[194] To "crack down" Hitler sent Heydrich to Prague in September 1941 and Neurath went on leave, refusing to resign for another two years.

At Nuremberg Neurath was sentenced to 15 years. Davidson says: "If one accepts the judgment's statements, it is difficult to see what was criminal in anything Neurath did as Foreign Minister".[195]

Hitler found a more pliable, if incompetent, replacement —the party "expert", Joachim von Ribbentrop, with champagne wealth obtained by marriage and with a reservoir of misinformation and prejudice that would cost Germany both peace and victory.

Ribbentrop was born in a small garrison town near the Dutch border, the son of a retired army officer. He dropped out of school at 16; by 18 he was working on construction crews in Canada where his charm brought him social acceptance. As a minor social success, Ribbentrop might have remained in the New World, but instead he returned when war broke out in 1914. He fought in the war as a lieutenant, receiving the Iron Cross, First Class. With his knowledge of French and English, he worked briefly with a cotton-importing firm in Berlin until he met wealth. He was married to Annelies Henkel, daughter of the owner of the champagne plant whose product he sold.

At first concerned only with social success (adding a "von" to his name), Ribbentrop watched the rise of the NSDAP which he joined in 1932. Since Hitler knew so little of the world outside Germany, he found the socially respectable Ribbentrop convincing, because whatever Hitler believed,

[194] Davidson, 172. [195] *Ibid.*, 176.

Ribbentrop confirmed. (Hitler's most fatal persuasion was in 1939 that England would not fight.)

In 1933 Ribbentrop set up a bureau of amateurs across from the Foreign Ministry, designed to supply Hitler with processed information that would please him. Ribbentrop's men edited foreign news for Hitler who had no other source (he read no other language). Ribbentrop was given much of the correspondence addressed to the Foreign Office before the Foreign Office got it and was even allowed to answer it. When made a "special Ambassador", he was responsible to Hitler alone. Despite his ineptness he was given the Anglo-German naval agreement by a Britain desperately striving to prevent a war.[196] This "success" brought Ribbentrop the job as Ambassador to England, where his series of mistakes began by greeting King George with a resounding "Heil Hitler".

Ribbentrop spent most of his 15 months as Ambassador in Berlin fighting for more power. Also in Berlin, he arranged the Anti-Comintern pact. When the British rejected his amateurish offer to guarantee the British Empire in return for German power in Eastern Europe, Ribbentrop changed from the *Mein Kampf* dream of alliance with Nordic Britain to an extreme Anglophobia; this was just before he became Foreign Minister.[197] This scorn of the rejected suitor equalled "proof" by 1939 that the British would not fight.

Ribbentrop's technique of power was to note what Hitler said and then to repeat the idea later to Hitler as his own, or to bring some evidence from the foreign press to support it. Besides his modest talent for languages, he brought to diplomacy an industriousness, working 14 hours or more a day. This substituted for skill, as did the vast expansion of staff, over fourfold, from 1938 to 1945. "It was a job for which he had not the slightest training or capacity. When he got the appointment it surprised even his wife. . . . In fact, Ribbentrop said it surprised him. . . ."[198]

He chose not to live in the Wilhelmstrasse quarters reserved for the Foreign Minister, but remained remote, except from Hitler. He largely abandoned his amateur party clique

[196] *Ibid.*, 157. [197] Seabury, 58. [198] Davidson, 151.

for the professional Beamten.[199] One exception to the isolation was Dr. Martin Luther, a neighborhood acquaintance and a local minor official who had met Frau Ribbentrop while collecting party dues. Luther was soon given the job of redecorating the villa, the stables, and the London Embassy. Hard-working, he rose to be an Embassy advisor, then Chief of the party advisory group. His transfer to the Civil Service was delayed by an indictment for embezzlement. He eventually headed the Foreign Office Section on "Deutschland".

As Minister, Ribbentrop took the side of the old-line diplomats against the party. Key personnel remained. He fought the party foreign policy leader, Bohle, and got rid of him when Hess left the country. On the defensive from the outside, he insisted on a total obedience from within. In return for his protection his Beamter had to join the party. On one occasion his entire corps of Beamten had to march like soldiers passed him at the Tempelhof airfield.[200]

In all the voluminous records of Nuremberg there is no word of respect for Ribbentrop. Even Hitler did not bother to consult him when he annexed Austria. Mussolini in 1939 thought him "a truly sinister man because he is an imbecile and presumptuous".[201] Krosigk agreed with Goebbels' evaluation: "you could find some good characteristic in all of the top clique, except Ribbentrop".[202] He was one of the very few in the government who urged Hitler toward a war. When at war he fully agreed with Hitler's every action, including the extermination of the Jews. The fanatic Luther was appointed to assist in the task of deportation.

Seabury concludes that the problem came down to the incessant intrigue in Hitler's court, where without repute in party circles, Ribbentrop was "totally dependent upon the Fuehrer's own continued grace".[203] Ergo his constant deferment to Hiter, and ergo his maintenance of his bureaucracy; "an insolvent and detested chief was bound to his contemptuous, but subordinate officialdom in a tenuous but persistent

[199] Seabury, 59. [200] Davidson, 152. [201] *Ibid.*, 158.
[202] Krosigk, 235. [203] Seabury, 166.

coalition of fear".[204] His defeat in 1941 by Rosenberg concerning power in Russia brought a singularly bitter scene with Hitler in July 1941, and his offer to resign.[205] Both were evidently made ill by the argument, and Ribbentrop promised never again to question the Fuehrer's judgment. Because the Foreign Minister stayed so close to Hitler and so far from his Ministry, its capacity for decision was crippled.

Krosigk noted that Ribbentrop spent so much energy in battling competitors for his prerogatives that it was a wonder he did anything else at all—which at least indicates great energy. Although Hitler made fun of him as a pompous ass, Goering, Goebbels, and Himmler all failed to get him removed.[206] Weizsaecker saw this energy as useful in defending the Ministry from attack:

> However much Ribbentrop may have pushed aside the Foreign Office when he was Hitler's unofficial collaborator, he now vigorously defended his own competence against the influence of all irregular advisors in foreign policy. He carried on a continual feud with Goebbels and Rosenberg. He challenged Hess' right of veto in matters of Foreign Office personnel. By means of large special funds, which he managed to procure, he escaped the control of the Minister of Finance. . . . With Himmler he attempted to keep on friendly terms because he was afraid of him.[207]

Dr. Luther had by 1940 acquired the Ministry's jurisdiction over Jewish affairs,[208] in particular the deportation directives sent to satellite countries. He developed a kind of independence and by 1943 delusions of grandeur. In a letter to Himmler, Luther revealed that Ribbentrop was insane.[209] This followed a financial investigation of Luther's office in December 1942. Luther's critical report to Himmler on Jan. 11, 1943 emphasized the mental infirmities of the Foreign Minister and the "decreasing" NS influence in the Ministry as

[204] *Ibid.*, 167. [205] *Ibid.*, 118.
[206] Weizsaecker, 278.
[207] *Ibid.*, 128. [208] Hilberg, 350. [209] Seabury, 131-32.

younger men went to the army, leaving behind the reactionaries. "Ribbentrop has completely turned away from the party and considers himself to be much above it, to need it no more and to be able to carry through his foreign policy with the old Beamten, even though they are still so reactionary."[210]

The SS-trusted Luther who had not seen Ribbentrop for six months, sent him a list of 168 Beamten who should be cleaned out, but Ribbentrop sent the entire list on to Hitler, knowing full well that Hitler would not throw out 168. "The Fuehrer had impressed on Ribbentrop that the filling of foreign positions in the Foreign Ministry cannot be with men with party decorations because of the fiasco in the South east area, but instead only with men who have the variety of technical skills qualifying them for these posts."[211] Himmler backed the leadership principle and Ribbentrop; Luther, instead of becoming Foreign Minister, was sent to a concentration camp where he died.

A purge followed, wreaking more havoc. The remaining younger party men finally took the long-delayed power, while the Ministry took over a hodgepodge of assignments. The center of gravity was gone; what remained was a vast undergrowth of new divisions and agencies. "The chain of command . . . had rusted and virtually disappeared."[212] Symbolically air raids were blowing up the Ministry piece by piece.

Although few diplomats were directly involved in the July 20, 1944 plot, reprisals were visited upon the Foreign Office as a whole because Hitler had never trusted it.[213] The long frustrated Gauleiter Bohle reported less than 10% had turned away from alien, that is Christian, creeds; the loyal 10% was only among the very young. Hitler ordered another purge; an executed conspirator had testified that 60% of the Beamten "unreliable".

The most significant of these reactionaries who played a double game was State Secretary Weizsaecker, replacing Mackensen, who could produce the testimony of the Roman church as well as top Protestants that he had been of enor-

[210] CGD, T175, R124, F9652-6.
[211] *Ibid.* [212] Seabury, 139. [213] *Ibid.*, 144ff.

mous assistance to them as well as to the Jews. A naval officer until 1918, without the usual university background, Weizsaecker was nationalist and monarchist. Ribbentrop had preferred him, thinking Weizsaecker would obey and not become a rival as a party man would.[214] He said on March 5, 1938 that he remained, "taking up this cross", hoping thereby to influence the unstable Ribbentrop to prevent war; "the only chance of doing that was in the Foreign Office, not outside it".[215] Weizsaecker resigned in 1943 to become Ambassador to the Vatican.

He was the ministry's liaison to the Resistance movement.[216] Beginning at the time of the Sudeten crisis, Weizsaecker was a party to General Beck's plans, who advised him to stay in office. Weizsaecker then sent secret advice to Chamberlain to stand fast, that Hitler would retreat.[217] This occurred though Weizsaecker regarded Germany's cause as just. Yet the involvement of the Ministry in the deportation of Jews from satellite countries brought him a seven-year sentence at Nuremberg.

There is no question that the Ministry of Justice became thousands of times over a dispenser of injustice, a fact that ignores the million-fold murder that circumvented the Ministry altogether.[218] Most of this probably occurred contrary to the convictions of the Minister of Justice Franz Guertner, who in 1924, as Bavarian Minister of Justice, had interfered with the process of Bavarian justice to help secure the earlier release of Hitler from prison. Despite the perversion of law during his time in office, the common conclusion of Guertner's associates was that he was not NS, but a conservative nationalist, who opposed the NS injustices but did not fight them. Bonn State Secretary Buelow defined him as "not a fighter"; others regarded him as "weak".

To the apparently obvious judgment of Guertner as more weak than evil, Krosigk observed that the supposedly colorless jurist was actually a man praised by Lawrence of Arabia

[214] Weizsaecker, 121.
[215] Seabury, 61.
[216] *TWC*, XII, 241-43.
[217] Seabury, 93ff.
[218] Ilse Staff, *Justiz im Dritten Reich*, Frankfurt, 1964.

as an opponent in World War I and credited by Lawrence with saving the Turkish army.[219] Krosigk regarded Guertner as possessed of an unshakable philosophical calm, a tough courage and humor, a man who had worked his way up from poverty with much sacrifice to achieve great learning, command of four languages, and fine skill as an organist.

Krosigk believed Guertner was aware from long contact with Hitler in Bavaria that the totalitarian demands of the party would attack his beloved domain of law and that his name would be used to cover up dealings contrary to that law, but that Guertner thought it cowardly to surrender the last bastions of justice even when his resistance had no hope of success.[220] On one occasion when a younger assistant begged that he either protest or resign, Guertner answered with a sad smile, "My dear colleague, I didn't start the revolution". He compared his career to that of Sisyphus constantly pushing the stone up the mountain only to see it roll down again before reaching the top. When a former associate met him shortly before Christmas 1940 on the steps of the ministry and commented how tired he seemed and whether he would resign, Guertner replied: "You cannot imagine . . . how happy, how eternally happy I would be, if I did not have to go into this building. But I must, I must. Look, there are the three who want in, Frank, Freisler and Thierack. One of them will get it. That's why I have to drag myself back in". In a few weeks he was dead.[221]

Long before that time, however, Guertner had no illusions about Hitler; concerning their infrequent meetings he reported: "One can't call it a conversation. He lets me say one sentence. Then he talks, without pause, without period or comma, like a torrent, which inundates everything in its path. The preconceived opinion against Justice is insurmountable. His very nature is anarchic, without any sense for the necessity of political order. We get along only when we talk about new novels".[222] Berlin Mayor Sahm quoted Guertner of 1934 as ashamed to meet foreign visitors who

[219] Krosigk, 317.
[220] *Ibid.*, 320. [221] *Ibid.*, 324. [222] *Ibid.*, 321.

were skeptical of any rule of law in Germany: "It is enough to drive one to despair. In the last weeks there have been six more murders in the concentration camps. When one tells Himmler that, one gets the answer, 'He must fight the Communist danger' ".[223] When Sahm asked about Frick's relationship to the Gestapo as Minister of Interior, Guertner answered, "Goering and Heydrich weigh much more than a hundred Fricks". Or as he told Frank shortly before his death: "Hitler loves cruelty. It pleases him . . . when he can torment someone. He has a devilish sadism. Otherwise he simply could not stand Himmler and Heydrich".[224]

This interpretation gains in credibility if one adds the contempt Hitler had for Guertner's ministry, occupied by the worst of the Beamten jurists.

> Our department of Justice frequently enraged me by its handling of crimes of treason. For instance on one occasion they recommended a traitor to mercy on the grounds that he was "primarily employed as a smuggler and should therefore be dealt with as such"! [A common Guertner trick to avoid death sentences.] It was only with the greatest difficulty that I was able to persuade Dr. Guertner . . . of the absolute necessity of exercising the utmost severity in cases of treason.[225]

Yet Hitler kept Guertner in office, although there were bloodthirsty judges at work who would pass out death sentences as though they were lottery tickets.

Guertner had been Bavarian Minister of Justice since 1922. He became Reich Minister of Justice in 1932 and stayed on in 1933. As Hitler described that decision: "It was I who had to make an effort of objectivity—and a great effort too—to call to the Ministry of Justice, the man who had me imprisoned. But when I had to choose amongst the men who were in the running, I could not find anyone better. Freisler was

[223] Quoted in Gert Buchheit, *Soldatentum und Rebellion*, Rastatt, 1961, 224.

[224] Frank, 132.

[225] *Hitler's Secret Conversations*, 7.6.42, 420.

nothing but a Bolshevik. As for the other [Schlegelberger], his face could not deceive me. It was enough to have seen him once".[226] Krosigk thought Hitler had chosen Guertner to avoid the impression that he was seeking revenge, and because he took men of ability, respecting each man's character and knowledge.[227]

That Guertner was serving on a sinking ship of justice is understandable from the fact that the punishment of crime of an NS, or nonpunishment of what the NS called "crime", was something that could not be hidden from prying eyes. Unlike financial wizardry, verdicts were so obvious that even Hitler in reading the newspapers could decide that justice had been "soft" and order a death penalty instead. Secondly, justice was confronted directly by the full force of Himmler's and Heydrich's police state—although the worst injustices were perpetrated by simply sending an accused person to Dachau without permitting the ministry jurisdiction. The impact of the NS dual power, propaganda and police, was directed at each judge involved in a case of interest to the party. The party was never content with its justice, no matter how horrible a verdict to an objective observer.

Guertner's most famous anti-law action was his post facto legalization of the "Roehm Putsch" murders. Guertner's rationale partly reflected the common conservative notion that Roehm represented the most serious threat to law and order, and secondly, he hoped to avoid the implication that the example of murder by the head of state would be an excuse for anyone else to murder; therefore it must be justified by "reason of state".[228]

Typical of the delaying action Guertner encouraged is the 1938 struggle with the party over the independence of judges. The key man in the struggle was Guertner's assistant, Hans von Dohnanyi, about whom Bormann bitterly complained to Lammers in July 1938: the man was half-Hungarian and one-fourth Jewish; he had flatly stated on his questionnaire his opposition to the NS racial policies as un-Chris-

[226] *Ibid.*, 310. [227] Krosigk, 318. [228] *Ibid.*, 324.

tian.[229] (Dohnanyi's wife was a Bonhoeffer; both Dohnanyi and Dietrich Bonhoeffer were major participants in the 1944 plot and both were executed.) Guertner had talked Hitler into keeping Dohnanyi. Lammers had taken Bormann's protest to Hitler on July 25, 1938, which led to a Hess statement that Lammers should regard the Bormann letter as not having been written. Lammers suggested the usual compromise: transferring Dohnanyi to a less exposed position, and Hitler so ordered.

What had brought on the party wrath was Dohnanyi's commentary in April 1938, written for Guertner and sent, to Lammers, on the theme that the judges must remain independent. He noted the contradiction between paragraph 71 of the 1933 Beamten Law—that the Fuehrer could release an official who was not wholeheartedly for the NS state—and paragraph 171, which added the sentence, "The release of a judge according to paragraph 71 cannot be based on the content of a decision made in the course of the judge's duties".[230] Dohnanyi saw great danger if the latter sentence were to be changed. Lammers reported to Guertner on April 27, 1938 that Hitler thought the law must be changed, that it was intolerable that a judge could not be fired if he showed a lack of the NS *Weltanschauung*. Lammers was to check with Interior Minister Wilhelm Frick.

Frick justified Guertner's judgment of him, that he lacked courage, by agreeing that there had been some "questionable verdicts" recently and that the sentence in paragraph 171 could easily be sacrificed. Guertner's defense (June 1, 1938) of the vital sentence to Lammers denied the necessity of using a judge's decision to show disloyalty; one could detect "disloyalty" in his nonofficial life. Cancelling the sentence "would mean the end of the office of judge".[231] Guertner suggested instead that Hitler strongly reaffirm the significance of paragraph 71. Frick feared that would cause unrest; Hitler should make a private emphasis to department heads.

Guertner seemed to have won when Lammers reported

[229] BA R43II/1145a. [230] BA R43II/1516. [231] *Ibid.*

on July 1, 1938 that Hitler accepted Guertner's position. (Hitler usually "agreed" but did something else.) In this case, the order of July 12 followed, which seemed to keep the Paragraph 171 sentence, but reaffirmed Paragraph 71 in such a way that it applied to judges: their release if, "the manner of his official activity, in particular through his decisions, or through his official or unofficial behavior . . . shows that he finds the NS *Weltanschauung* alien".[232] An example of such "behavior" was *giving the lowest penalty for "racial defilement"*.

Otto Thierack, pushing for Guertner's job, saw the problem clearly.[233] There were so many "wrong decisions" simply because (a) "our laws still have largely the expressions of the liberal period"; (b) the majority of judges refuse to interest themselves in political affairs. "The problem then is one of education and a leadership problem of the judges. Up to now nothing has been done in this direction and one can scarcely expect anything to be done now." The solution, other than the unmentioned appointment of Thierack as Minister of Justice, was to give his special "Peoples Courts" the right to intervene.[234]

Rather surprisingly, upon Guertner's death (Jan. 29, 1941) Hitler did not immediately accept a radical as Minister of Justice. Hans Frank, who headed the Reich Lawyers Association when his Bavarian Ministry of Justice was incorporated into that of the Reich, had made too many enemies.[235] Schlegelberger had been implicated too much with communism; Roland Freisler, although an NS since 1925, had absorbed "some respect for tradition" while serving in the Justice Ministry. (Freisler had been shunted to unimportant jobs by Guertner after Guertner was forced to accept him as State Secretary.) Heiber continued: "as so frequently when faced with a decision, Hitler did nothing". Schlegelberger was put in charge of operations.

Thierack, thus passed over, took advantage of a conflict

[232] IZG, NG285. [233] *Ibid.*, 17.9.38. [234] *Ibid.*

[235] Helmut Heiber, "Zur Justiz im Dritten Reich, Der Fall Elias", *Vierteljahresheft fuer Zeitgeschichte*, 1955, 276.

between the Justice Ministry and Heydrich, concerning the execution of Czech resistance fighters, to climb into office. Neurath and the Justice Ministry had been able to effect a halt of Hitler's order of execution for two years. Opposing this mercy were Bormann, Goebbels, and Heydrich. Heydrich went to Prague in September 1941 to clean house and found that a Czech official, Elias, protected by Neurath, had been in contact with the opposition. Heydrich consulted Thierack who saw his chance. Each stimulating the other, they decided to use the Peoples Court and the Gestapo, not the States Attorney as prosecution, thus avoiding the Ministry of Justice.

Thierack was playing the role of the legal Siegfried to slay the bureaucratic dragon.[236] Elias was arrested; Schlegelberger, learning of it in the papers, called Thierack for an interview and asked whether he realized that he was thus involving himself in Heydrich's "program". Thierack did, and planned to climb in the program. Schlegelberger tried to get allies such as Stuckart in the Interior Ministry and Lammers, but both deserted him. Thierack kept his promise; Elias was found guilty on flimsy evidence and there followed the quick execution of 150 to 200 Czechs by October 5, the executions continuing into November. Heydrich notified Hitler that despite the obstruction of Schlegelberger and thanks to the outstanding help of Thierack, he had achieved a quick trial and execution.[237]

Despite such recommendations, it took Thierack until August 1942 to become Minister of Justice, Freisler taking the chairmanship of the Peoples Courts. Thierack was appointed to the Ministry with the express permission of Hitler to deviate from the existing law when necessary. Thus died Justice after a long and painful accident of politics.

Goering

Although Hermann Goering does not fit neatly into any section of the administration, there would be a large gap if

[236] *Ibid.*, 281. [237] *Ibid.*, 290.

he were excluded, for he enjoyed the title "The Second Man in the Reich". Yet making a safe generalization about his role is more difficult than for any other NS leader; the safest is that he was usually important and usually ruthless.[238]

One can begin with the immediate oddity that Goering was significant on the national level as Hitler's second-in-command; in 1939 he was named successor to Hitler as well as becoming Air Minister. He was also significant on the regional level as Minister President of Prussia. Although "Reichminister" he was therefore significantly anti-centralization. He was of the party but also of the military, and he could speak for both; his Luftwaffe was the most party-oriented of the three services. Further, Goering was dominant in 1933-34 as organizer of the secret police, until he was eased out by the more patient Himmler. In 1936 he became a dominant force in the economic sphere with his "Four Year Plan". But like his Gestapo role, Goering's business role passed away, so that by 1940 it would be difficult to show exactly what part he was playing. Some assert he even tried to save the peace. It would be rash to say that by 1942 Goering played a dominant role anywhere but in the Luftwaffe. In 1933 among the most radical, he was in 1934 a destroyer of SA radicals; by 1939 he was regarded as "conservative", a hope for compromise at home and abroad. In 1941 Goering issued the order beginning "the final solution". On Hitler's orders he called the Wannsee Conference, which decided on destroying the Jews, and he selected Heydrich to direct the destruction.[239]

Among the most clever, ambitious, and brutal, Goering was outdistanced in each vice by the tortoises, Himmler and Bormann, who finally convinced Hitler of his treachery. His decline had begun when his Luftwaffe failed to defeat England. It is even possible that his vanity is responsible for the failure to destroy the British forces at Dunkirk. His position

[238] Bewley, who saw Goering through the eyes of Frau Goering and family, would not agree. See Charles Bewley, *Herman Goering and the Third Reich*, New York, 1962.

[239] Davidson, 62.

declined further when his Luftwaffe failed again at Stalingrad. On April 23, 1945 the SS, on Hitler's orders, arrested Goering and his family, with orders to kill them if Berlin fell. By then Goering was considered lazy, vain, arrogant; he was more scorned than feared. Everything he was supposed to control had fallen to pieces.

The paradox begins with Goering's having come from a respectable family, the son of a colonial official. The family lived for a time with Hermann von Epenstein, a rich friend of alleged Jewish descent, who was Hermann's godfather and who, by Davidson's account, was the mother's lover for 15 years.[240] The "Jew" paid for Hermann's education and left him considerable property, including a castle. A war ace of skill and reported gallantry, Goering left the new Germany for Sweden. After a romance and marriage in Sweden, he returned to Germany and took courses at the University of Munich. There he was attracted by Hitler's oratory. He was wounded in the 1923 Putsch attempt and again fled to Sweden and to morphine to escape the pain. His need for drugs returned during the stresses of the war (Bewley calls it "medication").

As a war hero and of the respectable middle-class, yet with an unswerving loyalty to Hitler, Goering was placed in the political forefront. This included the presidency of the last Reichstag, where he gleefully cooperated with the communists in making parliamentary government impossible. A cluster of jobs followed: he was in 1933 Minister without Portfolio, then quickly Minister President of Prussia and Prussian Minister of Interior to organize the secret police and the concentration camps. As an air ace he presided over the revival of an air force. More power was added as he took over the economy with the 1936 Four Year Plan.

Where there was intrigue and violence, there was Goering—in 1934 the miscellaneous killing over which he presided; in 1938 the ouster of Blomberg and Fritsch; even the

[240] So thinks Davidson, 64. See also Roger Manvell and Heinrich Fraenkel, *Goering*, New York, 1962, 23. Bewley denies it.

ouster of Gauleiter like Streicher in 1939. When Hitler needed a respectable bully he used Goering.

Goering cultivated the image of a moderate. He was used as a kind of troubleshooter, but seems generally to have been made uncomfortable by fanatics because they implied trouble. With foreigners he appeared more flexible and congenial than any other party leader. Yet he bullied Austria in 1938 and Poland in 1939. As Hitler said of him in 1943, when Goering was in eclipse: "He is ice cold in time of crisis. At such a time one can't have a better advisor—brutal and ice cold".[241] The brutal image changed to that of pampered aesthete. Perhaps Goering's preference for the fruits of power took him away from the roots of power. For example, in the middle of the war a plane brought rare fruits and wines to his private train.[242] His estate became a fabled Oriental castle of luxury; he pirated art on an unparalleled scale.

Buchheit sees Goering as more the friend of authoritarian order than of sadistic cruelties.[243] Unlike most of the top party men, he surrounded himself with middle-class types, perhaps because he was one of the very few who had emerged from a solid family background. He had a frequently expressed contempt for the political *Leiter* of the party and the SA rowdies, yet he ran with the pack.

Like Hitler, Goering was peripatetic. He was famous for his change of uniforms five times a day; he would also change offices, move from one office to the other, staying in each but an hour or so and dashing on to some other busy-ness. This multiplicity of Goering's offices was at once Goering's strength and weakness. He accumulated jobs, any of which would have taxed his abilities, then abandoned the real power to "subordinates" such as Himmler, "conceding" to him the command of the Gestapo. Buchheit assumes that Goering was afraid of the same fate that had fallen on Roehm, and found a security in the expansion of nominal powers. (His technique was to gather scandalous material, tapping telephones in his "Research Office", against potential ene-

241 Manvell, 296.

242 *Ibid.*, 297; Davidson, 87.

243 Buchheit, 73.

mies. Buchheit assumes that Goering's possession of Rosenberg's love letters to a Jewess gave him a "defense" against Rosenberg.) Yet this expansionist push brought a counterpush from the rest of the elite and aroused their fear, envy, and eventual scorn.

Buchheit agrees with the onetime Goering assistant in the Gestapo, Rudolph Diels, that Goering could have modified the brutality of the regime had he not been so cowardly, so afraid of Hitler's wrath, and so lazy. A resolve to persuade Hitler to a more reasonable course melted away as soon as Goering was in Hitler's presence. Although he enjoyed the nickname of "the iron Hermann", he was actually soft under the layers of fat—a soft personality covered with thunder and bluff.[244] On occasion, Goering could display something of the verve and energy of the authentic war hero, but he lacked the patience and ability to cooperate where necessary to assert a lasting influence.

[244] *Ibid.*, 76.

2 THE REICH MINISTRY OF INTERIOR

ANY of the Reich ministries would justify a study of the workings of a dictatorship. The Ministry of Interior was originally chosen on the assumption that it was the most important legal link between central and local government. It became apparent that the legal link was fragile, but that within and around this ministry were fought four key battles on these most important internal policies: (1) The party versus the state, (2) central versus local government, (3) the SS police versus the law, (4) racialism versus reason. It was the failure of the Interior Ministry to stop Hitler's anarchism that left the nation exposed to a mad caprice.

The fault was partly that the traditional ministerial organization was not equipped to deal with so much persuasive anti-reason, although it had a solid, legally trained staff able enough to provide the successor Bonn government with its top men. The fault was partly the hodgepodge character of the Ministry's assignment, and the absorption of new problems which did not fit into the other departments, e.g., the Jewish question which came to rest in the otherwise obscure section that decided matters of citizenship. One would expect party pressure on its otherwise quiet departments of police and Beamten, even on communal affairs, but what could be more innocuous than health and sport? Yet health got involved in the matter of euthanasia, and sport in the 1936 Olympics, as propaganda and whether Jewish athletes could participate for Germany (they did) and whether Hitler would honor the magnificent Negro athlete, Jesse Owens (he did not). For this mixture of services the Ministry was singled out by Hitler in his first cabinet to be the first (and only) ministry with an NS as minister, presumably to control the police —which, oddly, Wilhelm Frick never did.[1]

[1] The chart of organization is available in BA R43II/1134.

The Limits of Hitler's Power

Some of the Ministry's failure resulted from its formal dependence on Hitler's whim, as there was no Reichstag or even cabinet to appeal to. The ministry was not well equipped to deal with Hitler, partly because the personalities of its leaders were not those that inspired sufficient confidence from Hitler that when he granted plenipotentiary powers, he really would mean it the next day. Hitler despised bureaucrats; when looking for examples of their sins he resorted either to the Ministry of Justice or Interior: "We see a man of extreme mediocrity like Suren promoted to the rank of Under Secretary of State simply because he has served a stated number of years in the Ministry of Interior, and quite regardless of the fact that in all his activities he has generally done more harm than good."[2] His model of the jurist-bureaucrat-academician—all favorite epithets—was Frick. In 1942 Hitler conceded that Frick had been of enormous help during the 1924 trial as adjutant to the Munich Chief of Police. "I can even add that without him I would never have gotten out of prison. But as it is . . . there exists unfortunately, a particular type of NS who at a certain moment did great things for the party, but who is never capable of doing still better."[3] Then in the same breath came the famous Hitler quotation: "Every jurist must be regarded as a man deficient by nature, or else deformed by usage".[4]

State Secretary Wilhelm Stuckart, loyal NS, lamented the constant erosion of the Ministry's powers. "The decided bureaucratic attitude of the Ministry of Interior . . . were bureaucratic limits in Hitler's eyes and completely discredited the Ministry. . . . In the case of any difference of opinion we had to take into account in advance that Hitler would decide against the opinion of the Ministry of Interior. . . ."[5]

Dr. Wilhelm Frick

Like so many other party "greats", Frick began his career as a minor official in Bavaria. Of peasant stock, he was born on March 12, 1877 in the Palatinate, the son of a school-

[2] *Hitler's Secret Conversations*, 370.
[3] *Ibid.*, 306. [4] *Ibid.* [5] IZG, NG3710.

teacher and a farmer's daughter. He studied at various universities and received the doctorate from Heidelberg in 1901, though he was too poor to afford the prestige of publishing his thesis on Bavarian postal law. After three years in private law Frick served as a minor official of the Munich police and the county government. A weak chest prevented him from serving in World War I; he did his duty passing out ration books. After 10 years amid stacks of papers as a mere assistant Landrat, Frick returned to the Munich police. The communist revolution not only offended his sense of order but placed him briefly on a list of hostages; 10 others on the list were shot. Frick later came to know Hitler and his group when they sought permission for their meetings.

Frick was able with help from the Munich police chief, Poehner, to aid in protecting Hitler's party. At least once he had Hitler released after an arrest, but did not join the party until 1925. He took a leading part in the November 1923 putsch as head of the criminal section of the Munich police.[6] During the putsch Frick ordered the police not to intervene because they were too few to resist. Hitler also had assigned him to take over the police headquarters, but Frick was arrested before the march began. Frick then spent four months in prison under interrogation.

When he was elected to the Reichstag a month after his trial, Frick followed the imprisoned Hitler's policy of opposing the parliamentary system, and introduced the first of many bills to exclude Jews from public office and reduce their influence on the economy.[7] He denounced both socialism and capitalism. Although a poor speaker, he became the party's Reichstag leader.

In the election of December 1929, when the NS party became the third largest in Thuringia, Frick was elected Minister of Interior and Education. He cleaned out opposition officials, forbade the playing of "nigger jazz" in beer halls, and introduced NS-flavored prayers into the school system,

[6] Other than his assistance to the arrested Hitler, he is reported to have assisted in the escape of the Erzberger murderers.

[7] Davidson, 264.

three of which were found unconstitutional.[8] He tried to get citizenship for Hitler by making him a Gendarmerie Commissioner, but the effort failed. (With Frick's help, Hitler became a citizen in February 1932 by appointment as a State Councillor in Brunswick, by NS Minister Klagges.) Frick's extremist methods brought on the opposition of his own Thuringian government and the refusal of Berlin to pay the national subsidies to that state.

The Prussian police in 1930 ranked Frick as second to Hitler. He was the vital intermediary in the 1932 talks with the government and with the Centrist party in 1933.[9] As the only NS given a definite cabinet position in Hitler's first government, Frick formulated the decrees that ended the republic he had long denounced in the Reichstag. In name, Frick occupied the second most powerful position in Germany. But the person behind the title was destined for lesser things.

Frick's personnel file included a 1931 assessment by then second party leader to Hitler, Gregor Strasser—"A typical, average administrative Beamter, a kind of 'C+'. He has nothing of a real revolutionary or of a significant leader, but is rather a nice guy and a decent person".[10]

Although anti-Semitic, Frick was not a man of violence; he felt much more at home among his stacks of documents. Although he regarded Hitler as a Messiah come to save Germany, Frick was never at ease with the Fuehrer or with the beer hall rowdies dominant among the old fighters. By nature an authoritarian conservative, he could but regret the anarchic radicals with whom he had to deal. Although capable of anger and major campaigns for power, he could also be easily dismissed, as during the Roehm affair about which he had no foreknowledge, when he was simply told to go home, that "it did not concern him".[11] He was to accept the 1939 position of General Plenipotentiary for Administration, a glorious title which meant in fact that he chaired a committee which never met. He accepted the title of Protector Gen-

[8] BA R43II/1136a. See also Davidson, 265.

[9] Davidson, 266.

[10] BA NS26/1221, Frick Personalakt.

[11] IMT, IV, 213.

eral of Bohemia and Moravia after a determination to refuse had crumbled before Hitler's persuasiveness, only to be informed never to oppose the will of his "subordinate," K. H. Frank.

Frick's former colleagues agreed on his weakness, particularly in the face of resistance; yet he had a predilection for law and order.[12] Some regarded him as energetic, even after 10 difficult years in office, preferring to remain.[13] Others noted that he was rarely in his Ministry office, that he conducted most of his business from his official residence and later from an estate on the Starnberger Lake in southern Bavaria. Everyone agreed that his marriage to a much younger woman after divorcing a typical Beamten-Frau while in Thuringia, added greatly to his ambition while at the same time detracting vastly from his energy and attention to his duties. He rarely left home. Finally, the second Mrs. Frick was not the asset that her ambition had indicated; Hitler could not stand to hear her sing.[14]

Gen. von Grolman, Frick's adjutant, regarded Frick's unwillingness to meet Hitler and his clique socially as a major mistake. The best occasion was lunch with Hitler, but Frick was too proud, or perhaps he had noticed with what difficulty he could converse with Hitler, his mind filled with administrative details the very mention of which bored Hitler. Instead, Frick insisted on eating at home. Occasionally Grolman would call for an invitation from fellow-adjutant Julius Schaub for Hitler and then inform Frick that Hitler expected him to be there. Once there, Frick would likely find himself at the far end of the table, while some more exciting conversationalist had the Fuehrer's ear. On Frick's increased isolation, derived in part from a lack of social ease and conversational skill, may well rest the weakness of the Ministry of Interior.

Dr. Hans Pfundtner

Hans Pfundtner was probably even more the Beamter and less the party man than Frick. An East Prussian wounded at

[12] Globke, Vollert, Lex, Loesener, Grolman.
[13] Globke. [14] Martin.

Tannenberg, he entered the Interior Ministry in 1917. He was a sharp opponent of Marxism and refused to swear loyalty to the Weimar Constitution, returning, instead, to private law practice. A longtime member of the Nationalist party, he joined the NS only in March 1932; Aronson thought this action was a result of pressure from his wife.[15] Pfundtner's late entry into the party, and a lack of any strong party contacts or acceptance, weakened his position. He was made State Secretary in February 1933, on Frick's suggestion, and the two seem to have maintained a close relationship. Rather than party activity or even exceptional administrative exertion, Pfundtner continued publication in the field of administration, collaborating with Lammers on a scholarly explanation of the NS state. Loesener regarded him as unfit for the office, vain but pleasant, clever but careful,[16] and it is quite probable he had brighter young men on his staff. Pfundtner's function as State Secretary should have been to assist Frick in protecting his staff from outside pressures and to represent their views to his peers. This he did not do for much the same reason that Frick was "weak".

Pfundtner's lack of political ability is evident in one attempt to carry some weight. In March 1934 he wrote to Roehm, the enemy of order, saying that as acting secretary for a month he would like very much to see Roehm to discuss "difficulties". He thought, as two old soldiers, that they could settle any problems in a conversation.[17] Pfundtner was released when Himmler became Minister in 1943. In 1945, as the Russians took Berlin, he shot his wife and himself.

Dr. Wilhelm Stuckart

When Helmut Nicolai, an ardent reformer in the NS spirit was dismissed in February 1935 because of an alleged morals charge, Wilhelm Stuckart became a department head, although he retained the rank of State Secretary from his previous position in the Ministry of Education. Stuckart had the NS credentials, along with something of the personality to

[15] Aronson, 290. [16] IZG, NG1944.
[17] BDC—File Hans Pfundtner.

become the real power within the Ministry. He had learned his NS-style hatred in the Rhineland, fighting the French occupation there. Stuckart joined the party in 1922 and rejoined in 1930, ostensibly because he had been watched too closely by the French in the interval. From a poor family he had worked his way through school. Stuckart was much younger than his superiors and looked much more Nordic; some pictures show a handsome youth with blond wavy hair, but others show bulging eyes and lips.

Nearly cast into regional oblivion by his fight with Rust—wherein Stuckart charged superiors with tolerating adultery, comparing the NS to the Bolsheviks, and reorganizing the ministry in an illegal way—Stuckart was saved by Hitler's intervention.[18] Perhaps because of this effort to flaunt the authority of incompetent supervisors, Stuckart did not openly rebel against Frick or Pfundtner, although he was a rival for Pfundtner's position at scarcely more than half his age. Stuckart was the only leading figure in the Ministry who joined the SS (in 1934), and was regarded by some as Himmler's agent in the Ministry. Globke, who worked closely with him, thought Stuckart had less fear of Heydrich and resisted SS efforts to invade the operations of the Ministry. On this question, particularly, Stuckart was willing to battle "the wild ones". Although Stuckart was the most amenable to party ideology, he soon had his own problems because he had belonged to a Masonic-like lodge, a membership which could have cost him his position.[19]

Stuckart's formal assignment was Department I, which involved the Jewish question. Because he had fewer qualms about the legal persecution of the Jews, and then their forced evacuation, he was the Ministry's representative at such conferences (e.g., the infamous Wannsee conference of 1941). Upon Frick's resignation, Stuckart replaced Pfundtner as State Secretary under Himmler. At his postwar trial he testified that Himmler suspected him, that Himmler and Bormann had agreed in the spring of 1944 to replace him but

[18] BA R43II/1154.

[19] BA R43II/423.

could not agree on a successor. Over a period of nearly two years Stuckart was received only a few times by Himmler.[20] The Nuremberg court found him guilty.

The Ministry's Personnel

The great bulk of the old personnel remained in office throughout the NS period, although practically none was NS. Among the few NS brought in was the Bavarian, Dr. Buttmann, as department head for church affairs. He soon became disturbed at the lack of good faith shown by Hitler in the Concordat he had helped negotiate and returned to Munich in 1935 as a librarian. Buttmann had brought a war comrade with him, the devout Catholic, Ritter von Lex, who had organized a military Catholic organization to battle the SA. Lex remained remote enough from the party in his Sport Department to be given high office in the Bonn government and then presidency of the German Red Cross. He organized the German victory in the 1936 Olympics (keeping three Jews on the team while overcoming a Hitler protest). The Olympic success helped Lex stay, though distrusted.

Although Lex occupied a nearly nonpolitical position, he was able on occasion to help friends in the resistance. On one occasion, a Beamter, unhappily on Himmler's staff, came to him to get tickets for the Olympic games. Through the contact thus established, Lex was able to get resistance people out of concentration camps, including his close friend, later Bonn Finance Minister Fritz Schaeffer.

In more exposed positions were two friends of Lex, Dr. Bernhard Loesener, an old party member who was given the "Jewish office", and Dr. Hans Globke, whose work as legal advisor to Stuckart brought him into the field of Jewish legislation. Their famous products were the 1935 Nuremberg Laws. Loesener later resigned his office when he learned of Jewish murders in the east and surprisingly, was appointed advisor to the postwar United Jewish Committee. He had acted as liaison to the Protestant church, as Globke did to the Catholic church.

[20] IZG, NG3710.

Globke became Konrad Adenauer's chief assistant, remaining in office despite sharp attack, particularly from East Germany which staged a show trial for Globke, "the murderer of Jews". Adenauer's confidence rested on the sure knowledge that Globke had been in the Ministry as an agent of the Catholic church, cleverly using his position to help Catholics. He remained throughout 1933 to 1945 non-NS, although he applied for membership in 1941; he was turned down on Bormann's orders: "Globke belonged to the Center party from 1922 to 1933. He maintains connections to the leading men of that party. . . . He is a close colleague of Stuckart who values his work highly and believes that Globke is free of church-political connections. I am convinced, however, that the acceptance of Globke into the party would bring it no profit".[21] Globke maintained contact with like-minded persons in the Justice Ministry and was able on occasion to get pressures built up interdepartmentally to elicit or to stop action from Schlegelberger or Stuckart.[22] The technique was to assign roles in advance to each member of the conferring committee and plan the discussion in advance so that the desired conclusion would be reached.

Yet Globke's power for either good or evil was limited. Had he not later become politically significant as the chief aide to Adenauer, and therewith a vulnerable point of the Bonn regime, it is possible he would have become no more a "war criminal" than Loesener.[23] The unknown Loesener had a more important role as head of the Jewish section than did Globke, who was in the legal section primarily occupied in putting someone else's decisions into legal language. The literature found on Globke is little more than recitations from the laws he phrased (as is the trial record of the highly prejudiced East German "court"). This is known: Globke remained with Stuckart who pushed anti-Semitism and shared

[21] BDC—File Dr. Hans Globke.

[22] State Secretary Professor Dr. Buelow, Bundes Justiz Ministerium.

[23] The only source of information discovered is in the Institute fuer Zeitgeschichte, in a relatively small and repetitive collection. As Globke was not a party member and never actually on trial, there is little good evidence.

the knowledge and guilt of the extermination camps. What Globke did has not been fully investigated. His only quotes are from the laws in which he commented in the fashion described later in the chapter. The only other evidence is the favorable testimony of colleagues.

One Department Head, Dr. Ernst Vollert, who joined the party only in May 1933, earned his promotion by helping organize the surprisingly successful Saar plebiscite. He was fired by Himmler as unreliable in 1943 and arrested July 22, 1944 as a part of the resistance—a single conversation with Popitz had gotten his name on a list of resistance officeholders.

The Party Versus the State

The Beamten

The institution the NS party set out to conquer in 1933 had been the pride of Germany for two centuries, a professional career elite with the status of a caste. It was a group difficult to enter and governed by its own code, which commanded obedience to the state but also to the law.

The Beamtenstand, or class, had its distinct subgroupings from the "lower Beamten", the "middle Beamten", the "raised Beamten", and the "higher Beamten". Each had its own procedures of entry and promotion, the higher Beamten requiring a university education, a doctorate degree, and several state exams. The positions achieved with such difficulty brought an appointment for "life". These positions were not to be affected by changes in government; a Beamter could be released only on certain legal grounds with specified procedures and with a pension. A political spoils system had barely begun under the Weimar Republic and many a Beamter assumed that the NS would fully restore, as their early law stated, "The Professional Civil Service".

The long training, or apprenticeship, produced a tight but unworldly in group. The higher Beamten tended to be bookish, for the bulk of their training was in law, after a prep school training in the classics. They had relatively little knowledge of science, even of social science, or even specific training in administration. One could be a Beamter if one knew the law and could use the proper paragraph to support a decision.

Distinct not only by their legal training, but usually by class origins, frequently generations of Beamten followed each other; the Beamten tended to look on the people as something rather ignorant, to be commanded or helped from above. An arrogance had set in; it was a constant complaint of the NS that the Beamten were not polite.[24]

The Beamten felt ill at ease in democratic Weimar with its seeming instability of government, the seeming demand that they keep in step with changing majorities, and the disturbing rise of the masses, notably the Marxists, threatening the state. As a group, the Beamten were conservative and nationalist, likely monarchist, suspecting the NS for almost the same reasons they distrusted the Marxist socialists. They looked for legal orders from above, which they would legally carry out with their precious expertise. Jacobs described them as "meek men",[25] but it was the kind of meekness useful in the white-collar classes in an integrated society.

To capture this fortress of legal privilege the party used a wide variety of devices: putting NS in state offices, making any state decision subject to party veto, creating a parallel party organization, putting party men in comparable state offices or a "personal union", transferring state functions to party organizations, purging the state of "disloyal" Beamten, compelling repeated oaths to the Fuehrer instead of the constitution, infiltrating offices, compelling Beamten to special indoctrination, spying on them and their families, threatening them with dismissal or concentration camps. Despite all of these devices, it is questionable whether the party really won. Despite Hitler's boasts that the party commanded the state, and the imposed silence on any rivalry, a constant battle was in progress between party and state, which was fought in every office and ministry but fought more openly (in confidential letters) in the Ministry of Interior.

[24] BA R43II/423. [25] Jacobs, 201.

The Development of the Beamten Policy

Although numbers of Beamten joined the party after 1929, most from lower offices, the party had no Beamten policy.[26] Hans Mommsen shows that the pressure for conformity came first from nationalists, like Pfundtner in 1932, to force out socialists and Catholics.[27] This group and not the NS he regards as pushing hardest for constitutional reform in order to get increased power for Berlin. The nearly constant thread of Frick's policy, with his supposed central powers, was the defense of non-NS Beamten from local party attacks. Issued with artificial bluster, unlike Frick in person, Frick's orders insisting on Berlin's Beamten supremacy were directed against local NS purges. Party men denounced important officials as "politically unreliable", ergo Frick's strong prose on March 31, 1933 against those refusing to obey non-NS superiors: "Membership in the national parties does not give the Beamten more rights but higher duties. Who does not obey the commands and orders of a superior installed by me, or kept in office, refuses therewith obedience to me".[28] Disobedience to Frick became so commonplace that such early bombast appears laughable in retrospect.

As a compromise between traditional "order" and the "revolutionary" SA violence, which consisted of arresting Beamten capriciously, the Interior Ministry introduced in April 1933 its "Law for the Re-creation of the Professional Civil Service", to create a uniform legal framework as a guarantee to the Beamten. The law took into consideration the desires of the NS to purge a hostile state, yet defined and legalized its actions as a limited and extraordinary intrusion into Beamten law. Frick assumed that in a few months change would stop; "after a certain waiting period the normal Beamten law would be in full effect again, as so stated in the concluding paragraph of the law."[29] The law defined the groups which

[26] Hans Mommsen, *Beamtentum im Dritten Reich*, Stuttgart, 1966, 21.

[27] *Ibid.*, 29.

[28] Bracher, Schulz, Sauer, *Die Nationalsozialistische Machtergreifung*, Cologne, 1960, 496.

[29] *Ibid.*

would be released—those which could not show evidence by their previous activity that they would be completely loyal to the NS state, and those not of "Aryan" descent.

Its first effect would be to limit the party's effectiveness. Hess raised the question whether nonmembership in the party would be reason for discharge, to which Frick answered: obviously not. Hitler and the rest of the Cabinet agreed.[30] Krosigk and Schlegelberger strongly urged that all dismissals be ended by September 30, 1933, which was agreed "after a long discussion".

The law shows signs of haste and a lack of awareness of what it would mean to the million and a half Beamten. Its implementation immediately excluded a group sentimentalized by Hitler, the front-fighters and fathers of war dead, even those officials in service before 1914. A part of the compromise rested in the discretion left to the Minister of the Interior; one could interpret "Aryan" and "complete loyalty" in various ways. In late April 1933 Frick apologetically emphasized that the power to release was centralized to protect the Beamten.[31] He urged objectivity, great care in accusing anyone of lack of national loyalty, and generosity with pensions. By May 6 a questionnaire was issued as a guide, but it was applied only in individual cases in the Transportation, Labor, Finance, and Interior Ministries, systematically in Economics, Agriculture, and Justice.[32] Schulz concluded that the Interior Ministry recognized that these personnel questions were the vital questions, and decided to avoid either overt obeisance or open resistance to the NS.

The percentage of the Beamten released can be misleading, because many were transferred or reemployed after attention had shifted, but Jacobs and Dror estimated, in the case of Prussia that 12.5% of the higher civil servants were released for political or "racial" reasons, and 15.5% for lack of qualification. The average for other states Dror lists as 4.5% and 5%, respectively. (Mommsen explains the higher rate in Prussia by the previous SPD power and the fact that

30 BA R43I/1461, 103. 31 BSA, 66911. 32 Bracher, 500.

the other Laender were not compelled by Frick.[33]) Schulz placed the average at 4%.[34]

This was the only purge. The law was also used to improve quality; even NS were released under the terms of the law.[35] Those who could not be retained were Jews or those who had undeniably been active in the SPD or the Center party. Mommsen concludes there was little change,[36] but that there can be little doubt of the basic loyalty of the non-NS who remained. The subsequent struggle was less from a personal point of view of the individual Beamter, as from the "pressure of reality" (*Sachzwang*) on his group against the unrealistic decisions of Hitler and his group.[37] It was "an internal and external self-assertion" as opponent (*Gegenspieler*) to the NSDAP. The tension between party and Beamten was patched over with the usual patriotism.

What the Interior Ministry ordered had little relevance to what happened. There were long delays in implementation, as the bureaucracy delayed making decisions, waiting until the law would expire.[38] Any influx of NS was stronger on the local level, least among judges.[39]

Ludwig Grauert, in the Prussian Interior Ministry, lamented (18 Mar 33) the pressures against the good old Beamten tradition and appealed to everyone to abide by the old rule, to maintain the authority within the ministry, to keep secrets and not to denounce superiors.[40] Grauert also suggested, accurately, that the NSDAP had lost its major function with the "Seizure of Power", that it should be reduced to the training of a political elite.[41] The party angrily attacked the idea, but Goering protected Grauert.[42]

Frick pushed a law through the cabinet in late April 1933 which stated that the SA-SS were subject to the laws.[43] But in fact they were not, and their defiance of the state continued. Frick was able to get Hitler to declare, July 6, 1933, that the revolution was over, to which Hitler added

[33] Mommsen, 56.
[34] *Ibid.*, 504.
[35] *Ibid.*, 59.
[36] *Ibid.*, 13f.
[37] *Ibid.*, 15.
[38] *Ibid.*, 52.
[39] *Ibid.*, 59.
[40] HA—Rep. 77-1.
[41] IZG Fa 113.
[42] Mommsen, 36.
[43] BA R43I/1461, 391.

three days later in a decree that any kind of parallel government was rebellion.[44] By this, of course, was meant the SA Special Commissars, who continued to rule parts of the country for as much as a year. Frick tried (8 Sep 33) to keep to the previously announced September deadline for releasing Beamten, but local authorities wanted more time.[45] In September Hitler told the Reichsstatthalters, his own commissars, to stop their attacks on the state.[46] The Prussian Minister of Interior ordered on Nov. 10, 1933 that no more Beamten could be arrested without prior clearance from him, otherwise the image of the state would be damaged.[47] Frequently in the past officials were sent to concentration camps; now their superiors had to be informed; there was to be no interference with their property, and they were not to be charged for the legal costs of their arrests (this last a sad commentary on the fate of the non-Beamter).

On December 1, 1933 came the "Law for Security of the Unity of Party and State", which affirmed that the NSDAP was "the carrier of the German political thought and was permanently bound to the state". The very modest legal implementation of this unity was that Hess as party leader and Roehm as SA leader became members of the Reich government.

More important was the question whether non-NS could be promoted, which an interministerial conference on Jan. 17, 1934 took up.[48] The Postal Minister had protested the previous December the discrimination against a nonparty member. One of the Interior Ministry delegates referred to the legislation of the previous spring, which had conferred full rights on all Beamten retained in office, that it would be poor policy to have special categories. Support for a partially partisan Beamten came from the Justice Ministry, yet Goebbels' representative took the extreme position that only NS should be promoted and any non-Aryan should be fired. The other ministries (Foreign Office, War) either considered themselves not involved or took the intermediate position urged

[44] CGD T175, R340. [45] BSA, 66911. [46] *Ibid.*
[47] CGD, T175, R229. [48] BA R43II/421a.

by the Finance Ministry. Representatives of Interior, themselves in disagreement, compromised; they thought that temporarily non-NS and non-Aryan Beamten should not be promoted. The guideline had little effect, as each ministry did much as it pleased. Frick, under party pressure and local practice, permitted (Mar. 10, 1934) the exceptional promotion of specially deserving NS, assuming, of course, the requisite experience and skill.[49] A May order, that the party should pay for any city facility unless performing a city function,[50] was virtually ignored, as were most of Frick's orders.

On Feb. 2, 1934 Hitler impressed again on his assembled Gauleiter-Reichsstatthalter the absolute necessity of the party supporting the state.[51] Their three-fold task was: to prepare people for government measures; to help implement government measures; to support the government in every way. "They are fools who say that the revolution was not finished, who have only the intention of putting themselves into certain positions. . . . Others [meaning Roehm] understand the NS revolution as the constant condition of chaos. However, we need an administrative apparatus in every area which will make possible the immediate implementation of the NS ideology." The party must be absolutely obedient and never take action "against any office or against any man who incorporates a part of this authority".[52]

The "fools" who thought the state and the army could be replaced by the SA were better informed after the June murders of Roehm, of other SA "revolutionaries", old enemies like Kahr or Strasser, and anyone who happened to be on the Goering-Himmler list, including the unfortunate Willy Schmidt who was shot in Munich by mistake. This victory of the SS and the army was also a victory of the Beamter, who had been most disturbed by SA special commissars trying to govern from outside. That Himmler's victory would mean the rise of the SS, who would try to govern from within the state organization, was an unheeded black cloud on the

[49] *Ibid.*
[50] BA R36/51, 22.5.34.
[51] BA NS 26/1290.
[52] *Ibid.*

horizon. The brutal illegality of the murders, for which Hitler accepted full responsibility, was a frightening example of latent lawlessness, but it successfully frightened and it was superficially counterrevolutionary.

Perhaps to reassure the party faithful, Hitler boasted at the 1934 party convention: "The state does not command us, we command the state; the state did not create us, but we created the state."[53] Like most of Hitler's pronouncements, this one was at best a half-truth. The Beamten remained; Frick would usually defend them, as when he ordered in December 1934 that all personnel matters were to be decided by the administrative superior. "The NS Beamten organization are forbidden any interference in the affairs of the state or in local administration."[54]

1935 marked a resurgence of the bureaucratic spirit with two major pieces of legislation, the first the "German Community Law" (DGO), worked out by Goerdeler, then mayor of Leipzig and later leader of the resistance, and Fiehler, mayor of Munich. The Community Law had two general purposes, one the assertion of local autonomy, the second the autonomy of the local Beamter from the local party.[55] Dr. Matzerath, doing research for the postwar organization of local government, concluded that this clear intent was moderated by party pressure, during the evolution of the law, but that the effect of the legislation remained, to limit party or central government intervention. In 1935 there was a strong effort to rehire those released for political reasons. Frick asked on March 2, 1936 also for a loosening of the restrictions on promotions.[56] His effort for a conference was postponed by Hess who was supported by Popitz.

The other step backward was "The Second Law for the Security of the Unity of the Party and State," which in essence regularized, i.e., limited, the party's role. The most significant analysis of party-state relations, by Gauleiter

[53] See Dror, 40. [54] R43II/421.

[55] The unpublished research of Dr. Matzerath for the Forschungsstelle fuer Kommunale Politik, Berlin.

[56] Mommsen, 58.

Roever in 1942,[57] admitted that this law was a mistake. "I cannot describe it as other than an embarrassed product of a calcified jurist. . . . The fact is undeniable that the legal position of the party is still rooted in the old concept of law." It made possible, he saw, the eventual control of the party by the state. The drafts prepared by the Interior Ministry[58] show clearly the intent to bind the party up in laws: "The participation of the party in administration is only where specifically ordered by law. . . . The naming and releasing of Beamten, or the remaining disposition of Beamten is entirely the affair of the responsible office. . . . The party courts have no jurisdiction over Beamten. . . . The NSDAP has the obligation to obey the government. It is forbidden to exercise any criticism on the measures of the government or of its officials".[59]

The compromise solution gave the party Gauleiter the veto right in Beamten appointments on the local level and gave Hitler—or rather, Hess, his deputy, and Bormann, Hess's deputy—the veto on officials of the Reich government. The clinching argument was that otherwise one would undermine "discipline and order". In practice, the veto was limited only to the very top positions, as it meant otherwise thousands of cases which the centralized party officers were not willing to process.

In a two-year correspondence with his fellow ministers concerning his draft of a new Beamten law, Frick discovered a unanimity, even with the Propaganda Ministry, that party influence must be curtailed.[60] A minor victory was that a minister could transfer a Beamter if he held party office, even if this weakened the local party organization.

The major complaint of the state was against the proposed paragraph that permitted a Beamter to report to the party any action which might damage the NS. This was equivalent to denunciation of a superior and would thus lower discipline. Although the ministers agreed, in the spring of 1935

[57] CGD, T81, R7, F4509ff.

[58] CGD, T81, R185, F5537ff.

[59] *Ibid.*

[60] BA R43II/420.

the matter was stalled. Lammers wrote in June that Hitler wanted to discuss it with Hess before approving it.

Frick tried again in January of the next year, appealing for some action to halt the conflict of conscience between duties to party and to state and thus end the splintering of a Beamten law among the various Laender.[61] Hitler seemed to agree, but could not decide on Hess's powers, evidence to Mommsen that Hitler was actually a "weak dictator", and of "the notorious insecurity of Hitler when confronted with questions of principle".[62] The party, which had opposed any definition of administrative rights (Mommsen thinks to give them time to end disputes in the party), changed tactics in the fall of 1936.

By the end of 1936 Frick thought he had an agreement on the controversial paragraph, but it took Lammers, who was "state" but close enough to the Fuehrer to be accepted by the "party", to effect a compromise (Jan. 13, 1937): The Beamter could not tell the party, but only the Minister, who would tell the party through Lammers, unless the matter was "without importance". All personal complaints must follow Beamten channels. (At the last moment Hitler removed the special exception granted the Reichswehr.)[63] If this procedure was not enough to discourage an over-eager NS, he was required also to inform his immediate superior.

Lammers had kept it on the Cabinet agenda despite the party efforts to take it off. The German Civil Service Law of Jan. 26, 1937 was the only big law of the Interior Ministry directed against the party; their other attempted reforms died of "Institutional pluralism".[64] It had taken over two years of pushing, with the party pulling.

Bormann protested on Jan. 16, 1938: The law weakened the position of the party by forcing Beamten to absolute obedience to superiors; "the party member must obey the party first",[65] to which the Reich Chancellory commented, "Impossible!" The party criticism had been directed at the official secrecy, and at the marginal comment, "Is not the party go-

[61] *Ibid.*, 419a. [62] Mommsen, 98. [63] BA R43II/420a.
[64] Mommsen, 91. [65] BA R43II/420a.

ing to obey the Fuehrer's law?" The party wondered who had removed the requirement for Hitler Youth success in the school as a Beamten prerequisite. It was particularly upset that a Beamter could not communicate with Hess without telling his superior. This two-year debate should put in a somewhat different light the published law and the usual phrase, "The Beamter must at all times and without reservation stand up for the NS state".[66]

Another matter of party protest was the question whether a NS Beamter could be tried in party courts.[67] Frick wrote Hess on Dec. 31, 1937 that according to the Beamten law a Beamter could not be tried by both his superiors and a party court. Frick received an angry reply from Bormann, that no one would be brought before a party court if he followed his superior's orders. "This is no meeting of the party half-way, but the complete separation of party and state. . . . Frick's picture of the lack of backbone of the Beamter was scarcely pleasing. Beamten must have a terrible fear of the party courts and must be freed from this crippling fear by being removed from party justice. . . . This is not a kind of Cheka in front of which honest men need tremble".[68] Party court cases for Beamten were rare but Frick knew they had reason for fear.

Typical of the uncertainty of policy and disregard for Berlin rules was the question of "personal union," the holding of comparable state and party offices simultaneously. In the Reich government Hitler was the major example; the ministers, except for Darré, showed a fairly clear break from party obligations. On the Gau level the practice was common, partly because the Gauleiter could thus be paid out of the state treasury. At first Berlin encouraged unity at the county level, the Kreisleiter also becoming the Landrat. The practice varied from Gau to Gau, from 63.5% in Silesia to nearly zero in others, the average no more than 10%.[69]

But the party line doubled back; a law of Oct. 1, 1937 forbade such union on the county level. The explanation justi-

66 Dror, 43f. 67 BA R43II/426a. 68 *Ibid.*
69 Jacobs, 134.

fied it on higher levels, because "the political character of the leadership was dominant."[70] Yet change was slow; of the 78 unions 24 remained in 1942, half in one Gau—East Prussia.[71] It was widely used in the areas taken from Poland with disastrous results to all concerned.[72]

Roever made clear the reason for the change: "Personal union means advantage to the state and disadvantage to the party and contains dangers for the future".[73] Most of those who held state office "soon forget the party work and either become bureaucratized, i.e., move away from the people, or pursue the calm life of the Beamter". The party could only survive by remaining dynamic, by being close to the people.[74] Roever, like other Gauleiter, saw no danger of this happening on his level. Nor did Bormann who on August 7, 1942 echoed these sentiments: the Landrat should be one able to administer, the Kreisleiter able to lead people.[75] As late as February 1945 Bormann was reporting Hitler's absolute insistence (which local ambitions ignored) that such personal unions be ended because they tied the party leader to a desk and kept him from the people.[76]

With his official position fairly well stabilized the Beamter was yet subject to confusing orders concerning his private life. In 1937 Frick ordered Beamten not to send their children to private (religious) schools, an order which apparently was modified by the Education Minister. In the confusion, many did as they pleased.[77] The Finance Minister ordered his personnel not to accept party obligations that would interfere with official duties.[78] In January 1938 the Economics Minister opposed someone's order for Beamten not to buy in department stores.[79] And on July 12, 1938 Lammers reported that Hitler was concerned that the Beamten were not operating in a NS spirit, that they should be removed more strictly than heretofore, and "not only in those cases where they consciously reject the NS *Weltanschauung*".[80]

[70] BA R43II/703. [71] Jacobs, 135. [72] Mommsen, 110.
[73] CGD, T81, R7, F4514. [74] *Ibid.*
[75] HA, 320-318, 11. [76] GSA—Epp File 61.
[77] BA R43II/423. [78] BA R36/51. [79] BA R433II/423.
[80] IZG, NG285.

The party remained outside, looking in unhappily at the bulk of non- or latecomer NS occupying positions of power and wealth. This frustration is evident in Hess's order of March 10, 1939 to Frick that important positions must now be filled only with NS.[81] Instead of compliance, Hess received a flood of complaints and rejections. Dorpmueller thought it unfair, because "many had not joined the party to avoid the appearance of opportunism"; he needed able men; his best four men had been refused promotions; they would leave for private industry if forced to join the party. The complaints noted the weak point of Bormann's argument: the party membership he demanded was largely a formality, a point that was included in Lammers' strong argument on June 13, 1939.[82] Lammers had persuaded Hitler a week earlier that party membership was only "desirable". Frick regarded the order unenforceable "for the time being". Krosigk thought "exceptions will have to be made". Hitler, perhaps uninformed of the Oct. 10th order, agreed that there would have to be a three-year wait, and then one should see whether the Hess order could be implemented.[83] Another defeat for Bormann.[84]

Bormann tried through the party to maintain pressure on local governments. He observed in May 1939 that Frick, in a confidential order, had decreed no punishment to Beamten declining to join the party if the party did not report the reasons for refusal. Bormann told his staff to be sure to report the reasons.[85] He also ordered the party to do something about the many local councilmen who had refused to join the party.

The ordinance (Dec. 28, 1939) for the administrative leadership in the counties was a weakening of the party's local power, giving the Landrat greater autonomy vis-à-vis the Kreisleiter. The rule was that if the two could not get

[81] BA R43II/421a.

[82] Lammers' letter to Hess, Mommsen, 191.

[83] BA R43II/421a.

[84] Mommsen (81ff) describes these repeated Bormann defeats, primarily by Lammers' Beamten.

[85] NSA, P7.

along they would both be fired. This was a much greater threat to the Kreisleiter, since the Landrat could not be fired, only transferred.[86] The Kreisleiter, as leader of the people, was to concern himself only with morale (*Stimmung*) and the Landrat only with administration.

Hess could not wait. In an appeal to the ministers on March 6, 1940, he agreed that in 1933 there had not been enough NS Beamten, but in the seven years since then, some should have been forthcoming. "When these positions almost entirely are filled with Beamten who though loyal will show no particular NS initiative, the purpose of creating new Beamten positions will not be achieved."[87] After more ministerial protests, Bormann angrily observed that in the Transportation Ministry, of the 27 men proposed, not a single one had given any particular service to the party. Lammers replied on August 5, 1940 with a copy of Hitler's letter giving the ministries three more years. Four months later, Bormann expressed his anger that Lammers had told the ministers about the letter, and told him not to do it again.[88] To this defeat Bormann threatened, Feb. 2, 1941 a "clean-out" after the war. Frick issued orders that his ministry *not* be informed of this Bormann threat.

The war brought some relief to the Beamten, as they suddenly became endowed with war-necessary tasks. It also gave the Nationalists the opportunity to gain acceptance as a soldier, that one could not get as party "old fighter". Guertner and Frick tried and failed in October 1940 to have service at the front substitute for party service as evidence of political reliability for Beamten.[89] Hitler and his crew remained suspicious of mere Nationalists.

Frick tried to convince Hitler that only a jurist could be made Landrat, noting the high incidence of corruption among the party-installed officials in the east. Bormann gloated to Lammers in March 1941: "Hitler ordered me to report that the idea of Frick that the Landraete must be legally trained is

[86] GSA—Epp File 61; Frick order 24.1.40. Gottfried Neesse, *Staatsdienst und Staatsschicksal*, Hamburg, 1955, 47.

[87] BA R43II/421a. [88] BA R43II/424. [89] BA R43II/424.

false and is rejected by the Fuehrer; Frick should be happy to have such hardworking men, who have no legal training offered to him as Landraete".[90] Frick answered that he had insisted on qualification for office, not just legal training; men without even character qualifications had been appointed by Gauleiter in the east and the results had been catastrophic. Clearly fearful of Hitler's antipathy for the jurist, Frick also wrote to Lammers defending his position, noting that he had tried to get persons with administrative training, instead of the purely legal background, that the Gauleiter more than he had agitated for the legally trained.

Frick delayed a reply to Bormann's threat of cleaning out, probably hoping for an interview with Hitler. That he finally had to write a "memorial" instead indicates the weakening position of his ministry and Lammers' Reich Chancellory. The document on which both conferred tried to appeal to the Hitler mentality; it evidences instead the collapse of Frick's political conception.[91] It is symptomatic, Mommsen concluded, that this memorial, "the swansong of the civil service", did not even reach Hitler.

In November 1941 Frick thus wrote "Mein Fuehrer" a pathetic letter begging Hitler to show *some* respect for Beamten. He had hoped to make the professional civil service into a basic support of the state, next to the party and the army, but it had been "atomized" by rival party offices. For years he had attempted to imbue Beamten with the Prussian concept of duty and the NS character, but had lately come to doubt any success. "In ever increasing intensity come reports of an embittered officialdom because of a lack of appreciation for their accomplishments." This lack of respect and recognition would cripple the best will; it tragically inhibited the inclination of young men to enter the profession. "There can be no talk of any particular display of confidence shown by the state's leadership in its Beamten." Not only did they not receive medals that all other careers did, but they were publicly insulted by those using false information and prejudice reminiscent of the class struggle, although it is

[90] BA R43II/1136b.

[91] Mommsen, 90.

that career from which the politically unreliable have been removed, in which thousands of "old fighters" have found employment. "I beg a word of gratitude and recognition."

Frick had asked in September 1941 that any attack on Beamten be immediately reported to him personally.[92] Such criticism continued from Bormann in 1942, who angrily noted that Beamten with Jewish wives were still in state service.[93] Bormann reported on July 3, 1942 Hitler's anger that so many party officials were too lazy in evaluating Beamten, and threatened to punish them.[94] And there was Himmler's contempt, as in his one-line on August 16, 1942, "I order that there must never be a jurist as head of any SS court".[95]

Yet Himmler's two subordinates in 1944—Kaltenbrunner, chief of the security police, and Stuckart, in charge of the Ministry of Interior—specifically forbade the performance of Landrat functions by the party, or party interference in administrative decisions. They wrote to their subordinates: "The maxim: 'only one can lead' is the motto to be applied to town and county government". As Jacobs found curious, leadership was assigned to the bureaucracy.[96]

In 1941 the ministries retained power over personnel. There had been rare application of the paragraph requiring the firing of those "not completely loyal".[97] The struggle then revolved around appointment to the key positions within the ministries. Frick gave in to Bormann in 1941 and took Helm from Bormann's staff to head the Personnel Department. When Thierack was appointed successor to Guertner, it represented the first breakthrough in the classic internal ministries.[98] Before the end, Himmler had Frick's ministry.

As Mommsen analyzed the development, the ministries had successfully defended their administrative integrity, but there occurred in the process the internal undermining (*Aushoehlung*) of their power by a gradual sapping of the moral fibre of the individual Beamter and of the rational framework of

92 BA R36/51.
93 HA—320-318, 50.
94 GSA—Epp File 117.
95 CGD, T175, R131, F7691.
96 Jacobs, 136.
97 Mommsen, 105.
98 *Ibid.*, 107.

the group.[99] More immediate in its impact was the isolation the Beamten had created for themselves. The irony was that by staying fairly clear of the party and its fanatic drive, by retaining something of the traditions of the past, the Beamten were left far behind. The traditional world they had jealously guarded in their quiet offices had little relevance to the mass-death world of the SS bureaucracy.

The end of the story in 1945 is that under the occupation authorities, all officials above a certain rank were arrested automatically and usually detained for up to three years without a trial. Generally speaking, any Beamter—no matter how insignificant his position or nominal his membership—who had joined the party was fired, a purge which Hitler never tried. In short order even the Americans were forced to accept the Beamten return to office. They were as necessary to the occupation as they had been to Hitler.

The Reich Versus the Land

Immediately upon Hitler's accession to power he declared the coordination (*Gleichschaltung*) of the various states. A series of laws followed which convinced even the casual observer that power had indeed shifted to the central government. But in recent scholarship there is increasing evidence that the NS victory brought a weakening rather than a strengthening of central government. (The files are full of various projects occupying the party planners, under such titles as "Reich reform", "*Selbstverwaltung*" [local self-administration], or "*Vereinfachung der Verwaltung*" [simplification of administration].) There ensued a tug-of-war over the matter of centralization in which Hitler pulled first on one side then on the other, from the beginning to the end of the "Thousand Year" Reich.

Although Germany was united by Bismarck, it had not been unified. Considering the power of the Second Reich, diplomatically and militarily, it was surprisingly little more than a confederation of semi-autonomous states, a fact

[99] *Ibid.*, 121-22.

obscured by the brilliance of Bismarck and the braggadocio of Wilhelm II. The states themselves controlled all internal administration. To implement its command the Reich had to *ask* each state to execute its decision. They were diplomatically represented in Berlin and until 1918 possessed their own armies and occasionally diplomatic representation abroad.

Primarily to make sure that the minority NS would defeat local non-NS majorities, Hitler in March 1933 grandiosely appointed his personal commissars—Reichsstatthalters, as local despots, giving them plenipotentiary powers. Such "absolute powers", in actuality meant as much as the individual was willing and able to fight for.

The easy interpretation of dictatorship assumed that with Hitler's emissaries "in control" of each Land, the political story had ended, i.e., they all lived dictatorially ever after. But in fact the power struggle had just begun. Not only did the Reichsstatthalter, usually the party *Gauleiter*, have to contend with the SA, which marched to a different tune, but they had to deal with the agents of party and government. Local officials they tried to frighten, central officials they tried to ignore. This "centralization" actually intensified "decentralization," because Hitler lacked effective control over the men he had appointed.[100] These became, Renaissance-like, Gau-Princes, more independent of Berlin than were the previous federal parliaments.[101] As Hans Gisevius described the 1933 process: "It was easy to see that our allegedly highly centralized Fuehrer state had already begun to break up into dozens of satrapies and scores of tiny duchies. Each of the Nazi governors interpreted the law according to his own sweet will. These men succeeded in disrupting all local governments to an incredible extent and completely ruining the finances of these governments. What kept the state apparatus going—unfortunately—was the indefatigable devotion to duty of the despised bureaucrats".[102]

[100] Schaefer, 32.
[101] Walter Baum, "Die Reichsreform im Dritten Reich", *Vierteljahresheft fuer Zeitgeschichte*, 1955, 40.
[102] Gisevius, *To the Bitter End*, London, 1948, 210.

The Interior Ministry, with a vague responsibility for local governments, began a 12-year bafflement with centralization versus decentralization, the strongest tendency being toward the former. The man assigned the task during 1933 to 1935 was Helmut Nicolai, who was credited with having suggested the Reichsstatthalter idea in an NS book, ordered confiscated as early as December 1933. His efforts, best described by Schulz,[103] show another old party member who was distrusted by his party after he entered state service. Although in his early thirties, he was entrusted by Frick with the preparation of laws for the reconstruction of the Reich. With the massive power the country had given Hitler, with many Germans expecting the solution to the inherited hodgepodge of state jurisdictions, the road would appear to have been clear. Nicolai plunged ahead with a six-point plan as though the green light would stay on:[104] (1) a strong central government; (2) reorganization of the provinces; (3) a uniform administration; (4) self-administration locally with party aid; (5) an NS civil service; and (6) a new constitution. This was the logical solution to the traditional provinces which had grown dynastically and haphazardly over the centuries, and which were joined together so haphazardly by Bismarck, who was pleased to get unity in any form. Except for a very few, very minor, changes, Hitler showed an amazing hesitance: he left the boundaries untouched and periodically banned anyone even talking about changing them for fear of "stirring up unrest".

In 1933 the major barrier was the bulk of Goering, defending his Prussian prize. When Hitler implied the liquidation of the provinces in August of that year, the threat was nullified by Goering who announced in September that he would not subordinate his Prussia to the Reich Interior Ministry.[105] Hitler, in conference with his "loyal" Reichsstatthalter on Sept. 28, 1933, gave merely cautious vent to his frustrations over the local lawlessness that was disturbing his foreign relations. The speech was more pleading than threat-

[103] Bracher, 592ff.
[104] HA, Rep. 77, Pfundtner, 60.
[105] Baum, 70.

ening.[106] Hitler was angry that some of his emissaries had used the SA violence to further their own ends, that they had hired and fired state ministers—would they please consult him? He was angry that even his ministers were misquoting him concerning the political redivision of the country. His Statthalter should supervise but not intervene directly in the administration. Above all, there must be absolutely no intervention in the courts. Would they please obey the Concordat with the church and leave the confessional schools alone?

Such meetings with his loyal Statthalter became ever more infrequent, partly because the Gauleiter were so delighted with themselves, that they had "conquered" their Gaue, and, of course, knew best how to deal with them. They chose to believe that Hitler at heart agreed with them, that the words for moderation were not those of the true Hitler but his stupid Berlin bureaucrats.

Goering and Popitz led more rebellion by presenting the Frick Ministry with a *fait accompli*, a new law in December 1933 that was designed to foil a Reich unification of the practices of local government, a law actually more authoritarian and with less local influence than the later Reich law. Rather than fight over the matter and admit a successful rebellion, the Reich let the Prussian law remain until *its* law was ready in 1935.

As Hitler retreated from a direct confrontation with his Gauleiter, perhaps because he was more worried about the SA whose radicalism could have brought an alliance with radical Gauleiter, he left the battlefield to Frick. Doing the Fuehrer's apparent will, Frick tried to increase Berlin's powers, but was betrayed by Hitler and proven "weak".[107] He began a new campaign in November 1933 against the independence of the Laender, which Hitler "approved" but only with the provision that Frick must avoid any "unrest".[108] On Jan. 30, 1934 Frick pushed a new law through the Reichstag—"The Law for the Reconstruction of the Reich"—in

[106] BA R43II/1392.

[107] See Hofer, 22.

[108] HA, Rep. 77, Pfundtner, 53.

which the various states lost their sovereignty. It took the country by surprise, for Reichstag legislation had become a mechanical process. The Gauleiter discovered the law gave Frick the power of a super minister, able to intervene at will. He boasted that the law created a united state instead of a confederation. Two weeks later, the states lost their representation in the old *Reichsrat*.

Yet all of the central (Frick) power rested on one fragile reed—the support of Hitler. This Frick never obtained when the local *Gauleiter* resisted, as they had to do. Even in law the states survived nearly intact and remained the only available executors of the national government. When Frick proudly claimed his new rights on Feb. 19, 1934, emphasizing his central control over the police,[109] he immediately discovered a Goering-Himmler alliance barring the way.

The simplemindedness of the NS leadership is evident in the Cabinet's reaction to Frick's effort in late February 1934 to discuss a proposal for simplifying the administration, another of Hitler's constant slogans which he as constantly prevented.[110] The only recorded reaction was Goering's insistence that the small town (*Gumbinnen*) keep its postal headquarters. Hitler raised the question, important to him for sentimental reasons, whether small towns had to lose their governmental offices. The Cabinet agreed only that small towns should, if possible, keep their offices. That was the extent of the debate.

Equally ineffectual was Goering's reaction to a draft law on Reich reform, which included a sentiment that the Reich must have more powers, including those of the police and personnel, but the contrary sentiment that the Reich dare not centralize as "un-Germanic".[111] The same illogic persisted in Goering's surrender of some Prussian ministries to the comparable Reich minister, for example, Interior and Justice, but not the surrender of Popitz's Finance Ministry. He carefully kept the Prussian police out of the Interior

[109] BSA—In. Min. 74114. [110] BA R43II/495.
[111] *Ibid.*

Ministry given to Frick, bestowing it instead on the Bavarian police chief, Himmler.

A further illogic was the appointment by Hess of Adolf Wagner, Bavarian Interior Minister and Gauleiter, to represent the party on Reich reform to Frick. This was the same Wagner who in 1933-43 dared Frick to exercise the slightest authority in Bavaria. Frick tried to deal with the unruly Wagner, agreeing on May 4, 1934 that the Reich laws had poured from Berlin from a variety of sources and in bewildering quantity, that more care was needed, and that this control should logically come from his ministry. This was not Wagner's intent, nor that of the loudest of the Gauleiter, Fritz Sauckel, who suggested on May 15th that any disagreement between Reichsstatthalter and any Reich minister should go straight to Hitler to adjudicate, thus reducing the Reich ministers to the level of their supposed regional subordinates.[112] Frick replied June 4th that it would be absurd to bother Hitler with all of these differences of opinions, that the Reich ministerial decisions should be accepted. Hitler, horrified of constant wrangles, agreed with Frick, but weasled out again by permitting exceptions for "matters of great importance". A local prince could make a Reich-case out of any dispute by claiming a violation of the sacred NS program.

Frick, with someone's cleverness, then tried to build his ministerial power on an alliance with these local governments, by implication against his fellow Reich ministers. Such was expressed in a long letter on June 12, 1934 to Hitler, with copies to other Reich leaders, in which the major premise was the need to build up community "self-administration".[113] Using the NS slogan of the Fuehrer principle, i.e., one person with full command and responsibility, he lamented the serious splitting up of this authority by the various Reich ministries, or special Reich offices, neglecting to note, of course, that it was Hitler's fault because he delighted in creating new agencies and confounding any command structure. Frick listed the variety of Reich or NS agencies that were undermining local authority and that would end self-

[112] *Ibid.*

[113] BSA—In. Min. 74114.

administration if not stopped. The Frick solution was that there should be no Reich orders issued to a community without his approval as the natural protector of the communities; the only exceptions were those matters which were purely "technical, scientific or artistic".

Whatever logic this might contain escaped the locally powerful. Wagner responded on June 23rd by attacking Frick's plans as part of the Berlin bureaucracy—which every right-thinking German should hate.[114] As Gauleiter were wont to do, Wagner "spoke for the people" who would be delighted to see the state machinery, including the Laender, disappear, *but* they wanted the power not to go up to Berlin, but to return down to them. Recent developments had forced them to give up any hope of improvement, but the party must keep its promise and keep the bureaucracy close to the people. (An interesting party argument throughout was, "we speak for the people against the state".)

A legal step toward decentralization was the Municipal Code of January 1935, the product of the "German Municipal Organization" of Fiehler. This middle Beamter, made mayor of Munich because of his old-fighter status, made an effort throughout for local government; his organization becoming increasingly an advisory agency to mayors on how to avoid subordination. The Code, coauthored by Goerdeler, was a step toward city autonomy:

> All in all the new German municipal code does not disturb the scope of local powers as they formerly existed, although it eliminates all local check upon the mayor. German municipalities within their areas continue to have practically free control, subject of course to budget limitations, over housing, public works, health, municipal enterprises, transportation, libraries, theaters and other cultural activities. . . . The city does not now choose its own officials although they are at present selected in such a way as to represent local opinion.[115]

[114] BA R43II/495.

[115] James Pollock, *The Government of Greater Germany*, New York, 1940, 142.

The intent of Goerdeler is evident in his commentary of Jan. 11, 1935 on changes made to his draft, with the strongest objection to the party's participation in local self-government; it would bring "a complete destruction of every feeling of responsibility in the administration."[116] He noted that his NS city council saw no need of other NS intervening, lacking the council's insight, and opposed centralization in terms that Hitler would understand—it would not be the Minister but his little Beamten who would be poking about. Hitler mentioned at the Cabinet meeting on Jan. 24th that Goedeler's objections had made a strong impression on him. He accepted a limited party right to appoint the mayor, while noting the problem was that too many communal officials were from the old parties, but this situation would surely change in the next 20 to 30 years.[117]

The confused struggle in early 1935 is evident in Frick's effort to keep other ministries out of Laender affairs.[118] Pfundtner began the meeting of various Reich state secretaries and special-guest Wagner from Bavaria on Mar. 4, 1935 by hiding behind the sacred "Fuehrer principle". Therefore the Reich ministries should stop taking over Laender departments, although Justice had already been taken over. Wagner fully agreed; the Reich should stay out; the competences of the Reich ministries must be better defined, that is, limited. It was so "agreed". This ran counter, however, to the desires of Wagner's "superior", Epp, who on Mar. 7th requested the demolition of the Bavarian departments by transferring them to the Reich in order to weaken his Bavarian enemies, Wagner and Siebert. Frick informed everyone a week later that Hitler wanted all talk of Reich reform stopped. An Epp attempt to enlist Schacht's support failed, as he cleverly "agreed" but thought the matter would have to wait on a general Reich reform. Frick wrote to the Statthalter March 30th to stop reorganizing Laender governments. To make sure Epp got the point, Frick wrote them all again in April.

Darré, as usual unaware of the political winds, supported

[116] BA R43II/569. [117] *Ibid.* [118] R43II/496.

Epp's dead plan, writing Hitler on April 16, 1935 that the organization of agriculture was a mess because there were no agriculture ministries outside of Prussia. He complained the next month of his powerlessness, that the vital needs of agriculture required that he be given full powers all over the country immediately. This Frick opposed in a letter of June 15th, noting the great confusion in Darré's ministry and reporting himself barely able to hold off the hordes of such ministries.[119] The Reichsstatthalter must be built up by making them head of the Laender government, a process that was nearly complete. (The exception would be Bavaria, where Siebert and Wagner should be built up against Epp.)

The noted change toward the assumed centralization was that of state ministries of Justice (April 1, 1935) under the Reich Ministry. This piecemeal centralization was assumed to be a prelude to the absorption of the other ministries, the completion of a Frick effort for a central control over each ministry. But the tide was moving the other way, as shown by Sauckel's powerful attack on centralization in January 1936 in the holy name of the party. His 36-page attack on the central government marks a turning point in internal development, albeit, as in Hitler's mode of operation, a corner never completely turned.[120] The argument was: (1) The influence of the leading men of the party on local districts is on the verge of disappearing. (2) The power shift through the centralization has not gone to the Fuehrer personally but to the anonymous bureaucracy. (3) An overcentralization does not bring unity but inflates the administration, making it unmanageable and cumbersome; it creates a departmental particularism and splits the state's authority. The solution, of course, was to return all powers to the Gaue, that is, to Sauckel. The Gauleiter had the party virtues born in the fighting years—initiative, power of decision, and enjoyment of responsibility—all virtues lacking in the dried-up bureaucrats.

Sauckel noted that with the second law (Jan. 30, 1935)

[119] *Ibid.* [120] BA R43II/494.

defining the power of the Reichsstatthalter they had become useless appendages, dependent on the bureaucrats for bits of information which they were more likely to get first in the newspapers. The system had become ridiculous, the Thuringian Minister President requesting approval of the Statthalter, who must ask the Reichminister, who tells the Statthalter, who tells the Minister President. The delineation of the competence of one ministry from another was a hopeless jungle; every ministry had a different geographical organization. Instead of 17 federal states, there were 14 "bureaucratic states".

It was an impossible situation when a Beamter was threatened with release by a Reich ministry for being "too close to the Reichsstatthalter".[121] The latter's right to look into administration was nil because of regulations from Berlin. "An occasional request to see a file will be refused. . . . One sees behind the Reichsstatthalter the influence of the NSDAP." This proved how far in spirit the bureaucracy was from the party. "The entire procedure shows the unending, still and persistent drive for dominance of certain Beamten for a monopoly and for the unnoticed shelving of the leaders of the party".[122]

Sauckel's model for the state was the party, with its emphasis on regional leaders who had "close contact" with the people. Thus the "Germanic Fuehrer principle" would be dominant instead of the "Roman bureaucratic principle". Quoting Frick's earlier reform scheme while Frick was Thuringian Interior Minister, Sauckel urged a concentration of all administrative activity into one unified office, the Landrat. (This local dominance of the county Landrat was a recurring goal. The other plan was for this unity at the Gau-Land level. The reform ball bounced from one to another.) Sauckel ended by recalling that Hitler had told him and Frick that he did not want the "Parisian system", i.e., centralism.

Frick's efforts turned toward "Reich reform". He was able

[121] *Ibid.*, 27. [122] *Ibid.*, 30.

to get the reluctant Blomberg support in January 1937 for the creation of 19 Gaue as the basic pattern. But Hitler, either disinterested or unable to decide, again declared a moratorium on such talk; so that nothing was done before the war.[123] However logical, reform would have meant the sacrifice of half of his *Gauleiter*—and unrest therefrom.

With the defeat of this reform proposal, Frick shifted to Sauckel's idea. A new memorial, dated Nov. 22, 1937, contained the similar intent of a common organization of administrative units, although Sauckel wanted the Statthalter directly under the Fuehrer, and with the Beamten organization sharply reduced.[124] On Jan. 27, 1938 Frick sent a draft law, his reaction to the Sauckel proposal, to Lammers, agreeing that the Statthalter should be given greater powers, that he should have all the strings in his hand for the "intermediate government" (*Mittelinstanz*). Frick admitted that it would be very difficult to persuade the other ministers to go along with this change. The big problem would be, who would have the right to name Beamten?[125] He defended the change as necessary to halt the increasing splintering of administration, and linked the proposed change to his own long-standing effort to bring all Beamten under unified Reich administration.[126] Were this accomplished by Frick's ministry, the other ministers would have less fear of regional integration of the Gauleiter, because they would have to deal with the varied practices of 16 states. Frick's law would give his ministry the right to integrate the Beamten and define "spheres of administration".

Why Frick seems to have shifted from a policy of centralization to one of decentralization is not evident from the record, but it *is* evident that the Gauleiter were more powerful with Hitler than he was. It is possible Frick saw his chance with this decentralization, which would have as its major link to the Reich government not the 14 ministries but the Interior Ministry. (Perhaps the mutual enmity toward Himmler centralized police system was the uniting factor.) If Frick's

[123] Baum, 50. [124] BA R43II/1310b. [125] *Ibid.*
[126] HA 320-450, 31.

ministry gained control over the Reich Beamten, decentralization in effect would mean centralization for his ministry.

A new draft along these lines was sent to Lammers on March 1, 1938, along with a plea for an appointment to present his ideas to Hitler. The answer, a month later, was: The Fuehrer cannot grant the Reich Minister of Interior an audience until further notice.[127] In early April another of Lammers' polite answers informed Frick that Hitler would not talk about it then, but that Frick could explore the matter with the various ministers; he could also request special reports from the Reichsstatthalter.[128] As early as June, Pfundtner recorded that an agreement[129] pertaining to a proposed Frick reform of county organization had been reached with all concerned:

1. All powers to the self-administering Landrat—but subject to state controls (presumably the Interior Ministry).
2. No other special authorities (presumably other ministries). Landrat must know of all activities in his county.
3. An advisory council of citizens (not specifically NS).
4. An NS "place of important influence."
5. Larger counties, i.e., fewer counties.[130]

Hitler supposedly agreed to this, which suggests he had not read it carefully, but requested that Hess first be heard. Hess was a slow reader; he vaguely implied general agreement when he replied on Jan. 7, 1939.

In the meantime, Frick tried to push through Interior Ministry coordination of the Reich relationships with local government. By December 5 he claimed the Fuehrer had given him the right to supervise any changes of administration in the interest of unity. Frick then announced to his fellow ministers that the central authorities had increasingly endangered the unity of local administration, which was the most vital because it was closest to the people. Hitler emphasized on Dec. 23, 1938 the necessity of unity set forth in the municipal code. All efforts at dividing up that authority, in-

[127] BA R43II/1310b. [128] *Ibid.* [129] HA 320-450, 57.
[130] BA R43II/703a.

cluding those for defense, must be sharply resisted.[131] Lammers corroborated this disturbing bid. Frick was to coordinate all measures of "greater significance", which involved any "boundaries of administrative jurisdiction"; such measures were to be cleared with Frick before they became law.[132] Thus, by appealing to Hitler's dislike of bureaucratization, and by using Gauleiter discontent, Frick apparently created genuine reform and power to his ministry. But like so much with Hitler, it turned out to be illusion.

Frick pushed for a new law—as though laws would help. He wrote Lammers on March 23, 1939 concerning his draft of a "Law for the Unified Construction of the German Authorities," asking him to put it on the next cabinet agenda. If there was no such meeting in the near future, in view of the urgency he would obtain a decision by circulating the proposal. He argued that Hess, by not answering the request of 15 months before, had therewith agreed. The law was published on July 11, 1939,[133] but seems to have been ignored, perhaps because just prior to the war on Aug. 30, 1939, Hitler had issued another decree on "The Simplification of the Administration". For this, Frick was made plenipotentiary, Stuckart was made Chief of Staff, with a commission to represent Hess, Goering, Krosigk, Himmler, and the army.[134] Although this decree gave the Interior Ministry the right to issue "instructions", the right was to be used only when absolutely necessary; it was only to make sure there was a uniform organization. The decree also ordered the cessation of any work not necessary to the war, an order periodically reissued.

With wartime needs as his argument, Frick set off to slay the administrative dragon in a series of ordinances. He made another attempt to gain control over the Beamten by including all of them in the Reich budget. As Pfundtner commented on Dec. 8, 1939, the major resistance came from Popitz, who foresaw the loss of special funds he had long

[131] *Ibid.* [132] HA 320-450, 91. [133] *Ibid.*, 113.
[134] *Ibid.*, 125.

hidden in his budget by not filling all his authorized positions.[135]

At Stuckart's suggestion (Jan. 6, 1940), Frick wrote on February 23rd to top government and party leaders, requesting their support for his desired Reich control over personnel, as "necessary to defense". He noted the difficulties in finding qualified people to serve in the occupied territories, and the Laender delaying or finally refusing to answer Reich requests in long and wasteful correspondence. "The present situation is actually organized bureaucratism."[136] The 2,000 Beamten sent east were still carried in the Laender budgets. "It is manifest that when the entire personnel policy is implemented according to a unified principle, then one has the precondition for a thorough decentralization, which is the natural result of the attempted centralization of the budget." The administration was already broken into pieces. "Since it is impossible to restore the unity of administration in the administration of the Laender, the only solution is to restore it in Reich administration."[137] In a long and persuasive letter, Frick tried to show that his goal was their goal and Hitler's goal. Goering seemed to have seen danger in a duplication of agencies, but he emphasized that unity must be at the intermediate (i.e., *his*) level.

Popitz, one of the few ministers informed of the Frick plan, replied, "It is a complete absurdity and is contrary to the simplest requirements of an orderly financial operation".[138] Conti, one of Frick's own department heads, thought that the attempt to unite at the Landrat level was foolish; the district level was better.[139] Fiehler used the opportunity to make a pitch again for the mayor's or the Landrat's freedom from the confusing plenitude of Berlin superiors who were flooding him with contradictory orders.[140] For example, the Mayor of Augsburg complained on April 10, 1942 of the impossibility of even a simple thing like building barracks, which needed the approval of 13 different offices. His experience

[135] *Ibid.*, 169. [136] *Ibid.*, 219. [137] *Ibid.*, 247.
[138] BA R43II/703, 9.3.40.
[139] CGD, T175, R40. [140] *Ibid.*

proved "that all of the Reich decrees and orders about the simplification of administration are valueless, because the high and highest supervisory authorities continue to crush the communities with work".[141]

Lammers wrote Frick in May 1940 that Hitler wanted no changes in the Gaue or even any talk about change. Yet he then complained that the Reichsstatthalter were acting selfishly in economic matters and should obey the central government's orders for the common welfare.[142] There was further controversy in early 1941 about the "representatives" the Gauleiter had sent to Berlin, a revival of the diplomatic representation supposedly ended in 1933. Hess had ordered them closed on Nov. 11, 1939.[143] Another *Verbot* was issued Feb. 25, 1941, but the Gauleiter protested; Hitler promised a decision which was still waiting in 1944. Sauckel had claimed them necessary because of the obscurity and confusion among the Berlin ministries.

The party began another offensive on March 1, 1941 on the central government, with a blistering attack by Bormann on its "desolate centralism". The occasion was a Reich Finance Minister decision not to permit the Gaue to own confiscated property, the reason being given: "they could become independent". Bormann's reaction was: "Only bureaucrats could come up with such a childish excuse; in reality they want the Gauleiter and Reichsstatthalter to have no independence. The Fuehrer authorized me to inform you that this desolate centralism of many Berlin offices must be changed as fast as possible. If a Gauleiter or Reichsstatthalter wants to promote a goalie to goalie first class, he needs the approval of some petty Beamten".[144] The Fuehrer ordered that they must be given their own funds over which they could decide independently, but they were not.

Lammers seemed receptive to another Sauckel blast at the government and description of how beautifully, by contrast, Sauckel's party organization worked when not bothered by the Reich government;[145] further impetus was given to Frick

[141] ASA—120/03. [142] BA R43II/1310. [143] *Ibid.*
[144] BA R43II/703. [145] BA R43II/1394.

for action.[146] Although Frick issued a series of seven ordinances of a technical nature for the simplification of administration, Hitler remained dissatisfied and in March of 1941 wanted the effort intensified to return decision-making to lower levels, particularly the intermediate level, for a unity there of *all* administration.[147] Stuckart then wrote to selected provincial governors, Landraete, and mayors, asking them how best to decentralize.

The inquiry brought a flood of responses, first in modest amounts from ministers protesting they had done all possible for decentralization, then in massive reports from nearly all of the Gauleiter, who denounced the manifold sins of central government.[148] The bitter attacks on the government made the plight of the poor-but-honest party leader seem tragic.

Martin Mutschmann (Saxony), in 39 pages denounced the centralism, beginning with Himmler's police and continuing about the endless correspondence necessary for "every new tooth for a policeman or for every police dog's death". The heart of the problem was that the Reich Finance Minister controlled every *pfennig* of enormous budgets; it took two Reich ministers to approve even the smallest salary increase. The Reich ministers were bypassing the Reichsstatthalters and the Laender governments and dealing directly with the district presidents. The ministries were ideologically unsound, Mutschmann said, and gave the example of the wife of a Jew who wanted to change her name. Mutschmann had refused, saying: "a woman should know better than to marry a Jew". But the Reich Interior Ministry had agreed to the change.[149] Frick's order of May 19, 1941 for reports on Beamten concerning the poor excuse of need for them in the east, was dangerous because it would lead to "disloyal" Beamten getting undeserved promotions by dealing with the Interior Ministry.[150] Mutschmann had naturally refused to cooperate, as had Sauckel.

The 40-odd reports agree that the Interior Ministry was at

[146] *Ibid.*, 1394c.
[147] HA 320-450, 359.
[148] BA R43II/1394a, b, c.
[149] BA R43II/1394, 37.
[150] *Ibid.*

best a nuisance, and that the Reichsstatthalter should report directly to the Fuehrer. The Braunschweig Statthalter observed that Berlin issued short laws, then followed them up with long and crippling commentaries.[151] Mecklenburg complained that the Laender minister crippled operations by ordering the Beamten to report every conversation with the Statthalter, and were not even to see him unless the minister approved. The decay of the state brought ever-increasing complaints to the party. "Every attempt to activate the authorities by the party leads to a total united front of Landraete and mayors against the party."[152] The party, the friend of the people, was "confronted with a coldly calculating, administrative jurist . . . who is bringing the entire apparatus to stagnation".

The mass of reports, showing the extreme discontent of the local powerful, were faithfully summarized by Lammers. In June he termed yet another Sauckel memorial "very interesting", and noted the similar proposal of nearly four years before. Lammers had not given the earlier one to Hitler, "because unless I talk with him at length, it ends in the file", but Hitler was "aware of the general ideas".[153] A Frick order of June 24, 1941 "implemented" the sentiment: everyone was to clear (decentralization) with the Landrat and clear (centralization) with him; everyone was reminded of the Dec. 28, 1939 order to the same effect. The Reich Defense commissars were asked to see to it that his order was enforced.[154] What actual authority the order had is unclear, as is the question whether anyone heeded it.

The next reaction was that of the Interior Ministry, which noted on Sept. 9, 1941 the great Reichsstatthalter pressure on Hitler for decentralization. But there was so much difference of opinion among the Reich ministries about the need for and extent of decentralization that one did not know how to decentralize.[155] They would "decentralize", but the ministers all wanted the privilege of intervention.

After another three-months wait, during which the Interior

[151] *Ibid.* [152] *Ibid.* [153] BA R43II/1394.
[154] GSA, 105739. [155] BA R43II/707a.

Ministry Beamten worked out a series of heavily corrected draft decrees designed to resolve the unresolvable,[156] Stuckart wrote Lammers in December 1941, confessing the sin of centralizing. For Hitler's consideration he included a 15-page draft decree[157] which would sacrifice the Finance Ministry's budget controls, but Stuckart thought the barest minimum of centralization would require the Interior Ministry's control over personnel. The draft had a certain logic, the kind never fulfilled in Hitler's approved decrees: the lowest level was "to administer", the middle level, "to guide", the Reich level "to plan"; Reich decisions to be permitted only when absolutely necessary; the heretofore Reich right of approval and supervision to be given to the intermediate level; the middle and lower leadership to be united in one office, at Gau and county level; the technical and budgetary to remain with the Reich ministries.

In January 1942 Stuckart again accepted the party position, that centralism was "alien to life and the times",[158] but Pfundtner revived the matter of reform, talk of which was many times banned by Hitler. Pfundtner noted the savings to be achieved by disbanding the small counties and districts. At a conference of State Secretaries on Jan. 13, 1942, Stuckart pushed his draft decree by quoting Hitler's desire to end unnecessary centralism. The new law was necessary to implement the Aug. 28, 1939 law, because, "without the insertion of the authority of the Fuehrer the opposition from various offices could not be overcome".[159] The state secretaries glumly observed that it was a sad commentary when one had to have a new law to implement an old law, and that Frick already had the requisite authority. Stuckart noted that the year-long effort of that Plenipotentiary for Administration had always failed because of the resistance of individual ministries. All agreed that the intervention of Bormann's office had caused very serious delays and duplication of work.[160]

"The Decree of the Fuehrer for the further Simplification

[156] HA 320-450, 414ff.
[157] BA R43II/707a.
[158] HA 320-451.
[159] *Ibid.*, 129.
[160] BA R43II/707a.

of the Administration" (Jan. 25, 1942) avoided any clear reform such as Stuckart had logically assumed from the Hitler complaints. Instead, Hitler listed 15 pious hopes (e.g., more Beamten to the army, the Reich government "to govern" not "administer", and to perform no "unnecessary tasks", no more questionnaires; instead more service and polite explanations to the people).[161] Hitler's line of thought, or emotion, on the matter is evident in his remarks the day before issuance of the decree: "Goering wanted to get from me a decree conferring powers on Stuckart and Reinhardt so that they could undertake the reorganization of our administrative services with a view to simplifying them. I refused. Why entrust these men with such a mission when it's precisely the Ministry of Finance and Interior . . . whose administrations are plethorically swollen? There are two ways of revising the administration: a reduction of the budget or a reduction of personnel".[162] He then outlined a simplistic tax structure and noted, "If I explain this system to the Minister of Finance or to Reinhardt, the reply will be after an instant's reflection: 'My Fuehrer, you're right'. But within six months they'll have forgotten everything"! The problem was that the solution was too simple for "the gentlemen of the administration. What would have been the use of having been to a university? Where would one find jobs for the jurists? "If I now give a jurist the job of simplifying the mechanism of the administration, his first care will be to create an office of which he will be at the head, with the idea that finally it will entitle him to a minister's portfolio".[163]

Jurist-gentleman Frick tried in a burst of activity through February 1942 to overcome his education handicap. He listened patiently at a Reichsstatthalter conference on Feb. 2nd to the local governors' denunciations of central government.[164] They complained again about the Finance Ministry; they agreed that the district presidents were useless; they agreed with Gauleiter Jordan that centralism led to anarchy; they pointed accusing fingers at the police, the labor minis-

[161] *Ibid.*
[162] *Hitler's Secret Conversations*, 194.
[163] *Ibid.*
[164] HA 320-451, 167.

try, and the agriculture ministry, "geniuses in the issuing and the countermanding of orders". They complained about the Reich's "soft handling" of Poles who found it easier to get trains to go home for vacations than German soldiers to get home from the front, and the prisoners of war "stuffed with geese and ducks", while Germans did without. Instead of the Reich's distrust of the Gauleiter, they should be given a free hand; if they do things badly, "off with their heads".[165] Frick appealed to Lammers for help, trying to prove that all possible Beamten had been released.[166] Rejecting the obvious method of reducing Beamten, Hitler refused to change the Laender organization.[167]

Stuckart tried again in February 1942 to convince his fellow state secretaries that the Reich organization was completely unmanageable, noting the useless DAF studies of conditions in Belgian coal mines or of Borneo natives.[168] He went beyond the breast-beating to attack the parallel party organizations, with hundreds of thousands of men tied down with redundant work. "Everyone does this work just to be sure that some other office doesn't grab it." Before one could reduce state functions, one needed a strict agreement with Bormann that the party would not step in and expand its functions. Lammers promised to get Hitler's approval for such an agreement. Neumann noted that one must also be careful that the army did not grab up the agencies the civil authorities dropped. All agreed—what was needed was one man with authority to deal dictatorially. (The dictatorship needed a dictator!) Lammers recalled that Hitler had recently vetoed the idea of commissars. Neumann thought Frick should do it. Stuckart then tried to get Lammers to persuade Hitler to give Frick more authority, but Lammers was afraid of a Hitler outburst if more such laws were given for him to sign.[169]

All the furor and planning was nullified by Hitler's negative attitude. Frick was informed on Feb. 19, 1942 by Lam-

[165] *Ibid.*, 179.
[166] BA R43II/707a.
[167] BA R43II/1310, 11.2.42.
[168] HA Rep. 320-451, 197.
[169] *Ibid.*, 201.

mers that Lammers had been right; Hitler did not want any increase in Frick's powers; he wanted no massive reform but a series of minor changes, such as followed in March.[170] A Rust effort in late February to grab control of the universities as "simplification", was opposed by Stuckart and vetoed by Hitler.[171] Only one minister, Funk, knuckled under the pressure and released staff, by the simple device of abolishing all departments as an administrative level. Hitler ended the months of reform plans by appealing on March 10th to his state apparatus to consider things from the standpoint of the little towns. "For a little community the presence of a government office means so much that one should remove it only after long consideration and only when a proper substitute can be given. Combination of offices would not save personnel so much as to cause unrest in the affected communities."[172]

Hitler issued grand and vague orders, all the while preventing any significant changes as "disturbing to the people". The Interior Ministry painstakingly compiled a list of 419 measures for simplification[173] accomplished, but the real problem remained. Therefore the Fuehrer ordered a sharper implementation of his Jan. 25, 1942 decree.[174] The ministry's 14-page radical commentary showed the same lack of attention paid to the previous orders. "The administration is split into countless agencies and offices. Scarcely an agency can execute a decision without the participation of other offices. There is a constant double and counter work. . . There is a nearly complete incomprehensibility and the various companies and individuals frequently do not know to whom to apply".[175] The commentary blamed much of this on the party, which was using the war to increase its powers. It repeated a long list of reforms, all previously vetoed by Hitler, or too radical even to have been suggested to him: the incorporation into a ministry or the army of party organizations, including RAD, NSKK, and even Speer's munitions

170 HA 320-451, 201, 353.
171 BA R43II/707.
172 HA 320-451, 357.
173 BA R43II/1135a.
174 HA 320-452, 19.
175 *Ibid.*

authority; the end of the church ministry, which had only 27 officials anyway; the closing of 26 agencies, mostly party; a periodic cabinet meeting; abolition of parallel party organizations including the Kreisleiter.[176]

At a subsequent meeting under Lammers, with Bormann, Keitel, Frick, Pfundtner, Stuckart, Krosigk, Reinhardt, and Goebbels, Krosigk pursued the theme of simplification, noting that his measures were countered by the Labor Ministry.[177] He complained that the various plenipotentiaries, particularly with The Four Year Plan, War Construction, and the Army caused so much waste by pursuing common objectives without even knowing what the other was doing. Everyone agreed, but Lammers sadly remarked that they would have no success trying to get Hitler to make a general change. "Individual cases must be given him with an indication of the possibility of saving manpower in a concrete suggestion." Bormann agreed: this was the technique for approaching Hitler. Lammers added his example—the "East Ministry" had created an Economics Department, while the Economics Ministry had created an East Department.

When in August 1943 Himmler "the powerful" replaced Frick "the weak" as minister, long after undermining his power by seizing the police, Himmler's program embraced the hopeless muddle of central vs. local.[178] Himmler wrote on Jan. 28, 1943: "Hitler gave me this new task; my principles are":

> 1. A strong central force . . . a clear path of command from top to bottom uninterrupted by special offices.
> 2. A strong central force must be based on a voluntary liking for the Reich by all of its parts.
> 3. I attach therefore particular significance to self-administration.
> 4. Official decisions must be based simply on the facts, i.e., no legal formalism.
> 5. Authorities must treat people as equals.
> 6. Only work of war importance can be done.

[176] *Ibid.*
[177] HA 320-452, 227.
[178] GSA MA 105387.

7. All positions must be filled with convinced NS with appropriate skills and energy.

8. The Beamten must be united in the purest spirit. The authority of the Beamten is to be increased and protected.

9. The Beamter must be a model in his behavior.

Himmler, the man who himself had created a centralized agency as Reich Chief of Police, and himself a chief target of the Gauleiter, professed a pious belief in the importance of decentralization. In a long letter on Dec. 8, 1943, Bormann emphasized the need for strengthening the Landrat; meanwhile, Stuckart composed long essays on their virtues.[179] Fiehler, the defender of communal government, informed his mayors on December 25th that Himmler was a benefactor of their interests.[180] A news story on the significance of Himmler as Interior Ministry noted that it was a victory for "self-administration", that Himmler would free the country from lifeless bureaucratism.[181] As late as November 1944 Himmler's plans were continuing for weakening the central government.

The German Municipal League, DGT, wrote to the cities on May 26, 1944, encouraging them to take advantage of the Interior Ministry policy. Although the Bavarian government, for example, was trying to slow down the transference of power to the cities by setting deadlines for the communities to request the return of their rights, the pressure group urged each city to send in as long a list of rights as they could think of before the deadline.[182] The simplest way to do so would be to request that all police powers go to the Landrat or the mayor. They were not to worry about the stipulation that the mayors must show they were able to do the job; obviously they could do the job.

The sum of Himmler's administrative change was the releasing of a few Beamten with tainted pasts. As head of a ministry, he chose merely to denounce bureaucrats as men

[179] BA R18. [180] *Ibid.*
[181] BA R43II/1137, from *DAZ*, 28.2.44.
[182] ASA 120/03.

who climb to higher office by insisting their work justified more bureaucrats as their subordinates in an ever-growing pyramid (à la Parkinson).[183] Himmler behaved like the very bureaucrat stereotype he denounced, yet copied Hitler's preference for disorder, and like his master, appointed ever more men to do the same job. As Ohlendorf concluded, "He's really organizing disorder".[184] As it had been since 1933, what remained in the absence of law was, every man for himself.

The SS Police versus the Law

The most frightening aspect of the NS state was the rise of Himmler's SS and secret police, who managed in the midst of chaos and confusion to kill millions of innocent people so mechanically and efficiently as to have shocked humanity—hopefully for centuries to come. The SS and its concentration camp terror has been the subject of much study.[185] My purpose here is simply to sketch the struggle between Himmler and Frick, between the Himmler-created SS bureaucrat and the traditional Beamter.

The story could be traced back to the mid-1920s, when the highly romantic, insecure, physically weak, and intellectually undeveloped Heinrich Himmler, for the moment raising chickens, found a purpose in life—serving the Aryan race by serving the Fuehrer. Himmler's fanatic belief in the Aryan race (he was short, round-headed, darkhaired, slender-shouldered, wide-hipped), plus his nearly perfect record of loyalty to Hitler, "the loyal Heinrich" and the romantic attachment for things military, are the "principles" on which he built an empire. He was well described by Aronson, as the eternal schoolteacher, admonishing his men as though they were children with a scolding forefinger.[186] As the SA, the original bodyguard of Hitler, grew into bigger battles and uncertain Roehm obedience, the SS (*Schutzstaffel*) replaced

183 IZG, MA 313.

184 Kersten, 216.

185 Gerald Reitlinger, *Die Endloesung*, Berlin, 1956; Shlomo Aronson, *Heydrich und die Anfaenge des SD und der Gestapo*, dissertation, Berlin; Hans Buchheim, *SS und Polizei im NS Staat*, Duisdorf, 1964.

186 Aronson, 76.

it, capitalizing on its proximity to the person of Hitler—like many palace guards before.

Himmler had the ability to attract all kinds of men to his SS from the bullies to beat up the helpless to the intellectuals to plan and defend his campaigns to the many police Beamten from the middle ranks to organize his power. His key acquisition was a junior naval officer, unemployed in 1932 by virtue of a naval discharge for dishonorable conduct—Heydrich. First interviewed on the false assumption that he had had naval intelligence training, Heydrich became the central figure in the police empire. It was he who announced shortly after March 1933 the simple but successful plan for power: "Now we do not need the party any longer. It has played its role and opened up the way to power. Now the SS will infiltrate the police and create with it a new organization".[187] This was Himmler's secret of success: in the constant conflict between party and state, between the Gauleiter and Frick, he deftly, quietly, and persistently linked his party organization with the most powerful of the state organizations, the police, until suddenly both party and state found themselves semi-prisoners in the "SS state". It was Roehm's great mistake to try in 1933 and 34 to increase his power by threatening the state with his SA, never sure whether his SA should become a police organization. Himmler was the only one not confused; he would work within the state until it was crippled.[188] No preconception about party unity should blind anyone to the bitterest of rivalries within the party and the undoubted hatred of the old fighters for Himmler's hybrid organization.

The beginnings were obscure. While men soon to be shunted into obscurity were occupying the center of the stage, Himmler, unnoticed, on March 9, 1933 took the minor, degrading job of Munich police chief; he was only 33 and Heydrich 29. Gaining the confidence of the radical Gauleiter, who had been made Bavarian Interior Minister, Adolf Wagner, Himmler began recruiting non-NS Munich police Beamten like Heinrich Mueller, chief aide, who never gained the confi-

[187] *Ibid.*, 176. [188] *Ibid.*, 163.

dence of the party, but who as SS police-Beamten terrorized first Bavaria and then Germany. By March 20, 1933 Himmler had created the institution of the concentration camp at Dachau, close to Munich. The camp set up was to hold 5,000 prisoners. Though it lacked the statistical horror of the later Auschwitz, Dachau was for Germany *the* symbol of unrestrained violence against Himmler's enemies. Men were sent there by party, SA, or SS, in "protective custody", and remained there without trial until such time as they were capriciously killed, or just as capriciously released, by Himmler. In a typical case, Himmler seized two businessmen who then appealed to Statthalter Epp who, in turn, arranged a meeting with Himmler. Himmler did not come. Epp became angry and ordered Himmler to see him. Himmler answered that the affair was in the hands of Hitler personally, and there it ended.[189] Himmler would nearly always be able to say, "I'll see Hitler", and the opposition would fold.

By April 1st Wagner made him political police commander for Bavaria and before another month he had command over the Bavarian police and all Bavaria's concentration camps. His Bavarian political police became the prototype for the Reich Gestapo, as Aronson has effectively demonstrated. Amid the SA violence, which attracted more attention, Himmler's better planned cruelty for a time went unnoticed. The Bavarian government theoretically in charge had other problems and was never able to coerce either Himmler or Wagner, both of whom had better connections with Hitler. Its mounting protests invariably were ignored; on occasion Wagner, as Interior Minister, joined in the cruel fun.

In Berlin, Frick, diverted by a nationwide unlawlessness which he was trying to curb, became keenly aware of the particular Himmler menace as the tide of violence and illegal arrests receded, leaving behind the hardcore terror of the Bavarian political police. (Frick had seen as a model for the political police Goering's *Gestapa*, but the more radical Bavarian political police won.) Not only did Frick oppose the

[189] *Ibid.*, 168.

lawlessness of Himmler and other local extremists, but he had his own plans for a national political police. On May 25, 1933 he sent to Goering, then the head of the Prussian Police, "A Design for the Unification of the Criminal Police and the Political Police by the Reich".[190] His plan was premature, because all of the powers in Germany, especially Goering and Himmler, were based on the sovereignty of the Laender.

Frick tried again in October to regain control over the police as part of his centralizing,[191] but the attempt was foiled by the secretly prepared Prussian reforms in early December. Himmler, working even more cleverly and surely, spent the months of November, December, and January traveling to the various Gauleiter in their feudal domains and persuading one after the other to appoint him as head of their political police. This bit of salesmanship, and not Hitler's particular backing, won the battle. Why they appointed him can only be assumed, but he presented himself as one with more experience. He seemed too Milquetoast in character, too lacking in vanity, to present a danger, and he promised to accept each Reichsstatthalter as his superior, while making any concessions demanded. Himmler had the prestige of being the Reich commander of the SS, and the granting of high office in the SS was a widely used bait. After his travels he had nearly all of the political police under his command, except for Goering's *Gestapa.*

In the fall of 1933 Frick also failed to get Goering's police and the Bavarian Ministry of Justice failed to control Himmler's police. When the Bavarian Ministry tried to investigate the deaths of three prisoners at Dachau, i.e., obtain some state supervision of Himmler's operations, Himmler hid behind Roehm who told the investigator in December that these were political prisoners and their arrests had therefore been decided by "political agencies". "I will order Himmler that no investigation officials will be permitted to enter the camp and no member of the staff will be permitted to be interrogated"—

190 *Ibid.*, 141.

191 Gunther Plum, "Staatspolizei und innere Verwaltung", *Vierteljahresheft fuer Zeitgeschichte*, 1965, 193.

and the typical last line, "Tomorrow, I will see the Fuehrer".[192]

In January 1934, the confrontation between Frick and Himmler began. After a long and disregarded series of his notes in 1933 against the illegal defiance of the authorized government, Frick observed that from all reports, "protective custody" was being misused, that it should not be used as a punishment or substitute for a court's decision, only when really needed to protect the life of the individual or from a serious danger to the public.[193] In reply to this, Heydrich emphasized to his men, "I call particular attention to the fact that if there is an imminent danger, you should continue the practice of rapid and sharp action".

The January 30, 1934 law, which removed the sovereignty of the various lands, seemed to give Frick the power to intervene, and he quickly ordered that his approval was needed in any important matters.[194] In late February 1934 he tried to enforce rules, which if obeyed would have broken the Himmler terror: neither the SA nor the NS were authorized to make arrests; Gauleiter and Reichsstatthalter could only request arrests; anyone who arrested without authorization should be punished "no matter who it is"; the arrested and his family should be informed of the charge within 24 hours; there should be no arrests for exercise of civil rights, for personal matters such as insults, or for any economic activity; all prisoners should be placed in state, not SA-SS, prisons; the arrest should last no more than 8 days unless the Supreme Laender Court extended the period, and then only for three months.[195]

Frick hoped to use the nominal leader of Bavaria, General Epp, who in March 1934 denounced the highly irregular misuse of police power, and Goering whose Nov. 11, 1934 Order on Productive Custody seemed to close the door: "I have

[192] GSA, 381.

[193] Aronson, 310.

[194] 5.2.34. Hans Neufeldt, "Entstehung und Organisation des Hauptamtes Ordnungspolizei", in *Zur Geschichte der Ordnungspolizei, 1936-45*, Bundesarchiv, Cologne, 1963.

[195] Reich In.Min. Erlass, IZG Fa 183/1-305.

repeatedly emphasized the prerequisites for deprivation of liberty on political grounds. . . . I have also repeatedly observed that the subordinate offices have not always observed my guidelines but have used measures which must be described as a misuse of legal operation".[196] He listed his rules, like Frick's with the emphasis on protection of the arrested. Even Hitler said again (on March 22, 1934) that the revolution must stop.

Frick could not count on Goering or Hitler for support; although he was granted the Prussian Ministry of Interior, Goering emasculated it by removing the police which went instead to Himmler. If one is to believe Rudolf Diels, who was fired by Goering to make room for Himmler, Hitler was not at all pleased to have Goering bring Himmler to Berlin.[197] Goering's fateful surrender on April 20, 1934 of the last major police power has the same familiar source as the other surrenders of power—Himmler swore loyalty to him. Himmler's position was technically as Goering's deputy; the showdown with the SA was approaching and Goering needed Himmler's support. Although there is reason to believe that the deal included the promise that Heydrich would stay in Munich,[198] it brought to an end the period when the rivalry of the secret polices meant Heydrich could be arrested if he entered *Gestapa* territory.[199]

The killing of Roehm at the end of June produced a surface, conservative reaction not only against the rebellious SA but against the rebellious Gauleiter. Frick, ignored and angry at the violence, tried to ride the wave by requesting on July 2, 1934 that the political police be put back under the district presidents. Just before the putsch he had tried to eliminate "unofficial" (SS) people from the political police.[200] Gisevius quoted Frick as having told Hitler, "My Fuehrer, if you do not proceed at once against Himmler and his SS, as you have against Roehm and his SA, all you will have done is to have called in Beelzebub to drive out the devil."[201] Like

[196] CGD, T175, R229, F7517.
[197] Aronson, 315.
[198] *Ibid.*, 318.
[199] *Ibid.*, 314.
[200] 22.6.34. Aronson, 369.
[201] Gisevius, 173.

most of Frick's attacks on Himmler, this one was well aimed, but it would have required a different Fuehrer for success. In this case the attack was ill-timed; Himmler had been too useful to Goering and Hitler. Goering answered, "In recognition of the particular service which the political police have rendered in the last few days, the Reich chancellor has given me and the RFSS (Himmler) a free hand . . . over the political police".[202] He then informed the police to ignore Frick's order. (Gisevius noted that already in 1933 a secret police official was judged on how effectively he ignored the Minister of Interior.[203])

Again defeated, Frick took solace in another written order; despite the continuance of the "special political police", he must emphasize the importance of police reports, of secret police responsibility to the government, instead of his learning of their actions in foreign newspapers. Frick objected to Goering's July 6, 1934 decree for organizing the Gestapo, but "accepted" it as a temporary measure. He and Goering struggled over the decree for the next two years.[204]

In October the Beamten seemed to have scored a victory over Himmler, when Goering required that Himmler be responsible to "the Ministry". The victory of the month was over when Goering informed his officials that Himmler was responsible only to him.[205] The issue at hand was whether the Beamten could gain control over an SS concentration camp; Goering had promised to tell Hitler of the cruelties there, but feared offending Himmler.

Frick continued to issue orders. On Jan. 30, 1935 he informed the Bavarian government that its agent—Himmler, over whom it had nominal control—had in protective custody several hundred more people than all of the rest of the country together.[206] He ordered that only the Reichsstatthalter and the Bavarian Interior Minister, the Gestapo and the district presidents, were authorized to make arrests. If an arrest lasted more than 3 days, a report must go to the Bavarian Interior Minister. Frick forbade Wagner to delegate

202 *Ibid.* 203 IMT, XII, 211. 204 Aronson, 371.
205 *Ibid.*, 376. 206 CGD, T175, R70, F7701.

this power. He demanded a report by March 1 on who was still arrested and why. Although Frick's order was largely ignored, Himmler did order an increased rate of releases from Dachau.

Guertner proposed in May 1935 a return to the traditional methods, and listed the indefensible abuses of the concentration camps against communist prisoners. He hoped Frick would stop them.[207] Frick tried, but was informed by Himmler in November that he had asked Hitler about Frick's idea to get attorneys involved in protective-arrest cases, and Hitler forbade it. Concerning a Frank complaint about the deaths in the concentration camps, Himmler blandly observed, "Special measures are not regarded as necessary since the camp commanders are obviously conscientious".[208]

Himmler's victory has seemed in retrospect a foregone conclusion, and so it would have been were Frick the only enemy of Himmler's rise; but the many Gau princes regarded Himmler's centralization, which they had unwittingly furthered, with serious misgivings. Plum believed Frick's option of alliance with these local powers was practical in 1936: "The Ministry of Interior could put Himmler and Heydrich on the defensive. Supported by the complaints from the Laender the representatives of the internal administration could force them to negotiation concerning a new [10 Feb. 36] Prussian Gestapo Law".[209] The political police were to be kept subject to the district presidents, who regained the right to participate in the naming and firing of Beamten, and in the "executive regulations". A Gauleiter-Frick coalition became possible, because local princes were able to force a decentralization, albeit not of the police. But Frick's lack of influence in the party and his preference for his own type of centralization, in which Himmler had been an uncomfortable ally, precluded any firm alliance.

Instead, in 1936 Himmler achieved his long-sought goal—appointment, over Frick's opposition, as chief of the German police. Frick saved what he could; he prevented Himm-

[207] Aronson, 400.

[208] IZG FA 381/346, 49.

[209] Plum, 203.

ler's being named a Reich Minister, Himmler remained legally under Frick, and Frick was to have budgetary control. What pieces of police power that were not yet Himmler's, he picked up in the next years.

Frick retreated but did not give up the effort to introduce law into "his" police operations. New principles were declared on Jan. 25, 1938 which gave the Gestapo the right to arrest those "endangering" the state. With this major concession to Himmler, Frick added provisions that gave the prisoner less protection than the traditional (10-day arbitrary arrest), but these provisions would have done much to limit the police state within the state had they been obeyed. However, obedience was not a NS virtue or even a "loyal Heinrich" virtue.

Racism Versus Reason

In contrast to the other areas of conflict between Frick and the party, Frick agreed in principle with anti-Semitism. His much more muted argument was for a "moderate" anti-Semitism, a "legal" anti-Semitism—an attitude certainly not commendable; yet had Frick succeeded *his* anti-Semitism would have precluded violence. Another difference would be that in this dispute, unlike the others, he was not speaking for a united ministry, for this was not a matter of power but of morality. Another difference was that in this matter there was much less Hitlerian ambivalence. Hitler could have opted for a moderate policy only briefly and only if some other objective—e.g., a foreign policy success or economic recovery—outweighed his desire to punish Jews. For this reason, any argument, in order to have any effect on Hitler, had to show the practical harm of anti-Semitism to Germany. Obviously no humanitarian sentiment would work.

Racism was not logically pertinent to the work of the Interior Ministry, assuming that any part of the government has a legitimate reason to inquire into the religion or race of its citizens. It was delegated to the ministry because of its traditional handling of citizenship questions—in this case, could the Jew be a citizen? Out of such legal questions developed a section in the ministry devoted to Jewish affairs under Dr.

Bernhard Loesener, whose background included a position as a customs official. Loesener was brought to the ministry because his father and Pfundtner had been good friends. His friends testified, and his work may indicate, that he was not anti-Semitic.

The first ministerial position on anti-Semitism (Feb. 9, 1933) may have been that of Pfundtner's, who passed on to local governments the foreign office's strong belief that an NS racial policy vigorously pursued would have serious effects on relations with the non-Aryan countries such as Japan, India, and the Latin American countries.[210] These non-Aryans failed to appreciate that the Reich was concerned with racial "differences" and not racial "superiority". Although "the racial principles could not change", application of them must take into account the possible damage to foreign relations. Any action should be cleared with the minister involved, the Foreign Office, Frick, and Hess.

Yet acts of violence, much worse than Pfundtner would have supposed, occurred, despite the warning concerning foreign relations, as local despots indulged their sadism on the Jews. Goebbels' boycott of April 1, 1933, ostensibly to show foreign Jews that they should not boycott German goods, backfired. Even the new Beamten law supported by Frick hurt foreign relations, because it created a second-class legal status for the Jews. Reich anti-Semitism *was* inhibited by foreign reaction, but the Reich government had difficulty halting the local actions. Hitler told his Reichsstatthalter on Sept. 28, 1933 that actions such as the cutting off of a Nuremberg girl's braids, was bad, that the racial process must be slow; the approach was to be from the standpoint of citizenship.[211] The locally powerful could not believe he meant it. Against these doubters Frick made frequent complaints, but with no power to stop them.

Loesener's particular approach, which colored the Interior Ministry's policy throughout, was enunciated on Oct. 30, 1933, when he complained about the discrimination against

[210] IZG, NG2292.

[211] BA R43II/1392.

the "half-Jews" (included in Frick's original Beamten law).[212] He observed that the half-Jew, treated as a Jew in Germany, would not be accepted as a Jew elsewhere if he migrated. He began the interpretation of the half-Jew equated with Aryan, that found legal basis in the Nuremberg laws, an idea which was anathema to rabid anti-Semites such as Julius Streicher who feared one drop of "Jewish blood".

Frick seems to have accepted (Jan. 17, 1934) Loesener's suggestion that the sharp definition of the Jew found in his Beamten Law should not be applied elsewhere.[213] Although Frick had in January expressed the conviction that racial mixture was the basis of the decline of all peoples, by December his office argued that one-fourth Jews should be considered Aryans for purposes of the Beamten law.[214]

Almost all the Interior Ministry's significant "anti-Semitism" came in 1935, climaxing in the "Nuremberg Laws". It resulted from continued party pressures to hurt Jewish businesses, although Hitler had forbidden boycotts. The pressure was met head-on by the Economics Ministry in August and seemed to be defeated, until the volcano erupted again upon Hitler's command at the party convention.

Schacht called for a conference on August 20, 1935 to mobilize the Reich government against local excesses as being harmful to the economy.[215] At the conference Frick informed Schacht that the Ministry was preparing decrees against such local actions, but that only Hess could stop them. Hess's representative stated that Hess was trying to stop the local attacks, but that "80% of the people wanted some action" from the government against the Jews. Popitz agreed with Schacht about the damage to the nation and asked for a clear line that could be enforced. Guertner noted the difficulty in trying to enforce such a line as long as the belief persisted that the leaders, i.e., Hitler, did not want the law followed. The Foreign Ministry thought the matter too important to permit "every hotel owner to set national policy". All agreed that the state should tell the people, and not the

[212] IZG, Fasz 1. [213] IZG, Fasz 2. [214] *Ibid.*
[215] IZG, Fasz 3.

people the state, what should be done. That same day, Frick wrote all authorities that there must be no more "individual actions". "Whoever participates hereafter in 'individual-actions' against Jews, or encourages such, must be regarded as provocateur, rebel and enemy of the state."[216] The police should stop such actions, and Frick should be called or telegraphed at once.

Frick, the legalist, was having trouble with Frick, the anti-Semite, when he wrote Schacht on Sept. 3, 1935, asking that something be done to reduce Jewish influence in the economy.[217] There should be legal restrictions because one could, he thought, assume that "Jews could not be trusted". Action by local governments should be stopped, but the central government must do something positive as well as negative to remain in control, otherwise unauthorized persons would continue to take violent measures. The Frick-Schacht conference, held on Sept. 23rd, agreed on the following restrictions: no Jews to move to communities of less than 20,000 without permission; any restrictions would be on retailers, not on larger firms; there would be no new Jewish stores or concessions; Jewish apprentices could train only with Jews.[218] For these concessions to anti-Semitism, Frick agreed "to forbid" any discrimination against those of "mixed race", no insulting signs, no restrictions on attending theaters or use of swimming pools, no "guards" in front of Jewish stores or photographs of customers in Jewish stores and no mobs chanting insults. It was a faint hope of Frick that he could ever hope to stop these local decisions; his orders were naturally ignored.

Already Hitler had declared the infamous Nuremberg Laws at the party convention on Sept. 15, the most significant action taken by the Reich government vis-à-vis the Jews before the violence of November 1938. The major terms of the laws were: only persons with "German" or "related" blood were "members of the state"; marriage between Jews and citizens with such blood was forbidden; non marital sexual relations

[216] HA 320-513, 2.

[217] HA Rep. 320-513.

[218] *Ibid.*, 24.

between Jews and citizens with such blood was forbidden; and Jews were not permitted to employ in their homes females under 45 years of age with such blood.[219] This petty infamy was signed by Hitler, Frick, Guertner, and Hess.

The laws resulted from a direct command of Hitler's, quite probably because he had little to offer the party convention in the rather uneventful 1935, and because the radical anti-Semites in the party were chafing at the Reich restrictions on their persecution plans. Buchheim, observing Hitler's aversion to laws, was surprised that he even permitted his cherished anti-Semitism to be thus bound by law.[220] As strange as it would appear to the uninitiated, these cruel laws were widely regarded as a victory over the extremists, in the sense that they would replace the more frightful, unpredictable, and illegal local violence.

The terms of the law clearly resulted from a last-minute decision by Hitler and a demand that the Interior Ministry come up with something quickly.[221] The details are an excellent example of the chaos in Hitler's Reich. The '*Parteitag* began on Sunday, September 8, 1935, with Hitler planning for the Reichstag to declare a new Reich-flag law on the concluding Sunday. With its top men in Nuremberg, the ministry was enjoying a period of pleasant quiet. Friday evening at 11, Loesener was called by his wife to tell him that he was to take the plane early Saturday morning to Nuremberg. It concerned a new law for the Jews and would he please bring the necessary documents? With two hours' sleep he reached Nuremberg and the small room assigned Pfundtner and Stuckart at police headquarters the next morning. He was informed that Hitler the day before had ordered a new Jewish law to fill out the program for Sunday; the flag law alone was too "thin" compared to the gigantic preparations. His only instructions reflected the noise from party propaganda about intermarriage, sex relations, and Aryan female servants.

219 *Reichsgesetzblatt*, 16.9.35.

220 Buchheim, 15.

221 The best account is Dr. Bernhard Loesener, "Das Reichministerium des Innern und die Judengesetzgebung", *VZG*, 1961, 264-310.

Dr. Loesener wrote, "It was clear to me that here was a great chance to achieve a success through the formulation of the drafts which had not been possible in the discussions with the party".[222] He hoped that with Hitler's signature on a law the party would quiet down, and he received the approval of both Stuckart and Pfundter who were in sympathy with his aims to help those of mixed blood. The party chancellory sent a Dr. Sommer, who represented the radical viewpoint of Dr. Gerhard Wagner, "Reich doctor-leader," that, of course, people of mixed blood would be considered as full Jews, and that "mixed marriages" would either be dissolved or man and wife would both be considered Jews. Sommer bothered the Beamten little, regarding "the entire scribbling as 'too stupid'. He spent most of the time in another room playing with a toy tank which sprayed sparks and could climb over the piles of documents".

With a first draft that paid little heed to party demands, Loesener struggled through streets filled with columns of marching men to find Frick. After the loss of much time he gave the draft to Frick, who refused to accept any explanation for its wording. With Dr. Wagner always at Hitler's elbow, pushing for a tough version, Frick could not counter with facts. Frick had always refused to take either Stuckart or Pfundtner along when he saw Hitler, a refusal that seriously weakened the ministry's position. "One needed knowledge of the intricate problems, and this Frick in his incomprehensible and ever increasing indolence never possessed or even attempted to obtain."[223] Frick refused to join in any discussions of the law. All through Saturday the group revised a rejected draft, to give it to Frick, who passed it on to Hitler with no knowledge of why it was phrased thusly. Wagner pushed Hitler to object, and Frick returned with Hitler's orders to toughen the draft. The group moved to Frick's residence, the Haeberlein villa, to avoid delay. They worked in the music room, Pfundtner at the grand piano, Stuckart on the sofa. Frick was in the next room conversing with the lady of the house over wine and *Lebkuchen.*

[222] *Ibid.*, 273. [223] *Ibid.*, 274.

At midnight Frick returned from an interview with Hitler and announced that Hitler wanted to choose from four different drafts, from "A", the toughest, to "D", the mildest (which was supported by the Beamten). Hitler had also suddenly decided that he wanted a citizenship law ready by the next day. Pfundtner angrily demanded to know why Frick had not told Hitler such a law, for a "Thousand Year Reich", would need more than a few minutes time to prepare. Stuckart also complained, but Frick was undisturbed, saying: "It should merely be some pithy statement giving preference for those with German blood". He went back to the next room to his wine and Frau Haeberlein.

The group was exhausted from its fight with "the unseen opponent Gerhard Wagner" and cursed their lot in an uncommon fashion. They decided to make the draft as empty as possible so that the resulting law would remain useless. Evolving an idea of "superior citizenship", they agreed that the rights of citizens should not be touched, nor should the citizenship rights of the Jews. Something was thrown together and at 1:30 a.m. given to Frick who took it to Hitler; a constitutional law was composed in little more than an hour.

After an hour Frick returned—Hitler had approved the draft. The group was invited to a bottle of wine with Frau Haeberlein. Even then Frick made no comment about the laws. Loesener reached his bed at 4:30, only to be awakened at 6:30 by a police band under his window. At eight, clad in pajamas, he conferred with Pfundtner about a press release Frick had ordered, an impossible task, because they did not know which version Hitler had accepted. They tried to muster support for the mild "D" version. Since Frick would be useless, they tried to get Neurath and Guertner to intervene. Amid the din from early drinkers, Loesener wrote out various press releases on menus.

Barely reaching the Reichstag meeting in time, they were pleased to hear Hitler read version "D" as the final version, and disappointed that he had left off the important sentence —"This applies only to full-Jews".[224] Hitler had struck out

[224] *Ibid.*, 276.

the sentence personally, but, typically, had ordered that it appear in the newspaper stories. But they were pleased to see Streicher's angry face when Hitler announced "the final settlement of the position of the Jews". Most of the crowd had not heard the law read, as Goebbels, for some reason, had turned off the microphone at that juncture to broadcast music.

The work was not over. They had next to decide what the new law actually meant. For the next eight weeks there was a constant negotiation between the ministry and the party. The moderates' position was not helped by Dr. Guett, ministry department head for health, who prepared a "scientific" analysis emphasizing that Mendel's law shows that bad racial characteristics once in the blood would keep reappearing, ergo mixed marriages were bad.[225] Loesener credited only the active intervention of Stuckart, who freed himself of other duties to maintain the struggle, with saving the situation from the party. The party had the advantage of constant access to Hitler, while the ministry had contact only through Lammers. The party demanded that every "fourth-Jew or eighth-Jew" be considered a full-Jew, that all mixed marriages be dissolved, and that some Jews be sterilized.

Sensible men had to make some approximation of sense out of racist nonsense, the major debate whether the part-Jews could marry, and with whom. At Guertner's urging him to take a mild solution, although Hitler reputedly had already decided for the tougher, Pfundtner asked Loesener on Oct. 8, 1935 to put into writing the arguments to save the half-Jews, so that in case of an interview with Hitler he and Stuckart would be ready to answer all questions.[226] Loesener, realizing humanitarian arguments would be useless, emphasized harm to the German nation.[227] His report, "Material for the solution of the half-Jew question", argued strongly for classifying half-Jews as Aryan, and stretched for every possible argument to convince Hitler that 45,000 men would thus be lost to the army and that the Jews would be given valuable "German blood", making them a more dangerous enemy, al-

[225] HA 320-513, 33ff.

[226] HA 320-513, 132.

[227] *Ibid.*, 141-55.

though the small amount of "Jewish blood" coming into the national heritage was too small to matter.

This exercise in convincing an irrational man of a rational position was temporarily successful. Not only did Stuckart accept it, but Loesener was permitted to attend a party meeting where Hitler spoke for two hours on the subject and Loesener heard reflections of his own arguments. What surprised Loesener at the party meeting was the discourtesy shown the Fuehrer; the party lords were bored and behaved in an "incredible" fashion at their tables.[228] Hitler changed the subject and spoke of the war, for which he would be ready in four years.

Because the Beamten were struggling to come to an agreement with the party, the Economics Ministry warned against extreme action.[229] The Reichbank noted on Nov. 1, 1935 that the mark was sinking rapidly, implying that Jewish money was being smuggled out and could not be stopped. It was therefore necessary to clarify Reich plans in order to remove these fears. The situation was very dangerous; increased Jewish emigration would place an insupportable burden on the economy. Stuckart's department followed this on November 2nd with a long defense of a moderate position, adding arguments about the "front soldiers", always effective with Hitler, and using even the coming Olympics.[230] Schacht, on November 4th, joined in with another blast. He regarded any toughening of the laws as hazardous.[231] Loesener thought there might have been as many as 30 different drafts. Party men would bluff by saying Hitler had agreed to such and such point, but Stuckart once called Lammers and exposed the bluff.[232] Stuckart reported on November 7 that Hitler had agreed to his solution.

These commentaries were Stuckart's responsibility, though the moderate solution was largely the work of Loesener who had a nervous collapse when finished. Stuckart began to put them in final form, then called on Globke, then Loesener's deputy and the legal expert of the department, to finish them.

[228] Loesener, 281. [229] HA 320-514, 15. [230] *Ibid.*, 27.
[231] *Ibid.*, 40. [232] Loesener, 281.

He gave Globke the dubious honor of listing him as coauthor. Thus arose the Stuckart-Globke *Commentaries to the Racial Laws*, published in Berlin in book form in 1936. Stuckart's introduction was filled with racist phrases, in sharp contrast to the dryasdust pages of Globke's legal commentary which followed.

The sum of the evidence supports Globke's claim that the commentaries were written in such a way as to protect the unfortunate people involved, in particular those of "mixed race". Karl Marx, the editor of the leading Jewish newspaper in postwar Germany, came to Globke's defense. While foreign Jews were clamoring for his release as an Adenauer aide, Marx believed Globke had in fact saved many Jewish lives.[233] A former colleague of Globke in the ministry, Robert Kempner, joined the Nuremberg trial prosecution staff; he trusted Globke as a key witness. Loesener reported that he and Globke tried to moderate the implementation of the law's provision by putting a non-NS colleague in the office that decided "race" when there was a doubt.[234]

By February 1936 Frick had made another legalist effort; he called attention to the new law and listed those things local governments were forbidden to do against the Jews: disturb their property; post anti-Jewish signs; boycott Jewish businesses; annoy persons trading with Jews; discriminate in renting, pensions, or tax matters, in the use of theaters, parks, cemeteries, swimming pools, or the use of markets.[235] Yet his order was based on the shifting sands of the Fuehrer's ambivalence. As Frick wrote Pfundtner on March 13, 1936, the Fuehrer had often said that signs proclaiming "Jews unwelcome" were all right, but he had declined to make their entry into any city illegal. If Pfundtner wanted to push the draft law, apparently concerning the signs, it was all right with Frick.[236] In April Stuckart sent out just such an order.

The following June, Stuckart called a special meeting of his colleagues to discuss the banning of *Der Stuermer*. The

[233] *Time*, Vol. 88, No. 27, 41.
[234] See IZG, F71, for corroboration.
[235] HA 320-514, 157-62.
[236] *Ibid.*, 166.

group agreed that it excited sexual interest among the young, who were the only ones who looked at the displays anyway, that the magazine was in very bad taste, and that it would leave a bad impression on foreigners during the Olympics.

Yet propaganda pressure was gradually increasing and the new SS man, Stuckart, was moving with it. In a conference on Sept. 29, 1936 with the party and the Ministry of Economics, Stuckart assumed the leadership. He suggested something must be done about the Jews in the economy.[237] Hess's representative, Sommer, stated that the only solution would come when there were no more Jews in Germany; all else was a partial solution. Hans Posse (Economics) carefully suggested that any action must fit into economic reality; the Jews must do *something*, and business was all that was left to them. Stuckart concluded that everyone agreed the final solution must be emigration, the tempo to be determined by the Jews' usefulness to Germany. They should be able to support themselves, yet encouraged to emigrate. But each time Stuckart suggested a restriction, Schacht's men said it was impossible, that Schacht would not go along. Even the state would have to buy from some Jews, often the only firms in the field. How to get people to avoid Jewish stores was insoluble since the Fuehrer was opposed to signs as such.

Action lagged through 1937, the pertinent file referring only to Dr. Wagner's effort to get Jewish doctors out of their profession, which Hitler finally approved (Sept. 30, 1938) 15 months after it was first mentioned. Concern was expressed at a Frick conference in October 1937 because Jewish emigration had declined in the previous six months, which was attributed to difficulties in entering Palestine, the resistance of other countries to taking them, and increased prosperity in Germany.[238] This is one reason for the 1938 offensive which pushed beyond the Nuremberg laws, led to the one act of counterviolence—the murder of the German diplomat in Paris—and which in turn gave an excuse for the mass vio-

[237] *Ibid.*, HA 320-515, 199.
[238] IZG, F71, Loesener *Handakten.*

lence of November 9. The fact that Germany had become less dependent on foreign trade, with Goering's ersatz Four Year Plan eclipsing Schacht's economic ministry and that Hitler had improved his war preparedness, had the effect of releasing the economic brakes on extremism.

The avalanche began to move in October 1937, when Hitler asked for some action against Jews buying land in health resort areas.[239] The Justice Ministry and the Foreign Office objected. In February 1938 Stuckart suggested instead a general law providing a ban on Jewish land-buying, to be applied gradually.[240] In March Pfundtner issued a secret order against the granting of public contracts to Jews.[241] Also in March, Goering asked Pfundtner for a law forcing the Jews to report their property.[242] Frick promptly complied with a ministry decree on June 14, 1938 that formed the basis for the compulsory transfer of Jewish firms, its application broad enough to include as "Jewish firms" those in which merely a board member or branch manager was a Jew.[243] On the date of the decree Frick wrote all offices, noting that one need wait no longer for voluntary Jewish withdrawal from business. One could use force, but be careful. Since Jews would not be wanted on relief, every assistance for emigration should be given them.[244] On Aug. 17, 1938 Globke drafted and Stuckart and Guertner signed a name decree, which stipulated that Jewish men had to add the middle name of Israel and Jewish women the name of Sara. An approved list of names for newly-born Jewish men was included in the decree.[245]

Anti-Jewish action continued, with the major push coming from Goering's economic sphere. Goebbels' action of November—SA mobs destroying homes and synagogues—literally fanned the flames. Goering's fury at the costs of the night (insurance companies estimated the losses at twice that normal for an entire year) was great and genuine, but his forcing the Jews to pay for the damage done by the SA indicated the depth of his amorality. Finally, a decree dated

[239] HA 320-519. [240] *Ibid.* [241] *Ibid.*
[242] *Ibid.*, 117. [243] Hilberg, 59.
[244] *Ibid.*, 153. See also Hilberg, 82-83. [245] *Ibid.*, 98.

Nov. 19, 1938, from Frick, Krosigk, and Seldte, excluded Jews from public relief.

The record of ever-increasing cruelty, with Frick's and Stuckart's legalism nearly but not quite forgotten, therefore, is unrelenting. On Nov. 28 Heydrich issued an order authorizing the limitation of Jews to certain places and certain hours. Frick ordered a reversal of Heydrich's order, insisting that he had authority on the highest orders that there must be no more violence.[247] Ten days later Goering echoed the appeal to stop "individual actions".[248]

To reestablish order Frick called the Laender officials to meet with him on Dec. 16, 1938, at which meeting he tried to convince them that enough had been done to implement NS racial policy: the Jews were out of the state, out of politics, out of the army, the schools, and most occupations; they had no cultural influence; they could have no new stores, no advertisements, no tax relief. This was a period of transition, he said, until all Jews had left the country, the question, then, was how to encourage emigration. Everything must be legal; there must absolutely be no "individual actions". The rich Jews were necessary to Hitler; their wealth would be used to get the poor Jews into those countries which otherwise would not take them. Frick listed several restrictions on party plans to make life miserable for the Jews—the Heydrich ban on their free movement was removed; they were to be allowed to buy in German stores; they would not wear the Jewish star because Hitler said that this would make it impossible to prevent violence against them and make their purchasing in stores too difficult.[249]

The next step, made expedient by the war, which halted emigration, and the wartime pressure to force the Jews out, was Heydrich's letter of Sept. 21, 1939, a copy going to Stuckart, announcing the "final goal"—the transfer of all Jews from eastern Germany, just taken from Poland, to cities farther east. This became an order from Hitler on October 10th. The impetus had passed from the negative govern-

[246] *Ibid.*, 119. [247] *Ibid.*, 247. [248] *Ibid.*, 279.
[249] *Ibid.*, 325.

ment to the positive SS. The Beamten merely had the opportunity to work on the fringes of Jewish policy and its implementation.

Loesener tried to use the war as an excuse to save his project (mixed races and mixed marriages). With Stuckart's support he was able to create a privileged group of Jews living with Aryan spouses,[250] which lasted through the long series of discriminatory laws. It was even part of Himmler's order for deportation. They remained privileged until 1945;[251] nearly all of the Jews who survived did so by virtue of this privilege.

At the beginning of the war, Loesener also tried to end the restrictions on half-Jews, arguing that they would be needed as soldiers.[252] Unfortunately early successes in the war indicated otherwise. Tens of thousands of Jews were discharged as unfit for military service, a ridiculous and costly loss. Stuckart was able to make a grim compromise, saving them by suggesting instead their sterilization, which, he testified, he knew could be done only after the war and assumed would never be done.[253]

At the next conference, Sept. 16, 1941, there was renewed pressure from the party chancellory and Eichmann to evacuate half-Jews. Keitel noted to Hitler that there would be a morale problem with the soldier sons of half-Jews if their parents were evacuated. Loesener opposed toughening the practice in the eastern lands to include one-fourth-Jews for evacuation.[254] At a conference on Jan. 29, 1942 he conceded that his argument about the dangers of the German blood in the half-Jews did not apply to the eastern Jews, and as weakly conceded to the agreement that the Nuremberg law did not apply outside Germany and half-Jews living in mixed marriages would be considered Jews.[255] In May 1942 Frick sent a long argument (Loesener's) explaining why one should not discriminate against the half-Jews; they were too few to be of biological importance; one could not tear families apart;

250 HA 320-519, 439. 251 Loesener, 287. 252 *Ibid.*, 293.
253 *Ibid.*, 297; IZG, NG2982; IZG, Fasz 8.
254 IZG, Eichmann, 1355. 255 *Ibid.*, 1102.

they "felt German"; each case involved many German relatives; they were important to the war economy; they were loyal in the army and Hitler had promised them citizenship.[256] As late as January 1943 Loesener was still working on the problem, informing everyone of their protected rights.[257] Frick's changeability is evident in his ministry's effort to maintain relief payments to Jews in May 1942,[258] and his effort a year later to push the divorce of the half-Jews so they could be brought under "war-important" evacuation.[259]

The climax of the hatred began in August 1941 when Heydrich received from Goering "the assignment for the Final Solution of the Jewish Question".[260] As of September 1st, the Jews were required to wear the Jewish star. Pfundtner noted in December 4, 1941 that Heydrich had invited a group from those agencies, "who were participants in the Final Solution of the Jewish Question, among them Dr. Stuckart. . . ."[261] From a colleague who had accidentally observed the killing of thousands of Jews in Riga, Loesener became aware that the real intent was liquidation. He went to Stuckart on December 21, 1941 and reported the slaughter. Stuckart replied: "Do you not know, Herr Loesener, that this takes place on the highest order?" Loesener asked to be released from his office and Stuckart lamented that Loesener had not "changed with the times", that he was still thinking in terms of the 1935 laws, whereas time had marched on.[262] Fifteen months later, Loesener was transferred. (He was later arrested 11 Nov. 1944 for having hidden two persons involved in the attempt on Hitler's life, expelled from the party, then liberated by the Russians on entering Berlin.)

With SS trainloads of Jews moving steadily to Auschwitz there was little that could be done, but typical of the Beamter's devious way of being humane was his technique of raising a doubt about someone in danger being Jewish, e.g., pointing out that he did not attend a synagogue. If there was any doubt about a father, the Beamter assumed the man was

[256] HA 320-519, 479, 487. [257] *Ibid.*, 501.
[258] *Ibid.*, 497. [259] *Ibid.*, 513. [260] Loesener, 197.
[261] HA 320-519, 447. [262] IZG, NG1944.

Aryan. When the deportation went into high gear, the practice was to advise anyone to raise doubts about a person's biological status and say to the SS that his case was being checked by the Interior Ministry.

The Interior Ministry had failed; its cherished legal fortifications had become as valuable as the Maginot Line.

3 BAVARIA

ONE link between the Reich and the people was the intermediate government, the *Land* (state). The largest *Land,* other than Berlin's Prussia, was Munich's Bavaria. In its history can be observed one layer of the disruptive confusion and conflict. The basic confusion concerned Bavaria's place in the New Order, whether it would survive at all. One of its conflicts was within itself, a conflict that was unending and bitter. Another unending conflict, which has survived all regimes, was against Berlin. A further conflict and confused purpose concerned Bavaria's subordinate (or insubordinate) units of government, the districts and the cities like Nuremberg and Augsburg.

A short sketch of this Land of Bavaria is useful, because it represents an important facet of the problem of a state's demanding and receiving loyalty. It mirrors an unending petty struggle over personal privilege and power, a form of selfish resistance of the majority, combined with a monumental acquiescence while the Reich destroyed an entire minority. A brief examination of Bavaria's government should add a significant dimension to the multi-faceted, tedious, political reality of the NS party and state.

The Land of Bavaria, with its *Lederhosen* and yodeling, not to mention Munich's beery *Hofbraeuhaus* and *Oktoberfest,* has seemed typically German to the outside world, an evaluation most non-Bavarians resent. Bavaria, in the southeastern corner of Germany, is notable for its scenery, mountains, rolling land, and small-scale agriculture. Bavaria has been notoriously different in character from the rest of Germany. Staunchly Catholic in most areas, rural, and locally patriotic, it had pushed for autonomy since Bismarck's unification. The 1919-23 rise and fall of Hitler in Bavaria is best understood in the context of a concurrent Bavarian revolt against the "Red Prussians," also described by Bavarians as the "Sow Prussians".

Although much weaker than modern Protestant Prussia, Catholic Bavaria had for a long period, nearly two thousand years, played a significant role in the history of the Germans. Occupying the vital area between the Alps and the Danube, it was a border territory of the Roman Empire. For over 500 years—15 B.C. to A.D. 488—Roman power was maintained, the most deeply entrenched south of the Danube. By the year 500 Germanic, "Bavarian," tribes had settled in the area. By 739-741 a new civilizing order began with the foundation of bishoprics, including that of the now obscure *Eichstaett.* Thus was formed Bavaria's enduring bond to Italy and to the Catholic faith. The Bavarian peasants among the foothills of the Alps remained the truest children of the Papacy.

Also, one can regard Bavaria's predominantly mountainous character as a factor for freedom. Its peasants, like the neighboring Swiss, were able to resist unifying despots with better success than the flat-landers. Contemporary Bavarians would also prefer to regard these mountain villagers as egalitarian and democratic.[1]

Bavaria's function as border province was renewed during Charlemagne's reign, with the Bavarians defending Christian Europe against the Slavs and Magyars from the East. "The Age of Emperors" began in 826; the Duchy of Bavaria became an important segment of the empire in the tenth century. The most direct link of the duchy to the twentieth century was its Wittelsbach dynasty which began in 1180 and lasted until 1918. Bavaria fell prey to the crippling partition via inheritance from the fourteenth to sixteenth centuries. The most powerful late-medieval units were the rich city-states, Augsburg in Schwaben (Swabia) to the west of the Lech and Nuremberg in Franken (Franconia) to the north of the Danube. The duchy of Bavaria remained traditionally peasant, its Munich a drab village by comparison to

[1] As an example, see Franz Baumgaertner, *Bavaria,* Munich, 1963.

the proud cities of Augsburg and Nuremberg. Munich was not even the ducal capital until the early sixteenth century, when Albrecht the Wise (1465-1508) made it so. Like his princely contemporaries, he ended the dynastic subdividing by the rule of primogeniture.

The Renaissance princes began to play a marginal role in European politics, a role that reached its peak with Maximilian I in the crippling Thirty Years War. With only few more resources than those of a tough peasantry, Bavaria took part in victories over the Turks, as at Belgrade (1688), and in the last of the Louis XIV Wars against the neighboring south German Hapsburgs. This small state thus had the opportunity of playing—and surviving—the power game with the big powers of France and Austria.

Greater dangers and opportunities of alliance with France came with Napoleon. In 1803 Bavaria gained the secularized bishoprics of Augsburg, Bamburg, Freising, Wuerzburg, and regions of Franken and Schwaben, hitherto subject only to the emperor; Nuremberg was added in 1806. The Duke of Bavaria became a king. The accompanying danger was with the 30,000 Bavarians who marched with Napoleon to Moscow. This great reshapening of Germany (1803-1815) doubled the "Old Bavarian" domains with the vital additions of Franken and Schwaben, and formed, essentially the modern borders of Bavaria. In 1816 a section of the Palatinate west of the Rhine was added, which remained until 1945.

The liberal centralizing of the French was copied until 1817 by the ablest of Bavarian royal ministers, Montgelas. In his 10 years in office the task he began of welding these long-independent pieces into a state. Montgelas was the delayed "enlightened" despot of Bavaria, a liberal anti-clericalist. For example, in 1818 Bavaria became the first German state to write a constitution.

With these new territories also came a push for change with the early industrialization in Nuremberg and Augsburg. The first German railway was built in 1835 between Nuremberg and neighboring Fuerth. The railroad was a source of power and communication, but also a source of continuing concern to the peasants.

While modernization was finally reaching it, Bavaria had its two kings. Ludwig I (1825-1848) aimed to undo the work of Montgelas. His was the last period of undisguised reaction, an effort to retain the land of small peasants and artisans.[2] More impressive was his beautification of Munich, including the international beauty, Lola Montez. Both left during the 1848 uprising. Their departure opened the door to reforms that ended monarchical dominance; thereafter the ministerial cabinet was the dominant force. Succeeding kings were singularly unable to compete with their ministers.

To the strain of cosmopolitanism, which would permanently distinguish the capital, was added an element of romanticism in the shy figure of the spectacular Ludwig II (1864-1886), who reigned as medieval prince while Bavaria was undergoing the forces of industrialism and nationalism. There was something peculiarly Bavarian about the king's "squandering" its still limited assets in subsidizing the romantic Richard Wagner and in building Disneyland-like castles such as Neuschwanstein. This medieval throwback "ruled" while Bismarck was forcing Prussia into the creation of a militant nationalism, defeating Bavaria and Austria in 1866, France in 1870, and uniting Bavaria into the Second Reich. As consolation, Bavaria retained special rights, including a form of foreign policy, particularly to its ideological center, the Vatican.

In development Bavaria had fallen behind not only the Ruhr, but even Saxony and Silesia.[3] In 1900 it had only about 300 thousand industrial workers. Bavaria lacked coal, capital, and ambition. After 1871 its Catholic peasants gave parliamentary power to a conservative Bavarian church party, with the NS period almost the only exception to its predominance.[4] This meant Berlin was the central ally of the Prot-

[2] Allan Mitchell, *Revolution in Bavaria, 1918-1919*, Princeton, 1965, 8.

[3] *Ibid.*, 10.

[4] Karl Schwend, *Bayern zwischen Monarchie und Diktatur*, Munich, 1954, 19f.

estants and the liberals against local Catholics.[5] A spurt of industrialization after 1900 doubled the size of Munich and tripled that of Nuremberg. By 1914 this growth had given the socialists sufficient strength to make an alliance for reform with the more liberal of the Catholic party.

With the mysterious death of the fairy tale prince, Ludwig II, the dynasty began a long regency (1886-1912) which was a step closer to its doom. Yet in its last days, the dynasty's tolerant, cosmopolitan Munich, an important intellectual and artistic center, harbored such then obscure notables as Lenin and Hitler. In a Munich photograph of August 1914, in a scene of mass support for the war, there is the ecstatic face of the young Hitler.

By 1914 nationalism seemed dominant, and Bavaria joined wholeheartedly in what might have been considered Wilhelm's Prussian War. The war sharply increased the rate of industrialization and urbanization. It also increased the suspicion of bureaucrats and Berlin. By 1917 there was a dangerous disaffection among the workers and the lower middle class.[6] The long-drawn-out hope for victory and the rapid defeat ended the hapless Wittelsbach dynasty and brought a period of violent struggle in the industrial and socialist cities. After a fragile socialist government, Catholic Bavaria, in April 1919, had the only communist regime in Germany. A Soviet-style republic took over Munich on April 7, 1919. The enormous shock to the solid peasantry and small-town bourgeoisie began the emotional illness which later gave particular strength to the right-wing extremism of Hitler. The immediate reaction was that of the volunteer Free Corps soldiers who subsequently became the core of Hitler's movement. They quickly cleaned out the beleaguered Reds in the few industrial centers in the name of monarchism, middle-class Germanism, and Christianity.

With the local left wing effectively curbed by rural Bavaria, the conservatives found another threat in the Berlin government and its leading socialist party. Berlin was no longer just Prussian but "Red". Bavaria's freedom was in jeopardy.

[5] *Ibid.*, 40. [6] Mitchell, 23.

The new Weimar constitution meant a defeat for their beloved "federalism". Bavarian Catholics perforce split from the German Catholic (*Zentrum*) party. Their major goal was to regain financial sovereignty; a lesser goal was to maintain control over the army, postal, and railroad administration.[7] Bavarian conservative, "black" (Catholic), separatism became entangled with the radical ("brown") nationalism of the Munich-spawned National Socialist party.

Bavarian anti-Weimar extremism provided the first test of Hitler's strength. The core of the party—the oldest of the old fighters—were Bavarians, although some were of recent vintage, like Hitler himself. This core included Roehm, a staff officer for Epp, the minor bureaucrat Frick, the chicken-farmer Himmler, the Munich student Hess, the ex-hero, ex-addict, ex-émigré Goering, and the Baltic refugee-racist Rosenberg. The conspiracy of this unlikely coalescence of failures to seize the Munich government reached its comic opera climax in the November 1923 putsch, ever since a part of German and world history.

Gustav von Kahr, the Bavarian Commissar, deserted the alliance formed at Hitler's pistol point and gathered sufficient loyalty among the conservative army and police to halt the ragtag demonstration with Hitler and Ludendorff at its head. Had Bavaria maintained the resistance and given the arrested Hitler an appropriate sentence for the guilty verdict of treason, or had such judges as Justice Minister Guertner kept him in jail for the full five-year sentence, the party might well have been lost among the comparable lunatic fringes of the Munich underworld.

D. C. Watt, using Foreign Ministry documents, has been able to put in question the assumption that the bureaucrats were all that sympathetic and helpful to Hitler.[8] Bavarian Minister President Eugen von Knilling blamed the laymen

[7] See Schwend, 135-36, for the (18.9.20) party program. See also Heinz Gollwitzer, "Bayern 1918-33", *Vierteljahresheft fuer Zeitgeschichte*, 1955, 363-87.

[8] Watt, "Die Bayerische Bemuehung um Ausweisung Hitlers 1924", in *Vierteljahresheft fur Zeitgeschichte*, 1958, 270-80.

serving along with Beamten as judges, for the moderate sentence upon Hitler. These were petty bourgeois whom Watt describes as fanatical believers in Hitler and Ludendorff.[9] While Guertner was sympathetic, the Interior Ministry was hostile to Hitler. Furthermore, Watt has shown that the Munich police made a serious effort to keep Hitler from being released before his five-year sentence was completed, an effort that was defeated not so much by Guertner's intercession as by the refusal of Austria to permit its citizen—Hitler—to cross the border, as Munich had requested.

In December 1924 Bavaria released Hitler to prey on the more receptive north Germans. He found the Protestant soil there more congenial to his rabid nationalism. Bavaria retained its first loyalty to the church and the church-backed Bavarian Peoples party (BVP). With Minister President Heinrich Held leading a stabler government than that in Berlin, the NS party was no longer so direct a threat to Bavaria.[10] (As Schwend would have it, Bavaria was again conquered by Prussia in 1933.) The major battle of 1925-1930 was that of Bavarian states-righters versus a Weimar unitary centralism, a tragic misapplication of Bavarian conservatives' energies.

The assumption of many, that the scorned brownshirts would merely provide a service to the middle class by counter-bullying the militant communists, seemed to be working, but in 1930 the NS electoral power, which doubled in 1932, meant that the Bavarian Peoples party itself was placed on the defensive by the brownshirts. The choice was between the conservative Catholic party and the pseudo-conservative NS. The Bavarian tragedy was partly that middle-class leaders assumed until the last minute that it would be easier to deal with Hitler than with the hated left wing. Another tragedy is that these conservatives, blending traditional piety and confused monarchism, failed to adjust to appeals to a modern electorate.

The "confessional" problem, most acute in Bavaria, also

[9] *Ibid.*, 272.
[10] See Schwend, Chap. 17, "The Held Era".

played an unfortunate part. Actually, with the Catholic majority having the greater power of a democracy and restrained less by the cautious royal bureaucrats, the problem became more acute. The Protestants feared a perpetual Catholic rule, with only a rare Protestant gaining a ministerial post. The choice of the minority of the Bavarians was to vote "national", to look to Berlin to rescue them from suppression. And it was precisely this minority that was won by the NSDAP.

The 1932 presidential campaign flooded Bavaria with NS propaganda and threats, yet Hindenburg's vote in Bavaria was 2,630,000 to Hitler's 1,270,000.[11] In contrast to most of the nation, particularly Prussia, there remained one party stronger than the NS—Held's BVP—having since 1928 gained 200,000 voters in the elections for the Bavarian legislature. Unfortunately Held rejected a coalition cabinet with the socialists.

By 1932 there was little doubt in Held's party about the NS threat to their dominance. One late answer to SA violence was Ritter von Lex's *Bayernwacht*, an organization of young men to defend the Catholic party. Yet violence remained restrained, by Prussian standards; in Prussia 72 were killed and 477 seriously injured in the July campaign. Yet in one NS meeting, Held was threatened with murder.[12] When von Papen deposed the Prussian Socialist government on July 20, 1932, it first became clear to many Bavarian conservatives that the real Berlin threat to Bavarian autonomy came from the right, not the left.[13] The constitution thus became the hope, not the enemy, of federal rights.

In the November 1932 election the NS vote declined from 1,346,711 (July) to 1,163,210, but the BVP also declined, from 1,323,969 to 1,209,334; and the Socialists slipped. The relative lack of NS success was due partly to the party's increasing identification with Berlin, which Hitler took in January 1933. The last campaign, February 2 to March 5, was fought in Bavaria against Berlin, i.e., the use of Reichs Kommissars, as had occurred in Prussia. Held threatened to arrest

[11] *Ibid.*, 419. [12] *Ibid.*, 449. [13] *Ibid.*, 460ff.

any such commissar from the north, and was backed up by Hindenburg's renewed assurances all through February. Frick's sarcasm on Feb. 24, 1933 about these dreams of a new defense of "the Main Line" (the south from the north), announced the NS determination to make all states conform.[14] Four days later the Reichstag fire, which was blamed on the communists, brought on the panic "Emergency Decree for the Protection of the State and People". Thus the fear of communism, nowhere stronger than in Bavaria, gave Hitler the weapon with which to attack the states, at a time when old Hindenburg would protect them no longer.

The Takeover

The NSDAP had no clear mandate to rule Bavaria even on the basis of the Reichstag election of March 5, 1933. The NSDAP received 1,910,000 votes, or 43%. The BVP and SPD actually had increased their votes in this last election and might have maintained a Bavarian coalition government had Berlin not intervened.

The conservatives' failure to appreciate Hitler's danger is shown by President Held's trip to Berlin on March 1, 1933. Held hoped that Hitler could be dealt with.[15] Held began by promising cooperation so long as the demand was "not against his conscience". Hitler put him on the defensive by dragging out Held's anti-Berlin quotes, most of them against von Papen. Held disclaimed the quotes and insisted Bavaria would not oppose Berlin for the sake of opposition. Hitler said that were he not in the Berlin government, only a government by bayonets would be possible, because the communists could start a civil war at any time. He boasted that he had not asked for power. "He could have waited six months more"; "the alleged party difficulties" had been easily solved.

Held replied that Bavaria had led the way against the communists. Munich had tried to ban them, but the Berlin government had prevented it. Held insisted that any government must be bound by Christian principles. Hitler responded that

[14] *Ibid.*, 511. [15] GSA—MA 105247.

Rosenberg was a Protestant and Hitler, a Catholic, that the "anti-Christian" book of Rosenberg was a private not a party statement, that the NS was often closer to the Catholic interests than was the Catholic party. Berlin might have to intervene in "Red" Hamburg and Hesse, but no one would bother Bavaria. Reassured, Held left, inviting Hitler to visit him as Bavarian president soon, and Hitler promised to do so. Nine days later Hitler forced Held out of office.

Even before the national election victory of March 5, Held had expressed to President Hindenburg his concern over rumors about the declaration of an emergency, for which no reason existed in Bavaria. Hindenburg's answer was that there was no such plan, only some special laws to fight against communist acts of violence. At the March 7 Bavarian Ministerial Council (cabinet) meeting, Held duly reported that Hitler was considering intervening in Hamburg and Hesse, but that no one thought of intervening in conservative Bavaria which had done the most to stop the communists.[16]

Yet with Berlin under NS control, Bavaria's NS leaders seized the initiative and forced their way into power, assured that the national government would support them and that the army would not interfere. At noon March 9th, Roehm, clad in boots and spurs, appeared, together with Gauleiter Adolf Wagner. They gave Held an ultimatum concerning appointing Gen. Ritter von Epp as Commissar. They referred to "unrest" in the SA, which by coincidence was gathering outside the building. The cabinet appealed for Reichswehr support, as in 1923, but the commander inquired of his Berlin superiors, who ordered the commander not to intervene in internal politics.[17]

The bitter injustice of NS local tactics is reflected in Held's telegrams to Berlin, appealing for legality.[18] A mid-afternoon telegram on March 9th started the panic, when Held reported to Hitler that the Munich SA was threatening to take direct action. (An SA mob demonstrated outside as a hostile chorus

[16] *Sitzungen des Ministerrats von Bayern*, in *Geheim Staats Archiv*, Munich.

[17] Schwend, 538.

[18] BA—R 43II/1315.

to the drama within.) Held saw no need of violence; his party was ready to create a new government under NS leadership. He expressed his "confidence" that Hitler would stop any SA attack. The reply from Hindenburg was simply that Bavaria should solve its own problems. At 7:41 Held telegraphed again that the new parliament would select a NS government within two days and requested that there be no Reich intervention in the "quiet legal development in Bavaria". Six minutes later Held appealed to Hindenburg not to permit any application of Reich force; at 8:50 he protested to Hindenburg the appointment of Ritter von Epp as plenipotentiary. No reason existed for such an appointment, as there was no danger of a communist attack. Nine minutes later Held protested in a telegram to Hitler Epp's appointment, which was followed just after midnight of March 10 with another telegram which "expected" the retraction of "the unnecessary and illegal appointment" of Epp. The file ends with Hindenburg's request to Hitler to listen to the Bavarian emissary.

The public was notified the next day of Epp's appointment as commissar, to be assisted by Roehm, Wagner, and Esser—and that was that. (The BDC Epp file has an uncorroborated story that Hitler intended to appoint parliamentary NS leader Buttmann as Reichsstatthalter, but that Epp's supporters destroyed Hitler's telegram and presented Hitler with a *fait accompli.*)[19] Local power seizures used the tactic of pushing legally elected mayors out of office, accompanied by force, or rumor of force, from assembled SA men. With a pseudo-legality provided by Berlin, plus local NS will and action, the representatives of the old order left protesting, but they did leave; many were soon arrested "for their own protection".

At the March 10 meeting of the Bavarian cabinet, Held objected to the presence of Esser, Epp's emissary, but agreed to discuss it with Epp. Held also agreed to turn the police over to Epp, which meant to the relatively unknown Himmler that the rest of the government was to remain the same.

[19] BDC Epp File, the Wilhelm Staudinger papers.

The cabinet meeting concerned itself with the fate of one of its members who had been arrested by the SA and taken from his home in his nightshirt to the NS "Brown House," where he had been insulted and beaten. Esser apologized for the violence, noting that Wagner also "regretted the action" and that Frank had arranged for the minister's release.

That Epp was also confused about the future is evident in his March 12, 1933 press conference statement: "Now that that victory was achieved, one goes farther as in war. A victorious troop does not stand still . . . but keeps going and breaks through. . . .[20] Detailed instructions about the conduct of the administrative authorities could not be given. As with the army the most important was not the regulations, but 'healthy human reason'. If only the Beamter acted quickly he would not be criticized, only if he delayed to act. . . ."[21] The Beamter's power should end any worry about the future of Bavaria, which had gained "the full respect of the Reich" by its conduct in the war. Two high Beamten, Kollman and Rohmer, responded to the reassurance that there would be discipline, order, and respect for Bavarian differences, by pledging full loyalty "as they could not do after the 1918 revolution". Epp responded in kind: Bavaria had "a good corps" of Beamten; few improvements would be necessary and those only "at the very top". Esser ordered the Gauleiter to avoid any interference in the state organization; the Ministry of Interior, Wagner, would take any necessary action—an order that was ignored.[22]

Wagner made his rebellion clear by holding his own press conference an hour later, without Epp or Roehm. Unlike Epp, he would not be satisfied with a passive implementation of orders, only with action; "Our Movement is a soldiers' Movement".[23] Where he had seen "resistance", he had already acted. "In those measures which I consider necessary, I won't be held to any paragraph (of the law). If they were not Beamten but politicians, they would not be held by any paragraph either."[24] He quoted Hitler to the effect that with

[20] ASA—108/570.
[21] *Ibid.*
[22] *Ibid.*
[23] *Ibid.*
[24] *Ibid.*

the coordination (*Gleichschaltung*) of the policies in Reich and in the Laender, the latter could be given "the greatest autonomy", and like Hitler, he would give authority to those who agreed with him".

At the next week's meeting there was an entirely new line-up, all NS, with Epp as chairman; Adolf Wagner heading the Interior Ministry and its police; Hans Frank in charge of "justice"; mayor of a small town, Ludwig Siebert, in charge of finances; Gauleiter Schemm, Education Ministry. SA chief, Roehm, was left an important, though undefined role, as were Himmler and Esser, an obscure Herr Luber. Of these men, who in 1933 had charter member status in the new government: Frank moved to Berlin when the Bavarian Ministry was incorporated into the Reich Justice Ministry; Schemm showed promise of high party position until an airplane death in 1935; Roehm left the scene in the famous "night of the long knives" in June 1934, after providing the worst problems to his Bavarian government; Esser resigned in 1935 to live a shadowy existence in the travel business; Luber left quickly in 1933 in a hushed-up scandal. Himmler took his Bavarian police command to Berlin and became, to the bafflement of his erstwhile colleagues, the most feared man in Germany. The three remaining—Epp, Siebert, and Wagner—constituted a kind of triumvirate which dissolved within two years into a permanent feud.

The commissar who seemed to have won power in Bavaria was Gen. Ritter von Epp, then the most famous person in the Bavarian party. With a military mien and mustache, his "von" a military honor, and associated with the conservative Catholic elements, he was as respectable as an NS could be. He had a wide following in Bavaria, because of his Free Corps which had defeated the communists in 1919, no major task in view of the communists' marginal support, but a victory nonetheless, in a Germany overwhelmed by the 1918 defeat. (The percentage of Epp Free Corps in the early NS movement was very high. The party banned it in 1935.) A nationalist who hated "Red" disorder, Epp was NS because he wanted to restore order and because he so strongly supported the Catholic church. In NS circles his nickname was "The Mother-of-God General". Active in the BVP until it refused him a leading position, he shifted in 1928, to be elected to the Reichstag as an NS.[25]

Epp's contribution to the party was his name. He does not seem to have spoken or written anything significant. He was a military man, accustomed to giving orders, not to organizing popular support or rabble rousing like the usual party leader. He operated best behind a staff which prepared thoroughly for the commander's decisions. Epp was constantly requesting important matters to be submitted in writing. Any reports were then assimilated by his staff and an answer readied for his signature. He attracted able men to this staff, usually moderates who found his prestige their protection against party radicals. The former Nuremberg police Beamter, Schachinger, did much of his planning.

More prominent was Col. Hans Georg Hofmann, a slight person whose bearded appearance gave him the universal nickname "Trotsky". He was a soldier, able by virtue of his old-fighter status and SA role from 1931, to speak out for legality and restraint. (Hofmann had the distinction of "discovering" Hitler by first giving him the chance to speak to army officers.) He was wounded in a party battle, hit in the head by a communist-thrown stone.[26] Having the manner of an army sergeant, Hofmann lacked the tact and skill to maneuver his way through the party squabbles, but his opposition to Epp's enemies, who were also the Catholic church's enemies, was inflexible. A brief career as president of Franken ended with Streicher's firing him and Epp's failure to find him any other job except as his state secretary.

Unlike Epp, Hofmann was a hard worker. A story about his death in 1943 suggests the comparison between the two men. Hofmann entered Epp's office carrying a large stack of papers he had worked through, which he was to explain to Epp prior to a decision. As he was in the process of explain-

[25] Ludwig Volk, *Der Bayerische Episkopat und der Nationalsozialismus, 1930, 34*, Mainz, 1965, 62.

[26] BDC SA File, Hans Georg Hofmann.

ing matters to Epp, Hofmann suddenly sank to the floor and died. Epp had him carried to a couch, regarded him for several moments, then returned to the pile of papers that had fallen to the floor, picked them up, and said bitterly, "Now I'll have to do all of this damned dirty work myself".[27]

Ludwig Siebert, squat and bald, was the Beamter of the three, among the very few NS in all of Bavaria who had completed the required training as "higher Beamter". Although he was not particularly distinguished, having risen only to mayor of a fairly obscure town in Schwaben, Siebert was almost the automatic choice by default. He made satisfactory public appearances and speeches, and he knew something of finances, a crucial position, in which Beamten had to be trusted. Siebert seems to have had the Beamten qualities of thoroughness and hard work, but no important strength of character. He lacked Epp's propensity for command or Wagner's tendency to bully. In fact, he was usually bullied by Wagner. The only hope of maintaining himself against Wagner would have been an alliance with Epp, but these two "moderates" fought each other bitterly during nearly their entire official careers. Siebert accepted his inferior status to Wagner;[28] he was rarely in attendance at Wagner-organized state celebrations, although he was the president of Bavaria and head of two ministries.

No doubt the single most powerful person in Bavaria was non-Bavarian Interior Minister Adolf Wagner, who after 1935 headed the Education Ministry, and was also the Gauleiter of the Munich area. As such, he had close contact with the Munich national party headquarters. With a certain dash, unlike the general or the Beamter, Wagner was completely confident of his "nearness to the Gods".[29] Yet he was fanatically loyal to Hitler, swearing that he would have every finger cut off if Hitler ordered it. He copied Hitler's mannerisms, his voice, even the slapping of the knee. Wagner's real bailiwick was the Interior Ministry, where he refused to give up his voice in the police even when they came under

[27] Epp's adjutant Trillich's account to Dr. Martin.
[28] Robert Scherer. [29] *Ibid.*

the formal control of Berlin. His powers were expanded in the war; he was made "Defense Commissar" for nearly all of Bavaria.

Wagner's radicalism (he was the hater of Jews and Catholics in the Bavarian top hierarchy) came in part from his background. The son of a Lorraine miner, he had attended technical schools. He went to the front in 1914 and was twice wounded and gassed, gaining the Iron Cross and other medals. Wagner lost most of his right leg in the war and, like Hitler, emerged from the hospital in 1919 without a home. First active in miners' unions, he joined the NS party in 1923. (His opposition to the priests was despite—or because of—his strong Catholic beliefs. He would say on occasion: "I can't stand the priests, therefore I don't go to church".[30])

But Wagner's private life was too scandalous for his peers. Karl Wahl complained that "power had gone to his head", that Wagner became more brutal the longer he had power. He smoked 80 to 100 cigarettes a day and drank too much, which complicated the health problems derived from his severely wounded leg. The handicap did not, however, prevent him from secretary-chasing. His late hours were his creative ones; ideas came to him in the middle of the night, for which he would rouse Beamten from their beds to get them working.

Intelligent and somewhat belligerent, Wagner came as close as anyone in Bavaria to being its tyrant. Complaints about his woman-chasing did not suffice to shake his position with Hitler, though. If Wagner feared anyone in Bavaria, it was the rotund, stableboy bully, Christian Weber, who gained great wealth, in contrast to Wagner's pride in remaining "a poor dog", with an NS monopoly of the Munich garbage business. Weber, who was unpredictable and invariably rude, had created his own little empire in Munich, able by his closeness to Hitler—he was one of the few to address his old fellow street fighter comrade as Adolf—to counter Wagner's influence.

The Wagner clique was composed of elements such as the onetime student-secretary-made-State-Secretary Max Koeglmaier, who administered the Interior Ministry for Wagner.

[30] *Ibid.*

A Hitler Youth leader, Emil Klein, was used for odd jobs, like running the Education Ministry. Gauleiter duties were largely assigned to a deputy, Nippold, who battled against Wagner's major weakness—susceptibility to flattery—thereby incurring the hatred of the abundant flatterers.

In the State hierarchy as subordinates of Wagner, but in the party hierarchy his equals, were the five other Gauleiter, who had little part in the Bavarian government, but who ran their own Gaue with as little interference from Wagner as Wagner accepted from Berlin. They varied greatly in personality from the boyish-appearing Schemm in Bayreuth, to the professional-like dentist, Hellmuth, in Wuerzburg, to the restrained clerk, Wahl, in Augsburg, to the vicious anti-Semite, Streicher, in Nuremberg, to the openly rebellious Buerckel in his piece of Bavaria west of the Rhine. What they had in common was a pride in having won a great victory, and they were determined to exploit that victory in terms of personal power and, often, profit.

This lineup of state and party leaders was remarkably stable through the years of the Third Reich. Schemm's death brought in the Streicher-like Waechtler. Streicher, driven from power, was replaced by the equally fanatic but less powerful Holz. Wagner's illness and death in 1942-1943 brought in from the outside another fanatic, but one with a technical background—Paul Giesler. Compared to Wagner, Giesler was "more dangerous because he was less insane".[31] His background shows a 1928 membership and activity in the SA, where he was a close follower of Roehm. Giesler was tried by the highest party court after Roehm's death and charged with having turned the SA against his Gauleiter in Westphalia and involvement in the Roehm "plot". He was quoted as having promised his SA men their chance to kill their enemies in the party. "His dismissal from the SA, as from the party is absolutely essential."[32] The 21 charges brought against him in October 1934 read like the total indictment against the SA: corruption, violence against citizens, threats of violence against even Goering. Yet Giesler was found inno-

[31] Martin.

[32] BDC File Paul Giesler SA.

cent, and instead of execution, he later became the most powerful man in Bavaria.

State versus Party

Despite the victory heralded in the newspapers with a carefully cultivated public image of stability, there raged behind the scenes of the Bavarian government a constant battle, first for the survival of the state of Bavaria, then for the survival of each member. At the first meeting of the new government, Siebert, with a superior knowledge of events, took effective leadership of what was supposedly Epp's meeting.[33] The meeting displayed the lack of any constructive NS program on which to use their prized power, only a pettiness against "enemies". The normal state payment to the Jewish church was stopped; state orders would go only to "German" firms; socialist directors would be removed from the state-owned enterprises. Despite the public outcries of Weimar bankruptcy and corruption, the cabinet approved without question the budget drawn up by the ousted government.

Yet from the first, the conservatives battled the SA; Siebert noted that so many Beamten and mayors had been thrown out of office by local SA leaders that the pension funds were nearly exhausted; also their contracts would surely be upheld by the courts. "The Commissar Land government must therefore assure with every possible means that further invasions into the private and public legal affairs by local groups must stop."[34] Thus the opening shot was fired, which was echoed many times in every community by the Bavarian state against the local party illegalities called "revolution".

The ambivalent Wagner, both party and state leader, partly defended his fellow revolutionaries. He issued the March 18 order which appointed the commissars, but he also set limits to their rights—no taking of police or army weapons, no command over police units.[35] Wagner lamely excused the violence as an effort to get "greater respect for the new government", and suggested that the pensions could

[33] GSA *Ministerrat Sitzung*, 25.3.33. (Hereafter Min. Rat.)
[34] *Min. Rat.*, 25.3.33, 94. [35] IZG—FA 115, 1-2.

be reduced later. Then Epp began his unending requests for "information".

The NS device of warping the law from within, instead of attacking it from without, as the SA did, was evident when Frank suggested that a steward trusted by the party be put on the special courts to assure their "vigor". Himmler was to appoint the appropriate persons. Frank urged the other technique of putting party men in key offices; applicants for jobs should also be examined about their party service. (It is remarkable how in this first serious discussion the SA's open revolution was weighed and found wanting, and the more insidious, slower infiltration of the law was approved in its stead.) But on March 31, 1933 Roehm urged more action, regretting that his commissars were not active enough. "Basically the commissar must become master of his district, before whom everyone has submitted. Principle for him must be: "Not to do something is worse than a mistake in the selection of methods."[36]

At the next meeting, on April 7, Siebert began again with the financial problems of SA illegality, horrified that the SA auxiliary police was costing six to seven million marks. He requested that before anyone hired more police they ask the Finance Ministry whether the new police could be paid. Epp thought the national government should pay them. Frank began to show concern for the arrests under NS "justice". The prisons were overfilled, with 5,000 as of April 1 and thousands more expected. "With the application of protective arrest the reasons are often insufficiently defined, so that one cannot be sure that innocent persons are not in arrest."[37] Arrests for simple denunciations and arbitrary arrests must stop. He wanted immediate interrogation and immediate release if the grounds were insufficient. Like the jurist he was, Frank urged a formal process of ordered authority, with security to the arrested and opportunity for complaint; the police should be informed of all arrests. The Council approved and ordered Wagner to take the necessary steps. Epp also wanted to be kept informed.

[36] IZG—FA 115, 5-6.

[37] *Min. Rat.*, 7.4.33, 104.

The next day, April 8, 1933, in Hitler's name Epp ordered an end to such illegalities. "The work of the public authorities may not be bothered under any circumstances by anyone's effort to interfere."[38] The Bavarian government then ruled that only it could make commissars; any commissars assigned any economic organization were fired no matter who appointed them.[39]

The meeting of April 19 began the task of defining the "all-powerful" position of Epp, a task comparable to explaining a fifth wheel. Siebert was Minister President, already a chief executive. What should Epp do? A list of high Beamten positions was to be drawn up to which Epp could name persons, the rest to be named by each minister; he would be bothered only with major pardoning matters; the ministers were to deal with him only through the Minister President. These definitions actually put limits on his jurisdiction, but they were not the real source of Epp's weakness.

The council also limited the SA and the party: no SA was to interfere with state policy or administration; no party member was to act except through party channels to the top. On May 16 Epp protested the actions of the Munich police against the Jewish community. "The actions of the political police command (Himmler) had already repeatedly given much reason for concern."[40] The council voted its full support to Interior Minister Wagner, the most radical of the group, authorizing him to clean out radicals, "who had damaged the prestige of the Bavarian government". Wagner showed mild concern for the turbulent SA, suggesting a compulsory labor service, because "the SA need above all something to do in order to master the difficulties of adjustment". (Finance conquered fanaticism as the suggestion to have Hitler's picture put in every room was voted down as too costly.[41])

Siebert showed a growing disillusionment with the new order when he opposed in May the new Reich "Law for the Recreation of the Professional Civil Service", the key NS

[38] IZG—FA 115, 7-8.
[39] IZG—FA 115, 9-10.
[40] *Min. Rat.*, 16.5.33, 135.
[41] *Min. Rat.*, 25.3.33.

change, ostensibly to take Weimar politics out of the administration, but actually to get NS politics into it. Siebert frankly believed, "The changes signify as a whole the end of the professional civil service". Like other NS officials in power, Siebert had to fight off "Old Fighters" hoping to use their party "battles" as stepping-stones to soft state jobs. These NS promptly observed that but a few of their number, like Wagner and Siebert, had grabbed the top jobs, that the great bulk of the denounced Weimar elite in industry and in government remained in their old power and wealth, while the NS rank and file remained in their old poverty, "with only their brown shirts to their name".[42] This was the social force behind Roehm and the SA, and one which the conservative state and Siebert would beat down.

At the meeting of the Council on June 27, 1933 the issue was the action taken by Wagner against the BVP, which had brought the resignation of its representative, Quadt, as Economics Minister. In March Hitler had personally and repeatedly pressured the BVP Reichtag member Ritter von Lex, also commander of an embryonic Catholic guard, to take such a cabinet post. By June the Catholic party was of no use and their leaders were easily arrested. This action led to what the cabinet's record describes as a "lively discussion" that lasted for two hours.[43] The decision was to accept Quadt's resignation, Siebert to take his ministry. As an attempted restraint on Wagner, the ministers were "in all important questions of a political nature to inform their colleagues immediately", not to act unilaterally, as Wagner continued to do. The "exceptional SA action" in Landstuhl was to be reversed; a franker report stated that the SA leader there had arrested all officials and demanded 20% of their income.[44]

The July 4 cabinet meeting evidenced a further effort to brake "the movement", as the party preferred to call itself. The government would accept party "trustees" in the minis-

[42] CGD—T 580, R 340, Bav. SA leader, 19.6.33.
[43] *Min. Rat.*, 27.6.33.
[44] CGD—T 580, R 340, Memo 27.6.33.

tries, but they were to be surrounded with such restrictions as to make solid Beamten out of them. Siebert then recited a list of SA atrocities: the beating of 15 guests in a tavern; the mobilization of a unit by an SA commander in Kempten to demonstrate against a NS mayor, "because the Commissar saw the mayor as a competitor for the cherished position as district president."[45] From Wagner's Upper Bavaria, "a shocking report of encroachments of innumerable variety. . . . Things simply cannot continue this way". To stop the SA attacks, the Council considered abolishing the positions of all Commissars below the county level, for the difficulty came from local commisars, "not capable of their jobs".

Epp agreed with Siebert's denunciation of the SA and typically wanted it in writing so that he could complain in Berlin. He suggested an alliance of the government with the political leaders of the party against the SA, the Gauleiter to meet with the Council. The Council instead decided that Epp should appeal to Berlin to get "the necessary measures from the party administration for cooperation with state government". They agreed that Epp needed the authority to control the party. From this authority would follow the clean-up, then no more interference with the state and no more arrests except by authorized police—or so they hoped. The rub was noticeable as Siebert, like Epp, complained that he was not informed by Wagner of important acts of the political police. "It is an impossible situation when the Interior Minister several days after such actions still cannot give any information about them."

An SA commander's letter showed the SA-created chaos.[46] "Everyone arrests everyone. . . . Everyone threatens everyone with arrest. Everyone threatens everyone with Dachau." After noting this danger "from the street," "as every street-sweeper thinks he should intervene in matters he does not understand", the SA author noted that he had ordered all such activity unapproved by his office to cease. Anyone who

[45] *Min. Rat.*, 4.7.33, also on CGD—T 580, R 340.

[46] CGD—T 580, R 340, 1.7.33 letter to Siebert from SA Fuehrung in Oberbayern.

disobeyed this would be sent to Dachau. Siebert sadly wondered on what authority these further arrests would be made.

The government placed itself, as it must, as protector of its servants; at issue was an SA attack on a non-NS Beamter closely associated with the old regime. Yet in a sense no decision was taken, likely because of a fundamental difference between Wagner and the others. Each minister was to check his staff and decide who could not be defended; up to that point membership in the BVP was *not* to be considered damaging. "Against the demands from the street for the release of an official, the Council must take a position because of basic considerations. The responsible minister must put himself in front of his officials."[47]

Matters seemed to solidify as at the July 18 meeting Epp proudly reported that he was "the only Plenipotentiary and the last resort for all measures".[48] Since many an SA man had also the title of Plenipotentiary, the question of what one "all-powerful" would do vis-à-vis another "all-powerful" remained to be answered. Epp never came close to being all-powerful.

With the question of who was to be top dog apparently settled, the Council turned to Roehm's suggestion of a "State Council", presumably with heavy party, i.e., radical, membership. Quoting Frick, Siebert opposed the watering down of the traditional government. His solution was for an "Estates", a chamber which would include some "citizens" (business conservatives to balance out any additions from the party), a step back toward the kind of parliament they had disbanded. The only agreement was that the commissars must be ended: "Business demands it". Epp urged restraint by the centralizing of controls in party organizations, but the Council noted that each party organization had its national head, any of which could issue contrary instructions to another organization or to the state.

There was a tenser atmosphere at party headquarters at a Council meeting with the Gauleiter.[49] The Gauleiter were not

[47] *Min. Rat.*, 4.7.33.
[48] *Min. Rat.*, 18.7.33.
[49] CGD—T 580, R 340, 18.7.33.

so easily impressed, and were quite ready to test their pull with Hitler against Epp's. After a brief Epp sentiment for unity of party and state, Siebert had more to say, e.g., that the party talk of cleaning out disloyal officials was unrealistic. It was impossible to release everyone who had worked against the NS. This was not only Reich policy, but the money as well as suitable replacements was lacking. In case of complaint he must insist on proof; simple membership in the BVP was not enough. He continued that the ending of other parties had not solved the problems; the enemy had become unknown, the opposition continued but within the party's own ranks. The Gauleiter should be built into the government, but they also should deserve the power given them. "Since the authority of the State has been reestablished, all of the devices used during the revolutionary time must be abandoned; this is particularly true of the Commissars."

The Gauleiter answered distrustfully; Streicher thought Bavaria had shown no awareness of the danger; he could not understand the calm attitude of the Munich government; the Gauleiter could do their work only if they were not bothered from outside. But Wahl agreed and asked for help against the commissars who had "exhausted him more than five electoral campaigns". Buerckel complained about high Beamten salaries and announced the plan to integrate the SS into local administration, a plan which Epp quickly criticized. After more Gauleiter complaints, Epp and Siebert ended the meeting, apologizing for not having contacted them before, but they should "see how high they rated" in Munich.

At their evening meeting with other SA-SS leaders, Epp used the conservatives' favorite quote from Hitler—"The Revolution is over"—adding, "It is unnatural that NS in government positions do not experience the strongest help from other party members instead of the strongest resistance. To end this resistance was the purpose of the meeting". Epp used his trump card again, reading from Hitler's orders that Epp was all-powerful in Bavaria, that his decisions were to be binding on all party leaders. Epp said he had not used his absolute powers yet and hoped the party would not force him to.

This grand declaration of unused power evoked only a series of criticisms of the general lack of cooperation. An SA commander complained of the lack of state support. Streicher complained that the SA refused to cooperate with the Gauleiter. "The situation was disastrous." Streicher wanted larger Gaue created. This threatened Hellmuth, his neighbor, who warned against creating larger Gaue. Streicher complained about Berlin's protection of Jewish stores and about Catholic party men on city councils. After the chaotic griping session, Epp reminded the party great of what Hitler had said, and spoke vaguely of future meetings. That he later opposed the Gauleiter joining the government council is fully understandable. (Meanwhile Wagner had issued an order to his Beamter that none of them should ever have any personal contact with Epp, never make any complaint or suggestion to him. Unlike Epp's, Wagner's order would mean something.[50])

Another Cabinet meeting was called within a week, which indicated the seriousness of the situation. The meeting concerned SA police action against Jews in Nuremberg, for which Epp expressed his regret.[51] He reported that it was done without either his or Wagner's knowledge; Wagner had issued orders against a recurrence. Yet Wagner showed his ambivalence by adding that he was not so much against the action as its timing, and "much valuable material had been collected". Siebert urged that the Political Police should be headed by "an experienced administrative jurist", i.e., not by Himmler. Epp agreed, quoting Hitler that there were not enough NS with the proper training for all the necessary jobs. "Also in Bavaria it is necessary to put the Beamter back into authority. One must give them time to adjust to the new conditions. . . . Improper Beamter should be released, but one should not be too hard on the Beamten and one should not comply with the wishes of party leaders without further ado."

[50] ASA—102/0101, 4.8.33. [51] *Min. Rat.*, 26.7.33.

Roehm, a member of the Cabinet, and at least the godfather of all the lamented SA abuses, made his first Cabinet defense of his commissars. He quoted Hitler, that the SA was the "guarantor" of the revolution. "It is therefore impossible to take the SA out of the operation of the NS state and to leave its operation solely to the bureaucracy." The commissars had done "a good job"; he therefore begged that they be permitted to remain at the provincial and county level. Frank the conciliator praised Roehm for his assistance in keeping the commissars out of the courts. What must be done was to place clear legal limits on their power and clear up the legal position of the Jews. He was pleased when Roehm agreed that the police could arrest "provocateurs in SA uniforms".

Agreement was reached—and partially lived up to—that only the top commissars could remain. The Gauleiter, and not SA commanders, at the provincial level were to be the advisory organ for the police and for military questions, with the Bavarian government providing them with guidelines.[52] Strangely for a man killed a year later for plotting revolution, Roehm accepted this loss of local power, at least at the meeting. His pill was sweetened by the State's payment of a modest amount to his SA men. (Roehm's reasonableness was related to the financial difficulties of his vastly expanded SA; Siebert wrote in September 1933 of his hope to use this fact to keep them under control.[53])

On September 1 Roehm wrote a remarkable defense of his commissars in answering the Bavarian criticism: In every state the government needed a healthy opposition for its development and progress. Since other parties would be disruptive in the NS state, the SA must maintain this vital opposition. The NS revolution had been able to occupy only the very top offices of the state; the great majority of the middle and lower offices were in the hands of open or secret opponents of the NS or neutrals. The SA-SS had the requisite discipline (he dismissed the troublemakers as not truly SA-SS), and the SA-SS in contrast to the Beamten were not

[52] *Ibid.* [53] GSA—MA 105256.

bound by the law, and therefore much more useful to the revolution. Adjustment was a simple matter; all differences of opinion would go up the neat ladder of command to the top.[54] (If not Roehm's SA, Himmler's SS did become an opposition to the government.)

The September 19 Cabinet meeting rose above the mundane long enough to authorize Siebert to tell the Gauleiter Buerckel that he could not substitute his district for the national social security program.[55] Siebert expressed his constant frustration with the NS revolution: "We have in Bavaria in addition to the Reich government, the Land government, a government of the political police, a government of the SA and SS and an autonomous government of the Bavarian Interior Ministry".[56] He had waited, but his duty forced him to wait no more; "order must be reestablished". He resented the insulting manner of Wagner both to him and Epp, using press statements and accepting positions without asking or telling either of them. Strangely, Wagner apologized and offered to resign. (The offer, if serious, unfortunately was not accepted.) Frank noted the incredibly bad conditions in Munich and Nuremberg, so bad that the police offered no help to the courts in finding the facts. To this criticism, Epp's complaint that someone had removed his honor guard seems ludicrous, but he agreed that if law and order did not improve, he would call in the army.

The Cabinet next puzzled over what to do with Streicher, whose anti-Semitic, anti-Catholic *Der Stuermer* was also anti-government, having attacked the Ministry of Justice.[57] Instead of closing down the newspaper they agreed on a sharp warning, a report to Frick, and the promise of full support to the police "which was having some difficulties in the performance of its functions in Franken".

A special meeting on October 20 brought the argument about the commissars to open debate—Frank and Siebert

[54] IZG—FA 115, 1.9.33. [55] *Min. Rat.*, 19.9.33.
[56] GSA Folder, *"Die National Erhebung, Wahrung der Staatsautoritaet"*, 7.10.33.
[57] *Min. Rat.*, 10.10.33.

in opposition, Roehm and Himmler in defense, the latter displaying the secret of his future SS success: the commissars were the first step toward building the SA-SS into the State, a process no one dared reverse.[58] Such an organization was necessary to win in the villages and throughout the countryside. Roehm regarded the political situation as one for concern, because a majority of the party members in the Reich ministries did not recognize the true situation and thought the revolution could be stopped. He had informed Hitler that the Beamten were working hard to get everything back to the peaceful ways of the past. The police were not as NS as pictured; nothing had changed in the Reich Interior Ministry; the Catholics were there as before.

The next Council had Siebert listed as chairman, evidence of Epp decline,[59] but Epp was back November 21 to complain about the police: "He has the impression that their realm of operations had been expanded too rapidly, and they do not fully measure up to their duties. The political police are not the equals of the State ministries; they cannot simply be left to the Interior Ministry, for they are the executive organ of the entire government, in particular the justice administration. Someone will have to instruct the political police on these important facts." In response to such Cabinet criticism Himmler wrote Siebert about the complaint, that the commissars were still running a Munich newspaper, that this was Hitler's specific wish.[60] No more questions.

The November 29 meeting began with the casting from their midst of a high official, although an old NS, who had accepted the gift of an estate. (It was later decided that he was not an "old fighter" after all.) Such conduct was impossible, not in accord with NS principles, and would if tolerated destroy the authority of the state. Not even Wagner in the triumvirate enriched himself in office, although each had a villa as official residence beyond their previous means. The meeting ended with a debate over the continuance of the exuberant Munich carnival, *Fasching*. Should police restraint

[58] GSA Folder on *Sonderkommissaren*.
[59] *Min. Rat.*, 24.10.33. [60] IZG—FA 115.

be withdrawn? The Council solemnly agreed that because of economic reasons (tourists), the need to support "artists", and in "an affirmation of the right to a joy in life, the *Fasching* in Bavaria in the sense of the good old Munich tradition is approved".[61]

The December 19 meeting saw Siebert the Beamter vetoing Wagner the party man, in his request that four SA-Commissar Police-presidents be made Beamten. Siebert implied sympathy, but "unfortunately" the law prevented the making of an official without the requisite qualifications. By the February meeting Wagner conceded that contrary to party protests the "opponents" within the bureaucracy were indispensable.

Siebert expressed the false hope that the power of the Political Police was being limited sharply, that there was nothing to worry about.[62] The public problem was the struggle with the church, but private attention was paid to the Gauleiter, each more or less flaunting the authority of Munich. How could one integrate, i.e. control, them? Siebert wrote Epp on February 9th of his meeting with the Gauleiter, who had expressed the belief common in the party that opponents of the regime were still in high ministerial places.[63] The Gauleiter thought they should have more power over the government apparatus.

Siebert described the three sources of power—the state, the party, and the SA-SS—the total costs of which were causing protests. "I would reject Wagner's phrase that the party should order the state and not the reverse" Siebert said. He suggested that the Gauleiter enter the state government. They answered that he should know that a schoolteacher (Streicher) could not take over a finance ministry. Siebert concluded that they wished to support the government, but wished to remain where they were "because—as they say—they are absolutely necessary out there". Siebert reported that Frick had finally agreed to their inclusion in the Cabinet, because only in Bavaria the Gauleiter was not also the

[61] *Min. Rat.*, 29.11.33.
[62] *Min. Rat.*, 6.2.34.
[63] CGD—T 580, R 340, 9.2.34.

Reichsstatthalter. Epp, cognizant of his lack of authority within the party, opposed their inclusion saying, "the responsibility of the Gauleiter to the Reichsstatthalter is not given, their taking of an oath not anticipated. They could only prevent the Bavarian government's taking action".[64]

Although the Council agreed to let the Gauleiter attend, Epp at the next meeting still described the action as impossible; he asked for a delay until he could see Hitler. Roehm took advantage of the opening by asking that the SA and SS also be permitted representation on the Council. Siebert thought this was not necessary since they did not represent different areas as the Gauleiter did; Roehm as a member could appoint a deputy to meet with the Council. To Frick, further delay would raise party doubts about the state, but Siebert answered that they could not act contrary to Epp's wishes; they could only hope that the Gauleiter would understand.

There followed another "lively discussion" which the report summarized: (1) the party was still the necessary link be tween the state and the people; (2) ergo, there was a need to strengthen the position of the Gauleiter; (3) ergo, a need to strengthen the position of the political leadership, i.e., the party, which had been deliberately undermined by many new organizations—SA-SS—in the last year.[65]

By the meeting on February 27 Epp was back with his trump card. Hitler agreed with him completely: adding the Gauleiter to the government would weaken the party. There should be instead a wider "Senate" created with the opportunity to complain and to suggest, perhaps a "chamber" composed of the Landraete, i.e., Beamten. Siebert observed that no great problem should exist since party and state were one, but differences in personalities might carry a danger. Knowing as well as Epp the difficulties of dealing with local tyrants like Streicher, Siebert again suggested an advisory council of 25-30 representing various groups including the party. This Frank rejected, noting that it was historically difficult to keep the powers of such councils defined, or limited. It would also

[64] *Min. Rat.*, 15.2.34. [65] *Min. Rat.*, 20.2.34.

complicate the chain of command from the Reich Interior Ministry.

Everyone agreed something must be done to prevent arbitrary arrests. Siebert could only request the SA command to arrest an official only after clearing the arrest with that official's ministry. In early March Epp suggested that most of those under arrest be released.[66] Himmler grandly released a token number.

The Gauleiter

The question of what to do with the Gauleiter began to be solved in March 1934, as Siebert suggested making them district presidents for the area of their party Gau. But the decision in April was to make them political commissars instead, with the right to attend the Council meetings at a good salary. These party dignitaries met on April 24, 1934 with the ministers, one of the infrequent occasions, because the Beamten and party fanatics were incompatible. The gathering observed two Gauleiter fire their district presidents because they had tried to restrain the party. One of the two was Colonel Hofmann. Toward the end of the meeting Epp brought up the Hofmann matter again. He had ordered Hofmann not to leave his Franken post, and insisted that he be given the presidency of Wagner's upper Bavaria. Wagner expressed his surprise that Epp would promise Hofmann the job without checking with Wagner first. All agreed that Hofmann could not stay in Streicher's Franken, but that his firing would be kept secret except from the officials. So much for Epp's plenipotentiary powers.

Paradoxically Wagner took the occasion to scold Gauleiter Hellmuth for forbidding his Wuerzburg mayor to receive the local bishop. "Ignoring for the moment that the Gauleiter was not authorized to give an order to a state and communal official, the action was suited only to make enormous difficulties for the party and the Fuehrer."[68] Streicher added another proof why he would not be an addition to Council

[66] *Min. Rat.*, 13.3.34. [67] CGD—T 580, R 340, 10.4.34.
[68] *Min. Rat.*, 24.4.34.

meetings when he spoke irrelevantly of the importance of his *Der Stuermer* in foreign affairs. He predicted a crisis in which he would stand alone against world Jewry. Streicher predicted further that the new party members would prove a great danger to the party.

In May Siebert wrote Epp that Frick had asked for a conference before inserting the Gauleiter as political commissars, because doing so would create a new category of official in which it would be impossible to draw their lines of authority. How could they be able to distinguish between their political and nonpolitical functions? Frick reversed himself; Siebert's idea was best—to make them district presidents. Yet Frick would never approve Gauleiter Buerckel's appointment of a NS hack to this post. "That would be the end of the professional officialdom, which must definitely be preserved . . . the naming of directors as of all officials must under all circumstances remain in the hands of the government".[69]

Epp's worry about the hoped-for authoritarian "law-state" reached a new peak: "orders of ministers had no effect", because the SA command ignored them and continued the insanity of their own courts; they did not report to the police although ordered to do so; cases of mishandling and "unworthy happenings" in concentration camps continued; even the police were lied to; party leaders kept interfering in administration, Streicher and Wagner always "running off to Berlin" to protect their favorites. "Government cannot exist this way. Such a system is impossible. Every existing authority will be destroyed. . . . An irrational policy on all sides and at all levels. . . . The terrorist acts in Franken against the Jews are known in Berlin. Since there are no orders to intervene one must do good things secretly."[70] (This last phrase is a great truth about the Third Reich!) Epp candidly wrote that the nonparty member was helpless and terrorized; the people no longer dared speak and no one knew what they really thought. Thus spoke Epp, the man supposedly in charge, with 11 more years in which to regret.

[69] CGD—T 580, R 340, 17.5.34. [70] *Ibid.*

By June the matter of organization was settled. Frick came from Berlin to inform them that the Bavarian solution of having the Gauleiter as commissars was incompatible with basic principles of government.[71] To achieve clear responsibility they should be named district presidents. If anyone was unconvinced, Frick added that it was "the will of the Fuehrer". The Gauleiter must decide immediately, "yes or no". Wahl was the first to announce his willingness, on condition the SA commissars be stopped. Hellmuth, like Wahl, lacking the security of sharp elbows and brutal manners, quickly took the job, but Streicher preferred the commissar solution. He would not take the president's job, probably because he would not leave the big city Nuremberg for backwater Ansbach. He nominated an official he could trust, Dr. Martin, the man who later toppled him. Buerckel agreed with Streicher and named again Imbt, the man Frick had said was not qualified. Wagner saw no sense to the Frick ruling; the Gauleiter should remain as commissar advisors. Frick's solution "posed a great danger to the power of the party".

Beamter Siebert rejected Wagner's arguments. He said he had done all he could for the party, but he must accept Frick's order. "Concerning the attacks on the cooperation between the Land ministers with the existing officials, he pleads that they would finally cease. By pensioning off some of the old, he had given the chance for many young NS to be integrated in the state's operation. For the time being the state could not exist without the cooperation of the previous Beamten for financial and professional reasons."[72]

In the aftermath of the "Roehm Putsch", in which Hitler personally struck a blow at the commissar system, the atmosphere changed. Even Wagner criticized the violence in Franken, such as the case of an SA man's shooting a tavern keeper. Streicher promised to take care of it without favoritism to the party member. Frank demurred, saying the matter should be settled in the courts. The other Streicher case, his famous beating of a prisoner in jail with his ever-present whip, he limply explained as resulting from "the charged at-

[71] *Min. Rat.*, 12.6.34.

[72] *Min. Rat.*, 12.6.34.

mosphere" of June 30. Thus the use of commissars was ended again, first by Frick's order, then by the new subservient command of the SA. The state, the army, and the SS had won.

Party Preference

The other problem, of preference to party members for jobs, remained, the state resisting hordes of party men seeking offices as rewards. (Siebert privately regarded the creation of a NS Beamten organization as a declaration of a "state of war" between it and his government.[73]) In August 1933 Epp asked for a report on which positions were filled with "less than completely qualified people". Naturally each department head reported back that he had no one who did not deserve his position. Yet the pressure continued to make jobs and give promotions to the faithful. Siebert suggested retiring more old Beamten to make room for the young NS.[74] The suggestion was vetoed by the Reich Finance Minister who had no means with which to pay the pensions (he calculated them at over 200 million marks). The minister suggested instead a ban on promotions. Epp advocated that retirement be made voluntary at 60, thus preserving morale. Nothing was done.

In May 1934 Siebert warned against overly rapid promotions for NS worthies. By July he was emphasizing that promotions could go only to the "particularly deserving Old Fighters"; otherwise it was impossible. By January 1935 he noted that there were so many "old fighters" in Bavaria that their promotions would exclude promotions for large numbers of other deserving officials for the rest of their careers, making it impossible for morale.[75] "Since in the coming, certainly difficult days, a disturbance of the officialdom must be avoided at all costs", the "particularly deserving old fighters" should be promoted only as their seniority justified it. They should be cheaply bought off with increased pay, i.e., for two extra years longevity. As pressure continued Siebert had a magnificent chart created (15 Apr 1935) of all layers of

[73] GSA—105694, 105710; also CGD—T 580, R 340, 27.6.33.
[74] BA—R43II/447.
[75] GSA—105694, 16.1.35.

the officialdom in each department, showing how many "old fighters" there were (77), and in detail how impossible it would be to promote them.[76] Berlin could only suggest a much higher screening level; the "old fighter" had actually risked life and limb for the party. Party pressure from local party officials on a special visit in November 1935 brought a vigorous Siebert rejection. By late 1936 Siebert was even more definite in a letter to all departments: "as previously noted last July", there would be no more special promotions to "old fighters"; the only promotions were to be based on achievement.

With no housecleaning on the order of party desires, it remained only to make NS out of the old officials, or better yet, to propagandize the new. Either was difficult. Wagner wrote to Lammers of his surprise that Wagner's imposed added test for "middle Beamten" had had excellent results. To such questions as "Why must the official be a National Socialist?" and "What do you know of the racial question and its significance for Germany?" the answers had been first-rate. Any teacher could have told him that students when necessary can parrot answers without belief or understanding. The party knew better: the official deserved its suspicion and hatred.

The New Struggle for Power: Epp vs. Wagner

No sooner had the triumvirate defeated the SA in the name of the state than it began to quarrel over the spoils. With Wagner as party radical subverting the state, it remained for the outsider Epp to try to save law, order, and himself. Epp's defeat, likely inevitable in view of the semi-concealed radicalism of Hitler, was clearly a defeat for a more moderate policy. Other than petty concern for his own power and comfort, Epp's efforts to get a word in edgewise were also efforts to stop criminal abuses. Siebert retreated when Wagner attacked, either rejecting the illogic of the Reichsstatthalter position—the fifth wheel—or sensing Wagner's inevitable victory. Epp did not, some say because he had added to his staff the

[76] *Ibid.*

pious and vigorous Hofmann, whose experience with radical Streicher had been most unpleasant. Even before the fall of Roehm, Epp had demanded the end, no later than July 6, of the Bavarian Political Police's order that arrests of party members or SA-SS not be reported to the district attorney but to the Political Police, for favored treatment.[77] Heydrich's response on July 3, 1934 was a grudging "acceptance", but with a long new order requiring that in the event of such an arrest the party be informed immediately, the assumption of favoritism from extra NS pressure on the courts.[78] On July 17 Wagner offered a defense of this special rule: there were so many persons hostile to the party in the Ministry of Justice "who delighted in making punishment on NS extra harsh".[79]

Epp remained on an offensive of sorts through the remainder of 1934. He endeavored to gain support within the ministries, requesting Siebert to have all the important officials come to see him to get acquainted.[80] This logical campaign was futile, as the officials perforce remained much closer to their immediate superiors, who ordered them never to see Epp.

The new law of Jan. 30, 1935, superficially defining the powers of the Reichsstatthalter, gave Epp a better legal basis for supremacy. Yet Frick's intention to curb the Reichsstatthalter, elsewhere the more radical Gauleiter in the incessant struggle between the central and the local authorities, was evident immediately in his commentaries on the law. Frick wrote the Reichsstatthalter that they had the right to be informed, to suggest action to State officials, and to issue temporary orders, but only for the exceptional cases of imminent danger. "They did *not* have the right to issue orders to the Reich intermediate agencies (Land ministries)". If they ordered anything, Frick and the respective national minister were to be informed immediately. If a Reichsstatthalter did become active in any area, "he was subordinate to the technical orders of the Ministry". For efficiency of operations the Reichsstatthalter should keep out of the way. This interpreta-

77 GSA—105617, 29.6.34.

78 *Ibid.*

79 *Ibid.*

80 GSA—105349, 17.8.34.

tion of the new law represented Frick's alliance with the Beamten ministries. Unfortunately in Bavaria, the key Interior Ministry was controlled by the kind of radical Gauleiter Frick was elsewhere trying to restrain.

Epp's response shows better cognizance of the real danger—the Political Police, *i.e.*, Himmler. The political police should be subordinate to the state; yet in Bavaria they were involved in the anti-Jewish scandals in Nuremberg, the forbidding of Catholic youth activity, and the illegal favoritism toward party members.[81] "In the cases in which the Interior Minister actually knew of these actions, he neglected to inform the government." Epp's questions were either not answered or answers were so delayed and came in such a form as to be useless. An example: Epp had been told *after* the Roehm killing, which occurred in his Bavaria, that Himmler had forbidden anyone's being informed. Siebert had said he could do nothing. Wagner, although responsible for the police, said they should not interfere with SA or party members. He had turned over his responsibilities to the SA or the political police. As Gauleiter he set the party against the Beamten, so that they dared not act against the party aggressions. Epp continued, were he not given the authority, he could be held responsible for the collapse of the state's authority.[82]

Events of May 1935 made Epp's defeat the more unfortunate. On May 18 and 25, 1935, the SS attacked Jews and in the process attacked the police. After their arrest they told the authorities that they had been ordered by Wagner's Interior Ministry to perform the acts of violence. Wagner admitted this to Hess and the case was dropped.[83] Epp tried again on October 8 to stop the political police, but Wagner said that Himmler was in control; he could intervene only if Frick in Berlin had the authority.[84]

Siebert had come to Epp on Jan. 10, 1935 attempting to

[81] GSA, *ibid.* Document *Oberste Pflicht des Reichsstatthalters.*
[82] *Ibid.*
[83] BCD Adolf Wagner File, reference to Schade case.
[84] *Min. Rat.*, 8.10.35.

remedy the early split; he asked if he had done something to offend.[85] Epp complained that Siebert did not seem to be exerting influence on the government and listed several cases of incursions by radicals in which he had done nothing. Siebert accepted the complaint about Wagner, "who gabbed too much and did not run his ministry," but what occasioned his visit was the virtual declaration of independence from Bavaria by Gauleiter Buerckel in the noncontiguous piece of Bavaria west of the Rhine. There was talk of territorial divisions in which Bavaria might lose more lands; Berlin ministries were pushing to get more and more of Bavarian agencies under their direct control. Unsympathetic, Epp raised instead the question whether Bavaria still had a government, suggesting that Siebert was not in charge and asking what he planned to do to save the Bavarian government. Siebert, perhaps more aware of radical power than Epp in his isolation, said one should simply wait. Epp thought instead that they should tell Berlin at what point they would not retreat further and that this point had come. Neither had a chance; the yielding Siebert and the unyielding Epp drifted further apart.

Epp's isolation was already evident in Schemm's order to his staff that no one was to communicate with Epp except through Schemm.[86] It became a three-ring circus with letters bouncing from Epp to Frick to Siebert. Epp proposed in March that the Reich grab Bavarian agencies for economic, social, farm, and educational matters, inferring that Siebert could or should not handle them.[87] Yet Frick opposed this centralization, assuming that he had greater chances with Bavarian ministries through Siebert than through his fellow Reich ministers.

Two Ministries versus Four Ministries

With Esser's resignation and Schemm's death, Bavaria had two ministries open—Economics and Education. The NS "old fighters" in charge were Hans Dauser in Economics, and

[85] CGD—T 580, R 340. [86] GSA—105349, 16.1.35.
[87] BA—R43II/496, 7.3.35. See two chronologies CGD 580-340.

Dr. Ernst Boepple in Education. Although Frick had told Boepple he would be appointed minister and Epp formally proposed them both, the appointments became the bone over which the dogs barked for two years. The respective national ministers Schacht and Rust had approved, but Frick consulted with Siebert and Wagner, urging each of them to take on an extra ministry. The issue thus became either "two ministers or four". Frick reported on May 6 that Siebert and Wagner were to get the two jobs,[88] but Hofmann appeared two days later to stop them. Epp saw Hitler on May 9 and apparently got his support, with the reservation that Wagner, who agreed with Hitler's grandiose schemes for theater construction, would take over the theaters.[89]

By June 1, Lammers, at an impasse and apparently speaking for Hitler, urged the "two ministries" plan, but Epp refused on the grounds of the continuing "security disturbances", presumably the work of Wagner's friends.[90] Related to this was Wagner's angry note of June 5th denouncing Hofmann for having telephoned the government of Upper Bavaria to halt the distribution of anti-Jewish placards.[91] Wagner told officials to report only to him. "I formally protest the contact of the Reichsstatthalter with one of my subordinate agencies", he said.[92]

In August Frick agreed to Epp's "four ministries", but told only Siebert who kept it secret from Epp until November. To Frick the next month, Epp protested the illegality of all Bavarian laws as being improperly signed.[93] Dauser and Boepple's appointments were more deeply bogged down in October. Frick then told Epp he had long since ordered Siebert to propose them to Epp as ministers; Epp told Siebert to hurry up and send him Frick's August order. The order came on November 12, along with Siebert's observation that Frick had since changed his mind, that he again preferred the two ministries solution. Epp wrote on October 19 to Frick of

88 BA—R43II/1317. 89 BA—R43II/1316.
90 CGD—T 580, R 340, Chronology 2.
91 GSA—105349.
92 *Ibid.* 93 BA—R43II/1316.

Siebert's efforts to reduce his powers, quoting from the official Bavarian newspaper that only the Minister President could question an official.

Epp's and Frick's assistants met to reestablish communication. Frick claimed he had changed his mind after a conversation which Epp claimed never happened. Wagner entered the struggle, sending his man to Boepple in an attempt to force him to give the Education Ministry to Wagner.[94] Frick offered Boepple a job in the Reich Interior Ministry if he would, but Boepple declined, thus starting a five-year feud with Wagner. (Wagner expressed no objection to Dauser's getting Siebert's Economics Ministry.) Frick told Lammers that Epp could not veto the appointment; Siebert and Wagner were already ministers and Epp's signature was necessary only for *new* ministers; these were *old* ministers taking new jobs.[95]

Inevitably when party powers clashed, Frick went to Hitler. Lammers telephoned that evening to Epp that Hitler accepted the two ministries solution. That should have settled it, but it didn't. Lammers had reminded Hitler that Epp opposed to the two ministries solution, so the question must be Epp's prestige. Hitler did not seem otherwise to care, so long as Wagner helped him build theaters. Another day, after another reversal, Frick told Epp that the "four ministries" would survive; Lammers promised to see Hitler to stop further machinations; "Siebert would make difficulties", but they must be overcome.

Epp's "victory" faded away. First, Hitler was "about to sign" and then Lammers reported on December 4 that "he would not make it a definite decree."[96] Frick wrote Siebert that Wagner was to have authority over theaters, but somehow this should not complicate the competencies of the Reich Ministries. Boepple pointed up the logical absurdity of separating art (*Kunst*) from the related departments of his ministry. Perhaps Wagner could simply run one department within Boepple's ministry. But because the Fuehrer willed a change, they had to concur. Siebert suggested one grand unity

[94] *Ibid.*, 15.11.35. [95] BA—R43II/1316. [96] BA—R43II/1316.

of all ministries jointly led by Wagner and himself, which Epp rejected as contrary to Hitler's instructions.

In January 1936 Siebert blamed Epp for the long delay with the budget law. Epp answered that Siebert had been disloyal and insulting. Siebert then referred to the Frick order and said he would appreciate it if Epp would hurry up, because the Reich Finance Minister wanted the budget. The public would get an even worse image of the Bavarian government unless it did something soon. Epp's answer was that Siebert had acted illegally, hoping by giving Epp the law without the proper signatures to create a precedent for the two ministries solution. It was Siebert's fault; if he was concerned about public opinion, let Dauser and Boepple sign the laws; they were both ready. A budget could have been declared since September.[97] Siebert answered with more polite hostility: Epp was confused and Siebert would not be instructed on how to run his office.

A newspaper clipping attested to a temporary budget which had the four signatures Epp wanted. In early February Epp tried to get Siebert fired, charging him with falsification, having tried to issue a law pretending that Epp had seen it and then lying, and with disobedience to the Reichsstatthalter law.[98] It appears that Epp briefly had Hitler's ear in Berlin and told him that his major concern was to keep Wagner and Siebert from adding two more offices, thus destroying Epp's power. Such a combination would be tolerable only if he had the actual leadership, i.e., the Minister Presidency. Hitler seemed sympathetic, but "had to leave" before Epp could get a commitment from him.[99]

An attempt by Wagner to mediate failed; losing patience, he began to implement his claim to the theaters, which Boepple resisted. On March 23 Boepple called for a meeting with Hitler, to which Lammers replied drily: "About the situation in the Bavarian government, Hitler will scarcely want to hear anything from Boepple". He referred Boepple to

97 CGD—T 580, R 340, 22.1.36.

98 *Ibid.*

99 CGD—T 580, R 340, Chronology 2.

Frick.[100] To an appeal in April for a decision, Hitler refused to talk of it until after the election. He asked Epp and Frick to present a compromise solution, but they refused. Laws had to be signed by someone; Dauser and Boepple thought they could sign as heads of ministries. Until they could, Epp refused to sign any laws. Since Siebert had thrown down the gauntlet, Siebert must come to him. Their conference on April 8 began with Siebert declining to accept any Epp lecture because Siebert had not been the driving force behind the affair. On his word of honor, Frick had made the suggestion first. Siebert dared not lose face because many persons knew of the affair; therefore, he could not permit the four signatures to the law.

Wagner pushed ahead and announced his change to the press, although the Reich minister responsible for Boepple had not been informed. Boepple called on the hapless Rust to stop Wagner, but only Frick had a chance of doing so. After some negotiations, a conference between Epp and Frick was attained. Lammers observed that Epp would not talk to Frick except alone, and definitely not with Siebert and Wagner present. Epp asked whether Hitler had ordered the meeting; Lammers told him it was "desired".[101] Frick admitted to the two ministries idea, but thought Epp's argument about signatures a silly one. To Epp, the matter was simple—Hitler had decided that Epp would decide on any problems within the Bavarian government. Frick expressed his doubts about this. When Epp then asked whether Frick had read his report, Frick replied angrily that Epp sent too many reports, that he had too large a staff. Frick claimed that he had tried to strengthen Epp's position, but that Hitler would not agree. After a further exchange of denunciations, Frick stormed from the room saying that the next day's conference would not take place; "Heil Hitler".

There was a meeting without Epp but with Siebert, Wagner, Rust, and Boepple. After the meeting on May 12th, Frick wrote Lammers that the Fuehrer would sign Frick's way, but that Epp threatened to resign if not made Minister President.

[100] BA—R43II/1317a. [101] BA—R43II/1317a.

Epp defended this contention in a confidential letter of May 19, 1936 to Lammers, stating that since both Siebert and Wagner were already too busy with other jobs, giving them more to do would mean that Bavaria would be governed even more than before by their assisting Beamten (a shocking charge). After their efforts to cut Epp off from information, he would have to be crazy to permit these two enemies any more power.[102] Again Hitler wavered; he would not sign Frick's document, but was inclined to make Epp Minister President and asked Lammers how Epp would do.

Hofmann continued writing his long memoranda, but Lammers noted in July that Hitler would not decide until after the party convention in the fall. Boepple got the message, to save himself (which he did not) he swung to the Siebert-Wagner camp. The next-to-last Minister Council meeting for two years, on July 16th, was devoted to Boepple's refusal to sign the new law on school purchases, i.e., to act as minister, as Epp wanted. All except Epp agreed that Boepple was acting in accord with Frick's orders.[103] The final cabinet meeting was devoted to the price of beer.

In July Frick's representative told Epp to give up his demands and accept the compromise: all Frick communications would go through Epp; he should not bring the whole governmental apparatus to a standstill. But in September the question was still moot who would sign the 1936 budget. The best idea seemed to be to have no one sign it. By October a law appeared, signed only by Siebert and Wagner, announcing the latter's acquisition of the theaters.

Another ring of the circus was the struggle going on simultaneously between the other Epp ally, Dauser, against Siebert.[104] Dauser, a very "old fighter" but also a very good Catholic, proposed promoting some of his Catholic Beamten, although they were attacked by the party. Frick heard of this in January 1936 and asked Siebert to find out what was going on in Dauser's ministry, the one for which Epp

[102] BA—R43II/1317a. [103] *Min. Rat.*, 16.7.36.

[104] GSA—1936 Folder, *"Beschwerde des Staatsekretaers Dauser ueber Siebert"*.

wanted to make him minister. The report came back that "a number of the officials of the department are not solidly behind the NS state and do not deserve Dauser's trust". Dauser learned of this quite by chance from a tavern remark overheard by Esser's father. In a series of inconclusive meetings over several months Siebert claimed a kind of innocence as Dauser sharply protested Siebert's "spying". He thought Siebert had been out to get him for over a year, but that Hitler's loyalty to his "old fighters" had saved him. Dauser was indignant that the spy was not even a party member. He could explain Siebert's behavior only in that Siebert had joined the party so late, in 1931. Dauser's report in September backed up the officials in question as being professionals. Dauser denied the party's charge about his being too close to the Catholic church and Siebert's charge that he was dominated by one of his Beamten. "I do not let myself be advised by my Beamten, not more and not less than other party members in leading positions, perhaps including Siebert", he said. If Siebert was going to throw the mud of having non-party advisors, then Dauser would list the important anti-party men advising Siebert in his Finance Ministry, including one with a full-Jewess as wife.

In November Epp gave his full support to Dauser, noting that the officials in question had been kept in their jobs when Siebert had the ministry, that they had done their work correctly. One had a personal testimonial from Himmler. The Reich Labor Ministry had praised the department. Epp saw Hitler to save Dauser, but noted Frick's "malevolent attitude".[105]

Yet by the fall of 1936 Epp was fighting a rearguard action and he knew it. In October he wrote a long complaint[106] which traced the decline of the Reichsstatthalter's position to "the Second Law" of January 1935: "He has today vis-à-vis the Land government absolutely no positive authority, no force to push through his will. The weakness of the position is known and has already lead to circumventions and cutting him out, to passive resistance and to camouflaged work

[105] *Ibid.*

[106] CGD—T 580, R 340, 10.10.36.

against him." At best the Statthalter had a right to information, but the state ministers had tried to remove even this. With no right to decide on differences in the state government or to give any orders, the position was not a link between the Reich and state government, but off to one side and outside the positions of power in the Reich and Land governments. The Bavarian government was slipping backward toward independence and was entrenching this by the uniting of power into fewer and fewer hands.[107] Epp included a long file on the Beamten's defense of themselves from Siebert's charges, and showing the chaos brought in by the battle at the top.

Frick complained to Lammers in November 1936 that there was a complete halt to Bavarian legislation, that the budget was hopelessly delayed. "If the Fuehrer still could not decide, then I beg him to give me the right to declare these necessary laws."[108] Frick talked again with Hitler and still got no decision. By November 20 Frick reported that Hitler had finally decided for the two ministers; what would happen to Boepple and Dauser was unclear, but as old NS they must be treated well. Dauser got a promotion to State Secretary under Siebert and the Fuehrer was ready to appoint Boepple to the same position, but Wagner objected. His crony Koeglmaier should be promoted instead. Yet the personnel file showed that Boepple joined the party in 1919 and Koeglmaier not until 1923.

The epilogue was Epp's correspondence with other unhappy Reichsstatthalter, most of them Gauleiter radicals who hoped to demolish the state, because they could not control it, in order to return power to the local level, to the party, to themselves.[109] Wagner also joined this group of party dissidents against the state, agreeing that they should not be subordinate to Reich Ministries.[110] This no doubt reflects Wagner's battle at the time with Siebert and Frick.

The story would be incomplete without mentioning that

[107] *Ibid.* [108] BA—R43II/1317a.

[109] Epp letter to Mutschman, 29.10.37; letter to Sauckel, 15.12.37; Epp File GSA, *"Stellung des Reichsstatthalters"*.

[110] *Ibid.*, Wagner letter, 1.11.37.

scarcely was Epp pushed into an obscure opposition but the Siebert-Wagner problem began to plague Lammers. Siebert told Lammers in February 1938 that the situation with Wagner was so bad it could not continue, that he must soon talk with Hitler. Three days later he lamented that the impossible condition with Wagner caused state services to suffer, saying, "I must ask the Fuehrer to take a position". Lammers, who must have wondered whether the Bavarian government would ever settle down, begged the party to do something about the latest mess.[111] The Fuehrer, of course, did nothing. The final irony came when Lammers wrote to Epp in April 1939 curious about how the Reichsstatthalter technique could be applied to new territories in Czechoslovakia, only to hear Epp's bitter snort in reply that Reichsstatthalter were useless.[112]

This difficult effort to follow the petty and complex events in an important and simple struggle for power should prove that power was by no means stable in Hitler's state, but bounced at times wildly like a ball in the air for the lucky person to grab, and that Hitler frequently would not or could not intervene with the easy solution. The Bavarian government was in chaos for at least two years, with its leaders refusing to cooperate, exchanging charges of anti-party sabotage instead. It is scarcely an exaggeration to suggest that democracy with its open accusations can bring quicker settlements by an appeal to the public than an authoritarian state, particularly when authority is absent.

The incident is of further interest as an example of a defeat—Epp's—though he seemed to have the support of Hitler, as well as that of law and precedent. An interesting aspect of the story is the arrest of the best-informed observer, a Dr. Detig, a journalist who was fed stories by an assistant of Siebert until Detig was arrested for "betraying state secrets" and "diminishing the prestige of leading personalities".[113] Detig

[111] BA—R43II/1317a.
[112] GSA Epp File, "Reichsstatthalters".
[113] BDC Ludwig Siebert File Reichsstatthalter.

wrote in December 1935 that in a secret meeting Siebert decided on Epp's full isolation into a representational function. It had been Hofmann's tactless policy that brought Siebert and Wagner together, two men with little in common except an aversion to Epp's intrusions. Detig thought Epp was doomed, since Siebert had the greater experience in government and worked harder. Of further damage was Hofmann's close connections with the Catholic church and Epp's with the Wittelsbach dynasty; a common joke was that Epp was on better terms with them than with the party. Of particular note is Detig's comment on March 16, 1936: "Epp still shows no activity in the election campaign, while Wagner is working extremely hard".

Epp vs. Wagner: The Klein Case

Although Epp emerged with little more than the title of plenipotentiary, he did have the authority to sign papers, an authority which on occasion was important. An interesting case was Wagner's effort to have his henchman Klein made a Beamter. In late 1937 Wagner, unable to control the Education Beamten protected by Boepple, had created a "staff" of party cronies about him who attempted to dominate the ministry. Although Epp originally had shown only minor resistance to political firings of Beamten, he took a special interest in Wagner's desires. Hofmann wrote on Sept, 2, 1937 to Wagner concerning two SS leaders with scandal in their pasts, that the effort to make them Beamten was simply to assure their economic futures because they had no qualification for office, that Wagner could not pass out offices as poor relief—all put in so insulting a fashion that Wagner would be furious.[114] Wagner thought it shameful that such good SS men had to be employed as drivers.

Boepple was still fighting Wagner when he protested to Lammers in April 1939 that the non-Beamter Klein was the illegal deputy of Wagner as "staff chief".[115] When Wagner ordered that all communications to him should go through Klein, Boepple protested that such was impossible, something

[114] GSA Epp File, 101. [115] BA—R43II/1311.

he as "old fighter" did not deserve. Klein's office as "staff chief" would be unique in Germany.[116] Frick wrote Wagner that Klein could not appear officially, because the "staff chief" position was an illegal and undesired innovation. Epp also protested. Wagner's defense to Frick argued that Klein was to handle correspondence with the party, but that he planned to make Klein a Beamter at any rate. Wagner defended the title because he had used it in "his successful battle for Bavaria." This was a new track, one not liked by dry bureaucrats, but great in practice.[117] It was needed because his Ministry of Education had been criticized by the party for lack of effectiveness in dealing with the Catholics.

Siebert tried to head off the move without angering Wagner, noting that he would forward the request to Berlin, but it was obviously illegal and Klein's salary, one-half a special subsidy, was too large.[118] Hofmann declared that neither the position nor the included auto and driver could be approved. Rust and Frick were opposed, with the latter asking in October for the authority to demolish this illegal staff.[119] By November even Hess lined up with the Reich ministers to stop Wagner. Klein remained "staff chief".

Boepple wrote in October to Lammers that Wagner had not yet answered his letter of five months before. The "staff" had grown to seven people, all paid from treasury funds not allotted in the budget. Klein had been given an automobile from state funds, which he had quickly wrecked and then bought another with state funds. The staff naturally got the best rooms and costly redecoration. "Their ignorance exceeds all expectations. But just as large is the lack of inhibition with which they jump daily into the complex operations of educational administration." They had brought great insecurity to the Beamten and schools. Boepple was not kept informed, his countersignature no longer required, his actions constantly spied on. Although Boepple was Wagner's deputy, he had last seen Wagner in early March. Wagner let Boepple

[116] GSA Epp File on Klein case.

[117] BA—R43II/1311.

[118] R2 10877, 13.6.69.

[119] *Ibid.*

know that he could communicate with him only through Klein. Wagner was trying to break his nerve, Boepple thought, and trying to force him into the army, although he was 52, while Klein, only 33, would stay at home. This was incredible to Boepple, who had never heard any criticism from Wagner or had any argument with him.[120] Lammers answered that it was a matter for Rust, but he realistically took up the problem also with Frick.

In the meantime, Boepple wrote that an order firing him had come without any warning. The non-NS, strong Catholic Dr. Mayer, who had remained a top advisor to Boepple, explained the sudden release as derived from Boepple's support of Mayer's efforts to save theological schools. Wagner had intercepted a letter for that purpose and Boepple had refused to tell Wagner that Mayer was responsible. Mayer, who resigned in 1941 rather than join the party, regarded Boepple as neither very harmful nor very competent. He had not seen through Mayer's five-year-long delaying tactics which had kept the theological schools in operation by using pension technicalities as the excuse.

By November Boepple was forbidden to exercise his office. Boepple appealed to Hitler, Himmler, and Bormann to get the ministry for himself because he had been a party member since 1919. Hitler or Bormann decided against Boepple, and Lammers wrote him suggesting he withdraw his request. In mid-November Wagner protested to Lammers that Boepple had not taken his "suggestion" to resign. Two weeks later Hitler talked with Wagner, who agreed to drop the term "staff" and to make Klein a "councillor". In December Epp protested the firing, contending that Boepple's only fault was that Wagner did not like him.[121]

Boepple left one battlefield for another. He joined the army and sent this short note for Hitler: "My Fuehrer. I report obediently that I, having been vacationed as State Secretary, entered the army as first lieutenant and am leaving for the front February 15, 1940. Dr. Boepple".[122] This

[120] *Ibid.*
[121] GSA Epp File—Klein.
[122] BA—R43II/1311c.

grand gesture stirred someone; a Frick assistant talked of giving Boepple a job at the University of Vienna. Then came Hofmann's discovery in April 1940 of a money scandal in Klein's background; the Hitler Youth had fired him and would not take him back.[123] Wagner asked Epp's approval of Klein's appointment, to which Epp joyfully answered that after an investigation of Klein he could not recommend him. (A tragic footnote was the report to Lammers that Boepple's son had died for the Fuehrer as an infantry lieutenant.)

The matter rested until August, when Wagner got the Hitler Youth to recommend Klein. Epp answered in September that Wagner's report of Klein's Hitler Youth success was beside the point. On Aug. 26, 1940 Wagner ordered any district president, Landrat, mayor, or police chief to report personally to him if Epp or any member of his staff or any member of the Bavarian government should visit any office.[124] Bormann joined in, informing Epp that Klein was a worthy old party member, adding, "I am of the basic opinion that anyone worthy to be a member of the party is worthy to be a Beamter. . . . If you intend to oppose further, the matter will be brought to the Fuehrer for a decision. There can be no doubt that the Fuehrer will make the appointment immediately".[125] To counter this, Epp wrote Bormann's superior, Hess (12 Dec. 1940), that he would permit no one to interfere with his right to appoint, not even Wagner or Bormann; they should respect the law which stated that any appeal should go to Frick and not to Bormann.[126] Epp doubted that Hitler would ever appoint Klein and reviewed Klein's inglorious career, noting that he had not the slightest qualification, though he had usurped a position as State Secretary. Further, Munich was full of stories of Klein's behavior during the November 1938 pogrom; Klein would never get a job requiring character and ability if Epp could stop it.

There was another six months of impasse, until Lammers wrote Epp on June 22, 1941, referring to a court judgment acquitting Klein of extorting money from Jews, to which

[123] GSA File—Klein.
[124] ASA—102/0101.
[125] BA—R43II/1311c, 23.11.40.
[126] Epp File—Klein.

Epp added, "It was and remains extortion". Lammers answered that there was no reason to oppose the appointment and preferred not to bother Hitler with it. Epp was not to be moved. He wrote Lammers in August a long attack on both Klein and Wagner. Klein's action was criminal, but the greater problem was Wagner's choice and use of assistants. "These creatures have been given charge over affairs and create not only an added government, but the major government within the administration."[127] Wagner had made many poor judgments in selecting his assistants; as an example, he had promoted an adjutant to be a police major over Epp's protests; the man had since been downgraded and then thrown out of the party. Another Wagner appointment, over Epp's objection, was a man put in charge of all water construction projects. "The result was that the building of the Rhine-Main-Danube canal, with enormous importance to the war, experienced an irredeemable delay, because Fischer did not like the project as devised by the assembled experts." The Reich finally had to take over the project and revive the original plans.

Epp continued that Wagner's policy concerning Beamten was bad for their morale and bad for the public which usually learned of the fiascos. He then referred to Wagner's most famous blunder, the 1941 effort to take the crosses out of the schools, which had nearly led to a Bavarian revolution. Epp quoted the reports of public anger and added: "These give only a weak picture of the true attitude of the population as I know from countless protests".

Bormann's brief defense of Klein emphasized his virtues: Klein had fought for the party and therefore deserved to be an official. He might have chosen "the wrong methods", but this was not for personal gain, but rather to implement the party-desired action against the Jews.[128] Lammers told Epp to sign, since Bormann wanted it so much, and transmitted Bormann's rejection of the charges concerning "the crucifix order".[129]

[127] GSA Epp File—Klein. [128] *Ibid.*, 2.10.41.
[129] *Ibid.*, Lammers, 17.10.41, 24.10.41.

Wagner wrote in December and included a letter from Klein's army commander written upon Klein's receiving the Iron Cross, First Class after a brief army service. "I assume [Wagner said] very honored Herr Reichsstatthalter that this message . . . will suffice to end your opposition to Klein's appointment." But Epp, in his reply ignored Klein to attack Wagner, conceding Bormann's charge that Klein was not responsible for the crucifix order: "Wagner wanted with the order to give some tangible results to Bormann's teaching that National Socialism and Christianity are incompatible opposites and instead achieved demonstrations, school strikes and unrest throughout the land". The fault, Epp stated, was not the priests, but Wagner, who had created a permanent "front of intellectual resistance". The "Klein case" would tear open the wounds again and this, Epp argued, he knew much more about than did the remote Bormann. Epp reviewed: the only argument for Klein was that Wagner wanted him and Bormann supported it as party leader; but, Epp said, "I am also a Reich-leader".[130]

Siebert complained to Pfundtner in December that Epp, but primarily Hofmann, was mixing in matters which did not concern him.[131] It was intolerable, as was the Reich ministries' ignoring of the Bavarian government. He would see Hitler. In January 1942 Siebert appealed to Krosigk for help in stopping Epp's interference, but Krosigk would not report having had any problems with Epp.[132]

In March 1942 Epp was still blasting away at Klein with one juicy prediction: "The popular fear that Klein will simply be the instrument of Wagner's whims would be justified and would lower the depressed morale occasioned by last summer's attack on the crosses".[133] Klein was back in office, if illegally, giving evidence in April of his bad humor in a nasty note to an ideologically lax district president.[134] Although Rust mildly suggested that Epp was right, the newspapers carried word that Klein was Wagner's "spokesman" on school policy.

[130] *Ibid.* [131] BSA—66821. [132] *Ibid.*
[133] GSA Epp File—Klein. [134] *Ibid.*

Wagner's illness and succession by Giesler in 1942 left Klein illegally in charge. As late as August 1944 Klein had Giesler's authorization to represent him as leader of the Education Ministry. In September 1944, however, Epp rejected a Giesler request as he had Wagner's, because Klein was unqualified. Giesler then told Klein that since he could not be a Beamter he could not represent him in the Education Ministry. After a five-year struggle Epp got Klein out; but Klein was immediately given the corresponding party office on school policy.[135]

Saving Bavaria, Opposing Berlin

Although all of the Bavarian leaders were National Socialists, they were also loyal Bavarians. They wanted Bavaria to survive and they wanted their power vis-à-vis Berlin to survive. Even in their bitter fights among themselves, they only briefly forgot their opposition to centralization. It occupied much of the attention of the Ministerial Council during 1933 to 1935, which reacted worriedly to the plans for "Reich reform", some of which attacked the variance in size of the German states and implied their division along the party Gau lines into 30 to 40 states of equal size. For everyone profiting from such a change in terms of power there was someone losing from the change and Hitler could or would never make a choice, repeatedly forbidding Reich reform to be discussed but always it reappeared, sometimes under such guises as "simplification of the administration" or "self-administration".

Frank and Wagner had spoken up for Bavaria in October 1933 as "the oldest state in Europe".[136] Frick reported no Berlin intention to destroy it, but Siebert made a special trip to Berlin to state Bavaria's case. As a true Bavarian he observed: "The Reich reform was a question of the destruction of Prussia. With that policy the Prussians would not agree, they would rather absorb all of Germany into a Greater Prussia". In a "lively discussion" in November 1933 Frank thought that Frick planned first to hollow out the

[135] *Ibid.*

[136] *Min. Rat.*, 24.10.33.

state governments and then end them. Paradoxically Frank thought a centralization of the Justice Ministry quite useful.[137]

Siebert returned from Hitler with words of reassurance. Hitler saw three other problems coming before Reich reform —pacification of Europe, unemployment, and building the party into the state. A reorganization of the Reich must wait. The conversation with Frick was less reassuring, because in that ministry there was great activity for reform.[138] Siebert's five-point program of adjustment to increased central power accepted the principles that all power came from the Reich; states of less than one million should be absorbed; enclaves of one state in another should be absorbed; the states would act as agents of the central government; a Reichsstatthalter would be in charge of each, with the Fuehrer principle supreme.

Frank remained worried about Bavaria's future, since most Reich ministers were also Prussian ministers, that Bavaria would have too little personal influence on Berlin. Siebert worried more about the noncontiguous Palatinate west of the Rhine. Epp, most confident of all, observed that the revolution succeeded in Bavaria because Bavarians trusted Hitler; even so, it would be good tactics to ally with the very small states for mutual survival. Siebert thought that politically the Laender were "zeros", but that one should keep them as administrative, cultural, and historic units.[139]

Siebert was still worried in February 1934 over interference from the Reich ministries; he urgently argued that the Bavarian cabinet unite to defend itself. The immediate disturbance was that the Bavarian police had been put under Frick without Siebert's having been informed.[140] Siebert hoped to maintain the special ambassador in Berlin to counter Prussian influence, or perhaps a special Bavarian department in the Reich government. In June 1934 Siebert reported his conversation with Frick and Pfundtner to oppose their plan to divide Bavaria into three Gaue each with its Statthalter.[141]

[137] *Ibid.*, 14.11.33. [138] *Ibid.*, 29.11.33. [139] *Ibid.*
[140] *Min. Rat.*, 15.2.34. [141] GSA—MA 105246.

In 1935 Bavaria lost out to the Justice Ministry's centralization, and lost real control over the Palatinate to Gauleiter Buerckel's decentralization.[142] Epp lamented the disastrous condition of Bavaria, doubting that Bavaria had a government, and urged Siebert to stop his cowardly retreat.

With echoes of such laments about coordination, one could easily conclude that independence was at an end, that Bavarian obedience to Berlin was automatic. Yet with the exception of Himmler's police centralization, localism was stabilized until a counterreaction set in which was led openly by Gauleiters. This Reich Interior problem was treated in Chapter 2. Suffice it here to quote a letter of Wagner to Reichminister Rust, his nominal Berlin superior as Minister for Education:

> I report to you that since yesterday I took over the Bavarian State Ministry for Education and Culture. . . . May I tell you at the beginning of my activity, that I am used to working independently. Since in the Third Reich there can and will be no Land interests, the highest law of my action will be the NS idea and the Reich. None of my subordinates would under any conditions be permitted to break one of these laws, and it is clear that I will naturally make sure that these agencies will remain capable of action, i.e., it is obvious that I should never consider giving up any of my authority.[143]

Wagner then made the point that he was on the party staff, given the job of Reich reform, and knew Hitler did not wish any change; so one must accept things as they were.

> There is a state called Bavaria with state administration and state ministries. As Bavarian Minister of the Interior I have absolutely succeeded with the Reich Interior Minister, to the extent that from the Reich ministry no one interferes with the Bavarian Ministry. I regard it as obvious that you, dear party member Rust, since you know

[142] CGD—T 580, R340, 10.1.35.
[143] IZG—MA 103/1, Wagner 12.1.37.

> me and my work sufficiently, will see to it that no one in your ministry makes an effort to interfere in my Bavarian ministry. Naturally I obey in NS discipline all of your regulations. . . . On the other hand please tell your officials that I will never be their subordinate. I would be therefore grateful if you would spare me the usual trivia and superficial writing. . . . Heil Hitler. [signed Adolf Wagner, Gauleiter][144]

This insolent letter was typical of an "old fighter" dealing with a Reich official who ordinarily lacked his appeal to supreme power, Hitler's sentiment. The local communities were everywhere led by old fighters and the central ministries by scribblers whose superior might or might not be an old fighter. Wagner's was therefore no idle boast.

Yet there was the question of which Reich ministers and how many Wagner could defeat. Rust was easy, Frick at times tough, but the Reich Finance Ministry was always around trying to strangle Wagner's brainstorms with purse-strings. The Finance Ministry records show NS hopes often lost among "bourgeois, liberal" statistics. An example is Wagner's effort in April 1936 to promote his driver to Beamter, as "chief of the car pool". He emphasized the man's old fighter status, that he was his closest confidant, that he would aid in party-state relations.[145] The Finance Ministry turned him down as "only a mechanic". Koeglmaier threatened to go to Frick, but the Finance Beamter called his bluff: "if you really thought him qualified, why have you not asked Frick?"

The Eberstein case is another example.[146] In June 1938 Wagner began the process of getting the regional SS leader, Police President von Eberstein the top Beamten rank of State Secretary, although he had no particular police or Beamten background. This touched a point of acute sensitivity in Berlin—the Bavarian effort to get more top ranks and to make them equal to Berlin's in salary and prestige. The endless battle about these top positions is one facet of the complex-Berlin-Bavaria power struggle. Strangely, Epp objected while

[144] *Ibid.* [145] BSA—66855. [146] BA—R2 10883.

Frick wrote in support of the promotion, although he usually opposed such promotions. Himmler wanted it.

Wever, the Berlin Beamter who represented Krosigk, made an interesting series of objections. State Secretaries were very rare; Reichministers themselves had only one apiece. Bavaria already had five. Bavaria had been putting up heavy pressure to get equality, i.e., for a Bavarian official to be considered just as important and paid just as much as a Berlin official. He noted further that Bavaria had not obeyed the Reich Interior and Finance Ministry orders of two years before to shift their officials to lower ranks. Instead, their recent request was for 10 new high positions. From this Wever drew the logical conclusion: "These facts when taken together show clearly the fundamental meaning of this case. In Bavaria is growing the desire to avoid the consequences of the Reich law of January 30, 1934 which changed the basic constitutional position of the states. . . . This desire has already reached the level of an open disregarding of Reich issued orders. One need not explain the inevitable consequences of a continuing retreat of the highest Reich authorities in the face of such special strivings of these particularistic powers for the future of a healthy administration and reform".[147] Epp, for personal power and fear of Wagner's irrationality, supported these Reich restrictions on his government, adding the useful argument that the centralizing of the police had left Eberstein relatively little responsibility. Krosigk picked up the theme of Bavarian separatism, but Frick defended Bavaria: a "special situation" existed there. As a compromise one should give Eberstein a Ministerial Director position, for which a new one must be created. This was another moot point. The Finance Ministry suggested an insulting compromise—give Eberstein his new position, but then take two director positions from Bavaria, when their present tenants soon reached retirement.[148] This was agreed on. A short Wagner note, with a job for Eberstein after over a year's wait, was briefly grateful. In the note Wagner neglected to mention any promise to give up the two extra director posi-

[147] *Ibid.*, 23.6.38. [148] *Ibid.*, 13.3.39.

tions. In October 1939 the Finance Minister reminded Frick that the concession had been made only because of the special circumstances of Eberstein, that only he had the job level; any successor must be classified at a lower rank.

As long as Hitler could be interested in anything but war, there was hope for local control. Rust, along with the Finance Ministry, opposed "The School for Applied Arts" in Nuremberg, noting that only 85 people were involved and could be easily absorbed into other schools.[149] Rust added that Hitler desired fewer schools, that the Weimar republic had encouraged too many people to become artists, that the Reich wanted them to be handworkers with full craft training. But plans of mice and ministers often go astray. A few months later, after some Nuremberg protest, Rust could only say, "Hitler wants the school".[150]

The Reich Finance Ministry records indicate what Wagner really wanted—theaters—and how Reich resistance hounded his efforts to be a great patron of the arts and particularly of aspirant ballet girls. In one gigantic demonstration blessed by Hitler, "The Day of the German Arts", Wagner managed in three days to spend four million marks, leaving a string of finance Beamten, including Siebert, gasping in his wake.[151] The fate of an "Artist Festival" sponsored by Wagner in late 1939, with 50,000 marks for a "Night of the Amazons", is not clear from the finance reports, which ooze their disapproval.[152] Tearful pleas by Wagner concerning the desperate situation of artists during the war was enough to convince Siebert who said, "I didn't think I should say no". He also did not think he should say no to Wagner's pleas for writers who needed money with which to spread the glory of Germany.[153] In 1942 Wagner was still noteworthy in the records in his efforts to build up the Bavarian State Opera, but ran afoul of statisticians. A dry Beamter report proved that Wagner's claim that the Bavarian King had given 1,000,000 marks for the arts was simply not so.[154]

[149] BA—R2 10884, 20.11.38.
[150] *Ibid.*, 14.4.39.
[151] BA—R2 10884, 23.6.38.
[152] *Ibid.*, Anlage A.
[153] BA—R2 10886, 16.9.40.
[154] BA—R2 10891, 17.6.42.

Not Saving the Jews

What is remarkable in the various Bavarian documents is the relative lack of mention of the Jews, either to urge their salvation or their destruction, although there was more written to defend than to attack them. None of the leaders seem to have been without prejudice. Yet all but Wagner wrote that they opposed any acts of violence against the Jews.

At the first meetings of the NS Cabinet, Siebert reported that he had stopped payment from church taxes to the Jewish churches. Frank had ordered Jewish judges and state attorneys transferred into less important positions. In their next action, April 1934, the Bavarian government forbade the entry of Jewish attorneys to the courts; Jewish judges and attorneys were "vacationed" from state jobs.[155]

Epp opposed in May 1933 the Munich action of the police against the Jewish community, arguing that there must be no such local initiative. "The Munich actions against the Jews are to be disapproved because such steps can be implemented only nationally", he said.[156] (Perhaps he opposed it for better reasons.) Epp agreed with Faulhaber that baptized "Jews" should be accepted as "non-Jews".[157] Nor was the Economics Minister's stated motive for restraint laudable: so many Jews were resigning from boards of directors out of fear that a lack of capital had occurred which threatened more unemployment. The Cabinet agreed to encourage Jews to stay on.

July's outbreaks against Jews were also regretted in the Cabinet meetings by Epp, claiming that it was done without his or Wagner's knowledge. Wagner had issued "orders against recurrences", but expressed approval in principle, if not in timing. The next reference, reflecting the slowdown ordered from Berlin and the relative quiet, was July 1934, when the cabinet agreed to remove the party-sponsored anti-Jewish signs, at least on the major streets.[158] This seems to end the Cabinet's formal interest in the Jews, although it rarely met after 1936 and then concerned itself with trivia.

[155] BSA—66908. [156] *Min. Rat.*, 16.5.33. [157] Volk, 80.
[158] *Min. Rat.*, 17.7.34.

Epp's papers lament the violence against Jews in May 1935, as well as against the police who tried to protect them.[159] The Epp report of June 26, 1935 noted that with the helplessness of the police against the SS, Wagner appeared and ordered men to write down their names, which they refused to do. They sang songs calling for the hanging of the Jews, and when threatened with report to their commander, they replied that their commander was with them. There were no arrests during the violence, probably because Wagner had originally approved it.

The Epp papers, filled with protests and candid criticisms, make relatively little mention of the Jews, although Epp kept after Klein partly because he had extorted money from them. He is reported to have inquired of Hitler what was happening to the Jews being deported in 1942 and told that they were being sent to do war work in the East and not to bother with something "not his concern". At the very end of the war Epp is also reported to have known enough of the killings to have seen in them the enormous guilt which would attach to all NS, whether involved directly or not.[160]

District President reports varied from Streicher's mad cry to make his Franken "free of Jews" (many moving to Schwaben where life was more quietly desperate) to criticism of overt anti-Semitism by other presidents. The change to cruel exclusion before November 1938 passed largely without comment. Only the violence of that night brought strong criticism from a minority. The moral indignation of one district president, Regensburg, quickly led to his dismissal. In this NS objective, Bavaria and its district governments were bypassed. The order went straight to the local SA. The government per se was also bypassed in the evacuations. Trainloads of its residents were shipped east with the Bavarian government a not so innocent bystander.

Saving the Church

For all of the lack of effort and success in saving the Jews, the Bavarian government and people made strenuous efforts

[159] CGD—T 580, R 339. [160] Dr. Martin.

and achieved a major success in saving its Bavarian church, especially the dominant Roman Catholic. There can be little doubt that the effort came from such devout Catholics as Epp and Hofmann, with support from nearly everyone in a responsible state position except Wagner; it came even from a few high party leaders like Wahl. Other Gauleiter such as Hellmuth, Streicher, Waechtler, and Buerckel were radical on the church subject. These local radicals allied themselves with central radicals, particularly Bormann, while local conservatives allied with central conservatives, mostly Beamten.

What made the partial salvation of the churches possible was the obvious fact that the great majority of the country entered the Third Reich with a religious commitment, the major exception being the working class, which was excluded from power anyway. The party had a particularly confused program on the matter of religion, which gave reason for many devout Christians to be equally devout NS, at least at first. Although Hitler and some cohorts had commended a vague Nietzschean neo-Germanic religion, they had come out strongly as the saviors of Christianity from the much-feared Bolsheviks. It is still debatable what Hitler's policy toward religion in Germany was, although he publicly promised the churches support. The evidence strongly implies that, although Hitler was careful with this last organized center of a competing ideology, he came ever more to the conviction that the churches must be destroyed, and had decided to do so after the war.

That the great bulk of the population was involved in the church question and that the party was undecided and divided is the basis for the state's saving the church from the party, beginning as a part of the general salvation of the law from the commissars. Such local violence disturbed the early 1933 coalition with the Papen Centrists and the Concordat with the Papacy, which Catholics hoped would protect them. Bavarian Cardinal Faulhaber played a controversial role in this attempted adjustment.[161] Although Faulhaber showed

[161] Volk, *Bayerische Episkopat*; also L. Volk, "Paepstliche Laudatio auf Hitler?" *Stimmen der Zeit*, December 1963; L. Volk, "Der deut-

more monarchist than democratic sympathies during the Weimar period, he was early aware of the dangers to the church in the NS state. His defense tactics, which included protestations of loyalty and support of the new order, as well as protests against its extremes, was likely the politic wisdom in view of the danger, although such caution is easily criticized by persons in other and safer times and places. Such was his declaration reported by Siebert on April 24, 1933, that Faulhaber would support the new regime and had instructed the entire clergy to stand behind it.[162] Faulhaber's was the hope that good and not evil would emerge if one waited long enough. Yet in late June over 2,000 BVP leaders were arrested, plus 150 priests.[163] The bloodiest scenes occurred in Buerckel's Speyer, with 21 priests arrested, 26 fleeing their parishes, and six beaten so badly that the state forbade them to appear in church.[164]

The Concordat that Faulhaber hoped for made little difference in Himmler's Bavaria. Less than 10 days after its signing on September 10, Heydrich forbade any activity by Catholic organizations, defending this violation to Frick by an exaggerated account of their activity.[165] By the fall of 1933 it was obvious that loyalty had not assured the church's security. In its October 1933 "Memorial on the Implementation of the Concordat in Bavaria", the church protested that the police's forbidding of Catholic activity in June and further in September had made Bavaria the most restrictive of any German state.[166] Various towns were listed where NS had tried to force all youths out of Catholic organizations and where church property had been illegally seized and not returned.

In October the leading Bavarian NS-Catholic in the Reich

---

sche Episkopat im Maerz 1933", *Ibid.*, March 1964; L. Volk, "Kardinal Faulhabers Stellung zur Weimarer Republik und zum NS-Staat", *Ibid.*, March 1966.

[162] CGD—T 81, R 185, F 4922.

[163] Volk, *Bayerische Episkopat*, 104.

[164] *Ibid.*

[165] *Ibid.*, 137.

[166] CGD—T 81, R 185, R 4956ff.

Interior Ministry, Buttmann, inquired of Epp about the complaints of Catholic youth organizations. This brought a statement by the Bavarian cabinet that they were "prepared to do everything to implement the Concordat also in Bavaria". But they could not control Himmler. Heydrich for the Bavarian Political Police wrote on November 2 to Bavarian districts that the Reich Interior Ministry had lifted the order forbidding all Catholic organizations and meetings, but this was to be done privately with no public announcement.[167] He requested that any political activity of the Bavarian Political Police be reported immediately. Epp requested Wagner to see to it that the protests be investigated and any violations of the Concordat be ended immediately in accordance with the Bavarian cabinet decision.[168] Epp's requests were ignored. The cabinet meeting on November 14 expressed dissatisfaction with the actions of the Hitler Youth and ordered that there be no more disturbances of church services and that members of the Youth be permitted to attend Sunday services.[169]

At the next meeting on November 21, Siebert was angry about Faulhaber's defense of church rights. "The NS would share political power and the political training of the youth with no one", he said. In his opinion, most Catholics disagreed with the position taken by the bishops. In early December Faulhaber's sermon suggesting an opposition to anti-Semitism by denying that German blood was the source of salvation, raised hopes of a determined stand.[170] It brought hostile speeches from Wagner, Esser, and Schemm; shots were fired at the Cardinal's palace during the night of January 27-28. At the cabinet meeting Siebert noted that the speeches had caused excitement, that conflict had broken out which could be ended only if "the clerics gave up certain things".[171] Esser defended his speech by noting that Faulhaber in his four Advent sermons had attacked the party. Something more must be done against those "Blacks". Dauser

[167] *Ibid.*, F 4948.
[168] *Ibid.*, F 4949.
[169] *Min. Rat.*, 14.11.33.
[170] Volk, "Faulhaber".
[171] *Min. Rat.*, 6.2.34.

urged caution so that lay Catholics would not be driven to greater unity with the clerics.

March 1934 saw the return of the seized Catholic property.[172] It came after a meeting between Wagner and Faulhaber,[173] in which Wagner blamed the Catholic organizations for the difficulties, that they persisted in wearing uniforms and engaging in "military sport". Faulhaber agreed to end both. Wagner reported that Hitler Youth would have to have a greater time allotment, probably all day Saturday and the church could have the youth Sunday morning. They had agreed on liaison people when problems arose. The conference reportedly ended with a perfect "Heil Hitler" from Faulhaber.

Whatever Faulhaber's obeisance, the pressure mounted on the Catholic youth as a potential competitor in glamor. Epp's file noted the rearrest of a rural pastor who had been returned, despite the party's protest, to his original parish after his first arrest in January 1934 because "no one else was available".[174] His Wuerzburg bishop said he would "gladly be the first bishop taken into protective custody".[175] Epp appealed on April 26, 1934 to Frick for a definition of state policy in view of the growing tension. On April 28th occurred a demonstration by a party mob outside the bishop's residence. Two days later Himmler called Epp to ask about the demonstration and assigned a guard to protect the bishop, while also sending an investigating committee.[176] Frick said to Epp that he regretted "the unfortunate incident" as giving the party a bad image. He expressed the conviction that such things would end and that the guilty would be punished.[177]

The passing from the scene of the SA rowdies in mid-1934 released some of the local pressure, but the party kept up the crippling police restrictions on religious meetings other than church services themselves. Goebbels took over the campaign with the flagrantly publicized cases of "sex crimes" and "smuggling", (violation of intricate currency regulations).

[172] CGD—T 81, R 185, F 4938.
[173] *Ibid.*, F 5165.
[174] CGD—T 81, R 185, F 5129.
[175] *Ibid.*, F 5126.
[176] *Ibid.*, F 5113.
[177] *Ibid.*, F 5102.

Local party leaders kept nibbling away at church rights, with Epp trying to bar the way. In January 1935 an eager local party man tried to stop a "Mothers Society" from meeting.[178] The Passau bishop appealed to Epp who wrote to the District President for an explanation, with a reminder a month later that the request for information had not been answered. In March the District President was reported fired.

In April 1935 Epp tried in vain to get control of the Bavarian Police, to protect the churches, including the rebellious Protestants, from police pressure. He "ordered" that the Political Police clear with him before intervening against churches and to make no arrests without his permission.[179] Wagner simply refused, and blamed Berlin.

In June Epp tried to deal with a complaint from the Passau bishop that the police were interfering with the Corpus Christi celebrations, a major Catholic observance in Bavaria, and with a bishop's protest from Wuerzburg that the police demanded membership lists of youth and adult groups, that the groups could not meet until the confidential lists were turned in.[180] Epp's request for an explanation brought the reply from the Wuerzburg police that the "Men's Society" was led by an old Catholic party man and that no NS belonged to it. While Epp was trying to plug various holes of local pressures, the Political Police chief forbade in mid-1935 church uniforms or badges, or sports participation on grounds that this "provoked" the Hitler Youth.

With the suppression of religious meetings, the next Wagner target was the religious schools and teachers. Since 1936 there had been a systematic effort to force the nuns from their dominant position in the schools, particularly in girls' schools. The Council meeting on April 27, 1938 described the need to change from church to state schools; almost 90% of high schools for girls were run by the church. It was admittedly a big problem to prepare the people and the state to take over this vital church task. Of 30 such boys' schools,

[178] *Ibid.*, F 5068ff.
[179] *Min. Rat.*, 25.4.35.
[180] CGD—T 81, R 185, F 5035.

11 had been closed, of 81 girls' schools, 36 had been closed; no report on the middle schools, except that much work was needed. Resistance was reported strong from Nuremberg and from Faulhaber.[181] Local resistance was more effective than that of Epp, already battling with Wagner and Siebert. Epp was reduced to an inquiry for information on what the Bavarian Political Police were doing.

In early 1938 there was continued pressure on Catholic organizations, this time from the Gestapo. Himmler had ordered in August 1937 a limitation on meeting rights.[182] In February 1938 three groups were dissolved by the police, yet a compromise was reached, with some organizations still permitted, perhaps because local resistance continued.[183]

The war gave the moderates a chance to regroup as Hitler had to be more careful of public opinion. The war clearly increased popular interest in the churches, particularly among the women worried about husbands and sons. It gave Hofmann the chance to speak for the church. In January 1940 he wrote the Reich Church Minister Kerrl, and both agreed on a more moderate state policy. Hofmann's plea for toleration of religion is an eloquent one and unquestionably expressed the more sensible policy he and Epp had pushed for years.[184] He denounced the substitution of NS worship of race for Christianity, something "Hitler had repeatedly forbidden". The result had been a deep division in the nation, even enmity to the party, and an increase in loyalty to the church.

Hoping, or pretending, that his pleas had not only Kerrl's "support" but Hitler's, Hofmann wrote Wagner in March 1940 that Hofmann's ideas on church and state had been made known to Hitler by Lammers and that Hitler fully agreed.[185] (Here Hofmann was bluffing again.) He observed November reports of a meeting in Hesse, where anti-church pressure was the heaviest, at which a party leader had declared that the churches would disappear, that this was Hit-

181 *Min. Rat.*, 27.4.38.
182 CGD—T 81, R 185, F 5005.
183 *Ibid.*, F 4996.
184 *Ibid.*, F 4925.
185 *Ibid.*, F 5448.

ler's wish.[186] Evidence that this was the true Hitler wish came from harsh persecutions in the newly occupied territories in Poland and France, as well as from Bormann's renewed pressure in 1940-41.

A famous vocal protest came from the courageous Bishop Galen in Muenster in July 1941, attacking the Gestapo seizure of monasteries and nunneries a few days earlier. Galen's vigourous speech, with Epp underlining the best parts, denounced the internal decay in the Fatherland resulting from Gestapo activity.[187] The greatest storm in Bavaria came from Wagner's order to remove the cross from schools, to be discussed later.

The attack on the churches, to which Hitler probably had given imprecise support, was called off within a few days of Bishop Galen's sermon. Bormann wrote to Gauleiter Waechtler in July 1941 that the Fuehrer ordered no more confiscation of church or monastic property; even in "special cases" Hitler's approval via Bormann would be necessary.[188] In early September Heydrich ordered the cessation of the anti-church actions, noting that Hitler wanted nothing that would diminish unity. "It is therefore absolutely necessary that all measures must cease which would diminish the united morale of the people."[189]

The wave of anti-church activity, local and central, ebbed further as the hopes for a military victory ebbed. In January 1942 Rosenberg ordered that there be no more discussion in party schooling sessions of religious questions, noting that his order came also from Bormann.[190] Bormann wrote a series of moderate notes on church affairs in mid-1942, including the order of August 1, that local party leaders should not get involved with the churches, that any such matters be referred immediately to him, and that there should be no contact with the churches unless he was informed.[191] In August 1943 Bormann ordered that religious instruction be continued even for those schools moved after bombings.[192]

[186] *Ibid.*, F 5301. [187] *Ibid.*, F 5365. [188] *Ibid.*, F 5298.
[189] *Ibid.*, F 5297. [190] *Ibid.*, F 5359. [191] *Ibid.*, F 5354.
[192] *Ibid.*, F 5342.

The Limits of Hitler's Power

With major elements of the Bavarian state trying to ward off local and central attacks on the churches, the churches could maintain a fight for their own protection. Anyone doubting that many brave pastors had the courage to criticize the party from the pulpit—which was unthinkable in public—need only read the reports of what was said, and who was arrested.[193] For example, the Franken report of Jan. 7, 1937 describes 15 Protestant and nine Roman Catholic bitter attacks on the party. The wonder is that so few were arrested. Ordinarily, local pastor reactions to local party actions characterized the "struggle for men's minds" on occasion, although some Bavaria-wide state action precipitated a kind of Bavarian resistance. Such cases were the justly famous reaction to Wagner's order to remove the crosses from classrooms and the Protestant reaction led by Bishop Meiser against the Hitler-favored "German Christian Movement".

The Incident of the Crosses

Wagner's order dated 23 April 1941 was part of the Reich campaign of pressure against the church, begun in late 1940 and lasting into the summer of 1941. It was part of an order which included the changing of the customary school prayer into some NS statement or song: "At the same time I call your attention to the fact that religious pictures, as well as crosses, are out of place in the schools; I request that the effort be made that such wall decoration gradually be removed or replaced with fitting pictures. A suitable occasion for this would be, for example, during renovation or alteration of the rooms".[194] Wagner claimed in a letter to Siebert that there was direct sabotage of his order by its immediate and flagrant implementation, instead of the gradual and disguised implementation he had ordered. In some schools the order was immediately enforced; in others no one ever tried to enforce it; in still others the community prevented its en-

[193] For Bavaria the best source is the Regierungs-Praesident Berichte, *Geheim Staats Archiv*, Munich.

[194] Dr. Heinrich Hueber, *Dokumente einer Christlichen Widerstandsbewegung*, Munich, 1948, 10f.

forcement or forced the crosses back into the classrooms by threatening lynching of the person responsible, usually the teacher.

Siebert responded to the flood of protests by requesting an explanation from Wagner and then writing again, tactfully suggesting that the order was a serious mistake.[195] There is no doubt that the popular reaction was violently negative, nor that all the responsible leaders tried to have the order changed. "The great majority of the peasant population have no understanding for these anti-church measures. They regard it, despite all explanations that it is a war necessity, as religious and church hostility and fear that another war against the church will begin in earnest after the war."[196] The response was a marked increase in church attendance and observance of the banned church holidays. "A principal had over-eagerly removed the crosses, so that 25 persons assembled in front of the school and in excited tones demanded the release of their children from the school."[197] The Landrat returned the crosses to the school and scolded the principal. The women were writing husbands at the front about it. "The forbidding of processions led in many communities to the peasants, without priest and without cross, making the procession singing and praying."[198] A village denounced the action to the mayor, who referred them to the teacher, who referred them to the order, at which point the village declared a school strike; their children would not reenter the school until the cross was returned.[199] The closing of cloisters and the effort to stop religious holidays had led to threats to stop working altogether.

Protests mounted in July. When one principal died soon after removing a cross, the village believed it the just punishment of God.[200] 211 parents in one village signed a protest against the action, noting the promise made in 1937, when

[195] Hueber, 16-21.
[196] Ber. Reg. Pres. Oberbayern, June 1941. Hereafter BRP.
[197] BRP Niederbayern, June, 1941.
[198] BRP—Franken, June, 1941.
[199] *Ibid.*, Unterfranken, June 1941.
[200] *Ibid.*, Oberfranken, July 1941.

they accepted the "community", i.e., nonconfessional, school, that the crosses would remain. The principal returned the cross without notifying his superiors. School strikes were reported from lower Bavaria and threats in which even the party leaders expressed their opposition to the order.[201] The people feared the removal of religious instruction from the schools. The order "markedly increased the suspicion of party and state" and reduced the willingness to sacrifice.

In Franken: "The state's orders have been met by a certain passive resistance".[202] No one worked on the religious holiday supposedly shifted to Sunday, to save a workday, attending church services instead. Attendance increased to show opposition, from 85 to 100% of the village marching in the Corpus Christi procession. There was widespread disobedience of the Reich flag laws. A peasant with three sons at the front said that he would rather have them die at the front than return to suffer the attacks on the church after the war.[203] Anyone who touched the cross, it was widely said, should have his hands and feet rot away. A community which had ranked first in butter deliveries suddenly became last. Many mayors declared that they would rather resign than participate in the cross removals. Counties reported attendance at religious processions were even over 100% of the population in some communities.[204] The removal of the crosses could be scarcely done without serious incidents. Mothers had threatened a school strike plus the return of their mother medals. In another village the members of the NS women's organization threatened to resign en masse.

The reports of August saw continued incidents such as the invasion by the mothers of the school, demanding that the prayer be said as before, not leaving until the teacher complied.[205] When a pastor was arrested for calling the Wagner action "Bolshevistic", 50 women demonstrated in front of the mayor's house, demanding his dismissal and threatening

[201] *Ibid.*, Niederbayern, July 1941.
[202] *Ibid.*, Oberfranken, July 1941.
[203] *Ibid.*
[204] *Ibid.*, Unterfranken, July 1941.
[205] *Ibid.*, Oberbayern, August 1941.

not to work and not to bring anymore food to market, to throw away their mother medals and to demonstrate in front of the Landrat office.

On August 28 the order was reversed. This was part of the general withdrawal of the Reich's anti-church measures, but in view of the special unrest in Bavaria the reversal brought a dramatic appearance of Hitler.[206] Hitler upbraided his Gauleiter Wagner unmercifully for his stupidity and told him if he should do anything so stupid again, he would have him sent to Dachau. Yet local disobedience to the new ban not to remove crosses continued. A local party leader took the cross out two weeks after the order. A priest tried to stop him and was sent to Dachau for four years.[207] Incidents continued throughout August, the Franken report listing case after case of farmers taking the law into their own hands, storming the school buildings over the protests of the teacher and putting the cross back. During one of the incidents the peasants were heard to shout: "We won't let them take our Lord God away. The Lord God stays; no minister or school superintendent can do anything about it. The soldiers at the front also need their Lord God".[208] The report noted that the great majority agreed with the demonstrators.

One village was reported as particularly unpleasant.[209] The cross was allowed to disappear during renovation which was referred to by the pastor.

> After the church service a large group gathered, mostly women, in front of the school and demanded that the Principal, who is also the party leader, put the crosses back. The protesting crowd, which in the meantime had collected four crosses from neighboring houses, began to push toward the principal in a threatening manner, so that he had to retreat into the house. Other persons brought ladders to get into the locked school. The principal was roundly cursed and the affair could have easily led to blows. In the

206 Described by Robert Scherer, cultural advisor to Wagner.
207 Hueber, 14.
208 BRP, Oberfranken, September 1941.
209 *Ibid.*, Unterfranken, September 1941.

> crowd there were party members, including an old party member, even the leader of the HJ was prominent. Under the pressure of the mob, the crosses were put back. After singing the hymn, "O Holy Cross, we greet thee", the crowd left in a crusading spirit.[210]

Even after the stop-order, the unrest continued, because the order was supposedly secret, however, the people often heard of it before the local authority was officially informed. Much variation in its implementation continued. Actual increase in resentment was reported.[211] Crosses were still being taken out. In one attack 500 people demanded the key to the room with the removed crosses from the mayor. He tried to defend himself with a pistol which was taken from him. Mother medals and war medals appeared in the mayor's box in a dozen different places. In one town the sister of the party leader took the cross back to the school. School strikes continued.[212]

Through the fall the reports mentioned a slow ebbing of resentment, but demonstrations and school strikes continued, with the reports making it clear that the population was strongly on the side of the church, even linking the heavy losses in Russia to this irreligious action. A December report said: "It cannot be ignored that we are still suffering heavily from the results of the crucifix action. The entire affair brought clearly-felt losses to the authority of the party and state".[213] Another report noted the obvious victory of the church in gaining the loyalties of the rural population. Some protests continued in communities trying to get the crosses returned. The mayor of Regensburg thought that a quieting of the matter had not yet begun, that one could not mend such a breach in a people with either "a yes or a no".[214] The order to hand over church bells for the war effort was resisted as a further provocation.

[210] *Ibid.*
[211] *Ibid.*, Niederbayern, October 1941.
[212] *Ibid.*
[213] *Ibid.*, Oberbayern, December 1941.
[214] *Ibid.*, Niederbayern, December 1941.

A February report noted that a teacher had removed the cross during the Christmas vacation.[215] But more cases continued of parents in February forcing the crosses back in, only to have the school administration take them out again.[216] The removal of bells on a wider scale than in World War I brought violence in April. The report stated: "As two young workers began the preparation for removing the bells, the school children began ringing them. Thereby half the village appeared. Some women pushed their way to the scaffolding, threatened the workers and forced them to stop. In the church the workers were surrounded by the women, beaten and forcibly pushed out of the church; outside the church they were pelted with stones, so that they were forced to flee".[217]

Meiser against the "German Christians"

German Protestants, with no loyalty to a foreign pope and no likelihood of foreign support, were less likely to oppose the national policy and less likely to succeed. Yet there was a definite battle within the Bavarian minority Protestant church between the German Christians backed by the party and the Confessional (*Bekenntnis*) church linked with Pastor Niemoeller. The latter's success is obvious in the official reports.

The first warning came from Schwaben in November 1933 that the Evangelical church had rejected the German Christian movement and was united behind Bishop Meiser.[218] The party tried to defeat him, but the following April Meiser spoke to a large *Bekenntnis* meeting of over 7,000. His sermon was reported as a restrained attack on the Fuehrer principle and against the pressures on the church.[219] A report from Schwaben in August 1934 stated that the German Christians had not found any support.[220] Protestant Franken devoted a large part of its report for October 1934 to Meiser.

215 *Ibid.*, February 1942.
216 *Ibid.*, Schwaben, March 1942.
217 *Ibid.*, Oberfranken, May 1942.
218 *Ibid.*, Schwaben, December 1933.
219 *Ibid.*, 17.4.34.
220 *Ibid.*

With obvious reluctance the party had let Meiser speak, although he had publicly attacked Streicher. The report claimed that the great bulk of the Protestants, even old party members, were behind Meiser.[221]

Meiser's opposition brought his dismissal as Bavarian bishop in October 1934, but the reports agree that nearly all Protestants remained loyal to him.[222] The Franken report admitted that 95% of the Protestants backed Meiser. "The measures of the Reich government . . . were without success", it said.[223] What had helped was Streicher's "conciliation" forbidding party intervention in the Protestant's internal affairs, for which he got their promise not to attack party leaders. The report admitted that the newspaper report that there had been joy at Meiser's release was a lie and one which had had a bad effect on public opinion. The church leaders refused to resign their offices and got a court decision denying the validity of the Reich action.[224] Meiser remained.

The defeat of the German Christians led them to blame the Political Police ban on public meetings.[225] One of the very few German Christians, an old party member, committed suicide when reprimanded by the Bekenntnis-dominated Church leadership.[226] Further reports made clear the decline of the defeated German Christians and the success of Meiser who was touring Bavaria and speaking to overfilled churches.[227] In this period in Franken the Protestants were particularly active from the pulpit.[228] Twenty-five theology students tried to walk out of a party leader's speech as a protest. "Bible hours" (a cover for forbidden meetings) were reported as a great success visited by all ages and including party functionaries.

Meiser's criticisms continued. The Franken report of November 1937 devoted 14 pages to long critical quotes of the regime from Meiser and his assistant, Kern; but he was

[221] *Ibid.*, Franken, October 1934.

[222] *Ibid.*, Schwaben and Oberbayern, November 1934.

[223] *Ibid.*, Franken, 9.11.34.

[224] *Ibid.*

[225] *Ibid.*, January 1934.

[226] *Ibid.*, 13.2.34.

[227] *Ibid.*, 7.1.37.

[228] *Ibid.*

not stopped. Kern, wife, and daughter, were put on trial in August 1938 for having voted both "yes and no" on the Austrian-Anschluss plebiscite, where a "no" vote was comparable to treason.[229] A judge ruled in favor of Kern and against his German Christian critic who had accused him of treason and forbade the further distribution of the pamphlet against Kern. The report observed that Kern's staying in office showed how disloyal Meiser was.[230] The Gestapo then forbade Kern to speak or publish anything.[231] The same report quoted a confident Meiser: "We have lost today many supports, the state, the school and a part of the *Kultur*. But be not afraid, we will remain the victors, come what will".

The onset of the war reduced the battle with the Protestant church in Bavaria. Patriotism climbed with victory. Meiser was quoted after the victory over France as "God heard our prayers and gave us victory".[232] Perhaps by no coincidence there were no arrests of Protestant pastors that month, although one Catholic was arrested for saying Christianity and order were more necessary to Germany than victory. Protestants continued to be arrested, but in smaller numbers and less so than their Catholic colleagues; they had long since defeated the NS sponsored "German Christians".

[229] *Ibid.*, 6.8.38.
[230] *Ibid.*, 7.11.38.
[231] *Ibid.*
[232] *Ibid.*, 8.7.40.

4 NUREMBERG

TOURISTS visiting the prewar Nuremberg would have been delighted by the charming "old city" along the Pegnitz. They would have been told of the late-medieval poet Hans Sachs and the Renaissance painter Dürer. They would have learned that its medieval toy industry had been altered in the 19th century into a diversified industrial base justifying a population of some half-million. The guide would have observed sadly that this had been a free city until the Napoleonic period, when it was absorbed, along with surrounding Franken, into Munich-centered Bavaria. It had never felt at ease among the alien Bavarians with their atrocious dialect, and was notably uncomfortable as a Protestant outpost in a Catholic south. For that reason it had been inclined to ally with the northern national forces against the Bavarian.

Visitors to Hitler's Nuremberg would have been told that the city was beloved by the Fuehrer, who had chosen it for the site of the annual party *Tag* (convention). Here was built the massive stadium and halls. Here were staged the massive demonstrations of fanaticism. Here were declared the infamous Nuremberg laws, which made the Jews "uncitizens," for this was the domain of the greatest anti-Semite of them all, Gauleiter Julius Streicher.

The Nuremberg of 1946 was nearly flattened. The International Military Tribunal for Major War Criminals was meeting amid the rubble. Among the prisoners was Julius Streicher, found guilty of having created the hatred which had led to the deaths of millions of innocent Jews. Because of this bald-headed madman, Nuremberg had become the international symbol of Nazi evil.

This study of a city symbolic of National Socialism offers an insight into the working of city government, in this case one that had a strong local tyrant, one in conflict with the bureaucracy of the national tyrant. It should show one example of local reaction to contradictory pressures from above and from below, and therewith the compromises necessary in any community. The city of Nuremberg was one link in the chain of command. Strange things happened because of Streicher and in spite of him. How the city reacted may not have been "typical," but Nuremberg is an example of what can happen, good and bad, in a human situation, It is further evidence of how strong willful personalities maintain a form of political process within the dictatorial framework.

Streicher

"The King of Franken" was probably not the most dangerous party leader, aside from his anti-Semitic *Der Stuermer,* but his flamboyant brutality made him the best known. Although Streicher's name has become synonymous with anti-Semitism, there is reason to believe that he was part-Jewish (like so many of the worst anti-Semites). Streicher had his grandmother's records investigated and the possibly incriminating page thereupon disappeared from the files.[1] (This is also implied in the investigators' remarks in an official genealogy.)[2] Born the ninth child into the poor family of an elementary schoolteacher in Schwaben, Julius Streicher also became an elementary teacher, the group Hitler called the dumbest of all. (His 1945 IQ test registered 102.) As a teacher he came to Nuremberg in 1909. In 1914 he volunteered for the army and won a medal in the first month of the war, ending the war with both Iron Cross medals plus a Bavarian and Austrian Service Cross. Streicher rose from private to lieutenant of a machinegun company.

Back in Nuremberg he devoted his nonteaching hours to political organizing, creating an anti-Semitic party which he "gave to Hitler" in October 1922. This Franken party Hitler acclaimed as the "NS bridge to the north".[3] He was at Hitler's side in the disastrous Munich march in November 1923

[1] Dr. Bruno Martin. A brief description of his anti-Semitism is in Davidson, 39-57.

[2] *"Ahnen Tafel"*. Berlin, 12.7.43, in Akten des Berlin Polizei Praesidents, BDC Streicher file.

[3] *Ibid.*

that brought vast party prestige to the survivors. In 1925 Hitler publicly thanked Streicher for having saved his life during that march.[4] The party Tag and the Nuremberg laws were a reward for this loyalty. It is significant that the first person Hitler went to see on his release from the Landberg prison was Streicher; he was reputedly one of the very few, less than 6, permitted to use the familiar *Du* with Hitler.

Streicher battled for Franken with enormous energy and savage intolerance. Typical was his constant diatribe against Mayor Luppe for having bought in 1920 a coat in a used clothing store, one which had been meant as charity for the poor. Luppe "with strong nerves and sharp teeth" was quite capable of defending himself; but as a northerner he had difficulty in establishing rapport with his citizens. He defended himself with equal tenacity in a bitter duel lasting to the very end. Streicher's excessively abusive language against any members of the establishment during the 1920's brought him many arrests and 11 convictions for slander, but these failed to halt his vicious hate. During the frequent conflicts with the law Streicher was treated with remarkable consideration. One such case in 1927 was based on an alleged rape of a teacher in France in 1916. It was investigated by an obscure Beamter, later District President Dippold, who found reason to accept Streicher's version of the case.[5] Conflict with fellow teachers and school regulations, such as taking sick leave to attend party meetings, brought an 87-page report that his conduct was unbecoming a teacher and his dismissal in 1928. Thereafter his occupation was "journalist".

The heart of Streicher was his fanatic anti-Semitism. This fanaticism was his strength with Hitler who regarded him with awe as the pioneer of the movement. The utter absurdity of his argument was evident in his 1934 order forbidding the use of medicines discovered by Jews, an order doctors even in Nuremberg rejected.[6] Typical was his psychopathic association of anti-Semitism and sex, his totally unsupported assertion that a woman on having had sex relations with a Jew

[4] *Ibid.*
[5] BSA—Streicher Akten, 1732-33.
[6] BSA—1735, 44.

was permanently "infected" with Jewish blood. For such reasons Streicher urged his judges to make sex between Jew and non-Jew punishable by death. His use of sex stories, mixed with sadism, was one reason why his journal was read and his tirades were often to filled halls, including many women.[7] Such were his hate-filled talks to children, as to 2,000 at Christmas time: " 'Do you know who the Devil is,' he asked his breathlessly listening audience. 'The Jew, The Jew,' resounded from a thousand children's voices".[8]

Streicher's hatred of all things Jewish could take surprising turns, as when a lady friend wished to sing in a forbidden operetta by the Jewish Leo Fall. She persuaded Streicher to let the Nuremberg Theater perform the forbidden work. When someone logically protested, Streicher's answer was simple: "A Jew could not have written something so beautiful; he must have stolen it from a Christian".[9]

The nationally known symbol of Streicher was his ever-present riding whip, with which he cowed subordinates and in a few highly publicized cases beat opponents bloody. Fantastic was the scene when his frightened appointee as President of Franken (Dippold) gave Streicher a whip as a birthday present,[10] because it was not at all unthinkable that Streicher in a sudden rage would have beaten the president with it. At the slightest opposition, Streicher would threaten to beat or to shoot even his most loyal servants; in one famous case he ordered his closest cohort to shoot himself.

So brutal a person was the same who loved to paint nature in pleasant and soft colors early in the morning and who loved animals, gently feeding the deer in his own park.[11] Contrary to the accepted NS beerhall patterns, Streicher rarely drank and would tolerate no drunkenness among his otherwise morally corrupt clique.

His party colleagues feared him, for he would without hesitation denounce the highest party officials in his *Der Stuermer* for lack of anti-Semitic zeal. A foreign journalist wrote that Streicher was rarely seen publicly; he knew of

[7] Koetter. [8] IMT, v, 111. [9] Martin.
[10] BSA—1735, 125. [11] BSA—Streicher File, 1737, 44.

only one of the top NS who liked him—Hitler.[12] Probably more so than any of his peers, Streicher combined the elements of the dictator who would brook no opposition with those of the anarchist, the lover of chaos, who would accept no orders from superiors. This inability to fit into an organization, even his own, was his great weakness as Gauleiter. His lack of control made him enemies above, such as Goering and Himmler, and drove honorable men out of his organization below, leaving miserable toadies who had to crawl at his feet. There was constant turmoil in Franken because there was constant turmoil in Streicher.

Despite his furious energy, fanatical oratorical prowess, and closeness to Hitler, groups within the Franken party plotted against Streicher. In 1928 a group of disillusioned NS at a mass meeting denounced his corrupt deputy, Karl Holz, and accused Streicher of high living at party expense, of sabotaging the party convention by stealing money from it, and of raising the young SA and SS to be rowdies. They also thought him guilty of cooperation with priests and with the city administration.[13] The Old Fighter who led the revolt told the police in 1935 that the question had been Holz's use of party money for a 1927 love affair with a Bayreuth waitress. Streicher replied that he would never break with Holz, that Hitler also had his women and gave them presents. (Among the rumors was that of a Streicher attack on Frau Holz.[14]) A similar protest was that of Feder, the early economic theorist of the party, who in 1930 denounced Streicher's efforts to keep Feder's publication out of Nuremberg, to prevent any NS papers' competing with Streicher's lucrative *Der Stuermer*. He accused Streicher and Liebel, later mayor, of having lied constantly and of having stolen money.[15]

The worst crisis, the "Stegmann revolt", came on the verge of the NS seizure of power. Stegmann, an SA commander, rebelled when Streicher kept SA funds for his party organization. In January 1933 the two factions, largely the

[12] *Ibid.*, 48. [13] BSA—1733, 50ff. [14] BSA—1744, 331.
[15] *Ibid.*, 1734.

SA and the party, engaged in a civil war complete with rifles and the storming of party buildings. Streicher informed Hitler of the revolt while at the theater; Hitler, in a fury because he was so close to power, immediately fired Stegmann, thus giving Streicher a victory regretted by most of Franken. The matter remained an obsession with Streicher and deepened his hatred of the SA; he would leave when they marched to avoid seeing them. Stegmann was the first matter of discussion whenever Hitler came to Nuremberg in 1933. Streicher had Stegmann, now helpless, arrested March 26th on the charge of the attempted murder of Streicher.[16] Stegmann had friends, including his school comrade, Himmler. He claimed friendships with Epp, Esser, and Schemm, any of whom would certainly have preferred him to Streicher.[17] Stegmann was released by the Nuremberg police after two days, only to have the Special Commissar rearrest him in May on the suspicion (totally groundless) of having planned a new insurrection. The police quickly released Stegmann again on Himmler's order. In June an order to arrest him was thwarted by the Nuremberg police, this third order supposedly from Hitler himself, but Stegmann, who was out hunting, was not found until a reversal order arrived the next day and ordered the arrest order to be kept secret.[18] Stegmann was finally saved from Streicher's undying hatred when he was sent to north Germany.

Streicher made important enemies, such as Frick who reputedly prevented his being made Commissar of Franken, and Epp who was reported to have prevented his being made mayor of Nuremberg.[19] Streicher's journalistic excesses brought even the wrath of Hitler's executive secretary Lammers, who ordinarily avoided any conflict. After a Streicher telegram attacking a Reich decision not to dissolve student fraternities, Lammers replied that Hitler, not he, had made the decision:

[16] BDC File on Wilhelm Stegmann.
[17] *Ibid.*
[18] *Ibid.*
[19] Arndt Muller, *Juden in Nuernberg*, Nuremberg, 1967, 246.

> Your outrageous insults in your open telegram to me are rejected with all possible sharpness. If you are not ashamed to send such a telegram without any knowledge of the facts and not having taken the slightest effort to inform yourself of the facts, and if you are not ashamed in such ignorance to have attacked me without cause in *Der Stuermer* with such lies, then you are lacking in NS behavior and discipline and are damaging party and state. I shall report the matter to the Fuehrer and reserve further action.[20]

Streicher replied: "Just read your telegram. . . . You are a saboteur of the NS principles and playing the devil with the name of the Fuehrer. Julius Streicher".[21]

With a percentage of the March 5, 1933 vote of 41%, 115,000 out of 276,000, less than the national average but relatively high for an urban area, the Streicher group—one is almost compelled to speak of them as a "gang"—took over power in Franken. The official ceremony was the march of the SA and SS at 3 P.M. on March 9. Streicher ordered the swastika flag unfurled, at which all removed their hats and sang the national anthem and the Horst Wessel song; the church bells rang.[22] There was revenge on the arch enemy Mayor Luppe who was driven in degradation through the streets. The other arch enemy, the Jews, was treated to the boycott of April 1, but called off by the Reich government as economically dangerous. (In his trial in 1946, Streicher described the boycott as Hitler's reaction to attacks on a Germany of 1933, which "still had Hindenburg and a parliament", the boycott was to show them to go no further. There was no organized boycott as such, but a Goebbels trick—Goebbels had spoken only briefly with Streicher on the phone.[23])

Major violence came in June, which, Streicher insisted to Hess, was not his doing:

[20] BDC Hans Lammers File.
[21] *Ibid.*
[22] *Stadtchronik Nürnberg.*
[23] IMT, XII, 314.

> I believe that I can be counted among those who fully understand the situation. Because I am aware of the consequences of a clumsy action against the Jews, in this center of anti-Semitism I took the greatest care that there would be no stupidities. An example: on the second day after the seizure of power some SA people led a Galician Jew through the streets, followed by thousands who demanded his thrashing. I had him brought to me and then had him escorted by Koenig through a back door to his freedom. That same day I told the SA leaders that I would throw out of the party anyone who attacked a single Jew. I told them they did not know what they would start, that a single beaten Jew could arouse the entire world against us.[24]

The arrest of 50 Jews was by the SA and without his knowledge, he wrote. For all of the foul hatred spouted by Streicher the journalist, there was relatively little organized violence by Streicher the Gauleiter.

The crowd around Streicher was largely an assemblage of bullies, weak enough to let Streicher kick them at his pleasure and craven enough to treat their own subordinates just as meanly. The deputy Gauleiter was Karl Holz, editor of *Der Stuermer*, although having a grade school education. For his party biography[25] he reported that as a salesman he had become aware of "the Jewish question" in 1914. He joined the party in November 1922 attracting Streicher's attention in a letter of March 1924, when he shyly wrote that he had always wanted to talk to him after his speeches but Streicher had been so surrounded by idle chatterers that he had not wanted to be thought one of them. Holz felt a great need to speak for the party and in the most radical working class sections; he did not want a post, only a chance to help.

The city fired him the same year from a menial position. In that November he was a party candidate for the city council, and won. He distinguished himself thereafter as editor by "taking the rap" for Streicher in many libel cases and being

[24] Streicher to Hess, 12.10.33 in BDC Streicher Berlin Police File.
[25] BDC Karl Holz, Party Correspondence.

arrested 20 times, including 5 prison sentences. The police reported in September 1930 that Holz was a vulgar speaker, and was used mainly for the peasants.[26]

The other intimate crony was Hans Koenig who, the 1939 Goering commission reported, was generally known as "the evil spirit of Franken".[27] Like Holz, with no intellectual qualifications for high office, Koenig was an "adjutant", a military title admired by the NS party and used for muscle-men too obviously unqualified for formal positions. The accepted story on Koenig's background was that he was illegitimate, that his mother had had relations with a Jew and with a non-Jew, that likely she did not know who was the father. Some observers detected an increased evidence of "Jewish characteristics" as Koenig grew older. Koenig, not a writer or speaker, was used for more private violence, showing more interest in factories or in starlets at the city theater.

More messenger boy than bully boy were Fink, a grade school teacher put on the city council to deliver Streicher's whim and to clear Jews out of the schools, and Strobl who was illegally made president of the chamber of commerce, as well as Gau "Leader for the Economy", and gained the wrath of the Goering commission for his slavish enrichment of the local party from Jewish property.

Something of an outsider was the Nuremberg Kreisleiter Hans Zimmermann, an unemployed engineer who found work with the party in 1932. He proved himself an able speaker; his preferred theme was "the Jewish question". Though round and soft-faced Zimmerman impressed Streicher as "Aryan-looking", which qualified him as a leader. Generally regarded as much less dangerous than the remainder of the clique, in 1939 he had the courage to distance himself from the falling Streicher.

The Party and the City Government

The NS mayor throughout was Willy Liebel, whose family background implied a respectability otherwise lacking among

[26] BSA—1744.

[27] IMT Document 1757PS, Goering Kommission, 154.

NS and the only one regarded after the war with some respect. His public history began with a respected printing house, old Nuremberg family, some of whom privately deplored his party membership. Into the war in 1914, wounded at Verdun in 1916, Liebel returned in 1919 to lead a nationalist organization and then joined the party through contact with Roehm. In 1929, he was elected to the city council where in 1930 he became the NS party leader, engaging in the vicious attacks on Mayor Luppe.

Although ridiculed by Streicher as a good family man, Liebel almost had his career torpedoed in the late 1920s by an "affair". The police reported that an employee of the Liebel firm had complained that she had been fired after the affair ended; their intimacy had occurred after the death of Liebel's first wife.[28] The police reported him in 1930, with Holz leading catcalls at a joint meeting with the KPD, which had begun with a search for weapons.[29] More sensational was Liebel's beating up of a taxi driver for having interfered with a NS parade.[30]

Liebel was a most ambitious man, quite aware of his own ability, including that of a demagogue. He was not the toady Streicher preferred, but a danger. Perhaps for this reason, Streicher made the point when announcing him as the new mayor that Liebel would be most obedient, to which the mayor responded with a sour face. Liebel's luck was that Hitler had taken a personal interest in the city he loved; he considered Liebel the kind of mayor with the proper image. Liebel capitalized on this asset, praising Hitler excessively on any occasion.

Liebel was anxious to make a model city of his Nuremberg. For that reason he kept most of the experienced Beamten, although none could have been properly considered NS. Luppe was treated roughly, but Treu, the second mayor, was given his legal pension. (Treu returned in 1945 as mayor, but was discharged by the Americans because he refused to fire all NS officials.[31]) Of the 11 top officials (*Referenten)*

[28] BSA—1451, p. 349.
[29] BSA—1744, p. 265ff.
[30] BSA—1451.
[31] Rollwagen.

only two were dismissed, and because they were Socialist party leaders. One of these, Hans Rollwagen, was given a disguised employment "as a police consultant on Marxism," since his pension would have to be paid anyway, until 1935 when he was taken back into the government as an assistant to the treasurer. Liebel defended Rollwagen as a man who had not deserted his party and had therewith proven his character. Liebel protected him and the others from Streicher's interference; although Liebel had begun as a wild NS, "he had soon become a mayor".[32]

Another SPD, Fey, was kept undisturbed in office, with Liebel commenting that he would be "loyal".[33] The closest compatriot of Luppe, Duerr, a "typical liberal", was kept in charge of school and culture. Fink, the Gauleiter's messenger who took Duerr's place on his death in 1935, was relatively harsh but remained largely an outsider among the Referenten.[34] The remainder of the Referenten, with either bourgeois political or unpolitical inclinations, were kept in office, most of them having served the city since the Kaiser days. One brought down the wrath of the Gau on Liebel in 1935 when he unfortunately admitted that he preferred a church charity to the party NSV as the administrator of a city institution.[35] These administrators were gradually forced into the party, Rollwagen in 1940 being one of the last. By 1937 it was clear that non-NS would not be promoted. The hiring policy (with the exception of Fink)—showing that any incumbent kept his job and any new man was primarily judged on the basis of technical capacity—party membership soon understood.

With the city led by skilled men personally known to Liebel, the party played a limited role in city administration, in contrast to the lower levels where there was a rabid party policy and mass firings, mostly of socialists supposedly hired as favorites of the previous administration. This occurred among the city street car employees, apparently as the personal revenge of their former, scorned colleague, Gradl, who

[32] *Ibid.*
[33] Nuernberg Stadt Archiv DA/S, P22.
[34] Rollwagen.
[35] NSA, DA/S, 7.

was so frequently with Streicher that he was called his shadow. Out of about 8,200 city employees, by 1938, 1,036 Beamten, 197 employees, and 264 workers were party members.[36]

Kreisleiter Zimmermann was rewarded with the directorship of the city health insurance. He had no particular qualifications for the position and was regarded by his subordinates as incompetent but terrible, perhaps because he was incompetent. Zimmermann fired a large number of his employees as "reds" to make room for needy NS. Early in his regime he demanded that anyone who had left the church must reenter it; when the party line switched, he demanded that they leave the church again.[37] The work, which scarcely diverted him from party and personal affairs, provided a Mercedes, a villa, and parties.[38]

Beamten were encouraged, at first, to engage in party work. Liebel presented Streicher with a villa to express the city's gratitude. The city administration was active in implementing an anti-Semitic policy in advance of, and often contrary to, orders of the central government. Jewish doctors were fired from city jobs as early as March 1933.

Although Liebel was thus a fanatic NS and anti-Semite, his amibition and loyalty to Nuremberg brought him into increasing conflict with the party. He resisted the implication that Zimmermann was cleaning out non-NS from his department (35, with 20 more due to go). Liebel protested that he was not less revolutionary, but matters were "different" on the city council and that there should be no firing for "some thoughtless words".[39] In October a doctor not a party member, was hired to head a clinic; the top four candidates were not NS.[40] Eickemeyer, the finance Beamter made second mayor, rejected the Streicher attempt through Fink to get barracks

[36] *Verwaltungsbericht der Stadt Nuernberg*, Nuremberg Stadtarchiv, 1937-38, I-9.

[37] SK, Hans Zimmermann, 45ff.

[38] Postwar police report, *Ibid.*

[39] *Geheim Sitzung des Stadtrats Nuernberg*, 12.7.33.

[40] *Ibid.*, 25.10.33.

torn down by noting that the people living there had no place to go.[41] Eickemeyer's concern was city money.

Yet Streicher's choice for head of the conservatory was accepted, although the man had failed his examination and the musicians all wanted a recognized authority. Concluding that the examination was probably not fair, and because Streicher's candidate had spent two years at the front, the committee elected him unanimously.[42] Such reasoning prevailed in the selection of a doctor, against medical opinion, because the doctors' candidate had a "dark look".[43] The difficulties of such reasoning became apparent when a construction inspector, highly recommended as an old NS who had lost his job fighting for the party, then caused "the greatest of difficulties"; he had not "worked in", but instead had written huge reports complaining about how he was being disadvantaged by older and experienced Beamten. He had been told to stop complaining and had promised to, but after a few weeks had caused more trouble. After being again told to work in, he wrote a nasty letter to Liebel claiming that he "had been raped".[44]

In 1935 Streicher gave in, after repeated protests, to the reelection of the old Catholic party man, Plank, as Referent, but only after an insult to the man who had joined the NS party. "It is terribly difficult for us to support a man who had already proven a serious lack of character. . . . The joining of the party means nothing to me."[45] The matter of late party-joiners was more tolerantly handled by Liebel, who ordered that teachers were not to have their promotions delayed because they had once been SPD (socialists). That they had joined the NS party sufficiently demonstrated their loyalty. In obvious reference to Streicher's more rigid line, Liebel said: "I would like to call the attention particularly of those party members who occupy leading positions to the matter. For me it is naturally impossible to doubt the political reliability of a man belonging to the party". He thought the old party members had already gotten their reward through

[41] *Ibid.*, 17.1.34. [42] *Ibid.* [43] *Ibid.*, 27.6.34.
[44] *Ibid.*, 15.8.34. [45] *Ibid.*, 9.10.35.

promotions.[46] The mayor's pro-Beamter position was resisted by Fink who postponed the promotion of an ex-SPD teacher for three years, although admitting that he was extremely able.[47]

A more open debate developed over the head of the statistical office. In October 1937 Liebel opposed Streicher's candidate as unqualified, that he had caused great trouble in his early jobs, and that every Beamter in the office would be his superior in ability. Zimmermann replied that Koenig also supported the man, that he would learn his job in time, and anyway it would get him away from his present job, where he was not working out well. Liebel replied that Zimmermann was speaking for an old party member, but "I'm an old party member too." The man had never learned to subordinate himself, that in this job he must possess more than good will. Another party hack, Gradl, insisted, but Liebel merely announced that he would reserve his decision.[48]

Liebel showed some reason when the party demanded in February 1938 that Jews be barred from the municipal savings banks and from city streetcars. He noted that since 1933 no loans had been given Jews, but that having special streetcars for Jews was ridiculous. Concerning the complaint of an SS man about working for a Jew, Liebel observed that there were enough other jobs so that he could change if he were unhappy. At any rate, the city would not be told what it should do.[49]

Further resistance was shown in late 1938 when Fink reported the case of the teacher recommended by the SA but whose work had been inferior. Himmler's SD had called to favor the appointment, so Fink was prepared to recommend it. Liebel said there would be no promotion and hoped that the man would simply take the hint and leave.[50]

The wheel was turning by 1939, as Liebel said: "The city administration is repeatedly approached from a variety of places with the intention of getting people jobs . . . regarded as a welfare institution . . . to so great an extent that it is nec-

[46] *Ibid.*, 26.5.37.
[47] *Ibid.*, 7.7.37.
[48] *Ibid.*, 21.10.37.
[49] *Ibid.*, 16.2.38.
[50] *Ibid.*, 28.9.38.

essary to call a halt".[51] Liebel reported that he had protested to the Gauleitung which had shown understanding of the problem but, "Now there is a veritable pile of recommendations sent him by the Gauleitung." He protested, "The city is no welfare institution." It had taken in many NS including those over age, but these had quickly requested easier jobs. His sentiment crystallized with the remark that, "I no longer want to do what someone else wants," but the words were crossed out.[52] The wheel turned further when Fink at the start of the war requested the party to release all teachers from party jobs, so that they could devote themselves to their public duties.[53] Significantly, although most of the party leaders were arrested for corruption, no city leader was arrested, even in the scramble for Jewish property.

Liebel's ideal was the "free city" practice of earlier times. Other than occasional obedience to the Gauleitung until 1939, the city ran its affairs largely unhindered.[54] With the grace of Hitler upon the city, no one else interfered. One could literally ignore the Ansbach district government which wanted only to avoid trouble. Bavaria had powerful personalities like Wagner who avoided Streicher's domain. The large city was too much like a province itself, fortified with expert Beamten, to be easily overrun.

The two points of conflict were the building program and money. Hitler's dream to build a new Nuremberg for the party conventions was welcomed on the one hand as providing enormous prestige, but it caused problems with land scarcity and grumblings about the deplorable state of private housing while millions were poured into representational buildings. In one of the rare references to outside authority, the council showed anger with Bavaria in 1935 that it would not help in housing construction.[55] Liebel was supposed to go to Munich and "show some teeth" to Siebert. "The city administration would not think of letting things remain as Siebert wanted." Money was the occasion in 1937 for a city fight. Eickemeyer reported the increased tax diversion to the Reich, that he had to fight hard in Munich to keep Nurem-

[51] *Ibid.*, 25.1.39. [52] *Ibid.* [53] *Ibid.*, 11.10.39.
[54] Rollwagen. [55] *Ibid.*, 30.10.35.

berg from losing even more.[56] But real fighting was kept for the "in group".

Streicher and the Police

The third element of power in the city (after the party and the city itself) was the police force, which was formally removed from city jurisdiction in 1922 and removed from Land jurisdiction in the "nationalizing" of 1936. It was removed in 1934-39 from Streicher's control by the successful diplomacy of Dr. Martin, with the backing of Himmler.

The leadership of the police force until 1933 was conservative. It tried to avoid involvement in the turbulent politics of the city. Only two very minor members were NS, and none of its leadership. Though the police had constantly arrested Streicher, he had been treated so tactfully that no revenge was taken in 1933, nor were there firings comparable to those in the city administration. Streicher regarded the police with some fondness, as in his letter of Oct. 21, 1933 to Hess protesting Esser's and Frank's effort to suppress *Der Stuermer;* it was tragic that NS ministers were planning to stop it. "The high officials of the then Nuremberg police were able time and again to protect the freedom of *Der Stuermer*", Streicher said.[57] When the Jews had the power there was freedom of speech, he lamented, but now?

Although the two top conservatives, Schachinger and Gareis, had not particularly annoyed Streicher, they were too much Beamten to please him; Schachinger became the organizer on Epp's staff, Gareis the president of Wagner's Gau of Upper Bavaria-Munich. The Number 3 man, the younger and tougher Dr. Martin, stayed. For a very brief period in April 1933 Himmler was nominally police president; he remained Streicher's competitor for control.

The Malsen-Ponickau Interlude

Erasmus von Malsen-Ponickau, Himmler's SS police president from April to September 1933, is an example of how not to play the power game. Sent by Himmler to curb Streich-

[56] *Ibid.*, 15.1.37.
[57] BDC Streicher Berlin Police File, 12.10.33.

er, he was publicly cursed by the latter and therewith unceremoniously fired. His story is valuable as an example of how the early SS and Himmler could be routed.

Some of the treatment given Malsen-Ponickau was deserved. His attitude was surely cavalier, so much so that it is difficult to think of him away from horses. His horse ride every morning was one reason why he was too infrequently on the job. His SS file is a series of scoldings by Himmler.[58] Horses were involved in Himmler's scoldings of 1935, when it was noted that he somehow maintained two horses without noticeable funds and in 1943 when Himmler gave him 14 days house arrest for illegal horse dealings.

Women played a role in his problems, from Koenig's complaint in 1933 that Malsen-Ponickau should not bother the girls behind the scenes at the city theater to the adulterous relationship which led to the disgraced remarriage lamented by his former father-in-law and by the SS. Yet Himmler was ready as ever to bail out SS men in marital difficulties with a 25,000-mark settlement from his special account, from which Malsen-Ponickau was already getting 300 marks a month. A certain irrationality in the man is evident in his suggested settlement for the divorce in which each parent was to keep one child and the third to be given up for adoption.[59]

A certain ideological laxity is also evident in this SS man who had to be scolded by Himmler in 1936 that his wife had treated another party member's wife impolitely, demanding that she be addressed in the third person suitable to her noble station. The same snobbishness was criticized in his treatment of fellow SS men, whose vulgar company he preferred to avoid. Himmler was further annoyed that the Malsen-Ponickau family patronized a Jewish shoe store.[60]

With a massive file of such delinquencies, which Himmler patiently overlooked in making Malsen-Ponickau police president in one city after another, it is no wonder that he lasted such a short time in Nuremberg. His intentions, however,

58 BDC SS File of Malsen-Ponickau.

59 *Ibid.*

60 *Ibid.*

seem to have been honorable, although his lack of police experience, leadership ability, or even energy made them pathetic. As early as April 1933 Malsen-Ponickau refused a Gauleitung request to transfer a police official who had sharply attacked the party.[61] He ran afoul of the rabid Kreisleiter Sperber, even threatening to send Sperber to Dachau if he did not end his abuses.[62]

Another Kreisleiter, also a mayor of Fuerth ran into Ponickau's sense of justice. This party worthy was charged with indecent exposure. Streicher sent Koenig to convince the woman involved to withdraw the charges, which she prudently agreed to do. As Streicher reported it, Ponickau, "who does not feel like a party member", sent police officials, who got the lady in question drunk enough to repeat the accusations.[63] Ponickau then had the audacity to charge Koenig with having coerced her retraction. Streicher saw the ludicrousness of charging so heinous an act to Koenig, who had a letter from Hitler addressed to "My dear party member Hans Koenig". Out of his sure instinct for party justice, Streicher had sent more policemen to the unsure witness, who saw fit again to retract the story against the mayor. To Streicher all of this attested to Ponickau's "lack of character" in his unfriendliness to a party member.[64] That he was an aristocrat proved to Streicher his degeneracy.

During these months the police showed themselves least able to restrain SA violence, but this was mostly the result of the overall license given the SA to finish the revolution by local violence. Ponickau attempted to use his authority as SS commander. In July he spoke to the SS and observed that "the SS was always being misused by irresponsible political leaders to wild operations. These wild operations result in part from motives of personal hostility and are contrary to the expressed will of the Fuehrer". This correct observation led Ponickau to command all SS men to refuse to take part

61 BSA—1452, "Polizei Bericht: Dr. Martin-von Malsen-Ponickau".
62 *Ibid.*, 21.8.33.
63 Streicher report in BDC Malsen-Ponickau SS File.
64 *Ibid.*

in such actions. "The party leaders are not authorized to give orders to the SS for any such actions."[65] SS men involved would be arrested for violations of the law. To underline the challenge, Ponickau sent a copy of his order to Streicher.

Holz replied with cries of anguish at this Johnny-come-lately interference.[66] Ponickau did not understand because he had not participated in the 10-year fight to conquer Franken; he was endangering that great victory by driving a wedge between the SS and the party. "We must forbid such orders by you" Holz said, and sent a copy of his letter to Himmler.

The crisis reached a climax with conflicting reports of a conversation between Ponickau and Dr. Martin; Martin reported that Ponickau refused to come to a party meeting and had said that "he would fight with all resources against Gauleiter Streicher, and also against anyone sent to the police presidium to represent him." (Probably meaning Martin.[67]) Martin, aware of who was king in Franken, dutifully reported such remarks, later denied by Ponickau, to Streicher. Holz wrote in reply how awful it was for Ponickau to attack Streicher, "That we don't believe that you are angel-pure in everything and . . . that you are in your sentiments anything but an aristocrat. Aristocrats do not denounce, Herr von Malsen-Ponickau."[68] Martin reported that he had, because of his 10-year friendship with Streicher, felt compelled to report that Ponickau had "a certain hatred" for Streicher.

Ponickau's letter of Aug. 14, 1933 attacked that of Holz and denied the accusation that he had hated Streicher from the beginning; he wanted to talk with Holz to clear the matter up.[69] The meeting failed, as Holz preferred to believe the new party member Dr. Martin rather than SS man Ponickau, and the stage was set for the famous Streicher blow-up of August 18.

During preparations for the party Tag Martin stayed with

65 BSA—1452, 7.7.33.

66 *Ibid.*

67 BDC Malsen-Ponickau, SS File, Streicher report.

68 BSA—1452, Holz 10.8.33.

69 *Ibid.*

Streicher. Seeing them together and suspicious of a plot, Ponickau went up to Martin and told him loudly in front of the 50 party men gathered that his presence was no longer desired. Martin replied that he thought it was his duty to stay and he had been asked to do so by Streicher. Later observing that Martin had ridden in Streicher's car to the parade grounds, Ponickau shouted to Martin, "I observe that you have not obeyed an order of the police president; I will not put up with such conduct."[70]

At this treatment of Martin, who, Streicher reported, had served the party for 10 years, as Hitler knew, Streicher approached Ponickau with threatening gestures and the denunciation: "You are a degenerate *Schweinhund.* I'll beat you with my riding whip about the ears, if you continue to provoke me in my Gau. The police president for me is Dr. Martin. When I want to talk to Dr. Martin, you are not to issue any contrary orders. You are the meanest rascal I have ever met in a uniform. What business do you have here? Go home, and take care of your estate."[71] Streicher reported further that Ponickau, instead of "taking it like a man", simply took out a pen to copy down the insult, but Streicher had said he need not copy it down. "You want to be an aristocrat. . . . You are a cowardly dog." Somehow Ponickau got it down word for word. Streicher accepted his version, but noted that Ponickau had left out the word "degenerate". Hitler was a witness to the scene, but moved away as though he had not seen a Gauleiter treat a police president like a criminal.

Ponickau reported that only the presence of Hitler had kept him from knocking Streicher down on the spot. He demanded that Wagner fire Martin immediately. Martin, however, had chosen sides correctly; he remained and Ponickau left. After a short investigation Himmler agreed that Streicher was difficult but Ponickau was wrong to give Martin an order "which could not be carried out."[72]

70 BDC Malsen-Ponickau, Streicher report, see also BSA—1452, Martin report.

71 *Ibid.*

72 BDC Malsen-Ponickau, SS File, Himmler to Roehm, 10.2.34.

The Obernitz Interlude

From September 1, 1933 to July 5, 1934 Hans Guenther von Obernitz, SA special commissar, was police president, having demonstrated his fitness for the post by his anti-law and anti-police violence. A more brutal, soldierly type than his predecessor, Obernitz had left home at 16 to join the army. He became an officer and was wounded in 1918. He had remained with the marauding Free Corps and Erhard Brigade until forced to flee in 1923 to Italy where he remained until 1933. Obernitz became the SA commander of Franken in May 1933.

A condotierre type, with military-party inclinations instead of police experience, Obernitz was forced to rely on Dr. Martin as the actual executive. Martin reported that Obernitz's first act was to order a thorough cleaning out of the old Beamten and their replacement by SA members, which Martin thought a "brilliant idea". In fact, Martin found so many bureaucratic difficulties that the change became impossible. He hired only one SA man, who merely continued his drinking and "developed a taste for women", all the while carefully watched by the police he was supposed to be leading.[73] Martin knew how to avoid trouble. When Justice Minister Frank protested the beating to death of a socialist by two SA men, brutally and without cause, Martin's police could not cooperate in the investigation because they were "too busy preparing for the upcoming party convention".[74] The state's authority brushed past Obernitz's feeble defense of the action and the police cover-up, to show that the defense was obviously false.

Obernitz also avoided conflict with Streicher but so busied himself pushing a radical course in Franken that he gained the enmity of fellow solider-SA man, Colonel Hofmann. Hofmann became incensed at Obernitz's insubordination. Obernitz refused to send reports, to appear when so requested by the District President, and illegally asked to be placed directly under Wagner's Interior Ministry. Hofmann wrote in

[73] Martin. [74] BSA—Bav. In Min, 71719, 6.9.33.

the spring of 1934[75] that Obernitz had been appointed to restore authority but was actually further undermining it, i.e., his illegal SA activity took precedence over his police duties. Obernitz had deliberately refused a direct order of the president. For example, when Hofmann asked the reasons for two Obernitz-ordered arrests, the reply was that it was none of his business. When Hofmann asked for the dismissal of the SA commissar in Rothenburg for grand larceny, Obernitz simply answered, "I like the man. The man stays".[76] Obernitz had prevented a state attorney from investigating the mishandling of arrested persons by the SA.

Hofmann dwelt on the incident of the mayor of Bamberg who was attacked in the party press and had responded by criticizing *Der Stuermer.* Obernitz wrote the second mayor to have the mayor arrested, which was done, an action totally without authorization. Hoffmann said: "Some 14 days after the arrest Obernitz described it to the SA unit in Bamberg as the beginning of a new revolutionary wave in Bamberg and ordered the SA members to report further 'representatives of the old system' among the officials."[77] The "disloyal" Beamten were to be fired within 14 days. "As this demand brought the wish for the release of many city and state employees, Obernitz had to point out the impossibility of so many firings and to withdraw his demand. The result was confusion and bitterness among the officials and the disappointment in the ranks of the excited SA."[78] A member of the city council who opposed him was summarily fired by Obernitz. Hofmann's denunciation continued with the news that Obernitz had stolen a bronze candelabra after a reception at Hofmann's house and refused to return it. Obernitz had sung in a tavern with SA cronies to a text which included the lines, "should Siebert (Bavarian President) enter the bar, we'll kick him in the *Arschloch* once more".[79] The problem was that these actions "emerged from a basic denial of authority or a weakness of character".

[75] BDC SA File—v. Obernitz, 5.5.95. See also BSA—Bav. In. Min, 71885.

[76] *Ibid.* [77] *Ibid.* [78] *Ibid.* [79] *Ibid.*

Obernitz's reaction was to command Martin to draw up an order to have District President Hofmann arrested should he ever enter Nuremberg. This was comparable to his request for a threatening letter to Mayor Liebel, which Martin also declined to write because Liebel was the head of an office of government. Obernitz's reply was simply, "That is not an office but a manure pile".[80]

Like so many appeals to reason, Hofmann's brought his own downfall—in the spring of 1934. Yet the traits Hofmann described were those Hitler chose to eradicate in the top SA men in the "Roehm putsch". Obernitz was nearly killed with SA cronies. He would have had he been found on the fatal day. He appeared two days later in his office and was persuaded to beg Streicher's help, who saw the value of saving him in order to get his loyalty.[81] Streicher traveled to Berlin where he saw Hitler who agreed and sent him on to Goering. Obernitz was released as police president but kept as regional commander of the chastened SA. There he remained, loyal to Streicher, at least until Streicher's fall. The war brought a more natural outlet to his abilities; he died in an air crash in 1944.

The Steinrueck Affair

The international symbol of Streicher brutality and police complicity was his beating of Steinrueck in the city jail, which occurred in early July 1934 in the turgid climate after the death of Roehm. Streicher, who had not been privy to information about Roehm's death, was extremely nervous, possibly worried about his own fate with the death of that other close friend of Hitler, Roehm. Although he suspected the rival SA organization, their radicalism matched his own. While he was sitting in a restaurant with Martin, Holz, and Koenig, news came of Steinrueck's arrest for having allegedly said, "It would have been better to have killed Streicher than those in the SA". The enraged Streicher demanded that the man be brought immediately to the restaurant, but Holz and

[80] Martin. [81] Martin.

Martin talked him out of it, only to have Streicher spring to his feet and insist that they go to police headquarters.

In the cell Streicher began beating the man mercilessly. Streicher's letter of defense[82] said that Steinrueck had not apologized, but had "grinned cynically, and showed himself cowardly", i.e., he did not hit back. All of those involved, with the exception of Steinrueck, swore time and again that Dr. Martin was not in the cell at the time of the beating, "having been called away". How he could have stopped the maddened Streicher had he stayed is moot, but the incident brought embarrassing publicity to all concerned. Dr. Martin the same night wrote a report which led to the state's attorney investigation. The charges against Steinrueck were dropped; the doctor's report minimized the results of the beating as only bruises on the body and head. Steinrueck claimed that he had not behaved "cynically", but had been first abused as an "academician" by Streicher, then beaten without cause. Martin's defense emphasized that Streicher was his superior, which was factually but not legally true. Martin had later talked with the prisoner and had a low estimate of his character.[83] Steinrueck was released but not forgotten. The matter was brought up in 1939 in connection with the party investigation of Streicher, which described him as a sadist with his whip, and quoted him as having said afterwards, "Now I am relieved. I really needed that."[84]

The Rise of Dr. Martin

The most fascinating personality in Nuremberg's NS history was Dr. Martin, surely the most intelligent in the power struggle and probably one who used his power humanely. But as a man who chose to play the double-game, to serve the NS government, even the mad Streicher, but also to serve himself and to oppose the NS, his path between subservience to criminals and opposition to the crimes was so tortuous that no simple statement can suffice.

Martin's role was partly that of circumstance; had he been

82 BSA—Bav. In. Min., 71719, 21.7.34.

83 *Ibid.*

84 IMT, 1757PS, 148.

subject to a more reasonable Gauleiter, or had Streicher fewer wild men about him, Martin would have found conformity much easier.[85] On the other hand, had Streicher been less mad, resistance would have been that much more difficult. In Munich, directly involved with the national party headquarters, as well as Wagner, a personal policy would have been vastly more difficult. Nuremberg was close enough to have the affection of Hitler, but far enough away to play its own game.

Martin had the tools with which to play the dangerous game. His strong muscular figure, well over six feet, impressed the smaller men about him. Martin had the manners of a diplomat and the skill to take advantage of his appearance. He was from a family with a Beamter tradition of 300 years. Of a quick spirit, an engrossing conversationalist of flawless diction, he had the allure of the aristocrat. From this solid, law-abiding, family tradition, he had been cast along with his generation into the trenches of World War I, returning the disillusioned patriot like his close friend, the Nuremberg journalist, Dr. Koetter. He finished his training as a jurist, capturing the rare distinction of ranking "No. 1" on his exam. Choosing police work, Martin in the early twenties wrote a widely used textbook on police work. In a normal time and place he would have risen quickly to the top of his profession and to a respected retirement, but Nuremberg in the 1920s was no normal time and place; matters got worse.

As a flexible diplomat, Martin was at first thought too friendly to the Reds, and ever since too friendly to the NS Browns. Although *Der Stuermer* announced in January 1933 that Martin was "an annoyance who would have to disappear", Martin had dealt so skillfully with the NS during the twenties as the political liaison of the police to the party that he had their respect. Streicher announced in 1934, when defending his new police president who had just joined the party, that Martin had been of "great service" to the party. More precisely, Streicher praised his help in keeping *Der*

[85] Martin.

Stuermer from being stopped by law and in preparing for the party conventions. (Evidence of more serious assistance has not been discovered.) Martin explained Streicher's early affection as partly admiration for Martin's physique, but even more the sentiment of a man in jail in 1924. When the courtly Martin asked what he could do to make the cell more comfortable and Streicher asked for a blanket, he had pleasantly granted Streicher's request for "the second blanket".

Political conviction played a rather small part; Weimar politics likely bored Martin. He found politicians unpleasant companions, socially and intellectually his inferior. The NS gang was the most obviously Martin's inferior. As a patriot and a conservative, though, he shared their dreams of a strong Reich. Briefly in the Free Corps in its "liberation" of Munich in 1919, he had friendly contacts with the extremist Captain Erhard whose regiment was in part financed by his wife's family. Always the diplomat, Martin avoided emotional nationalism, and as carefully avoided public speaking or even a public statement. Hitler, almost alone of the NS leaders, commanded his partial respect as a man of demonic energy and ability. Martin's favorite comment, borrowed from Goethe, on Hitler was: "Don't paint the devil too small".

Martin's ability to survive depended also on social facility, such as the ability to drink Holz under the table or to entertain Hitler on his visits with charming stories or attentive listening. One technique was to prepare for Hitler's favorite subject of conversation, operettas, by reading up on an obscure operetta just before Hitler arrived. Martin's charm as a conversationalist contrasted sharply with the dullness of most of the bureaucrats Hitler despised. Once, on a visit to Berlin, Martin was invited to sit next to Hitler at dinner, while Frick, so much higher in the chain of command, was relegated to the opposite end of the long table.

Martin was equally skillful in gaining the respect of subordinates, some of whom were old friends from fraternities such as his close collaborator, Dr. Georg Kiessel, head of the local Gestapo, or from the army and Free Corps where ties were strengthened over sparkling wine and conversation. Like the patriarch of an estate, he could demand absolute loyalty of police officials and yet be courteous and concerned, as in asking a doorman about the wife and family.

Inventive in technique, Martin increased his influence over the Gestapo, which he did not clearly command, by keeping them in the same building on the pretense that "there was no place else to put them". He released prisoners delivered by party radicals on the grounds that they were too ill to be arrested, with a pious police doctor, Anton Wegner, ever ready to attest them "unfit for arrest". Under the cloak of police secrecy he could spy on the party, even on Streicher. Ostensibly for Streicher's protection, guards (spies) were stationed outside Streicher's palace; they delivered a detailed report of Streicher's political and social activity each morning to Martin's desk.

With his superiors transferred in 1933, Martin was left with Malsen-Ponickau and then Obernitz, neither of whom had the capacity to run a police department nor the ability to work satisfactorily with their superiors. Martin knew he could run the police better and that he could ingratiate himself with Streicher. This was his effort in 1933-34, as evidenced by Martin's letter to the SS sending in the necessary papers for application and including a news clipping which stated that he had long helped Streicher out of inner conviction, though unable to join the party, and had thereby made himself unpopular with his superiors.[86] That the latter statement was untrue is evidenced by a letter to Martin's former superior, Schachinger, commenting on Streicher's honoring him for "the many secret services" given the party before 1933, that is, for the many hours of conference with Holz and Streicher in his office. Then he thanked Schachinger for introducing him to the NS world of ideas.[87] In Martin's autobiography written for party files in 1935, he explained his late entry to the party,—August 1933—stating that Streicher had said he could be more useful outside the party.[88]

An associate, remembering that Martin had referred before

[86] BDC SS File, Dr. Martin. [87] *Ibid.* [88] *Ibid.*

1933 to Streicher as "the fool", observed to Martin in 1934 that the newspapers had made Streicher an "Old Fighter". Martin replied: "Do you think I could be friends with those fools?"[89] Zimmermann testified after the war that he and most of the party had always thought of Martin as an opponent, but Streicher had considered him a friend.[90] Surely Martin was never an NS; "no one could understand his SS promotions". He was always suspect, although an investigation in January 1936 reported that all charges against him from party elements "had been completely disproven".[91]

To achieve power in Nuremberg Martin had to become "Streicher's man", which he did publicly. At the same time, he needed the support of Himmler who regarded Martin as a check on Streicher's effort at Frankish autonomy. As Himmler told him, "You're the only one who can deal with those fools in Franken".[92]

It is nearly certain that Martin was ideologically unattracted either to the Weimar parties or to the NS except perhaps for its patriotic appeal for a stronger Germany. Yet he knew if he were to succeed in his chosen career he must cooperate with the powers that be. There is evidence that conservative elements, particularly his close friend, the journalist, Koetter and the manufacturer, Dr. Mayer, urged him to stay in power to keep the radicals in check.[93] Koetter described Martin's quandary about whether to stay or find a less exposed position, and Koetter's appeal: "You are our last hope". The alternative would have been the bully Koenig. It is certain that Martin used his power in part to moderate or deflect the action of the party radicals, and in time to end the power of his onetime protector, Streicher. Yet Martin's technique of doing so was so subtle that five postwar trials could not resolve the debate.

Perhaps the best analysis of Martin was that written by Heydrich to Himmler.

[89] Grafenberg, Martin Spruchkammer, II, 130.
[90] *Ibid.*, II, 142. [91] *Ibid.* [92] Martin.
[93] Koetter, Mayer.

> The technical work of Dr. Martin is in general satisfactory. His many years of experience assure a technically irreproachable conduct of the police business.
>
> But beyond the technical, may I express to the Reichsfuehrer my strongest doubts about the person of Dr. Martin, based primarily on the fact that Martin to a very great extent conducts his personal policies.
>
> He tolerates no strong personalities around him, instead only those obedient creatures totally subject to him. He prepares systematically for his personal domination and government of his realm and is already preparing politically for the expected appointment as the commanding SS officer.
>
> In the pursuit of his personal efforts, Martin has developed a persistent and tough perseverance which usually brings him success. It is unpleasantly apparent that he unhesitatingly follows various paths to reach his goal. Martin will never become in character a SS leader and National Socialist.[94]

Streicher was easier to convince, as was Himmler. Martin was made police president on Sept. 30, 1934, and remained in the post until promoted to SS commander in 1942. His nominal chief, Frick, gave him only one order—"Get along with Streicher".

Running his own police force meant keeping the Gauleiter from intervening, which Martin was usually able to do, although not in the Steinrueck case. Later Martin was reported ordered with a flick of the hand from his own office, while Streicher beat another helpless prisoner. The other interference could come from the Bavarian government, Wagner, or from Berlin. Lesser figures could be overawed by Martin, as was a subordinate of Wagner, by his dropping the names of Wagner, Streicher, Liebel, Reich ministers and even Hitler to inform him to stay out. He quoted Wagner: "no one in Munich would think to intervene in Nuremberg police affairs".[95]

[94] BDC SS File, Martin, Heydrich to Himmler, 21.3.42.

[95] Martin to Commander of Landespolizei, Schweinle, 7.10.35, in Martin SK, VI.

Streicher and the Frankish Government

Streicher's base of operations was the city of Nuremberg, which culturally and perhaps politically dominated the back country, a series of counties with scattered small towns as NS strongholds and hundreds of villages as strongholds of conservatism and religion. Streicher's main interest was the party organization, where he kept close check on his Kreisleiter, most of whom tried to emulate the tough belligerence of their chief. Like him, they had emotional problems. To work for Streicher meant for most a cringing loyalty to him and a flamboyant bullying of the local party which tried to bully the population.

Streicher's relation to the governmental structure was less congenial because he had an inborn distrust of the bureaucrat. Most Gauleiter shared this dislike, but most of the others became the nominal presidents of their provinces, if for no other reason than to have the state salary. Streicher could not tolerate the 18th-century, small-town atmosphere of Ansbach, nor the daily contact with the despised officials. He would "not let himself be squeezed into the limited confines of a bureaucrat".[96] He had less need of the salary, reportedly getting 5,000 marks a month as Gauleiter; his real income came as publisher of *Der Stuermer*, which had made him a millionaire.

Colonel Hofmann was made President on April 1, 1933. Although a convinced NS, Hofmann tried in vain to restrain Streicher and Obernitz in their acts of violence against the leftists and the Jews. A Landrat regarded Hofmann as much more concerned with upholding the state than the party; an example was his stopping the party's efforts to increase the required percentage of party members on town councils.[97] For this reason the party came to distrust and ignore him. Not a politician, and with an army sergeant personality, Hofmann assumed that orders would be obeyed; when they were not, he lacked the flexibility and diplomatic skills to win obliquely.

Streicher forced Hofmann out and took over "the political leadership of the government", but refused the permanent

[96] Landrat Dr. Heinz. [97] Heinz.

honor, choosing instead Dr. Hans Dippold, an obscure official who remained almost as obscure as President. The major apparent reason for his choice was that in 1927 as school Beamter, Dippold had handled a case for Streicher sympathetically (they had no other contact before 1933, Dippold testified). Streicher defended him as "absolutely honorable", with "the instincts of a born National Socialist", though not a member until 1933.[98] The police view of Dippold's abject dependence on Streicher showed through during the investigation of Streicher in 1939: "Dippold because of his personality was never in a position to in any way talk back to the lords of the Gauleitung or to oppose them. One cannot wonder therefore that by the opening of the Autobahn in February, 1938 he permitted himself to be called by Streicher "*Arschloch*" in front of a large group of important people".[99] Privately to his driver, Dippold had similar disregard for Streicher whom he thought "a complete fool". "It is a horror to have anything to do with him."[100] There was talk of firing Dippold in 1939; Seiler, the party official involved, convinced Streicher that in view of the strained relations with Wagner, both he and Frick would have refused.[101]

Dr. Hilger, another Landrat, thought Dippold's view of the Jews agreed with Streicher's, therefore, the latter trusted him in office. On occasion, Dippold could use this "trust" to protect a Landrat. His reports to the Bavarian government support Hilger's view that Dippold helped by passing on with emphasis their complaints about party excesses, and the party-caused problems with the church and foreign workers. After a standard sentence or so of highest praise for Der Fuehrer, Dippold's reports contain large batches of open criticism, with remarkable quotations of criticism from pastors left unarrested. (The exception is Dippold's praise for the anti-Jewish violence of November 1938.) Yet an open support of the Landraete against Streicher was unthinkable; on one occasion Streicher denounced the group to their faces;

[98] BSA—1735, p. 312.
[99] IMT, 1757PS, 227.
[100] Stark, SK—Dippold.
[101] Seiler, SK—Dippold.

several left the room, but Dippold did nothing.[102] The next closest thing to a Dippold action was his report of anti-NS criticism, with the vague suggestion that the critics be more effectively silenced.[103]

There are indications that Ansbach played only a nominal role in the governing process; no evidence has been discovered of a significant intervention, positive or negative. In his defense, Dippold reported the following opposition to the party: (1) The transfer of a rural school teacher for an affair with an SS man. Streicher's attitude was, why discipline her if she had a good German baby? (2) The reversal of a Liebel order forbidding a Jew a tailor's license. Streicher called Dippold to Nuremberg to scold him, but Dippold diverted any punishment from his officials. (3) Preventing his other Gauleiter, Waechtler from firing 21 of 23 city councilmen in Bayreuth.[104]

Intervention in local politics came either from the Gau, so long as Streicher was in power, or from the Gestapo with regional headquarters at Nuremberg. Both Hilger and Heinz agreed that Martin helped where he could to soften the blow. In one case in 1935-36, the Gestapo came to arrest a pastor. The people gathered in front of his house to protect him. When the Landrat protested, Martin kept his promise of no more such actions. Streicher rarely visited the rural areas, so that pressure depended primarily on the Kreisleiter. Wagner had little to do with local government; on one occasion he entered a meeting with Landraete, "struck his usual Mussolini pose, looked about the room, said angrily, 'These are supposed to be my Landraete, with only three in uniform', and left".[105]

The older Landraete were deep in the Beamten tradition, i.e., they were legal technicians. Their dealings with the many rural mayors under them were conducted pretty much as they had been and would continue to be—rather informally and about earthy rural problems. Landrat Heinz estimated that in 1933 only five or six of his 51 mayors were convinced

[102] Heinz.
[103] BRP, Franken, 6.8.36.
[104] SK, Hans Dippold, 7ff.
[105] Hilger.

NS. With the improved economic conditions, he guessed that the percentage might have reached a peak of 60 or 70%. Landrat Hilger estimated that at most 50% of his mayors were members. The fear of war brought a terribly low morale in 1938, which prompted Streicher to a flaming speech. Even the events of November 9, 1938, caused little enthusiasm. In Hilpolstein Kreis, there were only three Jews; a local party leader broke some of their windows, which prompted the legalistic Kreisleiter to express his regrets to Hilger the next morning and to fire the overly exuberant underling.[106]

The Killing of Strauss

A case of small-town violence occurred in Guenzenhausen, with a relatively large Jewish population, in early 1934. It seems to have had no counterpart in Franken, perhaps because it seriously embarrassed Streicher who had to explain it to the Bavarian government. The incident suggests the kind of terror that occurred particularly in small towns, the kind that was held in restraint until November 1938, and then transferred from Germany to the conquered territories.[107] Violence began in April and May 1933 with the breaking of windows. In June there was a mass demonstration of the SA against the Jews, which a policeman tried to restrain; the policeman was transferred. In August a peasant was attacked after leaving a tavern owned by a Jew named Strauss, "arrested", and led through the streets with two placards—"I am a scoundrel" and "I am a *Stahlhelm* leader and drink my beer at a Jew's". In January 1934 a group of 60 to 80 people gathered outside the tavern which the SA leader Baer closed for a time. In February more windows were broken and demonstrations occurred against an attorney who had represented a Jew. Also in February a mob of 200 SA demonstrated against a pastor in a neighboring village, chanting "The *Pfaff* [priest] must leave, the *Pfaff* must leave, Traitor

[106] Hilger.

[107] BSA—Bay. In. Min., Document 73708, "Anti-Juden Demonstration in Guenzenhausen".

to the People, Fat Belly, Jew-friend". After an hour's demonstration they tried to break in. In early March a night watchman who checked Jewish stores among others was beaten up.

The climax came on March 25th, when two SA leaders, Baer and Kaiser, coming home from an SA meeting saw a bicycle outside Strauss's tavern and were told that it belonged to a rural mayor inside. They entered the tavern. Baer had a grudge against the tavern anyway, because he had been thrown out of it a few years before. Kaiser hit the offending mayor and Baer knocked the glass from his hand as he tried to empty it.

The mayor left the tavern, but Baer returned several times to be sure that he had not come back. He asked for a Jewish man named Jacob Rosenfelder, who had also fled the bar. Baer hit Strauss's son who tried to flee but was taken prisoner again by Baer, who was armed with a pistol, dragged down the stairs and beaten again, then beaten by members of a mob in front of the house until unconscious, carried back into the house and revived with a bucket of water. When the parents tried to help, they were forced into the next room.

Baer then spoke to the mob, reminding them that "the Jews had killed the Lord God", that they were responsible for the two million dead in World War I and for the 400 dead and 10,000 injured in the Nazi NS rise to power. (The first is a Christian legend; the rest was invented by the NS.) He appealed to them to think of how many "innocent girls had been raped by Jews", with so many Jewish bastards resulting. Baer claimed that Strauss had spit at him, which all witnesses later denied. If the police were too cowardly to arrest such criminals, the SA were not. The SA report noted excited calls from the crowd demanding action; the official account reported no such denunciations of Strauss or demands for his arrest, that instead the crowd was opposed to any violence.

Baer ordered the SA to clear the streets. When they failed to do so, he reentered the house and arrested the family. The boy was still unconscious as he was carried to jail. There Baer hit Frau Strauss in the face when she protested that she had not done anything, then hit her again when she tried to hide behind the jail warden. Baer ordered everything in the house destroyed. Then 33 more Jews were arrested.

The mob also caught Rosenfelder who was beaten, then dragged up the steps by Baer and asked whether he was a coward, to which he answered "*Ja*". He was beaten again and sent home under SA guard. When the mob chanted anti-Jewish slogans outside his house and prepared to break in with an axe, Rosenfelder was found dead by hanging in a shed. The official report accepted it as a suicide, although his sister said that he had had no rope. The SA continued entering and "searching" Jewish homes through the night. Another Jew was found a "suicide victim", stabbed but with no knife near him.

The next morning the investigation began. The SA report blamed it on the Jews, "who were just as fresh as before", and on "certain lack of character among broad sections of the population" (those who were not anti-Semitic and dealt with the Jews as before). It was also the fault of the Landrat, who was not NS but a member of the old Nationalist party and therefore incompetent; if he were fired, there would be no more difficulties. The mayor said the solution was to close the Jewish shops.

Hofmann in Ansbach denounced the violence as surely not Hitler's intent; he had forbidden such "individual actions". It was contrary to the law forbidding assault and battery, a danger to Germany's foreign policy and contrary to the Roehm order of January 15 ordering the SA to help keep law and order. It was Hofmann's opinion that Baer ordered the attack because he wanted Strauss's bar for himself. Hofmann added that in the spring of 1933 the Fuehrer gave him the job of cleaning up the Franken SA, and Baer had already behaved badly toward him in public. He blamed the violence primarily on Baer who had no sense of proper behavior and order. Twenty-three people were brought to trial, mostly new members of the SA.

The further ramifications included the firing of Hofmann.

Baer was released from the SA and the party, probably in June. A report of the SA (July 15, 1934) states that Baer had entered the Strauss tavern and shot both father and son, killing the father, and said he would kill 20 more if the convicted SA men were not released. Streicher passed it off as the action of an ex-SA man for whom no one could be held responsible. The SA report came closer to the truth by emphasizing the hatred created by Streicher, Baer's age (22), and the possible belief that the violence they were doing was what the government secretly wanted.[108] Streicher, embarrassed because of his claim that no Jew was in danger in his Gau, denounced the action. Baer was given a long sentence but placed on probation and forbidden to return to the county; he reportedly died in a Russian prison camp.[109]

The Church in Nuremberg

The Protestant church in Nuremberg became in 1934-1935 a real center of opposition to the NS church policy by its support of Bishop Meiser and his opposition to Reich Bishop Mueller, despite the clearly anti-church stand of the feared Streicher. Although Meiser may have shared some of the hopes of other Protestants that NS power would mean a strong Germany free of anti-religion pressures, there is no doubt that he was disillusioned by 1934 and promptly became a daring foe of NS church policy. His two lieutenants in Nuremberg were pastors Schieder and Oscar Daumiller. The latter wrote of his contacts with his state from the time in 1933 he was sent to lead the "*Kirchenkampf*".[110] Daumiller first visited Liebel, Obernitz, and Martin; he said: "The only one with whom I could deal was Martin. Almost every third day I saw him to try to find out what was planned against us. I noticed very soon that he was actually on our side. He gave me names of pastors who were in particular danger". From Martin, Daumiller learned of planned German Christian

108 BSA—*Ibid.*, Guenzenhausen.

109 Kirsch.

110 Oscar Daumiller, *Gefuehrt im Schatten zweier Kriegen*, Munich, 1961.

disturbances; Martin returned an incriminating letter sent by an unwise deaconess. Daumiller said: "He told me that he had orders to arrest me. We came to the agreement that it would be better if he permitted me to remain free and through me maintained contact with the entire Protestant church. He told me that he would permit us a free hand in the churches, but he would have to intervene, if we appeared in public on the streets or squares to demonstrate".[111]

The crisis began when the local NS newspaper, *Tageszeitung* ran a headline on Sept. 14, 1934, stating: "Throw Bishop Meiser Out". The NS charged that he had been elected in January promising loyalty to the Third Reich, yet only three months later he had betrayed his promise by joining the *Bekenntnis* movement. He was therefore a traitor.[112] Three days later the competing *Kurier* (generally thought to have been made as critical of the NS as possible by Dr. Koetter, with Martin's protection) simply reprinted the church defense of Meiser, which should have convinced any nonbigot.[113]

In late 1934 the campaign against Meiser mounted in intensity. Daumiller reported that they had learned in October that Meiser was to be arrested when his train arrived in Rothenburg. Meiser was spirited from the train earlier by Augsburg friends and brought by car to the church where he spoke to thousands.[114] A demonstration was planned in Nuremberg for October 12. Light was streaming from the churches which were filled to the last corner. Thousands gathered on the Marktplatz and demanded that Meiser speak to them. According to the agreement with Martin, Daumiller asked them to return to their homes and not demonstrate.

The next day Martin invited the Protestant pastors to meet in his office. When Martin and Streicher came, they brought along four "German Christian" pastors. Daumiller told Streicher that if he wished to talk, these four would have to leave. Streicher complied. Then Daumiller asked Streicher whether he had made a comparison (as was done in *Der Stuermer*) between the Last Supper and "ritual murder".

[111] *Ibid.*, 64.
[112] NSA—DA/S 7 *Kirchenstreit.*
[113] *Ibid.*
[114] Daumiller, 66.

Streicher said that he had not nor did he approve. Martin said afterward that he had never seen anyone take Streicher's breath away in such a frontal attack. Streicher blamed Holz and said that the state would not intervene in church affairs because the state needed the church.[115]

The struggle was quickly won within the church organization in Nuremberg by the NS-opposed *Bekenntnis* group. When Hitler's Reich Bishop Mueller tried to speak in Nuremberg on March 25, 1935, Liebel had to report that he could not use the significant churches because Meiser controlled them. Schieder said there was only one church on the outskirts controlled by a non-*Bekenntnis*. Liebel said he could do nothing.[116] Schieder wrote Liebel that 268 of the 308 pastors in Nuremberg had replied that Mueller was unwelcome; only the minority, which was actually "church-hostile", favored Mueller.

Daumiller wrote of a Mueller attempt to speak in the Marktplatz. He went to Martin who agreed to help. He called Streicher and told him that the Marktplatz was so dedicated to party meetings by Hitler at the party conference that it would be improper for Mueller to use it. Streicher bought the argument.[117] Also in 1935 the party attempted to create an incident giving an excuse for the arrest of Meiser; intensive propaganda worked up popular emotion and a mob gathered outside the St. Egidien church. The hill was black with the angry and the curious. To be sure Meiser would be safe, Dr. Martin sent his own police limousine, which spirited Meiser out to safety.

In 1935 the Protestants requested a national church gathering in Nuremberg. Although Himmler and Heydrich were opposed, Martin promised to put the request through. His technique was to first get the backing of Kerrl, the "Minister for Church Affairs", who was not sympathetic to the meeting. While in Nuremberg Kerrl was taken to a charming cabaret and plied with champagne and introduced to a pretty dancer. While Kerrl was trying to converse with the dancer, Mar-

[115] *Ibid.* [116] NSA DA/S 7. [117] Daumiller, 72.

tin kept nagging about the church conference, until Kerrl became annoyed enough to say "Oh, go ahead and have your conference". Although Heydrich was incensed, Kerrl stood by his permission and the conference was held,[118] which brought unwelcome praise from pastors farther north about the tolerance of the Nuremberg police.

Police doctor Wegner reported that Martin told the police to ignore the forbidden "Bible hours" held outside the church, or the church's "theater evenings".[119] Schieder testified that such meetings were left undisturbed though banned in Augsburg and Munich.[120] Daumiller reported that frequently Gestapo men wanted to help the church. For example, a police car was deliberately driven in the wrong direction to avoid catching Meiser. Another high official, later executed by the French, had always helped; the prison Beamter, whom Daumiller asked whether he believed in God, had answered "yes" and wept when Daumiller said that he would have to stand before God and answer for what he was doing.[12]

In 1937 Martin, according to Wegner, heard of the arrest of the Eichstaett priest Kraus. He called Wegner and suggested that an old man always had some body defect and happily received Wegner's report two hours later that the man was "physically incapable of being arrested". He called Wegner again and noted that "his appetite had increased with the eating", and could Wegner issue a certificate that the old man was too ill to have been arrested when they arrested him —it worked.[122]

In Munich Wagner fumed at the liberties taken by or given to the Meiser group. On one occasion, to prevent a Protestant gathering in Nuremberg, he called Martin and ordered him to arrest all the incoming delegates from the train, an impossible task of identifying, much less arresting, so many people. Order ignored. In 1940 Wagner heard from a blond lady friend about a pastor who had expressed defeatist sentiments and sent the name to Martin with a large green crayoned order: "Off with his head". Martin simply sent the

118 Martin. 119 Wegner, 77. 120 SK, Martin, VII, II, 7.
121 Daumiller, 72-75. 122 Wegner, 73.

order to various superiors in Berlin requesting instructions. No one replied and the matter was forgotten.[123] Direct pressures against the church after 1938 took more the form of competition for youth, until the famous crucifix order of Wagner. Wagner reported that Martin tried to sabotage this infamous order by exaggerating the reports of disorder and sending out police agents as provocateurs of church resistance.[124] Drummer, of the Nuremberg Lutheran *Dekanat*, testified that no pastor or priest was arrested in Martin's area in all of the years he was in power.[125]

The Jews in Nuremberg

Nuremberg will forever be associated with the senseless and incredibly cruel persecution of the Jews. The Streicher work of hate, and the 1935 Nuremberg laws against the Jews, to honor Streicher, justify the infamy. Yet his was not the only anti-Semitic journal; and many party leaders were unhappy about *Der Stuermer* because of its pornographic tendencies, and because Streicher did not shrink from attacking the party powerful. As early as 1933 Streicher wrote Hess that Esser and Frank, in the Bavarian government, were trying to suppress the magazine.[126] An issue in 1934 had to be forbidden and Hitler reportedly screamed so loudly at Streicher that it could be heard two floors away.[127] Streicher again complained to Hess in 1935: "I know the Gauleiter who think they should get excited about *Der Stuermer*. These are the Gauleiter in whose realms the explanation about the Jewish question is in a bad state and where they could not in part for personal reasons have a particular interest to put the explanation of the Jewish question too much in the foreground."[128]

Streicher claimed then, as later at his Nuremberg trial, that

[123] Martin.
[124] Wegner, 79.
[125] SK, Martin, VII, II, 2.
[126] BDC Berlin Police File, Streicher to Hess, 12.10.33.
[127] Martin. So reported as police chief and confidant of journalists. A partial file of the infamous paper is in the Nuremberg Staatsarchiv.
[128] BDC, Berlin Police File. Streicher to Hess, 20.2.35.

Der Stuermer did not incite but instead inhibited violence against the Jews.[129] He testified that Bormann had tried to ban the paper in 1939,[130] and claimed it was banned by the HJ, SA, and SS, who had their own publications.[131] The circulation rose from 3,000 in 1932 to 600,000 in 1938, sinking to 150,000 during the war. Although the paper was not an official party organ, but Streicher's private paper, he was able to force copies in large numbers on the fearful or the ambitious; his defense in 1946 reported that many bundles were later found in the original wrappings.[132]

According to the Goering Commission report the significant writer for *Der Stuermer* was the Jewish merchant, Jonas Wolk who had an Aryan wife. Partly because Streicher liked Frau Wolk, he employed Wolk at a high salary under the name Fritz Brand. Streicher was frequently together with his assistant but refused to shake hands. Wolk wrote informed articles about his people until he fled the country in 1939 to Switzerland, supposedly later dying in a French prison.[133]

The Early Violence

Nuremberg, probably even more than the rest of Germany, was like a pressure cooker of the Jewish question; constant party harangues called "schooling", and vicious lies in hundreds of newspapers all created an intense hatred that demanded some expression. The lid popped off briefly in 1933 and was put back on with difficulty. The hatred then supposedly formed an outlet in more restrained "legal" outlets. It blew off again, mostly on command, in November 1938, with a persecution of the Jews, mild only in comparison to what awaited them when they were subsequently shipped east.

Persecution of the Jews in Nuremberg had horrible medieval precedents. The banishment of the Jews from the city had lasted from 1498 to 1813.[134] Jews reentered the city,

129 *Ibid.* 130 IMT, XII, 329. 131 IMT, XVIII, 210.
132 IMT, XVIIV, 204. 133 Martin.
134 Nuernberg Stadt Archiv, *Schicksal juedischer Mitbuerger in Nuernberg*, 1850-1945.

particularly after 1871, and become important in business and intellectual enterprises. Before Streicher's blatant hate poured over the city, they had been able to assimilate well into the city's population. That their pledge of loyalty to Epp in March 1933 was sincere is beyond doubt.[135] A spokesman, Blum, was reassured in 1933 when Streicher was not given a state position and Blum's major industrial clients continued to show their high regard.[136]

Beginning in March 1933, a few politically prominent Jews were arrested and sent to Dachau, where they were beaten, forced to eat their own feces and to drink their own urine. Nine were killed there in these early years, their bodies returned with bullet holes in the back.[137] A Nuremberg police officer on a visit to Dachau saw a guard order a Jewish prisoner to pick up something close to the fence and coldly shoot him "for attempting to escape".[138] The Jews in Nuremberg would experience private SA beatings or continued private friendship; but mostly they met with public apathy.

Public action was the nationwide boycott of Jewish stores for April 1, 1933. A thousand SA men in Nuremberg pasted up posters proclaiming the boycott. It accomplished relatively little because in the large city most people could anonymously patronize Jewish stores with relative impunity. From Berlin, Streicher was ordered to stop the boycotting.

An example of the kind of SA violence, held largely in check until 1938, was the outburst in July 1933. Obernitz's SA arrested 300 Jews, including elderly and highly respected citizens, herded them together on their sporting field and indulged in such sport as forcing them to tear out grass with their teeth. Similar fun was the driving of a non-Jewess through the streets with head shaven and a sign saying she had had relations with Jews. Protesting the SA action, Martin called Schachinger, who told Siebert.[139] The police could do nothing; the SA threatened to arrest them. Martin had got-

[135] Arndt Mueller, *Juden in Nürnberg*, manuscript Nuremberg Stadt Archiv, 245.

[136] *Ibid.*, 246. [137] *Ibid.*, 252. [138] Wurdak.

[139] GSA—MA, 105256.

ten Obernitz to promise to turn the Jews and confiscated materials over to the police. Obernitz admitted to Wagner that he had been ordered by the SA-SS to the action contrary to state orders; he obeyed orders gladly but often wondered which orders.[140] (By mid-June over 700 of Nuremberg's 8,266 Jews had left the city.[141])

The local party, acting on the assumed wishes of party superiors but contrary to the often reaffirmed law and desire of the central government, made life as uncomfortable as possible for the Jews, though major violence does not seem to have occurred until 1938. Injury to Jewish businesses was largely successful in the small towns, less so in Nuremberg. Dippold's report in 1934 considered the propaganda against Jewish stores as successful, yet in many areas problems existed because there was no replacement for the service the Jew had provided. He complained that the Jews showed how mean they were when they stopped delivery to towns that had put up placards saying Jews were unwelcome.[142] In September 1934, 300 to 400 SA demonstrated in front of the central Nuremberg synagogue, tacking copies of *Der Stuermer* on the door and trying to climb in. The Gau declared a Christmas boycott in 1934, contrary to the Economic Ministry orders.[143] Isolated efforts at a boycott in January 1935 were reported at the same time that Jewish war veterans announced: "I am German-born and I will die German", that they supported the German acquisition of the Saar, and that their loyalty to Germany remained their highest loyalty.[144]

Schacht seemed to have thwarted the new effort to attack the Jews in the economy when the sudden decision came for some anti-Jewish laws to be declared at the Party Convention. Until these laws, Schacht urged his Nuremberg banker friend, Kohn, to stay in Germany; then he urged Kohn to leave and save what he could.[145] The city government did what it could to cripple Jewish business: Blum described how Schacht had made sure that businessmen had the necessary identity card for leaving the city, but when he fell from power in 1937

140 *Ibid.*
141 Mueller, 257.
142 BRP, Franken, 6.4.34.
143 *Ibid.*
144 BRP—Franken, 9.2.35.
145 Mueller, 290.

Liebel refused to let Jews leave the city for business purposes, which meant the end of their businesses. Streicher put his cronies into the businesses the Jews were thus forced to sell.[146]

The law was used confusingly to arrest: (1) a teacher for having his class chant a U.S. Jew out of town, (2) a zealot for sending a letter demanding that Jewish stores be closed one day, (3) a Jew for "insulting the state", (4) a Jew for "fraud", and (5) a worker for breaking into a Jewish store.[147] Fifty-six arrests for "racial violation" were made in Nuremberg; the most famous case was Judge Rothaug's misuse of the law against the elderly Katzenberger.[148] By the end of 1937, 3,000 Jews were left in the city; 3,000, a high percentage, had emigrated. Streicher's brutality saved lives by frightening Nurembergers away before the worst came.

Some Who Helped

While the majority apparently either implemented or passively tolerated the emiseration of their fellow citizens, there were some who helped. One Jewish emigré noted the great bitterness among fellow refugees, but each could remember someone who proved his friendship. She compiled a list of 106 Nuremberg citizens who had helped, including some high officials.[149] Most help was private and secret, yet one brave statement early in the regime is worthy of note. The Reich government had ordered all "non-Aryans" out of state service, which meant out of the state church. In September 1933, 16 Nuremberg pastors publicly rejected the application of the "Aryan paragraph" to the churches, noting that neither Peter nor Paul could therewith qualify for church service, not to mention Jesus.[150]

Although prior to 1933 Martin had organized a club which included two Jews, he seems on occasion to have run with the anti-Semitic hounds, as in 1934 when he suggested to Munich that Jews be forbidden to collect money.[151] Yet there is much evidence that he helped privately, the best from the head of the Nuremberg Jewish community, Dr. Walter Ber-

[146] *Ibid.*, 263.
[147] BRP, Franken, 7.3.36.
[148] Mueller, 293.
[149] Frau Steuerwald from Chile, in Mueller, 250.
[150] Mueller, 252.
[151] Mueller, 283.

lin, who escaped to London. He testified in 1946 that his friendly contact with Martin had begun before 1933 and lasted until his departure. Martin always showed a great understanding for the problems of the persecuted Jews and had done everything possible to deflect party policy.[152] In March 1933 Martin heard of SA attacks and sent the police to protect Jews. On March 29th he sent the police to search a Dr. Berlin's house, but with orders to limit the search so that Berlin's wife and children did not realize the police were even there, a farce designed to have negative results and protect Berlin from further searches. In the same month Martin warned a series of other Jews of police searches. He got Jews released from arrest, observing to Dr. Berlin that he could protect them in 90% of the cases, but the pressures were too great in the rest. In 1935, when a pistol was found in the possession of a Jewess (a dangerous "offense"), Martin had his police certify falsely that the pistol was not subject to reporting. When the Gau was planning to seize a Jewish business, Martin warned them of the party plans. Of all Martin's promises to help, only one was not kept: to protect Jewish stores in 1936 (or 1937) during the party *Tag*.

After the evil night of November 9, 1938 Berlin's house was sacked and he was arrested, though not by the police. When Martin learned of it, he immediately got passes for the entire family to leave the country and Berlin's release. He urged Berlin to emigrate, that he might not be able to save him again. The police found the stolen jewelry and returned it. Martin gave what help he could to Jews who wanted to emigrate. More careful as the hate increased, Martin continued to receive Berlin in his office, but asked when possible that he come during the noon hour or late afternoons. Berlin after comparing notes with colleagues from other cities concluded that Gau Franken was the worst, but that the Nuremberg police were the best, protecting the Jews after the courts had stopped.[153]

[152] SK, Martin, VII, I, 1.
[153] *Ibid.*

The Beginning of the End—1938

A new wave of persecution was noticeable in Nuremberg early in 1938 and in the economic sphere. Dippold reported in March that there was joy in Franken that the Jews were leaving; a matter of pride for a county was to be "free of Jews".[154] To facilitate the buying of Jewish property at absurdly low prices, the Jews were ordered to report all of their property.[155] In June there was a wave of arrests of Jews.[156]

In August, Liebel and Streicher showed that Franken would lead again, by decreeing the demolition of the central synagogue on the specious grounds that its Byzantine architecture was offensive to the architectural picture of old Nuremberg. After Liebel and Streicher insulted the Jews lavishly, members of the crowd cheered to see the first blow struck to the synagogue. (Others report the crowd horror-struck; only a claque applauded.[157]) Liebel had promised that the structure would be removed before the party *Tag*, but he failed; it survived into November, requiring a special fund of 50,000 marks to finish the demolition.[158]

Dippold reported that a party member—Frisch—had helped the Jews remove the 500-pound stone that commemorated the burning of the synagogue 500 years before. Dippold added that Frisch, who had joined the party in 1937, was thrown out "for lack of character".[159] Frisch's son testified after the war that Martin kept his father out of a concentration camp by having him declared physically unable to be arrested, a diagnosis obviously exaggerated, and brought him home the same evening.[160] The stone was discovered in the spring of 1946 in the cellar of the police headquarters.[161] Wegner explained that Streicher had wanted the stone but Martin had the Gestapo hide it, first in the furnace room of police headquarters, then with the bombings, in the air raid

154 BRP, Franken, 9.3.38. 155 Mueller, 304.
156 *Schicksal*, 35. 157 Nadler.
158 *Geheim Sitzung Nuremberg*, 30.11.38.
159 BRP, Franken, 7.9.38. 160 SK, Martin, VII, I, 7.
161 Mueller, 303.

shelter; he had seen many policemen, even Martin, angry because they had stumbled over it in the dark.[162]

As another warm-up for the violence of November, during the night of October 17 in Leutershausen, near Ansbach, the synagogue was destroyed and Jews mishandled.[163] Dippold reported "traitorous" Jews were sad because of the Munich agreement; a Nuremberg Jew was sentenced to 18 months imprisonment for having expressed doubts about German justice; a Jewish factory-owner was arrested and his factory turned over to the DAF; 140 Jews had left that month; 443 Jews from Poland had been dumped on the Polish border by order of Himmler.[164]

The Night of Terror

Although Streicher was the No. 1 anti-Semite in Germany, the oddity of the "*Kristallnacht*" on November 9, 1938 is that he knew almost nothing of the action and took no part in it. The violence seems to have been planned and organized the same day in Munich by Goebbels, together with Lutze and his SA. Obernitz received the late-evening order from Munich and went to the sleeping Streicher and told him. "Streicher without emotion replied, 'If Goebbels wants it, then it should be all right with me', rolled over and went back to sleep." While Streicher slept, men whom he had taught to hate all things Jewish behaved like madmen, destroying Jewish property with maniacal zeal and terrorizing families of young and old who could scarcely believe the hate hysteria of supposedly civilized men, leaders of the community, even judges. Synagogues were set afire, in one case with a woman's voice screaming "Throw the Jewish pack into the fire". The downtown streets were filled with broken glass from store windows.[165] Jews were beaten without reason; during that night nine Jews were killed.[166]

The police acted as though nothing were happening. Kreisleiter Zimmermann, apparently not previously informed of

[162] Wegner, 92.
[163] *Schicksal*, 35.
[164] BRP, Franken, 7.11.38.
[165] *Schicksal*, 61-65.
[166] Mueller, 305.

the SA action, recalled that the police would not open their doors or answer the phone.[167] Martin returned from Munich between two and three in the morning and hesitated, not knowing whether Hitler personally had ordered the action. The police reaction then was to arrest many male Jews for their protection. When the violence had subsided they were sent home, or wherever they wished to be taken, in Martin's own limousine and police cars. On Liebel's order city hospitals were closed to the injured Jews, although he was quoted as saying the violence was a "scandal."[168] The police hospital was the only non-Jewish hospital that accepted the injured.

Martin's police reported the following results: 70 stores, including one Aryan store, destroyed, 256 dwellings damaged; this nearly all in Nuremberg and Fuerth, little damage in the rest of Franken. There had been some plunder, one looter arrested by the police was given a 21-month sentence. An SS man was arrested for robbery of the Jewish mother of the Swedish consul and the home of the attorney Berlin. The Gauleitung returned 46,000 marks plus property valued at 30,000 marks.[169]

The public's morning-after reaction to the partial ruins of their old city is usually reported as negative, an impression borne out by Streicher's telling the people that they should not have so much sympathy with the Jews.[170] Martin was quoted as saying that he was ashamed to go out on the streets or to belong to a people who could do such things.[171] A police official was appointed to handle all Jewish complaints concerning the night of November 9, with strict instructions to follow the law, to help find the missing Jews, and to return stolen property. He was also to help Jews leave the city by falsifying their police record if necessary.[172] A more public reaction was the pastor's denunciation of the action in the central Lorenz church, followed by the marching to the front of the church by the entire staff to recite in unison the Ten Commandments.[173]

167 SK, Martin, II, 144.
168 Fries.
169 CGD, T 81, R 57, RO275.
170 IMT, XII, 327.
171 Engel, SK, Martin, II, 144.
172 Steigleder, SK, Martin, VII, 95.
173 Mueller, 313.

The Aryanization

Streicher's anti-Semitism led to the attack on Jewish stores which in Nuremberg led to "the Aryanization", i.e., the stealing of the remaining property, which in turn led to the fall of Streicher. To the party, November 9 meant that the long awaited chance to exploit the helpless Jews had arrived. The Gauleitung had already been after Jewish businesses; Holz approached Streicher and suggested that they remedy the housing shortage by taking away the Jewish houses and putting the Jews in internment camps. Streicher rejected this idea as impossible to implement. Holz had a second proposal, that since it was unthinkable that the Jews own houses and land, their houses, land and remaining businesses be taken from them, to which Streicher answered, "If you think you can, go ahead", explaining later that he hoped to use the proceeds for a new Gau school. Holz began the infamous action the same afternoon. Streicher claimed to have taken no further interest.

Thus offhandedly began the operation that ruined the Gauleitung. The technique was in the best gangster tradition. Jews with property were called to the DAF headquarters where they were humiliated and intimidated into surrendering their property at one tenth of its value or less.[175] All but one, a foreign Jewess, agreed to do so. By November 14 the property of "The Israelite Community", including a synagogue worth much more than 100,000 marks, was sold for 100 marks. The same day, a document of sale of property worth more than 20,000 marks was to be registered with its sale price—180 marks. The official report of the buying orgy listed 569 pieces of land and buildings sold in less than a month. The difference in its real value and the sale value was 21,000,000 marks.[176] Holz, defending the cheating to a NS court, claimed that the Jews had gotten the property cheaply during the inflation, but the police promptly showed the

[174] IMT, Document 1757PS, 68.

[175] CGD, T 81, R 57, FO275; IZG NG 358; IMT Document 1757PS.

[176] IMT, 1757PS, 94.

falsity of the claim. The national party broke Streicher out of greed of his ill-gotten gains, but the Jews remained impoverished, the money from the sales in inaccessible bank accounts, the party faithful quarreling over the spoils.

The only hope was to escape, which Martin helped; but with their lack of property and reluctance to leave, few Jews escaped. A Jewish offer to arrange a mass emigration with the Jewish community to raise enough to pay for all its members, got insufficient support.[177] Condemned to stay, the Jews experienced an increasingly vicious discrimination, from which some actually hoped to escape via the evacuation to the east. By September 1939 they were subject to an eight p.m. curfew and severely limited as to where they could buy. They were forced to turn in radios and telephones and forbidden to read newspapers. In 1941 they were subject to forced labor and forced to wear "the Jewish star" which led to a competition among denunciators which the Gestapo largely ignored.[178] In 1942 the restrictions spread. The Jews were forbidden use of public transportation, possession of pets, forced to turn in any extra clothing; they lost ration cards for meat, fish, fowl, fruit, eggs, milk, and canned food.

The Evacuation

By November 29, 1941 the tragic evacuation of the Jews from Nuremberg had begun, ostensibly to new settlements in the east, but actually to mass extermination. The initiative came from Berlin; Streicher was out of power, as was Holz. Zimmermann testified that he knew of the action only by the accident that from his window he saw the Jews being loaded on trucks. The police were assigned the task of organizing the first shipment. Martin let the Jewish community choose who should go and arranged for the use of regular passenger trains instead of the cattle cars used later. Yet the misery of the departure could be exceeded only by the misery of the arrival. Later shipments were organized completely from Berlin.

[177] Mueller, 330. [178] *Ibid.*, 354.

The total horror of the "final solution" might be better comprehended if one uses the local statistics of evacuations published conscientiously by the postwar Nuremberg government.[179]

Nov. 29, 1941	to: Riga	512	of which	17 survived
March 25, 1942	to: Lublin	426	of which	0 survived
April 23, 1942	to: Lublin	23	of which	0 survived
Sept. 10, 1942	to: Theresienstadt	533	of which	26 survived
June 18, 1943	to: Theresienstadt	14	of which	4 survived
June 18, 1943	to: Auschwitz	16	of which	0 survived
Jan. 17, 1944	to: Theresienstadt	10	of which	5 survived

Of only minor consolation was the sabotage of the order that all half-Jews be taken for forced labor in mines. Martin prepared an inaccurate list and then removed the names of professional men, professors, doctors, dentists, and their wives from the list.[180] This was comparable to the list found by the new commander of the Nuremberg Gestapo, with the name of all Jewesses in "mixed marriages" whom Martin wished to be informed if they were in danger.[181]

The last order—to send all Jews living in mixed marriages to Theresienstadt—was totally sabotaged. The Gestapo's man in charge of the Jewish department hid the list, possibly on Martin's orders.[182] Two Jews tried to avoid evacuation by hiding, and one succeeded. A certain kind of revenge was achieved with the Allied bombing of Nuremberg, which flattened nearly every building in the "old city" near the "offending" synagogue.

The Plot to Oust Streicher

Of the three local seats of power—party, city, and police—Liebel and Martin were forced into an uneasy coalition to halt the Frankish Nero. The means were devious, not always pleasant, but easing Streicher from power not only meant their own power and likely survival, but the greater security of the entire population.

[179] *Ibid.*, 72.
[180] Wegner, 102.
[181] SK, Martin, VII, I, 14.
[182] Mueller, 378; Wegner, 102.

Liebel's Role

As a loyal NS with beliefs comparable to Streicher's, Liebel's part in the ouster arose from his anger at Streicher's intervention in his city business, possibly his mockery of Liebel's private life of family virtue, and Liebel's ambition to become Gauleiter or more. The official record hints of the struggle only late in the game, Liebel having given Streicher a house acquired from a Jew in February 1938. In April 1937 Liebel strongly protested a Streicher action against a member of the business community, a colleague of Liebel's.[183] In January 1939 Liebel declared a kind of independence from the Gauleitung in his personnel policy.[184] In April, two of his top officials without party service credits were rehired. The first admittance of the fight was only after Streicher had lost; on March 20, 1940 Liebel begged the city council to trust him, and gave this view of the recent past: "The conditions in Nuremberg from the political point of view had become in the last years very unhappy and have had a most unfavorable effect on the operations of the city administration. These conditions became more difficult from month to month, week to week. A man whom I was forced to dismiss and to forbid even entering the city hall was made but a few hours later a bureau chief in the Gauleitung. . . . In the last half-year I was risking not only my position and my honor but also my head. . . ."[185]

Two months before, Streicher was much more explicit in his report on his fight against the "disloyal" Liebel.[186] Streicher argued that Liebel had been rotten from the beginning, when he had deserted the party upon Hitler's arrest and started his own party. When Streicher returned from prison, Liebel had attacked him and followed Ludendorff instead. He had rejoined the party in November 1925, but had quit again when his intuition told him the party would not climb as fast as his ambition. He left again in March 1926, despite

183 NSA—DA/S P13.
184 NSA—*Geheime Sitzung Stadtrat*, 25.1.39.
185 NSA—*Geheime Sitzung Stadtrat*, 20.3.40.
186 BDC Willy Liebel, Streicher's *Denkschrift*, January 1940.

a "brilliant" Hitler speech, which had "left him cold". Only with the fall of Ludendorff did Liebel once again join the NS—in October 1928—demanding that he be made a party candidate immediately. In 1929 Liebel had tried to get Holz's cooperation to dump Streicher.

His disloyalty, Streicher believed, was further shown in 1934 in Liebel's collaboration with Roehm, when Liebel invited Roehm in May to be his guest during the party convention. That Liebel knew of the plot was "evidenced" by a remark of his wife to a party man: "Remain loyal to my husband. In a few days the government will no longer exist". Frau Liebel had also criticized Hitler's action against Roehm; Liebel was not seen for days thereafter.

That Liebel always planned to revolt against Streicher when the right moment arrived was proved to Streicher by such things as his constantly referring to his support in Berlin, that Hitler regarded him as "the best mayor in Germany", the hundreds of postcards sent out with Liebel escorting Hitler about the Nuremberg zoo, or the many pictures of Hitler holding the Liebel baby. Wagner had warned Streicher on Jan. 6, 1937 of the danger: "I cannot stand to see Liebel's methods, which no Jew could exceed, and I beg you to stop him".

The "Stock affair" in 1935 showed this perfidy: an old party man and anti-Semite, trusted by Streicher, had been fired in the presence of three "Weimar" Beamten; Streicher had forced Liebel to take Stock back, but he was treated as an alien. Without cause in August 1939, Stock was fired again; Liebel demanded back a book and even a movie ticket given him. He had charged Stock with tattling on the mayor to Streicher and having criticized Liebel in the presence of other officials. "We aren't slaves," Streicher fumed, "why should not he be permitted to criticize a superior?"[187] A party court had shown that Stock's only crime was loyalty to Streicher.

In August 1939 Liebel had also refused the resignation of Obernitz as a councilman with an insolent letter making it

[187] *Ibid.*, Beilage 7.

clear that the mayor and not the Gauleiter decided who could resign from the city council. To a Gauleitung protest, Liebel had answered that he was not about to let Streicher lecture him, an old NS, on the meaning of the law on local government. "It has the signature of Hess and Hitler and should make impossible the interference of party subordinates. . . . The law was quite definite on what the party can and cannot do. . . . The mayor has the exclusive responsibility for the operation of the administration." Liebel claimed that not he but Streicher had damaged the image of the party and state. In October 1939 Liebel had been the only mayor not to co-operate with the party, by refusing to give the party the names of officials transferred to Poland, thus making it impossible for the party to issue the necessary political evaluations.

The climax came in 1940 with the shameful treatment of the Streicher confidant Fritz Fink, the only old party member among Liebel's top 12 officials. Fink was called to Liebel's office on March 13 and scolded for his closeness to Streicher. Liebel told Fink that he had informed Hitler and Wagner of the shameful happenings in the party meetings. "The Gauleiter in these meetings had lied shamelessly and slandered me in the foulest manner. He had dragged my entire work in the dirt." Liebel had then screamed, "When the Fuehrer drops him, then I'll destroy him!"[188] Fink, caught between his two bosses, stood on his loyalty to both party and state, but this last radical in a top position was fired by Liebel by the end of the year; so departed the last Gauleitung agent.

These attacks came after Streicher's position was already badly shaken, mostly from Martin's police, but Liebel's party prestige and contacts in Berlin covered his flanks.

Police versus Party

Martin's cooperation with Streicher, for whatever reason of saving himself and the city from "the fool", became increasingly a disguise for a remarkable effort to drive Streicher

[188] *Ibid.*, Beilage 10.

from the city. Although Streicher became more corrupted by his power, it was the greed of underlings, particularly Koenig, which widened the gap. By 1937 Koenig was using his influence to force the sale of a brickworks; he then forced its resale when he proved incompetent to operate it. Such was the occasion for Martin's remark that year that he feared that the radical, not the moderate NS, course would win.[189]

With his police and allied Gestapo working behind a veil of secrecy, Martin gathered material for the ouster of Streicher and gang. As early as 1934 he gave the assignment to Heigl to compile material for the eventual ouster.[190] In January 1934 the SPD leader, post-1945 Nuremberg's second mayor, Lossman, was visited at Dachau by Streicher who swore that Lossman would never leave Dachau alive. Lossman was out four weeks later, after Martin got Epp to work on it. (A second arrest of Lossman in August 1944 was also reversed by Martin.[191]) A police official was assigned in 1935 the task of determining how the police could stop *Der Stuermer*.[192]

The police kept a special "black list" of party member delinquencies, and the resulting arrests of Streicher's men are remarkable: (1) in 1934, 15 SS men from Dachau, (2) in 1935, arrests for embezzlement of NSV and WHW officials with sentences up to 10 years, (3) in 1936, more SS men, from Muggendorf, (4) in 1937, two mayors, (5) in 1938, another mayor and a rural party leader, (6) in 1939, a Kreisleiter for child-murder, (7) a local party leader for a swindle, (8) also in 1939, nearly the entire Gauleitung was arrested for theft in the "Aryanization" process, (9) in 1940, the arrest of Deeg, Streicher's most profitable anti-Semitic writer, (10) another Streicher collaborator for drunken-driving manslaughter, (11) another mayor for rape.[193]

The surveillance of Streicher approximated that of an enemy at war. The police guard observed his every coming and

[189] Pastor Schoenweiss, SK, Martin, VII, II, 9.
[190] Heigl, SK, Martin, VII, XIII, 121.
[191] Lossman, SK, Martin, VII, 94.
[192] Korn, *ibid.*, VII, X, 5.
[193] Greiner, SK, Martin, VII, XIII, 102.

going and reported them to the police chief. Cameras recorded his movements; a microphone built into his desk taped his conversations, including some damaging comments about Goering and doubts about his fatherhood of a child; during the height of the crisis, Martin had Himmler's permission to tap Streicher's phone. The temporary ban on *Der Stuermer* in August 1938 led Streicher to tell Fink that one must accumulate capital since one did not know what would happen next.[194]

The immediate target was Koenig, the most aggressive and suspicious of the gang. The party version of the conflict placed the emphasis on the alleged rivalry between the mistress of Koenig, Fraeulein B., and a friend of Martin, Frau G., both at the Nuremberg Theater and sharing the same dressing room.[195] Fraeulein B.'s career was furthered by Koenig, and the party accused Martin of wishing to help the career of Frau G. In early 1937 Fraeulein B. became pregnant from Koenig and feared the scandal would force her from the stage; she soon received anonymous notes telling her that her condition was known. In early May, Fraeulein B. obtained the services of a Dr. Simon, an abortionist known to the police. She promptly received another note, threatening prison for the abortion. Continuing on the stage, she received pictures of herself with the inscriptions, "the abortionist, E.B." and "before or after the abortion?"

The letters were traced, the party report continued, to the office of Kiessel's secretary. After this the party and Martin accounts agree. "For the *Reichsparteitag* in 1938 all of the leading persons of the party and the state received anonymous abusive lampoons", on the one side concerning Koenig's private affairs, titled "The Saint and the Fool"; the face of the fool was Koenig's. On the other side were the sins of Streicher. "The list of the addresses to which the abusive cards were sent was available in only two places—the organizational headquarters of the *Parteitag* and at police headquar-

194 IMT, 1757 PS, 139.
195 BDC Martin File, Partei Kanzlei Korrespondenz.

ters." Dr. Martin was given the job of finding out who had sent them, but reported no success.

Dr. Martin indeed sent the cards to dislodge Koenig just as he sent the hundreds of similar denunciations of Streicher's gang to Nuremberg stores.[196] The typewriter had been bought in Berlin, and was later destroyed by driving over it and then throwing it into the canal.[197] The scandal now known to every one of importance in the country did not unseat Streicher, but it did lead to the death of Koenig during the "Aryanization" scandal. Since Streicher had known of the abortion and since abortion was one of the crimes frowned on by Hitler, Streicher sent a pistol from the theater to Koenig in early February 1939, with a note telling him to kill himself; Koenig obeyed immediately. Friends of Koenig blamed it on Martin and Kiessel, quoting him to the effect that these two were "the worst scoundrels in Franken". Martin attended the massive state funeral for Koenig, but because of a threatening letter kept his right hand on a pistol in his pocket throughout the ceremony.[198]

Sometime in early 1939 Streicher became convinced that it was Martin who had plagued Koenig for two years, a conviction shared by SS commander Schmauser and SA Obernitz.[199] Streicher concluded the indictment by stating that neither Martin nor Kiessel had any belief in the party. "Both share in the life of the party only insofar as they are forced to by their offices . . . the feeling for comradeship and the feeling for the community of the movement is completely lacking."[200] In 1938 Heydrich, whose SD agents had Martin and Kiessel under surveillance, sent a report to Himmler suggesting that the two were homosexuals, to which Himmler replied: "Nonsense".[201]

November 9th, the action against the Jews gave the opportunity and the reason for removing Streicher. When the

196 Marchot, SK, Martin, VII, X, 7.
197 Martin.
198 Wegner, 138.
199 BDC Martin, *Partei Korrespondenz.*
200 *Ibid.*
201 Schallermaier, SK, Martin, VII, XI, 13.

Jewish community reported the terror of the Aryanization to Martin, he forwarded the report to Berlin, but received no answer. Himmler, who regarded Martin as a balance against Streicher, had repeatedly promised Martin full backing whenever Martin tried to resign. The question, however, was what would Himmler do once Martin had been beaten or killed. Martin first went to Himmler's office but was informed that Himmler was away. He caught him in the lunchroom and got his approval to see Guertner. Guertner was shocked by the latest horror but could not believe its extent. He requested Martin to bring the evidence. This presented a problem, as the police were forbidden by Streicher from even entering the DAF building where the records were kept. Martin arranged to have the Gestapo seize a bundle of incriminating documents during the night. These he took to Guertner, then, through his contact, Bodenschatz, to Goering, whom he got in the mood by telling him of the malicious jokes Streicher told about "father Goering." Goering was less incensed at the maltreatment of Jews than at the fact that his authority had been challenged, that the Gau was profiting instead of the Reich. His orders to desist had been disobeyed by the Gau, which instead hastened to push through the registration of the expropriated properties, a disobedience that angered Goering more. After Martin obtained support from the greedy party treasurer, Schwarz, and even Hess, he got Goering to appoint a commission, Goering gleefully rubbing his fat hands at the idea.

Chaired by the SD police Beamter Meisinger, and with officials from the Finance and Economic Ministries, the commission accumulated evidence, mostly from Martin's file. Its case was much bolstered by the fearful statements of a cast-off Streicher mistress whom Streicher had had arrested, thinking her involved in the plot. Martin transferred her to the police hospital where she talked compulsively about Streicher's dealings.[202] For example, Streicher had had the local NS newspaper give her a salary, though her services were to Streicher. For these her father was given a job at the paper and a car.

[202] Wegner, 136.

Another relative was given a car. Fink had been ordered to build a villa and to reserve one room for the trysts. The most famous incident involving the mistress was Streicher's order that all of his associates donate their wedding rings, which were melted down to make a jewel box for his mistress; Dippold found the courage to demand his ring back.

The commission uncovered so many illegal actions centering on the acquisition of Jewish property going back for two years that nearly all of the gang, particularly Holz, should have been given long prison sentences. For example, anyone wishing to buy Jewish firms cheaply was forced to give a voluntary contribution to the party, or more precisely, to Koenig.[203] Not only did Streicher profit by shares purchased at 5% of true value, but he got rid of an estate he had mismanaged into debt, by permitting the sale of a Jewish firm only if the buyer paid him a good price, sight unseen, for this estate. He ordered councilman Fink to lie under oath, to say that the stock purchases had been for his newspaper, by flooding him with threats such as "I'll shoot you down like a dog."[204] The hapless Fink, damned if he lied and damned if he did not, was further told in April that "someday the police would come for Streicher, but when he returned he would shoot all of the traitors."[205] The list of persons incriminated in no uncertain terms by the commission was the honor role of the party; only Zimmermann was uninvolved. The lesser men were fired or arrested. Streicher, who placed the blame on Holz, was left untouched, and even Holz remained for the time in full power.

Martin, who had tried to remain publicly uninvolved, received a letter in March threatening to kill him and Liebel if anything should happen to Holz.[206] He appealed to the party's top judge, Buch, who was indifferent. He sent two volumes of crimes to Frick, who listened patiently for 45 minutes to the record of crime but could only say, "Ja, Ja, Herr Martin, you have a difficult job in Franken, but stick it out."[207] Mar-

[203] IMT, 1757PS, 141ff.
[204] *Ibid.*, 205.
[205] *Ibid.*, 154.
[206] BSA—1744, signature, "J.H."
[207] Martin, SK, Martin, II, 47.

tin sent a copy to Epp, who was disgusted but helpless, and to Wagner, asking what he planned to do; the answer was, "Nothing".[208]

In June Streicher sent a report of the "disloyal" conduct of Martin and Liebel to Lammers, who the same day gave it to Hitler.[209] That Streicher was forced to a written report and had to go through Lammers supports Streicher's later claim that he had very little contact with Hitler; it enraged Streicher to hear Liebel brag that even when Hitler came to Nuremberg he saw Liebel and did not even inquire about Streicher. Streicher testified that it was very difficult to make friends with Hitler; to approach him "some manly deed" was necessary. (Streicher had almost no contact with Himmler; he never knew Heydrich or Eichmann.)[210]

A new scandal removed Holz from the scene. In August 1939 Holz took a mistress to Italy. There, in a chance meeting with an Italian fascist who knew Nuremberg, Holz introduced her as his wife and the next day came the glad tidings of the visit of the important Holz and wife in the newspapers. There were repercussions, first that Streicher had been amused by Holz's report from Italy, then that he was angry. "Unfortunately the affair is already widely known. 'Good friends' [Liebel and Martin] took care of its widest circulation."[211] It became more than a moral issue when the Nuremberg police noted that he had given his companion foreign exchange, contrary to the law.[212] The matter was taken to the highest party court. To avoid further trouble, Holz enlisted in the army, but even there the police were worrisome. Streicher wrote to Private Karl Holz: "I learned that certain people (you know who they are) have the intention of tightening the rope. You supposedly got a meal at the Grand Hotel without ration coupons. G. thinks you should give the coupons to the Grand Hotel immediately, so that they won't have the chance to hurt you."[213]

208 Martin. 209 BDC Holz, 9.6.39, to Streicher.
210 IMT, XII, 313, 332.
211 BDC Holz, File, *Partei Korrespondenz*, Seiler, 10.8.39.
212 *Ibid.*, Holz report, 31.10.39.
213 BDC Holz, *Partei Korrespondenz*, 21.11.39.

The crisis reached a climax in the winter of 1939-40. Liebel said Martin and he had agreed to shoot Streicher if necessary as defense against his usual methods. They planned to arrange such an act of "defense" unless Streicher was soon removed.[214] Holz heard of a pre-1933 letter of Martin to the Jew Kohn to form a club; Holz demanded it to destroy Martin, but witness Stauder had burned it. With Liebel's connections to Berlin giving added weight, Martin finally got some definite action. Streicher had recently made some unguarded statements which could be construed as betraying military secrets. On February 13, 1940 Streicher's "hearing" began, with six Gauleiters, his peers, three of whom were chosen by him.

There were but three witnesses, Liebel, Martin and Meisinger, each with instructions from Hitler that any lie would be their deaths.[215] Martin testified that Streicher was so abusive that Martin had drawn a pistol and said, "One more insult and I'll shoot".[216] The court gave Streicher no punishment, simply the evaluation that he was "unfit for leadership". He was banished from Nuremberg for five years, remaining Gauleiter in name only. At first he returned briefly to the city, but Martin's complaints got the banishment tightly enforced. Streicher remained on a country estate and received very few visitors.

Himmler, whose desire to be free of Streicher made him a benevolent but cautious supporter of Martin, did not jump into the matter until the decision was made. Heydrich worried about Martin's role; he made an effort to get Martin out of Nuremberg, to have him made president of a remote province.[217] With Streicher settled, Himmler wrote Martin, referring to party complaints about a lack of support from "state officials". He reminded Martin that the rule was, if a Gauleitung wished action there was to be action unless there were conflicting state-police needs. If a lower party authority made a request, it was to be refused unless there were state-police

214 Stauder in Martin, SK, I, 4.10.47.

215 SK, Martin, II, 47.

216 *Ibid.*

217 Martin, SK, Martin, II, 92.

needs which made it advisable.[218] There was the added note that Himmler was to be informed of any action *before* it was taken. Himmler orders were rare; one was to place a wreath on his grandmother's grave, the other to wipe out the Stauffenbergs.

Post-Streicher

With nearly all of Streicher's group driven out, life became much quieter. For a time the three powers—Martin, Liebel, and acting Gauleiter Zimmermann—cooperated, but it was easier for each to rule his own realm, with the party no longer able to intervene in city hall or the police. Zimmermann's only action noted at his postwar trial was his inquiry concerning the euthanasia program of which he had gotten reports that relatives had received identical notes on the death of different patients. Bormann answered curtly that the commission was authorized; an effort was made to make the letters different, but by chance similar letters had reached the same neighborhood; it was obvious that the church would oppose the action, but all good NS must support it.[219] Zimmermann was no competitor for Liebel and Martin; he left for the army in January 1942.

The ambitious Liebel found wartime life in Nuremberg a bit provincial. The city lost the spotlight as the party Tag was cancelled, even that of 1939, despite elaborate preparations up to the very outbreak of the war. He tried in 1940 to gobble up the neighboring city of Fuerth, the traditional rival of Nuremberg, but Hitler turned it down for the duration of the war.[220] In April 1942 his friend Speer called him to Berlin and he had the glory of opening an exhibition in Madrid. He returned to Nuremberg in August after the first air raid on the city, although he remained a "special agent" for Speer's munition ministry. He seemed earlier to have wanted the job of Gauleiter, yet Bormann wrote in August 1943 that Speer thought him more important in his present job and that Lie-

218 BSA—1615, 29.3.40.

219 SK, Zimmermann, III.

220 BA—R43II/575, 19.3.40.

bel was not up to handling the job, "which had already broken two men".[221]

Martin tried to get a Gauleiter as ally against Liebel. Through SS contacts, he attempted to bring in Gauleiter Forster from Danzig, a former employee of his wife's family. He wrote to Hildebrandt on Jan. 19, 1942 that it would be a mistake to have another temporary appointment; this would likely mean Liebel, the worst solution; would Hildebrandt see Bormann or Himmler?[222] Another letter in January emphasized the need for a strong personality to bring some balance of power "to reduce the arrogance, megalomania and bumptiousness to a tolerable level".[223] He wrote Hildebrandt again in March for Forster, who had indicated he would be "grateful for Martin's advice".[224] Bormann saw that Forster would have supported Martin against Liebel.[225] Holz was made acting Gauleiter in April; Martin observed that since it was Hitler's own decision, he would not interfere. Martin had had a talk with Holz and things were going smoothly.[226] Liebel had shown his disappointment by sending no one to the ceremony, and had quickly announced his departure for Speer's office.

Holz, who had left the Gau under several clouds of scandal, had begun his army career insubordinate enough to need an army trial; yet he behaved so bravely on the Russian front that his sins, civilian and military, were forgotten. When he returned, a preoccupation with women and drinking made him less difficult for Martin to handle. His method of operation owed much to his mentor, Streicher, and shows the NS mentality.[227] One issue was Sandreuter, a feared member of the old Streicher crowd, still a member of the Fuerth city

[221] Bormann memo, in BDC Liebel, 19.8.43.
[222] BDC Martin, SS File, 2193.
[223] *Ibid.*
[224] *Ibid.*, Hildebrandt; Wolff IZG—MA 328.
[225] BA, R43II/575, Bormann, 19.3.40.
[226] Martin-Hildebrandt, BDC, SS File, 2193, 29.4.42; IZG, MA 328, Wolff, 8.4.42.
[227] Martin report to Wolff, 26.5.42, CGD, T 175, R 406, F 8975-9028.

council, and, like Holz, deeply involved in the Aryanization scandal. The mayor, Dr. Haeupler, was pressured by Epp's assistants, Hofmann and Schachinger, to fire Sandreuter and bring him to trial; Zimmermann told Haeupler that Sandreuter was impossible. Zimmermann thought him a Jew; Liebel ordered his officials never to deal with Sandreuter.

Holz called Haeupler to the Gauhaus, where he adhered to the custom of having someone else in the room as a half-threat, but refused Haeupler the usual handshake. Holz told Haeupler that he had behaved not like a NS but like a jurist. Holz became angrier when Haeupler passed on the Dippold suggestion that the matter be settled by Sandreuter's permanent transfer to the east. Holz observed bitterly that this showed what ice-cold people jurists were. Haeupler, to Dippold's defense, said that the suggestion was made only to help Sandreuter keep his honor. Holz began to scream that Haeupler had no right to correct a Gauleiter; that he had passed on the case without consulting the Gauleitung proved that Haeupler was no NS and that he had no heart, that he did not care about the misery he had caused Sandreuter for the last two years which had caused his hair to turn gray; Sandreuter was an old party member, but he, Haeupler, knew only paragraphs and thought like a formal jurist. Holz was further angered: "That you did not stand up to Liebel, when he would not recognize a member of the Fuerth city council, shows what a weak mayor you are". Holz then turned to his cronies and observed, "Liebel had used every opportunity to act like the Gauleiter and to brag about his close connections to the Fuehrer". Back to the hapless Haeupler: "there he sits, the ice-cold jurist, with no interest in National socialism". Haeupler said that he had not come to be insulted, and left.

Sandreuter came to try to smooth things over, noting that with Holz one had to let him rant and rave for a time but a reconciliation would come in time, that Haeupler could get another interview if he wrote that he had not meant to insult Holz. At the second interview, Haeupler observed several of Holz's staff taking notes, and again no one offered a handshake. He made the necessary apology, but Holz refused to accept it and insulted Haeupler again as lacking in any discipline and not being an NS. Haeupler left again. The incident suggests how the party exerted its pressure on good members put into state positions.

In another celebrated case, Holz used party pressure to get a train depot's book store for an ex-mistress.[228] The party was mobilized to denounce the proprietor who was sent to the army to die in Russia. The railroad director appealed to Martin; Holz went through Bormann to Himmler's office to get the director arrested. Martin and the Reich Minister of Transport got the man out of jail again, though he had to leave the city.

For all Holz's aberration he was much less difficult to deal with than Streicher—so Himmler was informed by Martin, who was reacting to rumors of Streicher's return from exile.[229] The sympathy of the party, he reported, was completely on the side of Holz, who despite certain "awkwardness", had managed to pull "the totally disorganized party" back together. Goebbels and Ley had visited Streicher to persuade him to make Holz Gauleiter, which Streicher refused because he had always regarded him unfit for leadership. "Even though he had publicly proclaimed a friendship with Holz, internally he had always treated him with contempt." Holz was therefore now so angry that he would rather die than work for Streicher again.[230]

Dr. Martin's Last Years

After so successful and dangerous a campaign against his local tyrant, albeit with the support of Himmler, a central and greater tyrant, Martin's inclination was surely to avoid trouble. As the SD reported in late 1941, relations were good: "For over a year there have been no difficulties. One major cause has been the departure of Dr. Kiessel, the acting Gestapo leader. K. showed no understanding of the SD work

[228] Geyer, SK, Martin, VII, V, 19.
[229] Martin to Himmler, 7.6.44, BDC Martin, *Partei Korrespondenz.*
[230] *Ibid.*

and let no opportunity go by to play off the Gestapo and SD against each other".[231] Martin had to deal with a Gestapo leader, Otto, not so trustworthy, whom he later discharged for brutality.

What had been a confused responsibility, because the Gestapo office had no formal head, became more confused as Martin was promoted regional SS commander. He regarded this at the time as a kick upstairs to limit his authority,[232] since the position was created by Himmler as a sinecure. The total command was a dozen men, although the rank approximated that of a general. Rather few of his peers occupied their time in other than trivia, but Martin exerted influence because of his ability to persuade his old police force, and simply to bluff.

The appointment of the man suspect in party and SS circles was ill-received. (Martin's full promotion was delayed by Wagner until the latter's death in 1943.) He had the enmity of the local Waffen SS leader.[233] Heydrich's distrust, as in the quoted letter of March 1942, was followed by Daluege praise for his technical skills, with no word devoted to his ideological obedience.[234] In the spring of 1942 Martin attempted to overcome Heydrich's suspicion with a get-well message and package of Nuremberg *Lebkuchen* after the wounding of Heydrich in Prague. A posthumous thanks was relayed by an assistant.[235] Perhaps as an effort to demonstrate Martin's dependability, his letter complained that a Nuremberg court had permitted a Jewess to testify against an Aryan.[236]

In 1941 the Nuremberg police carried out orders to discover the Communist commissars among the Russian prisoners of war. These were sent in crowded and unheated boxcars in mid-winter to Dachau where they were shot.[237] A former police subordinate, Betz, became commander of a nearby camp for Russian POW's; with the cooperation of the

[231] CGD T 175 R 406, F8966ff.
[232] Schiel, SK, Martin, VII, XI, 13.
[233] CGD T 175, R 406, F 8966.
[234] Daluege to "Lieber Heinrich", SK, Martin, VII, XIII, 125.
[235] CGD T 175, R 406, F9032ff.
[236] *Ibid.*, 9028.
[237] Ohler, IZG NO 4773.

Gestapo chief, Otto, permitted horrible conditions, including the beating of prisoners. Both were fired immediately and Betz was imprisoned, when Martin became aware from Dr. Wegner of the conditions, though both had long been in his top group of coworkers.[238]

SS commander Martin had no command over the area concentration camp at Flossenburg. It was directly responsible to Pohl in Himmler's Berlin RSHA. He could not enter the camp without express permission from Berlin. Once he gained permission to deliver a package to a Countess von Bismarck. He was conducted straight to the cell, permitted a short conversation, and taken straight out. Martin heard from Kiessel in RSHA that his visit had been timed to the second and reported to Berlin.[239]

A civilian friend informed Martin in 1944 that beatings at the camp could be seen from the street, so he tried to use his high SS rank to effect improvements. Citing the danger of epidemic he got Dr. Wegner into the camp for a carefully limited examination. He then arranged a conference to discuss "the medical problems" of the camp with a reluctant commander, Koegel. When Koegel reported things in order, Wegner exploded, "You're telling us fairy tales. The conditions in your camp shriek to high heaven. If we Germans ever want to claim to be a civilized country. . . ." Koegel jumped to his feet, answering that he had not come to be insulted. Martin reported that conditions had improved slightly.[240] When Koegel was ordered in March 1945 not to let any of his 7,000 prisoners fall into Allied hands, Martin advised him simply to march them to the south, instead of killing them, correctly assuming they would be captured.

Wagner testified that Martin had few of the many foreign workers who fled their jobs reported, since this meant a concentration camp. When pressed, he investigated instead the working conditions causing the flight, helped at times by the local DAF. A direct order from Martin was that there would

[238] SK, Martin, I, 30, 31, and VII, XIII, 95.
[239] Wegner, 57; Hofmann in SK, Martin, VII, III, 6.
[240] Wegner, 60.

be no foreigner reported for plundering to the RSHA because this meant certain death. He sabotaged the order to report all Slav workers having relations with German women, for which was the death penalty. The one loophole was that if they did not look "east", but "Aryan", they could be pronounced marriageable and live.[241] Martin showed the Gestapo how to lead such interviews to avoid finding guilt, but this failed when there was a pregnancy or a family argument. The guilty were then declared "Aryan" and their lives were saved. Then the RSHA appointed 23 "race-deciders", who demanded pictures. One case was particularly hopeless; a worker with no redeeming Aryan features had made a "nymphomaniac" pregnant. Martin suggested that they get an anti-NS professor from the University to draw up a report. He brought along an anthropologist friend, and together they produced 20 pages of scientific misinformation, which brought delight to Martin; but the carefully contrived report failed to convince the RSHA of his "Aryanism"; the unfortunate man was ordered to a concentration camp.

As SS leader for northern Bavaria, Martin had another Gauleiter to deal with—Waechtler—who in his way was more dangerous than Streicher. Waechtler's weakness was excessive drinking; Martin tried without success to have tales of his drunken orgies bring his ouster. Failing this, he delighted in foiling Waechtler by working with the mayor of Bayreuth, an avowed Waechtler foe. He also protected two high finance and economic officials, Drs. Graf and Rauch, who were thorns in the Gauleiter's side, because they limited his exploitation. On one occasion, Waechtler got party approval to have his own economic office, but Martin located Himmler's train and convinced him to cancel the order.[242] In 1943 Waechtler envied some castles, including that of the Countess Schoenborn. The mayor of Bayreuth alerted Martin who immediately confiscated the castles for the police, giving special protection to the valuables and forbade the party to enter the building. In another "confiscation", the party ar-

[241] *Ibid.*, 52ff. [242] *Ibid.*, 115.

rived to find the castle a "Police Clothing Office", which meant that two rooms were used to store winter clothing.[243]

The Resistance Groups

Dr. Martin regarded the local resistance of little consequence. It represented mostly critics of the regime, though they risked their lives for any word of criticism. His friend, Dr. Alexis Mayer, denounced the regime so loud and long in Martin's own office that the police guard knocked politely on the door and informed Dr. Martin that Herr Dr. Mayer should please keep his denunciation to a lower volume because passersby on the sidewalk could easily hear it.[244]

Several Nurembergers generally accepted as part of the resistance testified for Martin. Hanswolf Obermueller testified that as far back as 1929 Martin had delivered anti-NS material for his newspaper, and continued to deliver such material to the resistance group. Martin had given him foreign books and articles against Hitler from the Gestapo collection and warned him of any danger.[245] Two other leaders, Drexel and Weller, were saved by his intervention.[246]

Martin was regarded as a confidant of another group of conspirators. Dr. Otto Graf, an old BVP supporter operating within the Frankish economic officialdom was linked to the Goerdeler group, his coworkers killed after July 20, 1944. (Working under Graf in an obscure scholarly research position was Dr. Ludwig Erhard.) Dr. Rauch, finance official and also BVP, was the contact man to the Catholic church and to the former Chancellor Wirth in Switzerland. The group counted among their number one of the later millionaires, Schickedanz, who had business contacts in the outside world forbidden the others.

Another in the group was Dr. Koetter, a very close friend of Martin, who kept a non-NS paper alive in Nuremberg with the help of Martin and Ruhr industrialist Reusch, his publisher. Koetter, an ardent patriot and conservative who for a

[243] *Ibid.*, 109f. [244] Wegner, Mayer, and Martin.
[245] Hanswolf Obermueller, SK, Martin, VII, IV, 1.
[246] *Ibid.*, II, 65; VII, III, 8.

time could not understand Martin's friendship with Jews, played the Martin game to stay alive, as an editor, and yet maintain some integrity. Many Nurembergers delighted in his careful digs such as the announcement of the death of an honored teacher who happened to be Jewish, or a slight typographical error which changed "Hail Hitler" to "Heal Hitler". Whatever patriotic feelings may have led him to follow the NS crowd were disrupted by two incidents—the fact that he had an English wife, a distant relative of Churchill. This brought such heavy party pressure that he sent her to Italy for her protection. Even there she was not safe, and only Martin's tearing up a Berlin order to have her arrested saved her from a concentration camp.[247] In November 1938, along with 60 other journalists, Koetter was permitted a secret session with Hitler who told them that until then he had been forced to talk of peace, but now the journalists must prepare the people for war; there would be one generation for conquest and the next to hold what was conquered.[248]

Like many such courageous but largely futile groups, this one talked. Their conversation differed somewhat from comparable groups in that the area SS commander provided them with the latest secret information. The obvious effort at resistance was the Stauffenberg attempt to kill Hitler on July 20, 1944 which brought not Hitler's death but that of hundreds of patriots, including Stauffenberg. The reaction from Himmler, who had toyed with the idea of allying himself to resistance before, was that not only the conspirators but also their families should be destroyed and their property seized. He gave specific orders to Martin to destroy all the Stauffenbergs. As the family testified, Martin did precisely the opposite; he saved everyone, going so far as to hide some in a hotel room registered under his own name. He personally took the family treasures for safekeeping from one hiding place to another, finally leaving them in an Eichstaett vault, with a note to the approaching Americans about the ownership.[249]

Less newsworthy after the war was Martin's aid to the wife

[247] Betty Anson-Koetter, SK, Martin, III.
[248] Koetter. [249] Wegner, 148.

of the executed Colonel Hansen, Canaris' agent for Upper Bavaria. Hansen's wife was ordered arrested and taken from her five children, including a newborn baby. When Martin discovered the arrest, he had the baby brought to her and both transferred to a hospital, where she was given the best room. After a short while, Dr. Wegner declared her "incapable of arrest" and she returned to her family.[250]

After the abortive attempt to assassinate Hitler came the failure of resistance to the Allied bombers and armies. While inner Nuremberg was flattened, the American army closed in. As usual, the orders from Berlin were for Nuremberg to die to the last man. These orders were accepted by Holz who refused every plea for sanity. Any hope of a retreat from the city was nullified by the encircling American troops. Among the many who fell with Nuremberg was Holz. Liebel died also, presumably by his own hand. Streicher was hanged in 1946 in the city he had been forbidden to enter. Kiessel was executed after the war by the Yugoslavs. Zimmermann survived, only to commit suicide in 1966; it was thought he did so at the rumor of a new trial.

Dr. Martin was taken prisoner by the Americans. His first interview, by his account, was shocking. The American officer interrogated him about the Jews in Nuremberg and at the end of the story erupted in an enormous rage. Martin asked later what he had said that had brought on such an outburst and the interpreter supposedly answered, "You didn't kill all of the Jews." His wife understood from an American officer that both her husband and son were dead. Much less robust than her husband, she took her life with poison. The fate of the only son remained obscure for years; the 17-year-old boy was killed in the last days of the war and his father informed of it years later. Dr. Martin was kept in camps, including Dachau, for three years and then tried five different times, acquitted repeatedly of any crime. During his trials he received help from the Catholic church, even the support of the Pope, because he had saved the Bamberg cathedral.

[250] Wegner, 152-54, Frau Hansen, and Deaconess Loschel, SK, Martin, VII, II, 1b, and III, 5.

5 EICHSTAETT

AS comforting as it might be, one could scarcely call Eichstaett a typical German small town of the 1930s, but it may represent in a heightened fashion the civil cold war between a radical party and a conservative church, a tendency present in many or most communities. Though atypical, Eichstaett serves as a reminder that uniformity is a rarity even in the state that gives top priority to uniformity.

Some of Eichstaett's surprising development was a result of its fairly remote location and nonindustrial economy, though it is surrounded by three major industrial centers—Nuremberg, Augsburg, and Munich. Its relative isolation was evident in the mid-1960s despite the determined efforts of its enlightened mayor to bring progress to a lovely medieval and baroque town. As one drove into Eichstaett, down into the lovely valley of the Altmuehl, one could almost believe that a time machine was taking him back several decades.

As a county seat, the town was a Beamten city, significant particularly in the NS period because Beamten in small towns were forced into the forefront by the party. It was a school city, filled with three high schools, triple the customary number for a city of 8,000—two "middle schools" for girls and a Catholic teachers college. The number of teachers in the city, particularly professors at the higher Catholic schools, was a vital element in the opposition to the Third Reich. Of most significance was the fact that the small town had its own bishop, and this rural bishopric county had been through a quirk of history joined to a Protestant Franken. The NS never had the pieces on this local chessboard to match the oblique slants of a bishop, or the knights of priestly teachers, all surrounded by loyal pawn-believers.

There was little industry, one reason for the town's medieval atmosphere. Despite its intellectual wealth, it was otherwise among the poorest for the region. Therefore, long after the NS had come and gone, the mentality of Eichstaett still moved as slowly as its meandering, albeit romantic, Altmuehl. What industry existed was a quarry atop a bordering hill. On occasion the workers of the quarry, outsiders in a bourgeois Beamten city, could express their alienation via SA extremism.

Eichstaett was in Franken legally under the rural political center of Ansbach, like itself, baroque in spirit. Real power in the NS period came from party and police headquarters, both located in "faraway" Nuremberg. Roads were bad, train connections difficult (the only train station was in a suburb), so that where possible people avoided the trip. Streicher was almost never seen. Voting patterns, heavily for the Bavarians People's Party BVP, and sentiment were much more like that of the Old Bavarian counties to the south than the Franken counties to the north, the Eichstaetters regarding their fellow Franconians with suspicion and scorn; and it was in the rest of Franken that Hitler garnered real support. Eichstaett, led by Wohlmuth, church official turned Bavarian politician, had given steady support to conservatives, not radicals.

The Party Leadership

One of the real joys of Eichstaett to a historian is the character of the Kreisleiter, Dr. Walter Krauss. Streicher, a prototype of irrationality, regarded the mouse-like Krauss as a truly strange man.

Although Krauss became the plague of the devout Catholics in Eichstaett, the oddity is that he came to the city precisely because he was so good a Catholic, as evidenced to his army chaplain during their service together at the front. During the 1920s he remained devout, attending services as the house doctor for the nunnery up to 1933. Somewhere he developed a violent hatred of the Catholic church. One theory advanced later by a rather sympathetic priest, Kurzinger, was that Krauss's women problems and various divorces was the source of the split. Kurzinger thought the church went out of its way in an unusual public excommunication on the occasion of Krauss's first divorce. Krauss allegedly declared at this juncture: "Now I'll make it hot for the priests". Although Krauss left the church in 1937 during the party-pressured mass exodus, he returned after the war in reconciliation. Bishop Rackl showed such tenderness toward his former NS enemies that the de-Nazification courts reprimanded his generosity. Kurzinger administered last rites to Krauss, although his last wife objected.

This pious Catholic turned bitter anti-clericalist was also an anti-Semite, although he treated Jewish patients until 1933. In what is a fairly common pattern with the most rabid NS, there was evidence that Krauss was half-Jewish. It was commonly believed by the town and on occasion was put to his face. More significant, however, was that Streicher came to think so too.[1]

Another facet to his character, and an explanation for his power in the community, was the fact that he helped the poor, charging them no fees and often paying for their medicines himself. Despite his fanaticism, he did not distinguish in his practice between NS and non-NS. During the war he treated the foreign workers as well as Germans. He always called a priest when a patient was in danger of death. He saved a boy from being drafted into the SS by putting him down as "sick".[2]

Krauss was appointed Kreisleiter almost immediately upon his joining the party in 1930, primarily because he had no real competition. Like so many of the "intellectuals" in the NS grassroots organization, his education was a technical one, but he had a *Doktor* title. His crew was markedly inept, not one having ability commensurate with the authority they seized in 1933. The man most often linked with Krauss was the city hall, low-Beamter A., known because of his short stature and bowed legs as the "city hall dachshund". During the Krauss heyday as mayor, A. rose to the front office, rewarding his promotion in power with absolute loyalty to Krauss, doing much of his dirty work. Typical was

1 SK, Dr. Walter Krauss, I, 24. 2 Verdict, SK, Krauss, 20.7.48.

his 1936 report complete with snapshot of a new Catholic student whom A. thought must be Jewish, because of his nose and walk.

Less typical was A.'s involvement in scuffles, for he was particularly unimposing physically. In 1934 he was guilty of the only known assault on a Jew in Eichstaett, attacking a traveling merchant, Schimmel, in the marketplace, scolding the customer for dealing with a Jew, and then reporting the Jew to the police. The police quoted the law, recently emphasized by Wagner, and refused the arrest A. demanded. (His defense at his postwar trial was that it was a personal matter with Schimmel, who had for years called him "scribbler".[3]) On another occasion he participated in the beating up of a town "police character" for having attacked another man who had not shown sufficient respect toward a religious procession (not removing his hat and continuing to smoke).

Opinions on A. were nearly universally bad, although Bishop Rackl went far out of his way to help him in 1948. His statement observed that "everyone has a good side to his character and this would likely apply to A. too". That A. acted more out of ambition than conviction is suggested by the fact that when he returned to his home village for a vacation, he sang in the choir every Sunday morning. In Eichstaett there were a few who could report that he had been tolerant to them, such as when he helped someone to get out of a concentration camp. (The denazification punishment was relatively mild, reflecting the fact that he had been away from his home for nine years, six as a soldier and three in a detention camp, that his family of five children was living on charity, his wife was ill, and he himself was partially crippled.)

A similar punishment was given Hans Roesch, successor to Krauss as mayor and a long-standing commander of the local DAF, who had been interned 23 months before his trial. Roesch's powerful positions had little to do with his training as a masseur, more to his loyalty to Krauss and to a 1931 motorcycle injury "in the service of the party" which injured

[3] SK, "A", 1948, 64.

his skull and an eye nerve, leaving him partially blind. Roesch's personality was heavy-handed; perhaps like A. he compensated for inferiorities by threatening violence and imprisonment to a relatively large group. Some of these threats were to asocial elements, like wife-beaters. His trial suggests little real activity or ability, but on occasion a social conscience, for example, an effort to get clothing for foreign workers.

Another member of the ruling clique, Gregor H., a journalist, was the pseudo-intellectual of the group. That he was fanatic seems certain; with the Americans already in Nuremberg, his wife said in April 1945 that Hitler would still win the war by defeating the Americans when they reached Munich. He gave important service to the party; some reported him as arrogant, hiding behind a civil manner while actually the author of the terror. Others reported that although he was anti-Semitic, he criticized the 1938 violence, and that though critical of the papacy, he remained otherwise a good Catholic, refusing to leave the church, as most of his party colleagues did, and publicly standing up to refuse the party's demand. He was, therefore, not trusted by the party headquarters in Nuremberg; the Gestapo checked on him in 1941. H. did not belong to Krauss's inner clique, which prevented his becoming Kreisleiter. His friends testified that during the war he did not report to the Gestapo two girls he knew were intimate with French POW's; he was reported decent to POW's, having been one for three years in World War I. After the war he was contrite. He stated privately that it was good that Germany had not won, once one knew what crimes the NS had committed. H. was in a detention camp until June 1948 until his trial. The sentence was for two of the three years served.[4]

The seizure of power in Eichstaett was accomplished with the frequent NS combination of bluster and hesitancy. The NS vote, about 30%, was much lower than the national average, so the NS power seizure was external to the city. Al-

[4] SK, Gregor H., 7.12.49.

though Krauss began early with the assertion, "Whoever doesn't line up will be run over", relatively little was changed at city hall. Fairly well absorbing the literate party members of the town, the NS took over the city council, but very late —May 4, 1933. The arrests of the ousted BVP councilmen came in June as ordered from above, and, as elsewhere, meant confinement of only a few days. The BVP mayor, Betz, was left in office partly because he was solidly conservative and partly because the party had no one in the community remotely qualified to take his place. The Landrat office was taken over in May by a Dr. Georg Roth, one of the very few NS among the Bavarian "higher Beamten".

The most obvious change was the beginning of an anti-Semitism that seems to have scarcely existed before. Almost the entire Jewish community, less than 10 families, was made up of respected professional men or merchants whose assimilation into the community was typified by the weekly card games involving both Jews and NS before 1933. There does not seem to have been even the usual ambivalence toward the "cattle-dealer Jew" among the peasants, because "the Jewish prices were good".[5] What anti-Semitism existed came from Streicher's fulminations and its local echo from Krauss and his cohorts. In June 1933 Krauss expressed the view that the death sentence was fitting for "racial violation" (sexual relations between Jew and non-Jew, a Streicher obsession). His further statement that one with Jewish blood could not be a citizen is doubly interesting when it is noted that the town assumed Krauss was half-Jewish. In January 1934 he compared the Jews to the locusts at harvest. To avoid such "parasites" he thought citizens should prove no Jewish blood in ancestors back to 1800. He complained bitterly that the peasants still dealt with Jews; if an NS "lost patience" with a Jew, as A. had done, "public opinion was on the side of the Jew!"[6]

Although there was relatively little violence against Jewish families, the smallness of the community made it extremely

[5] Mayor Dr. Hutter.

[6] *Eichstaetter Anzeiger*, 6.1.34.

difficult for the Jews to withstand a boycott. In July 1935 two merchants were arrested and SA were stationed outside their stores. With effective spying on who entered a Jewish store or spoke to them on the street, economic and social pressure forced most of the Jews out of business and the town in the first two or three years. It was Betz's loyalty to a Jewish friend that contributed to the fall of the non-NS mayor—he attended the friend's funeral. A picture of him in attendance was then posted outside the city hall—rumor said by A.—with the scornful inscription, "this friend of the Jews".

One family remained for the night of violence, November 9, 1938. The Landrat testified being informed at 5 a.m. that the SA had called demanding that Franken become "free of Jews", that there was nothing he could do. He heard noises in the town and called the police. They found a mob of 20 men, obviously under orders, trying to break into the Jewish home. The police intervened. The Kreisleiter came and it was agreed that the Jews were to be arrested instead of mobbed. The Landrat arranged for them to join relations in Augsburg. The railway would not sell them a ticket, so the Landrat got them a taxi. They later sold the house and emigrated.[7] The inability of a minority to survive in a small town sharply contrasts with the ability of a majority, i.e., Catholics, to do more than survive.

The Incident of the High Cross

Krauss achieved a sort of regional fame with a senseless and unhappy effort to replace a Christian monument, a cross situated on the highest hill overlooking Eichstaett, with a *Thing*, a monument with obscure Germanic origins which Eichstaetters assumed meant that Krauss had become a sun-worshipper. On the night of September 7-8, 1933, Krauss organized a crew of workers and shovels and in the darkness took them to the cross with orders to take it down before dawn. But word leaked out. City officials alerted the police, who caught the Kreisleiter with the High Cross far from down. Krauss agreed to stop the work and disbanded his

[7] Baeuml, Miller, Eisenschink in SK, Josef Baeuml.

crew. Later the same night, Krauss pulled the crew out of bed again and sent them back to work. Soon the crew realized that the cross, set in a heavy concrete base, would require another day's labor to move. Any chance for a *fait accompli* was gone, and Krauss had to give up.

The official report sent by Colonel Hofmann, was a clear call for Krauss's removal. "In the area the incident brought forth a great indignation, considerably increasing the already strong dislike of Dr. Krauss."[8] Not only was this a disgrace to the party, in Hofmann's opinion, but Krauss was scandalizing the community by already having two divorced wives, and, to public knowledge, being involved in two affairs. Hofmann hinted further at other Krauss affairs with two young men of his entourage. Hofmann requested that the bishop's report on Krauss be read and that he be immediately dismissed as Kreisleiter; otherwise Hofmann must consider arresting him.[9]

Hofmann was not the only NS disgusted with Krauss. Subterranean infighting persisted in the Eichstaett party through the winter of 1933-34. A Baron von Egloffstein was arrested in late November by the SA for spreading the story that Krauss was a homosexual. (He was later rearrested for saying after the killing of Roehm and his followers that someone had overlooked Krauss.) Landrat Roth reported to Hofmann that among the old NS the feeling was strong against Krauss, who had therefore not been able to enlist a NS city councilman acceptable to his own party. He had been "vacationed" but then reinstated by Holz.[10] Hofmann told Roth if Krauss caused any more trouble—arrest him.

The Landrat intervened in November 1933 when Krauss tried to force all officials to attend a NS convention in Nuremberg. Bavarian Beamten rules forbade such attendance.[11] Roth complained again about Krauss to his superiors, state and SA, in early December. The SA Special Commissar for Bavaria told Roth to mind his own business and leave po-

[8] Hofmann report to Obernitz, 12.10.33, in SK, Krauss, II.
[9] *Ibid.*
[10] Roth to Hofmann, 30.11.33, SK, Walter Krauss, II.
[11] BSA Innen Ministerium 73437.

litical matters to the party and the SA. Roth replied that there would be no peace in Eichstaett until the Gauleiter installed someone who had the confidence of the local party. Holz had defended Krauss's behavior concerning the High Cross which had caused further doubts about the law. Roth's report further complained of Hitler Youth violence, invading a church boy scout clubhouse by brutal measures; Roth bitterly noted that the police were ordered not to intervene.[12]

In a similar incident in February 1934, the HJ said they wanted to rent a Catholic youth home, but the HJ leader seized the key and threw out the Catholic equipment. The Landrat wanted to give them police protection, but the Special Commissar again intervened.[13] Landrat Roth then asked for Ansbach support but was told not to intervene, to which he answered with a strong protest at this danger to the state: "The Law must remain the law, particularly in the NS state". In his report, Hofmann agreed with Roth.

Krauss was brought to trial for having damaged the foundation of the cross. His defense was that he only wanted to move the cross, and that anyway when a true NS saw a problem, he immediately did something about it. The court, unimpressed by such logic, noted that it would have been impossible to "move" the cross with its base with so few men and at night. The sentence was 250 marks or 10 days.

In March 1934 the community replied in nearly the only way possible, by staying away from party meetings in great numbers. The point was not lost on Krauss and Uhl, an SA leader later killed with Roehm. In their indignation at the Catholics, they practiced target shooting with their pistols at the picture of former Bishop Merkl, and for good measure tore up the picture of the reigning bishop, Preysing. The hotel owner, not accustomed to pistol shooting, called the police and the ill-fated Fischer appeared. For his efforts Fischer was threatened by the party leaders with dire punishment if he intervened. Yet, with the support of Mayor Betz, Fischer took the matter to court.

12 Roth to Hofmann, 6.12.33, SK, Krauss, II.

13 BSA, Innen Ministerium 71719.

Krauss's attack on the cross and bishop added to the division within the party. Relations with NS Landrat Roth worsened permanently. Roth's wife was fired as leader of the women's auxiliary. Much of the city council apparently opposed Krauss. At the meeting of May 12, three of the 10 present were informed by a phone call from Streicher that they were to quit the council. When they hesitated, they were informed that they had been thrown out of the party. After a stormy session they left at 11 p.m. At midnight an agent of the Special Commissar appeared to arrest them.

The non-NS mayor Betz was treated with more consideration; he was forced out but not arrested. Krauss asked him to resign several times, charging him with conspiracy with the priests because he had been observed speaking with them on the street. Krauss was even angrier because Betz had not attended party functions, that he had not stopped the charges concerning the High Cross or the target-shooting at the bishop's picture. Betz declined the suggestion and tried to get support from the Munich officials, but was told that Interior Minister Wagner insisted; the matter, therefore, was hopeless.[14]

As a reward for his model behavior Krauss became mayor to drive the priests from power. Streicher's logic was to put Krauss in because he had so many weaknesses and yet was an "academician", i.e., he had a doctor's degree, which the old grade-school teacher Streicher did not. "Then these Academicians, these *Schweinhunde*, who have led degenerate lives at the expense of the peasants do not deserve such positions."[15]

The local NS paper reported the "enormous public joy" at the selection of "the beloved" Krauss. The headline of his first speech as mayor (May 15, 1934) observed less ecstatically, "Whoever is not for us is against us". He noted obliquely that there had been the opinion that he would have to be replaced, but that such opposition from councilmen who wanted to show off would no longer be tolerated. The NS fight would be especially hard in Eichstaett. "We must make

[14] Betz, SK, Krauss, II.

[15] Nussler, SK, Krauss, I, 289.

it clear that the opponents, always strong in Eichstaett, are far from giving up", Krauss said. The socialists had been beaten to their knees, but not the Catholics, for example; a priest had said it was wrong that the youth were no longer in church, but instead were singing blasphemous songs. "We forbid most energetically anyone calling our fighting songs blasphemous." Anyone who thought that the NS would bother religion was a liar. Krauss thought it very strange that a priest would defend the Jews, the source of all enmity among peoples, saying: "We leave no doubt that now also in Eichstaett 'The Jewish Question' must be regarded more sharply".

In a speech on May 30, Streicher gave his blessing to Krauss. He noted the unfair attacks by the church on him, i.e., the High Cross, since he only wanted a proper place for a party symbol; Krauss had been publicly insulted, that his enemies had gone so far as to boycott Krauss and taught others to hate him. Streicher scorned the "cowardly parents" who would not let their children join the HJ, and the "cowardly churchmen" who would not accept the party's hand of friendship.[16] Streicher's private opinion was more perceptive; he was overheard telling Holz during Krauss' inauguration: "One can't rely on Krauss. He is a born fool".[17]

The Matter of the Flags

One of the biggest fusses in the early years came over the matter of a few Catholic flags. The Catholic youth, still quite active, had been given a breather by the Concordat with Rome, but were forbidden to conduct parades and public meetings. Scuffles with the Hitler Youth, "led by a fanatic young man from a good family, who tried to restrain him" were not uncommon. The Catholic boys planned a meeting for Whitsuntide and had Catholic banners attached to their bicycles. An auto passed them and stopped in front; HJ leaders got out and after an argument seized the flags and took them to their headquarters to make HJ flags out of them. The priest-advisor, Rieder, went to the HJ to get the flags, where-

16 Personal Akt, Dr. Krauss, Stadt Archiv, Eichstaett.
17 J. E. in SK, Krauss, 1949, Appeal.

upon the HJ ran to the police to stop him. While they were gone, Rieder simply picked up the flags and took them home. Krauss appeared soon and demanded the flags back, but was refused.

The next day the NS mobilized its forces. Groups of party and HJ appeared before the priest's house and demanded the flags, meanwhile denouncing the reactionary "blacks". When the mob broke down the door, the bishop went for help. The police curbed the demonstration by arresting the HJ leaders, but Krauss released them. In the afternoon girls demonstrated against Rieder. At midnight the police searched the priest's quarters and arrested him. He was released with orders to surrender the flags by 9 p.m. After an early conference with Bishop Preysing, who said they must not be returned, Rieder left town briefly to avoid more mobs.[18]

The police submitted an objective report of the HJ attacks which was rejected by Krauss, who demanded a new report. But Fischer and his superior, Boehm, refused to sign a false version. Krauss's first act as mayor was to fire Policeman Fischer. Fischer was acquitted in a Munich trial of any dereliction of duty; even Krauss admitted that he had done his duty, but claimed Fischer was "not NS in spirit". (With difficulty Fischer found a new job in Wuerzburg, where he died in the Allied bombing attacks in early 1945.) At his own trial in 1948 Krauss reported that Streicher had insisted that Fischer be fired. Krauss then had asked Streicher to listen to Fischer. Streicher instead had hit the table with his riding whip and said, "Am I or am I not Gauleiter, you booby?"[19]

Mayor Krauss was made an "honorary" mayor, i.e., he was unpaid, either because he was not qualified for a legal appointment or because he preferred the image of self-sacrifice. Actually the obliging city council, notably his staunch ally, A., gave him compensation at considerable expense to the city. In 1935 A. bought him a 60,000-mark insurance policy for the city, with careful notation that the arrangement would be in effect even if he were mayor only for a short time.

[18] Rieder in SK, Krauss, 277, and interview.
[19] E. in SK, Krauss, Appeal.

His "expense account" was about half the normal salary. He was given a rent-free house with electricity paid, and a promise of a pension of 500 marks a month if at any time he should not be able to work.[20] The Bavarian Interior Ministry protested these arrangements and finally declared them illegal. A bitter correspondence ensued over several years with the insurance company disturbed that a lucrative policy was cancelled and Krauss disturbed that they would not return the 1,636 marks already paid as premiums. In late 1937 the Bavarian Ministry forced through a 400-mark compromise with the company for the inept city government. Then the bitter Krauss discovered, once out of office, that he was supposed to pay the coal bills, by then years in arrears.

With Krauss as mayor, revolutionary changes would have been expected, but administration remained with the Beamten. A. was placed in the front office, regarded by his colleagues as the eyes and ears of the party. The city had two Jews arrested and their stores boycotted. A few days later, a citizen accused Krauss of being a half-Jew; he was also arrested for his opinion. More city money was available for party projects, including the *Thing* monument. A few more "old fighters" were hired for menial tasks at the city hall. Likely prompted by one of his ex-wives, a cleaning woman was fired for spreading scandal about the mayor. Yet because of his own inexperience and A.'s limited ability, in September 1934 various "full powers" were given to experienced Beamten.[21]

The most significant of these officials was Josef Meier, in the town's opinion too good a Catholic to have been an NS. His long-time foe at city hall, A., conceded that Meier was a powerful opponent. In his position as city treasurer and plenipotentiary for the city school, Meier had undue powers, while the party frantically tried to get some trustworthy NS to pass the necessary Beamten tests for his job. Meier was able to delay his joining the party until 1938. The church's lawyer, who had fought NS pressure with success, gave Meier a clean

20 Personal Akt, Krauss, Stadt Archiv.
21 *Sitzungsprotokoll der Stadtraete*, Eichstaett.

anti-NS bill of health at his trial, adding that by 1937 a declining portion of the town was NS, but that the declining minority tried that much more to terrorize the majority.[22]

Meier regarded his NS superiors as blanks, so incompetent that he could run his office very much as before. He preferred to hire non-NS teachers, including one whose employment in Bavaria had been forbidden by Wagner.[23] The postwar mayor of Eichstaett agreed that Meier had helped save the Catholic girls school, which was ordered closed by the government, on the fictitious grounds that the city did not have the money to replace it.[24]

Most upsetting to Meier the accountant was the waste of city money by the party. He estimated that the city had squandered its 60,000-mark reserve in the first few years; the *Thing* monument had cost another 40,000. Meier was proudest of having violated Wagner's order to buy Reich treasury notes, which were worthless in 1945, thereby saving an estimated 850,000 marks for the city. Whatever value these good works were, they were outweighed by Meier's panicky counterdenunciation of a former family friend who had spread an anti-NS rumor, saying that Frau Meier had told her. The rumor-monger was given a year's jail sentence; the Gestapo on its own added two more years in a concentration camp. Meier's overreaction could not be "made good" after the war, and cost him his job for two years and a heavy fine.

The position as Krauss's nominal superior as Landrat was not easy either. The old NS, Dr. Roth, who failed to get Krauss fired in a test of strength of the Bavarian government against Streicher's party, was transferred after more fights. It was rumored that the last straw was Krauss's demand for money for a Hitler Youth home from a city savings bank. Roth's replacement was Dr. Max Foerderreuther (from July 1936 to December 1937). The judgment of his party unit in Munich was: "For party work he is completely unsuited, as his short service in the lowest rank proved. He is a typical Paragraph-Beamter. He gives the impression of the

22 Lawyer Riedl, SK, Josef Meier, I, 60.

23 *Ibid.*

24 Mayor Blei, *Ibid.*

bureaucrat who does his duty wherever he is. What government is in power is of no importance to him. . . . He certainly is not an opponent to be feared. For that he is much too harmless and bourgeois".[25] Even the worst foes of the party could agree that Foerderreuther was not an NS.[26] Foerderreuther had been forewarned of Krauss's county, but no one could have predicated the kind of battle which he found himself in the middle of.

Party Against Church

The two years, 1936-38, in Eichstaett's history were probably unique in the Third Reich. The irrational determination of Mayor Krauss found its match in the cool recklessness of the priest Johannes Kraus.

Before Kraus came, matters were relatively quiet, although in October 1935 some 15 boys of the Catholic youth group were arrested. Father Rieder was interrogated again and charged with "contact with the Austrian government". Unluckily, one of the boys—Neubrand—had kept a diary that quoted Rieder's critical remarks, so that he could be accused of misleading the youth.[27] A party mass meeting demanded his arrest. The Hitler Youth had placed a spy among the Catholic youth, but the state attorney broke down his testimony. The freed priest was forced to leave town on the next train. Diarist Neubrand was arrested because of Krauss's charge and became one of the approximately 50 from Eichstaett who were arrested, and among the few sent to a concentration camp. In his five months at Dachau he was never questioned; his only communication from his captors was the day before his release when he was given his discharge paper. The Eichstaett Prioress and Bishop had used Catholic contacts to get his release. After a second arrest and jailing for 30 days, and indignities suffered by his widowed mother, the Neubrands left Eichstaett until after the war. Father Rieder

[25] BDC, Foerderreuther File, 4.5.36.

[26] Johannes Kraus, *Erinnerung aus Meinem Leben*, unpub. manuscript, Eichstaett, 199.

[27] Rieder and Neubrand.

returned quietly after Krauss had lost power and was not bothered.

With Johannes Kraus as the spearhead, the local church took the offensive. By similar bravery he had won the highest Bavarian medal in World War I, even beyond the Iron Cross, that NS regarded with holy awe. His being a war hero made dealing with him more difficult, as did his position as army chaplain, which gave him some kind of army legal status. Eichstaett also had a new bishop, Michael Rackl, who was pushed into a determined battle by his new preacher and a staff of brilliant teachers at the seminary. These teachers were a remarkable group; even before 1933 they had foreseen the Hitler menace much more accurately than their superiors.

The tradition of opposition began with Father Ingbert Naab and former journalist Fritz Gerlich, who together had published journals for Catholic youth, which were distributed throughout Germany. Naab's devastating attack on the NS as "the worst thing that could happen to Germany, next to communism", was reprinted many times in newspapers and reached an estimated 20 million readers.[28] Naab's and Gerlich's journal, *Der Gerade Weg*, was so incisive that the NS got Munich to suppress it in July 1932. One striking title was "National Socialism is a plague".[29] Naab, saddened that the church leaders seemed blind to the dangers, was the religious and moral thinker, while Gerlich was the driving spirit and organizer of the attack on the rising NS.

Gerlich had been editor of a leading Munich paper before his conversion. Otto Strasser wrote that Gerlich was one of Hitler's most dangerous opponents. He had collected information on the mysterious death of Geli Raubal in 1931, Hitler's niece and alleged mistress.[30] Guertner allegedly stopped the investigation. This would explain why Gerlich was selected to die on "the night of the long knives", June 30, 1934.

[28] L. Volk, *Der Bayerische Episkopat und der Nationalsozialismus, 1930-34*, Mainz, 1965, 42.

[29] James Donohoe, *Hitler's Conservative Opponents in Bavaria, 1930-45*, Leiden, 1961, 35ff.

[30] Quoted by Donohoe, 39.

The enmity of Gerlich and Naab to the NS was so apparent that Gerlich was arrested in March 1933 and sent to Dachau. Naab was spirited out of the country in April 1933 by shaving his beard and borrowing a friend's passport in a well-planned, locally-executed escape. He died in exile in Alsace in 1935; his remains were brought back by Mayor Hutter to Eichstaett after the war.

The zeal and insight of these two remained with their students and was a factor in the continued conspiracy. The remaining conspirators included the Old Testament scholar, Professor Wutz, who combined a genius for languages with enormous energy, working hard through the day and conversing brilliantly through the evening. His ally was Dr. Josef Lechner, a sharp lawyer of wide cultural background and the author of one of the most famous, clandestine, anti-NS publications, "The Goebbels Letters".

Bishop Preysing, Rackl's predecessor, had been very close to Naab, visiting him every day and apparently agreeing with his anti-NS position, but by nature a cautious diplomat. Like other bishops Preysing could not ask people to become martyrs, and like the rest of the bishops, he was not politically trained, and thought that the first concern of the church was for men's souls, a job he hoped would be better accomplished if he kept a distance from "politics".[31] Bishop Preysing narrowed this distance as a leader of the resistance in Berlin.

The unusual public opposition of Bishop Rackl resulted from the crisis which Father Kraus's candidness created—the proddings of his professors, especially Wutz, and the increased pressure on the church by Goebbel's mounting attack on priestly "crimes", and Wagner's effort to force the Catholic church back from its dominance of education. Kraus was a believer in direct action, such as arrogantly providing the Gestapo man he observed taking notes of his sermon with a copy before the next service. He went to Kreisleiter Krauss soon after his arrival on Ash Wednesday, 1936 and offered him a "quiet and reasonable settlement of problems". Mayor

31 The analysis of the church leaders depends heavily on the observations of Mayor Dr. Hutter, their good friend and student.

Krauss agreed, so Father Kraus as war hero attended the "Hero's Memorial Day". All was in order until the SA marched from the meeting singing an anti-church song. (One such ditty commonly sung implied that priests should be hung and Jews shot.) The agreement was obviously dead.

Yet 1936 was for the church in Eichstaett a year of building. Kraus's memoirs describes many well-attended meetings of the youth, one with 1,800.[32] In July 1936 a battle between Rackl and the party began over a rural pastor, which made the county well noted, if two critical Rackl sermons had not already done so. In May the Bishop had complained about the new *Kulturkampf* in progress. The official report for June noted Rackl's decrying the lack of freedom and suggesting that one could be either NS or Catholic, but not both.[33]

The Battle of Pollenfeld

The problem in the village of Pollenfeld was a priest, Schmalzl, who had his domain so well in hand that the party was forced to try to take it by storm. The Eichstaetter newspaper reported a mass meeting in Pollenfeld on June 22, 1936, ignoring that it was largely SA imports from outside, and emphasizing that everyone was there but Father Schmalzl who had been warned by an Eichstaett contact and had left. To be sure the "cowardly" priest would be properly impressed, a loudspeaker was used which could be heard for 500 yards. The Kreisleiter attacked the priest as the enemy of the party and no true friend of the Catholic people.

Whatever terror the assembled NS and blaring loudspeaker were intended to create failed. The August report from Franken noted that on July 18 the NS had staged another meeting in Pollenfeld that was extremely poorly attended.[34] Krauss wrote to the Gauleitung that when he arrived he found only the teacher-NS cell leader and the school children who had been ordered there; even the mayor was missing.[35] The pastor had scheduled a service that Saturday and the peasants

[32] Kraus, 15.
[33] BRP, Franken, 1.7.36.
[34] *Ibid.*, 6.8.36.
[35] SK, Krauss, Vol. II, Krauss to Gauleitung, 22.7.36.

were going to church. Pollenfeld had always been "the worst village"; one could not even put a NS flag on the school because of Schmalzl. Every Sunday he preached against the party. The teacher-NS cell leader was fired as choir director and Schmalzl took over the choir himself, in a clear continuation of the forbidden youth organization. Krauss continued his lament: once a week the youth of the village came to Eichstaett in a group, ostensibly to learn shorthand.[36]

Therefore on July 21, in this "community in which the NS had still not established itself",[37] the Kreisleiter called a new meeting and brought in outside units to be sure someone was there. At the meeting, amid threats on Schmalzl, Krauss announced that the priest had "fled". On the 22nd Bishop Rackl came from Eichstaett and spoke to the village. He told them not to let their children be used to put a crown of thorns on the priest's head. Any act against Schmalzl and the entire village would suffer. He threatened the medieval interdict: "I will take the Holy of Holies out of the church and extinguish the eternal light".

The village rallied around the church. Krauss wrote the Gau on July 26, 1936 Schmalzl when he entered the classroom had been welcomed by a spokesman for the class: "The school children greet you as their spiritual teacher and the shepherd of their souls. They had the most heartfelt sympathy for you on the days of your heavy trial. The children stand united behind their spiritual teacher and shepherd of their souls, who is training us to be strong Catholics and good German citizens. God bless you and our school".[38] A Pollenfeld mother said she would rather kill her five children than let them join the Hitler Youth, because only she would go to hell, not all five.[39]

The teacher observed how un-NS Schmalzl was.[40] Schmalzl had taught children that all men are equal because they had all come from Adam and Eve. The difference in the races had come from the different circumstances where they lived.

[36] *Ibid.*

[37] BRP, Franken, 6.8.36.

[38] SK, Krauss, *ibid.*, II, 26.7.36.

[39] *Ibid.*

[40] *Ibid.*, letter, 12.8.36.

Neither did Schmalzl give the necessary "Heil Hitler". The party leader reported that when on July 27 Schmalzl entered the classroom, the children, instead of "Heil Hitler", had said "Praised be Jesus Christ". "Right in front of him I gave him the 'Heil Hitler', which he did not answer with word or arm movement. I left but told the class to greet their teacher with 'Heil Hitler' ". A few did because they "feared" the teacher. The other teacher reported that in every sermon Schmalzl brought in criticism of the state which the peasants were clearly aware of. It was also reported that in 1934 Schmalzl had said salvation came from the Jews because Jesus and Mary were both Jews, and not from the Nordic race.

On the 28th Deputy Gauleiter Holz drove out to Pollenfeld and tried to calm the village down. The priest remained, but his foe, the NS mayor, was sent away.[41] When a year later, in April 1937 Schmalzl was forbidden to enter the school, Pollenfeld declared a school strike. When Krauss had to report on April 10, 1938 on who voted on a plebiscite, the highest percentage came from Pollenfeld and included Johann Schmalzl.

The Kraus Crisis

Kraus took the 1936 unrest as an occasion to deliver a series of sermons which lasted into the fall and denounced the state attacks as making the 19th-century *Kulturkampf* look like "child's play". He also tried to organize a group of priests with similar views. In Augsburg he found a few willing to join him.[42] At a meeting in Frankfurt Kraus got a list of 70 names, later useful for spreading material; but as Kraus lamented, too few of the priests and bishops were ready to act.

In the fall of 1936 came a serious blow to the Bavarian Catholic church—Wagner's effort to close the "confessional" schools and replace them with community (*Gemeinschaft*) schools, i.e., to take elementary and intermediate education out of the hands of the church. The Franken government sent down the order for the sisters teaching in the elementary schools to be replaced by lay teachers. (The relative over-

[41] *Ibid.* [42] Kraus, 25.

supply of lay teachers made the banishment of the nuns a pleasant economic prospect, and was one reason why rural teachers were party agents.[43]) For Eichstaett this meant that all of the teachers in the grade school would be replaced. The Prioress objected strenuously to the order and to the government's answer. The District President backed up Mayor Krauss, as did the official in the Bavarian Education Ministry, Fischer, who described the action as "legal". Mayor Krauss, so anxious to be rid of the nuns, most of whom then emigrated, discovered in December that the city could not afford to pay the salaries of the replacements and required a Bavarian subsidy. The Prioress maintained a foothold by an agreement in which the nuns, in return for taking care of the buildings, could stay and were to receive a small compensation.[44]

Rackl made his position clear in the case of Father Heuberger, a village priest in his diocese who had the patriotism to write a letter affirming that Christianity and Nazism were not incompatible.[45] Rackl requested the errant priest to retract this mistaken point of view, and the retraction was then read from all pulpits in the diocese. The Bishop used the occasion to answer the unfortunate Father Heuberger's assertions in his pastoral bulletin.

This provided further impetus for Father Kraus's attack of 1937, beginning with the sermon on January 31, 1937. These criticisms of the NS anti-church policy brought on the crisis of April and May when both party and state tried to drive Kraus out of town. When the news spread of Kraus's impending ouster, the cathedral was packed with a reported 5,600 of the faithful, or two-thirds of the town. Bishop Rackl went to the pulpit and noted the unfortunate reason why so many had assembled. "But when he made clear that he had given Kraus an official order not to leave his pastorate, an applause broke loose, such as the cathedral had never heard before".[46] During his 45-minute talk, Rackl had to stop fre-

[43] Eichstaett Stadtraete, Akt, 1429.

[44] *Ibid.*

[45] Donohoe, 73.

[46] Kraus, 29; see also BRP, Franken, 5.5.37.

quently for the applause from the congregation, pleased to hear that someone was going to resist. During that evening, 1,800 persons signed a petition against Kraus's removal.

While loyal Catholics were enjoying their defiance inside the cathedral, the police force, plus SA and SS, was marching about outside to "protect" the worshipers inside from mob violence—odd because the great majority of the town was inside. They did prevent the townspeople from giving the Bishop a street ovation.[47] Party units arrested some of those showing defiance. All through the night and into the next day lines of those praying for the retention of Kraus wound through the cathedral.

Landrat Foerderreuther deluged the Gestapo and his superiors with appeals to do something to prevent the potential battle between church and party. He tried to prevent the expected imminent arrest of Kraus on April 13. He asked the support of A. to prevent any arrests, but that ally of Krauss thought driving the bishop and priest out of town was a first-rate idea. Foerderreuther called Dippold to warn that the arrest of the two could lead to bloodshed. He was worried about violence coming from the quarry workers, who were being plied with liquor by the NS. He made the frightening suggestion that the army be called in; after all Kraus was a war hero and an army chaplain. Foerderreuther asked for the army in order to save the Concordat with Rome. The Franken government answered that the army would not be used against the SA and the party—a thought that horrified Streicher.[48]

The arrest, if planned, did not occur. Instead, Holz came from Nuremberg to settle matters once more. His view of the crisis was evident when he climbed out of his car. Instead of leading the charge on the church, he turned on Krauss in typical "old fighter" vulgarity and asked, "You, *Aschloch,* what mess have you gotten yourself into now?"[49] In a tame speech, Holz reassured the aroused citizenry that no harm would come to Father Kraus or the church. The official re-

[47] BRP, Franken, 5.5.37.

[48] Foerderreuther, SK, Krauss, I.

[49] Kraus, 30.

port noted that very few citizens bothered to hear him, that the audience was composed of party units.[50] By April 14 the petition with 2,582 names, was given to the state; it opposed the Gestapo action and claimed that Kraus "had never said one word against the state".

The state, better informed, took the view that Kraus had indeed attacked the state. On April 23, in an unusual display of legal nicety, it introduced court charges against Kraus. In the meantime he was forbidden to give the usual religious instruction in the school. Kraus wrote that this was not so serious, because the students came to him anyway. He was amused by the simple-minded efforts of the party to indoctrinate the students, including those of Deputy Kreisleiter Haberl who had gotten a nun's teaching job and who avoided the quick-witted Kraus after an incident at the vocational school. Haberl was asking "tricky questions" about the rise of the NS party, and Kraus lost his temper, saying: "Hitler was also found guilty of high treason in 1923 and the verdict has not yet been reversed". Kraus reported his remark to Foerderreuther who threw his hands together over his head and said: "But Herr Cathedral pastor, you simply can't say things like that".[51] Haberl took no action except to stay out of Kraus's way. He left the room before the priest appeared so that a "Heil Hitler" would not be necessary.

The Franken government's report for May noted that Rackl assumed he had won a victory over Kraus, and Rackl "does not show any gratitude".[52] Instead, Rackl was causing further trouble in a neighboring village of Ochsenfeld. Again it concerned a priest the NS wanted to remove. The bishop simply refused to send in a replacement for Father Heinloth, the priest in question, when the party forced him out. "Unrest in the population is growing ever larger."[53] Rackl came to the village on May 6 to conduct a funeral, and used the occasion to discuss the affair. On May 15 Heinloth was permitted to return. The population had told the police, "We won't let our priest be taken away again". The people stood

[50] BRP, Franken, 5.5.37.
[51] Kraus, 29ff.
[52] BRP, Franken, 5.6.37.
[53] *Ibid.*

guard the entire night in front of his house.[54] On May 25 Heinloth was arrested, which caused "great excitement" in the village, that was directed against the only village NS, the two teachers who were also the mayor and NS cell leader. Some peasants entered the mayor's house; others entered the school and took the children out, all the while scolding the teacher. A crowd gathered in the streets. With such a popular protest the state retreated; Heinloth was released after promising not to return to Ochsenfeld. The report concluded: "therewith the Heinloth Case can be regarded as finally settled. The authority of the state emerged with a full victory".[55]

The correspondence between the Munich Gestapo and Mayor Krauss, asking why he had forbidden Catholic women to meet monthly when it was legal, suggests the role of the state's Gestapo vis-à-vis the local party. Krauss listed his reasons: the excitement because of "the moral cases" involving priests and the anti-state behavior of Kraus and Rackl. The Gestapo answered that a general forbidding was not legal, therefore he should approve their meeting. Yet in view of the particular circumstances in Eichstaett, forbidden individual meetings would be permissible.

In these angry days, Goebbels' speech of May 23 prompted the famous reply—"The Goebbels Letters by Michael Germanicus", the author, Eichstaett's Dr. Lechner, turning Goebbels' attack on the church into a counterattack. The brochure, mimeographed in an attic room of the seminary, luckily was distributed far from Eichstaett. Although there were many Gestapo searches for copies, the attic room was not discovered. Yet Kraus reflected later that had the group known how many persons outside Eichstaett would lose liberty and life for having been caught with the brochure, they would have likely foregone the pleasure of answering the hated Goebbels.[56]

In June a sermon by Rackl denounced the NS attacks on the church as being as bad as those in Bolshevik Russia,

[54] *Ibid.*, 5.6.37. [55] *Ibid.*

[56] Kraus, 52. Donohoe provides a full discussion of the incident and includes the full letter in English; Donohoe, 68ff.

that "the moral cases" were an effort to make the priests criminals instead of martyrs, that only one of a thousand priests were involved, but the propaganda campaign by having highly publicized trials deliberately created a false impression.[57] A biographer counted 45 fighting sermons from Rackl in 1937, speeches copied not only by the Gestapo but by believers and passed from hand to hand. One included the following: "I have always emphasized that the fight is not political. We are not being punished because we have undertaken something against the politics of the state. . . . The fight involves two *Weltanschauungen*, which are to each other as fire and water. In this fight, the church sees what kind of terrible opponent the state is. . . . We are always loyal and want to be obedient to the state, but one thing we will not permit any power of the world to take from us [is] our holy Catholic faith".[58]

Rackl and Kraus continued the fight into 1938. Rackl worked against the "Community" schools with sermons sent to mayors and teachers and letters to priests, urging all to fight for freedom. Yet 1937 was the high point. In 1938 came the fall of their most active and least successful foe, Krauss, and the arrival of a Landrat, Baeuml, more restrained but more feared by Father Kraus because of his ability to entangle the church in laws instead of demonstrations. When Baeuml got Kraus transferred, matters quieted down. With the coming of the war the bishop took a more loyal position, which was less dangerous because the war brought the people even closer to the church as a means of survival.

Anni Spiegl

Typical of what devout and somewhat reckless young Catholics *could* do in small towns was Anni Spiegl, a petite, bright-eyed, intelligent owner-operator of a butcher shop. Fraeulein Spiegl not only distinguished herself by her activity as Catholic, but by close contact with one of the "miracles"

57 BRP, Gestapo, München, 1.7.37.

58 Andreas Bauch, *Im Dienste von Glaube und Leben*, Eichstaett, 1959, 11.

of the twentieth century, the world-famous Therese Neumann, who considered Eichstaett a second home. The miraculous reports of Neumann's life can only be mentioned in passing—the wounds on hands, feet, and side comparable to Christ's and appearing at Easter, the testimony that she lived for some 20 years without food or water. Although science would likely reject these miracles, most Eichstaetters did not, and some believe that even Hitler was afraid of Therese's mysterious powers. As a close friend of Neumann, Spiegl wrote a fervent biography after her death.

Even before 1933 Anni Spiegl was a leader of the Catholic girls organization, "The White Rose". In Eichstaett the organization was forbidden repeatedly, but it continued. At first it was completely religious in nature, but soon took on strong political overtones, became critical of national socialism. There were also discussions of race contrary to the NS position. Miss Spiegl thought that two-thirds of the 15-30 age group remained loyal from beginning to end. Many parents, particularly those self-employed, refused to send their children to the competing Hitler Youth. The countering instruction was, she thought, effective because it was so personal, a close association of student with religious instructors, and intensive.

In addition to the intellectual leaders already mentioned, Anni Spiegl emphasized the role of the Prioress, a world-travelled lady of aristocratic background who commanded five languages, the single most impressive personality in Eichstaett. Anni also emphasized the daring of the group—"permitting themselves everything". They collected opposition sermons, mimeographed them in Kraus's attic and at night carried them from house to house. Anni packed contraband material in with packages of meat as another distribution technique. Some of the early action was simple youthful exuberance. They got together evenings and decided what they might try. Once they agreed to beat up the feared party spy in City Hall. A truck driver slugged him, put a sack over his head and threw him over a garden wall. On another occasion Wutz and Neumann's brother attacked

Streicher's *Der Stuermer*; they pasted heads of Hitler and Goebbels onto the magazine's display of anti-Jewish propaganda.

Anni Spiegl was taken for interrogation by the Gestapo 10 times, but never overnight. After one of the rousing Catholic mass meetings in Eichstaett, the Gestapo took Miss Spiegl to City Hall and began by asking her, "What is going on here?" Her answer was that if she told them what the people really thought, she would be arrested. When they promised not to arrest her, she told them how they all hated Krauss. They let her go, as promised, but told her she dare not tell anyone else what she had told them. She agreed on the condition that the song which included the charming phrase "the priests to the gallows" would no longer be sung.

In the affair of "the Goebbels Letters", Anni Spiegl was arrested again, but customers who were wives of NS leaders had warned her of the impending house search. Since her father worried she sent a letter to the Kreisleiter, informing him that she knew there would be a search and not to bother because they would find nothing. The Gestapo arrested her the next day and asked repeatedly who had warned her, but, of course, she did not know.

Once she heard stories about the Landrat hoarding eggs. She sent an ironic postcard with a hen and eggs and the inscription: "Everyone works for the Landrat". The Gestapo appeared again, but she took advantage of the party split to suggest that it must have come from the mayor, and she was released.

Having exercised the right to vote no on a plebiscite led to another arrest and another quick release. Her shop was then boycotted and so announced at the NS meeting. The Beamten were placed under the greatest pressure, but the boycott did not work. The "first lady" of Eichstaett, whose husband was the bemedalled commandant of the local garrison, kept coming and others took courage and continued coming too, including most of the Beamten.

Krauss's successors were able to get her, along with Kraus, expelled from the city during the early war years. After a few weeks with Neumann, she worked in a butcher shop in Wuerttemberg. When Baeuml left, she returned in peace to Eichstaett. But the battle had not been without its losses; the cost had been not only financial but the drafting of her brother, who was singled out as the town's only butcher, "not necessary for the war effort"; he was killed in Italy.[59]

The Fall of Krauss

Although Krauss would seem to have been radical enough to suit Streicher, he was surely not a successful radical. The local party was sharply divided, the more rational members distancing themselves from Krauss, thus leaving a small clique sharing his power so long as Streicher backed him.

Indicative of the party disunity is the case against Krauss which reached the Highest Party Court in October 1937.[60] The record begins with Krauss explaining why he forced out Seyler, a former party assistant. He could not work with him. Seyler no longer attended the leadership meetings or even greeted Krauss when they met. He had protested to the Gau about Krauss and was particularly critical of Krauss's tax problems. Krauss, while defending his unorthodox finances, admitted that when he had refered to *Schweinhund* recently in a party meeting, he was talking about Seyler. Yes, he had once borrowed from a city employee to help pay for a car, but the latter's subsequent promotion in the city was "according to the rules".

Krauss admitted that his wife frequently made jealous public scenes and that his city hall stooge, A., had been given a love letter to deliver to a local lady hairdresser, which had been intercepted by her husband and returned. It was true that he had raised party charges against Landrat Roth, but he had not pressed them when Roth apologized and agreed to work with him. Krauss admitted that he had had sexual relations, but not "adultery", with the daughter of a city employee. It was not true that the father was a drunkard

[59] The foregoing Spiegl account is supported by available records and testimony and the high reputation of Fraeulein Spiegl in the town.

[60] BDC File, Krauss, 18.10.37.

or that Krauss had promoted him because of the daughter. The promotion had been deserved, Krauss insisted, because the father had worked so hard for the party before 1933—a frequent claim of the less able party faithful—that he had, therefore, not gotten the pre-1933 promotion he then deserved. This was true, he insisted, although the father joined the party first in 1933. Another Seyler charge, that Krauss had immorally approached yet another man's wife, was "slanderous". In a second hearing of the case, Krauss again discussed his tangled financial affairs, insisting that he had not known he was supposed to pay for coal delivered to the house supplied by the city. He added a serious charge against Seyler—that Seyler daily saw "the State-enemy", the local army commander, who was so suspect that his mail had to be checked.[61]

Although Krauss's tangled story of money and women would ordinarily suffice to unseat a mayor and party leader, such matters could not even be publicly criticized. Only Streicher could dump Krauss, and Streicher was equally interested (therefore vulnerable) in money and women. Yet Streicher is frequently quoted as being dubious of Krauss. A Krauss lieutenant recalled a trip to Nuremberg during the Father Kraus crisis to explain matters to Streicher, who first demanded to know why Mayor Krauss himself had not come, but then said: "I'm glad that I don't have to see him".[62] When told that Father Kraus had put on his old uniform and put himself under the protection of the Eichstaett military detachment, Streicher flew into a rage and compared it to the Munich disaster in 1923. "This was the blackest day in his Gau", he said. Streicher lamented that he learned only from the police president what was really going on in his Gau; his Kreisleiters told him nothing. Streicher was to be informed if something like that ever happened in Eichstaett again and if Krauss did not report it . . . "I'll clean his shoes!"

Two weeks later Krauss went along to Nuremberg and was greeted by Streicher's rough bodyguard, including Holz and Koenig: "There you are, you *Scheisskerle* from Eichs-

[61] *Ibid.*, 3.11.37.

[62] Flieger, SK, Krauss, I.

taett". There followed a flood of cursing, and Krauss was thrown bodily out of the office. The local conclusion was that, "From then on the relationship between Gauleitung and Kreisleitung was no longer what it should be".[63]

Another source of Krauss's weakened position was the appointment of a real party man as Landrat, one who could compete. Foerderreuther had been brought to Eichstaett in July 1936 as a result of a conversation of Krauss with Wagner's Koeglmaier and the Kreisleiter of a neighboring county. Since the latter wanted to get rid of Foerderreuther, and Krauss would have taken him, Koeglmaier decided: "You take Foerderreuther along".[64] Now Krauss wanted to be rid of him; Streicher considered him a weakling, though Dippold found nothing wrong with his administration. Koeglmaier bowed to Streicher. But Streicher was told that this, the fourth Landrat in less than four years, would have to stay; Bavaria would send in no more.

Baeuml, a young Beamter, slender, intellectual, with ascetic, steel-rimmed glasses, had the advantage of being an old party member and having the explicit promise of Munich support. His first meeting with Krauss, in January 1938, was weird, for Krauss had the habit of constantly looking behind himself. After perfunctory remarks they sat in silence for what seemed like five minutes, then Krauss suddenly left. Baeuml avoided him and seems to have played a minor role in the fall of Krauss.

Krauss had to leave because of his third divorce and his fourth marriage in 1938. His first wife had agreed to a divorce only on the condition that he not marry the woman who eventually became his third wife. To outwit the first wife, he married a 19-year-old druggist's assistant whom he then divorced after four weeks. This somehow enabled him to marry his original choice, wife number three. By late 1937 this marriage was also ruined and Krauss was desperate to divorce and marry again, except his third wife demanded too high a price for his freedom.

Streicher gave his version of Krauss's problem to the party

63 *Ibid.*

64 Schroeder, SK, Krauss, I, 302.

treasurer, Schwarz, to get the divorce: Krauss in "black" (Catholic) Eichstaett had accomplished a great deal, but he had been married three times and wanted to marry again, "a girl who was thirty years younger. All of my protests were in vain. Finally I gave him the choice, either to marry the fourth time and to give up his office as Kreisleiter or to remain Kreisleiter and in the interest of the general public to give up the idea to marry again at his age, something that everyone would laugh at". If he chose to resign, Streicher promised Krauss 25,000 marks to pay off the third wife. Streicher noted further that Hitler had already recognized Krauss's outstanding service to the party and had previously agreed to Hess's payment of 4,000 marks to take care of Krauss's debts.[65] Schwarz agreed. Actually, letters to Koenig, the third wife demanded 30,000 to refrain from making public charges of adultery against Krauss.[66] Krauss expressed his gratitude to Streicher in March 1939 and mentioned that his fourth wife was soon to be a mother.[67] (In his trial, Krauss emphasized Streicher's belief that Krauss was half-Jewish.[68])

The offices of Kreisleiter and mayor were divided again. Schoolteacher Haberl became Kreisleiter and worked closely with Krauss. Some regarded Haberl as more difficult to deal with, but matters remained relatively calm. The third new man, the mayor, was Dr. Edgar Emmert, who was sent in by the Gauleitung from Nuremberg. An émigré from Lorraine, Emmert had painfully made his way up in the Beamten hierarchy, serving since 1936 on the party Gau courts and participating in its obeisance to anti-Semitism and Streicher.[69] His appointment by the party was without the public competition required by law.

At his first meeting with the city council in March 1939, Mayor Emmert announced his policies. He admonished his councilmen to bring to him the wishes of the people so as to link them to the administration which could then decide wisely and justly.[70] That one would not regard this as Weimar-

[65] SK, Krauss, v.

[66] *Ibid.*, letter, 7.10.38.

[67] *Ibid.*, Krauss letter, 24.3.39.

[68] SK, Krauss, I, 22.

[69] BDC, Dr. E. Emmert File.

[70] *Sitzungsprotokoll des Stadtrats* Eichstaett, 8.3.39.

democratic, he added, such advice must, of course, follow the right *Weltanschauung*. Emmert promised to be objective at all times, to be just, and to explain his decisions to the people. He hoped for a "vigorous exchange of opinions". He outlined his plans for the city, improvements that would remind people that Krauss, other than the *Thing*, had left the city almost as he had found it. Emmert gave the initial impression of someone who would pay attention to the job of mayor and get something done. The meeting in April left a less exhilarating impression; action meant money; it became necessary to pay more expenses for a mayor with plans, for his car and representational funds. He made an immediate hit with the Beamten by putting Krauss's much disliked crony out of the front office and into a less dangerous rear office.

Opinion is largely that Emmert was not really an NS enthusiast. As a *Doktor* he remained aloof from party affairs and even from social contact with the NS families. The city budget was no longer the private preserve of the party; the party now had to pay some of its bills to the city.[71] Any criticism of Emmert's year-and-a-half tenure is not that he was too active for the party, but rather that he was not active enough for the city.

In the party-state troika, Landrat Baeuml, Kreisleiter Haberl, and Mayor Emmert, Baeuml was the most able, and attracted the most enmity from the Catholic church. Although he also remained officially and socially isolated from local party circles, he was a convinced NS and implemented the increased pressure from Bavaria, such as the forbidding of a pilgrimage (party orders keeping religious processions off the roads were circumvented by the use of side roads). Some Eichstaetters regard the former Catholic Baeuml as less an enemy of the church than his very young Protestant wife, an officer's daughter with intellectual aspirations, but unhappy in conservative, pious Eichstaett. Kurzinger, a sympathetic priest, did not regard Baeuml as dangerous (e.g., that he had promised to warn the priest if he were in any

[71] Meier in SK, Emmert, 16.

danger). Baeuml rejoined the church after the war and was remarried to his Protestant wife, this time by the church. Father Rieder found Baeuml a person one could talk with, and thought that fear of Krauss led him to a strong implementation of party pressures. Rieder was amused by the fact that when Baeuml's devout mother visited the Landrat, the crosses were put on the walls and taken down when she left.

Baeuml's clash with Father Kraus indicates the importance of personality. In October 1938 Kraus was busily organizing "Youth Week", for which he got the cooperation of the Hitler Youth leader, who agreed not to schedule conflicting meetings, and to which Kraus hoped to attract 90% of the girls and 50% of the boys. He went to the Landrat's house to be sure that their maid could attend, a brazen act to the Protestant and NS wife. The words exchanged when these opposites met became the basis of a bitter correspondence.[72] The Landrat wrote indignantly "in the future, visit my wife only when I am there". Father Kraus, doubtless enjoying the other's anger, replied at length that the meeting should give no one reason for complaint. Further annoyed by such amused tolerance, the Landrat replied that he did not withdraw his objection and that he wished no more letters from Kraus. "I need my time for the work of reconstruction" he said. But Father Kraus had the last word: "I thought I was conducting a discussion with a man of honor and who would behave accordingly. That this seems not to be the case, I will naturally avoid any further correspondence. Kraus".

Kraus did write again denouncing a vicious party speech to which Baeuml had been a passive witness, and which threatened to end the relative peace since Krauss had left office. "I see this break in the civil peace without fear. Whether you, Herr Landrat . . . can regard the end of peace with the same quiet . . . must be doubted."[73] Over a year later Kraus was arrested, but immediately released by the local judge when the witness changed his story. Another arrest followed an incident in Eichstaett during which a cross from one of the medieval bridge statues was thrown into the water late at night.

[72] Kraus, 75f.

[73] *Ibid.*, 77f.

Kraus commented: "I fear that the guilty party will again not be found, although we have so many police in the city".[74] After this arrest Kraus was sent to Munich on Gestapo orders. The Gestapo agent was apologetic; years later, after the man had served years in Allied prisons, he came back to visit Kraus, but refused to enter the room or to accept the extended hand until Kraus would forgive him for the arrest. They talked of the agent's years of forced labor in France.[75]

The desecrated cross became a cause célèbre and brought action. The state's attorney found a girl who had witnessed a half-drunken SS man urinate on the bishop's door. When she had tried to shame him, he replied, "You should see the bridge". Confronted by his commanding officer with the accusation, the young SS man confessed and committed suicide, apparently on command; he had been a theology student.

Kraus did not long remain in jail. A state's attorney and loyal Catholic had him freed with a masterful case. Riedl, though assigned to the feared "special courts", arranged for nothing to happen in the six Kraus cases. It may have helped that the local Gestapo were not Kraus's intellectual equals; to help them he dictated the report they had to submit.[76] He was transferred to another diocese until after the war.

The war moderated the church's problem with the state. In one minor case the police reported a church service in December 1939, in which the priests called for love of mankind and an end to the war.[77] Later, an ex-officer even denounced the war. The church was ever full, mostly women, but some soldiers and officers. The reports agree that almost everyone attended services. Attendance at party meetings withered away.

The State versus the Party

Along with other small cities, Eichstaett lost its close connection to the district in 1941. Its connection to Ansbach was now through the Landrat. This is the official reason

[74] *Ibid.*, 97. [75] *Ibid.*, 119. [76] Hutter.
[77] T 81, R 184, F 3960-4121.

for Emmert's leaving as mayor.[78] (The last reference to the once ambitious planner is of bills, which he said he had not paid because Krauss had not paid them before and he assumed it went with the job.[79]) Emmert's replacement was the ex-masseur Roesch the county DAF leader and confidant of Krauss. This job permitted Roesch to have some concern for a few of the area unfortunates, as well as power. His de-Nazification verdict agreed with most of the witnesses—that he had not behaved badly as mayor, i.e., had done very little either good or bad. Meier judged that Roesch did not like his job and much preferred to let the Beamten run city hall.

The position of Kreisleiter withered after Haberl left for the army, to be killed in Russia. His successor for six months, Gregor H., lacked Gau support; his successor commuted from a neighboring county. Effective party pressure—the denunciations, the power—left to the party remained with the Krauss clique. Its major target was not the Catholic church, but NS Landrat Baeuml.

The fight which, like so many others, had to go to the Highest Party Court to be settled, was traced by Krauss back to late 1938 when Baeuml protected the pious rural teacher Schmalzl, throwing out of office instead the NS teacher who had criticized him.[80] Krauss's memory reached back also to the end of 1939 when he had sat down at Baeuml's table in a restaurant and Baeuml had promptly left. An earlier discourtesy Krauss excused as being a result of Baeuml's "frequent drunkenness". Baeuml refused to let Roesch's DAF agents into his Landrat office and spoke bitterly of Krauss's spies in that office. Krauss accused Baeuml of treating his staff, particularly those friendly to Krauss, with such cruelty that they came crying to him for protection.

The real crisis began in early June 1941 when a worker in the Landrat's kitchen saw some 30 to 40 eggs without the official stamp, which made them black market. He saw but did not count others in the pantry. Soon the word was all over the county that the Landrat was black-marketeering.

[78] *Sitzung Protokoll*, 30.8.41. [79] *Ibid.*, 8.10.41.
[80] BDC, Josef Baeuml File, Partei Korrespondenz.

Baeuml countered that Krauss had long been gathering material against him in order to get him fired, that Krauss and Roesch were responsible for spreading all the stories. He hinted darkly that the worker was very close to the Catholic church and that his daughter had been involved with "The Goebbels Letters" affair. Each side accused the other of being pro-Catholic. Baeuml noted that Roesch had protested his having arrested some Catholics in a procession. Roesch claimed he was only concerned with the popular discontent, but Baeuml answered that morale was the job of the Kreisleiter, not the Mayor.

The worker was brought to "trial", such as it was, by an ambitious Beamter in city hall. He noted that the worker had not examined each and every egg, so that he could not swear that all were unmarked. The court scolded the worker for snooping and gave him four months for insulting the Landrat. Had Krauss not been interested in the affair, this would have died as the normal justice of the time. Instead, there was a flood of anonymous cards insulting Baeuml and demanding that he resign.

Baeuml accused Roesch of a lack of party solidarity in listening to the Catholic and non-NS secretary (a Krauss spy) whom Baeuml had transferred to another county. Various party leaders, Baeuml said, had openly admitted that the intent of the rumors was to rid the county of Baeuml; Roesch had even offered Baeuml's job to another Beamter, who questioned a transfer not decided by the Interior Ministry, but Roesch assured him that the Gauleitung would take care of everything. The candidate had been called in August 1941 with the message, "The bomb has gone off", the day the Landrat office had been smeared.

It thus became an even more public scandal when someone smeared a tar sign on the Landrat's office wall, stating that he was a black marketeer and should be sent to the gallows. The Landrat called in the Gestapo to find the culprits. First on his list was the mayor, who was "arrested" by the Gestapo and subjected to handwriting analysis to see whether he had written the many postcards. They discovered that Krauss's friends, the secretaries Baeuml had fired, had written some. (Anni Spiegl had written others). The Gestapo reported that the sale of an adjunct of the "*Thing*" memorial had led to the tar smearing.[81]

Krauss played his trump when he denounced Baeuml as hateful to the party,[82] saying: "As a doctor I've come to know how hated Baeuml is". Baeuml had treated women employees and wives of soldiers so badly that they left his office in tears. (The people Krauss referred to were probably his spies.) Even Mayor Roesch, trying to save the people from so brutal a Landrat, was nearly destroyed. Krauss again reported Baeuml's cruelty, the punitive transfer of the Pollenfeld teacher for opposing Schmalzl. Then had come the evidence of Baeuml's black-marketeering.

Baeuml appealed to the Gau and got a September conference by Gau-organizer Haberkern, who insisted on unity. Baeuml wrote that Roesch was notoriously close to the Catholic church, that Roesch had also raised false charges of black market activity against the deputy Landrat. Yet Roesch was but a tool of Krauss, the center of all troublesome elements.[83] Baeuml refused any personal contact with Krauss, who then started a legal action with the Gau court.[84] In October Haberkern talked Krauss into withdrawing his charges, arguing that Eichstaett with its bishop was so difficult that, more than any place else, comradeliness was a necessity. As Haberl had fallen in Russia, the Eichstaett party must finally be rebuilt into a dependable organization. Krauss complained to Haberkern[85] that matters had gotten much worse, that there was now a storm let loose against the old NS because of Baeuml's victory. Haberkern lamented bitterly that the matter had to be brought up again. It was to be hoped that after so long a time the Eichstaetter party members would come to their senses. They should think of the war and let these petty grievances rest.[86] Haberkern fully supported Baeuml's

[81] SK, Krauss, II, 15.12.41.
[82] BDC, Baeuml, letter 24.8.41.
[83] Baeuml letter in SK, Krauss, II.
[84] BDC, Baeuml File report, 17.9.41.
[85] *Ibid.*
[86] *Ibid.*, 30.10.41.

report, adding that no one had tried harder than Haberkern to get some unity in the Eichstaett party. "All of the good words and all of the sharp reprimands, whether in a meeting of the party members, or in a private discussion unfortunately fell on stony ground. One always promised finally to respect the simplest duty of every NS, but unfortunately these promises were never kept."[87]

As in so many such disputes, both sides lost. Baeuml gave his troubles with Krauss as the reason for his leaving for the army in 1942. Krauss, failing to get Gau support, subsided into inaction. With most of the vigorous people called into the army and the war absorbing extra energies, the party and state in Eichstaett went through the motions of power, but the population showed its inner loyalty by going instead en masse to the church.

The fall of Eichstaett to the Americans suggests again who actually led the city. The Prioress took the leading role. There was no Kreisleiter or Landrat; the mayor had fled, more afraid of the SS than the Allies. As a fitting tribute to the unreasoning cruelty of the party in Eichstaett, two "deserters" were hanged at the last moment in the town square.

The city lamented that its first American military governor was more than unusually harsh on all Germans as "Nazis"; Eichstaetters thought they deserved better. Krauss and A. served three years in detention camps, then returned, the doctor to an interrupted practice and church reconciliation and the low-Beamter to the church's gracious forgiveness and a low position in the Catholic party's city hall. Baeuml lived for a time in poverty after his three years in a detention camp, through a difficult denazification, but was granted in time a Beamter position elsewhere in Bavaria. Kraus and Spiegl continued in their proud and victorious faith. The dominant political figure, Dr. Hans Hutter, was the devout student of Naab and successors. He became mayor after his return from five years as a prisoner of war in Russia.

[87] *Ibid.*

6 AUGSBURG

AUGSBURG is a proud city, with the conviction that its historic liberal and dynamic character survived the NS period of "alien" domination. It is one of the very oldest German cities, 1,100 years older than its long-scorned traditional rival, Munich. The city is named for Caesar Augustus. The Romans used its location on the Lech River south of the junction with the Danube as a frontier fort against the Barbarians to the east and north. It became such again after the Roman empire was in local ruins. In a turning point in European history in 955 at Lechfeld, just south of the city, the Germans drove the Magyars back toward Hungary. Thereafter south German Swabians went on the offensive, pushing east to Austria and beyond to settlements that lasted until 1945.

Augsburg remained a frontier fort, of "progressive" Swabians against the "backward" Bavarians, on the other side of the Lech River. Augsburg's location on the plain just north of the Alps provided for its early recovery as the most significant center for traders coming north from Italy. This commercial, and later manufacturing, function was added to the older function as bishopric. The city thus occupied an important role in Catholic history and an even more important role in the Reformation. Its wealth provided for a rich culture and for a record of freedom from 1276 until 1805.

To medieval and Reformation Augsburg should be added its development as a focus of Renaissance power and glory. By 1500 it had become an important international economic center in Europe. The name most often associated with this golden age was Jakob Fugger, probably Augsburg's most famous citizen, and certainly Europe's most famous banker under Charles V and in the politics of the Hapsburg Empire. During the sixteenth century this Protestant city gained fame as the center of religious decision, the "Augsburg Confession" and the "Peace of Augsburg". The prosperity, based on north-south trade, was then retarded by the shifting trade routes and the Thirty Years War. Yet the city survived, becoming the place where famous people were born, from Leopold Mozart to Bertolt Brecht, or the place visited by famous people such as Goethe and Beethoven.

The city's atmosphere of a quiet cultural center was altered by the political and economic events of the nineteenth century. The splendid isolation of a thousand years of independence was ended by Napoleon's absorption of Augsburg into Bavaria, against which the city had stood guard for hundreds of years. Accustomed in a generation to Bavarian rule, it resisted Prussian incursions in 1866; yet with the unification in 1871 it became loyally German, in some ways more akin to the urban Protestant north than to old Bavaria to the east.

Forced into a politically larger German world, Augsburg was among the first to be brought into the economic world with the early railroad to Munich, built between 1835-40. To its old textile industry, rapidly mechanized, came a new basis of rapid growth in a large-scale, machine tool industry. Industry brought to the enriched patricians of the city a disturbing element, a working class made proletariat by the harsh conditions of early industrialism. Their socialist party grew with difficulty, politically outweighed by the entrenched burgers and the devout Swabian peasants. The beautiful façade of the city was bourgeois and seemed solid.

There had been the simultaneous amalgamation of the dozens of petty jurisdictions into a Schwaben from the Danube to the Alps, between Wuerttemberg and Bavaria, with Augsburg as capital. The city was the only significant industrial center. Other than small towns, albeit one-time "imperial free cities" such as Memmingen and Kempten, Schwaben was an idyllic series of villages of Alpine dairy farmers. The rural areas were and are predominantly Catholic, with a few scattered Protestant towns. Augsburg was in Reformation times largely Protestant, but with the rise of industry in the nineteenth century an influx of peasants led to the rise in the number of Catholics and a fairly peaceful balance between Catholicism and Protestantism. Politically the area was predominantly Bavarian Catholic *BVP*, with some socialist party strength in Augsburg's industries.

The war of 1914 was more of a shock to bourgeois society than were the occasional strikes. The proud burghers joined in the enthusiasm, the suffering, and the bitter defeat. Shaken by defeat they found themselves briefly in the hands of the long-suffering workers, some of whom seized the city briefly in April 1919. The burghers rose in righteous wrath, supporting the violence of the Free Corps. Victory over the small numbers of Soviet-led workers "liberated" the city, but left hate and fear that was useful to the NS party then being born in neighboring Munich.

Whether for reasons of its Catholicism or the usual conservatism, Schwaben was one of the areas least NS before 1933, despite the fact that it was close to the NS power center in Munich and played a role in the earliest party history. At the 1929 election in Augsburg, where the party was strongest, the NS got only three of 50 seats in the city council. Of neighboring towns, only one—Friedberg—had any NS representation in city government. In the last free election, on March 5, 1933, the NS received only 32.3% of the vote, compared to 27% for the BVP and 23% for the SPD. In the plebiscites after 1933, Schwaben voted about 10% less NS than the national average. In contrast to some northern areas that were nearly 66% NS in 1933, there was no NS victory on the local Augsburg level; it was national and was imposed on local government from the outside. This influenced the local reaction—a feeling that the NS were somewhat alien, northern, and "un-Swabian" in their radicalism.

The Rise of the NS Party in Augsburg

With but scattered pockets of radicalism and no financial support from outside, and speakers sent from the central office to preach the gospel of hope and hate, the district party depended on determined personalities. The three who held the movement together were the Gauleiter, Karl Wahl, a minor official in the city slaughterhouse, the Kreisleiter Gallus

Schneider, an engineer, and Josef Mayr, a city middle-Beamter. Their fanaticism kept the party in motion, which meant first and foremost continual attendance at meetings and parades to attract attention and demonstrate NS vigor, therewith to build up local parties and local leadership.

The marches through the cities were not only signs of manly vigor but signs of financial weakness. With no industrial financing, with but scattered small-scale offerings from the lower middle class, the local NS had little choice but to march with drums and trumpets to reach the masses. Wahl, Schneider, and Mayr had been able to get a newspaper started in 1931, which acquired few readers, primarily because it lacked the graces of a sellable paper. With a debt of 60,000 marks by 1933, its furniture pawned, and no help from the national organization, the newspaper was close to the end. Only the national victory that year saved it from bankruptcy.

Because most people were unwilling to sacrifice, creating an organization was quite difficult. Not even the Gauleiter got a salary. Getting someone "to lead" meant, Wahl reminisced in 1964, many compromises. Persons were given titles, which by 1933 meant real power, simply because they were the only ones who would take the jobs; many would prove unworthy later.

What most NS recalled with nostalgic pride was "the battle," the street and barroom brawls with the communists or occasionally the socialists. Each side blamed the other for "aggression", but the pattern was clear—enemy meetings must be disrupted by heckling or violence, parades attacked with eggs, stones, or clubs. To these army veterans, sick with the 1918 defeat, or as they preferred to think, "betrayal", it was invigorating to fight again and win.

The police fought, too, with as little reluctance to club National Socialists as communists. Wahl recalled having been beaten four or five times, once by the police. A socialist observer recalled a political meeting in which, at a table of NS, Wahl and Schneider created a disturbance. The police intervened, grabbing Wahl and beating him across the face with rubber clubs until the blood flowed, tore open his shirt, and threw him through the doors to others waiting outside, who threw him down the stairs.[1] Political meetings were no gentle debating sessions, one reason why activists were often more adept with their fists than with their minds, why they gloried in Hitler's description of them as the "old fighters".

What is obvious from the newspapers and police reports is that the NS party out-met all contenders.[2] Most obvious in the campaigns of 1932-33 is the 10-1 ratio in meetings between the NS and any other party. The NS meetings were often ill-attended and simplemindedly repetitive, but the Nazis met and met and met. Travel was difficult; only old cars were available, which meant constant breakdowns and flat tires. If the speaker was lucky, the local agent, usually a Beamter, had arranged a time and place of meeting with someone to talk to.[3]

To Wahl the emphasis was on a show. The value of brochures was dubious; "People don't read". They preferred to watch, but would listen if the subject touched them. Peasants would listen to talks on the farm problem, on order, discipline, or authority in the state. It was important to let them smoke during the meeting.

Hitler's "appointment" as Chancellor came as a near miracle for the local party; salvation was in sight. (The non-NS paper paid much more attention to the pre-Easter Carnival.) The election in March was the signal for local offensives. While the BVP remained fairly passive, the NS by great exertion attracted the usual nonvoter and the percentage of participation rose from 74.9% to 91.9%.[4] Among Swabian cities, the NS percentage was lowest in Augsburg—38%—with Noerdlingen on the northern edge having 60%, the highest. The act celebrated as a symbol of great bravery and national significance was Wahl's symbolic raising of the swastika flag over the city hall on March 9, 1933. The challenge to the old order brought confused reaction. Rather than risk violence with the armed SA guards, the decision

[1] Nerdinger.
[2] *Tagebuch der Aussendienstpolizei*, Augsburg Police Hdqs.
[3] Wahl.
[4] *Neue Augsburger Zeitung*, 6.3.33.

of the city's leaders was simply to raise other flags including the Bavarian.

The next day the NS took effective control of the Munich government. Epp was appointed Reich commissar simultaneous with the announcement that the elected communists would not sit in the new Reichstag, but in concentration camps instead. The local arrests of leftists began under the leadership of the district SA commissar, Ritter von Schoepf. Arrests continued for months, with people going to and coming from prison amid the sarcasm of the NS newspaper. The Reich Law on Coordination of the Laender (April 7, 1933) ordered the reconstitution of the local governments on the basis of the Reichstag election, i.e., with NS majorities despite the local voting results. With arrests of town leftists (230 were noted on April 5) and the ominous notice of the establishment of a concentration camp at Dachau, an hour's drive away, the city council was steadily revamped. Mayr became assistant mayor. By April 22 the NS had seized the council majority.

The Reich "Enabling Act" was optimistically reported by the leading non-NS newspaper *(Neue Augsburger Zeitung)* with its newly acquired carefulness, "as an opening to constitutional reform". It also nearly brought the demise of the paper which was forbidden for six days while the editors pleaded with the local authorities, notably Schoepf, for permission to resume publication. Permission was granted, but at the cost of the small voice of criticism the paper had permitted itself since the March election. It remained a better written, more popular echo of the drab NS paper, with a slight tendency toward a more factual approach, until closed by wartime shortages in 1944.

The socialist paper had shut down in April 1933 without ceremony, but with savage violence and plunder by NS rowdies. A local book-burning in May 1933 gave further evidence of the end of "unpatriotic" (critical) information. Further steps toward the end of democracy in Augsburg was the destruction of the unions on May 2nd. On May 12 the remaining SPD were removed from the city council, and by

June 26 the remaining non-NS on the council had resigned in hopes of escaping concentration camps or worse.

The changes, accompanied by propaganda about the new free Germany and arrests of any "treacherous" objectors, were irresistible. Young socialists waited for orders to pour into the streets and battle the hated Nazis. They have ever since questioned the caution of their leaders, many of whom were already arrested. Although a similar attitude has been described by many young priests looking in vain for some signal to resist the NS takeover, it would have likely been a bloodbath, as Hitler had a mass following, army and state support, a claim to legality, a unity of command and purpose, with every likelihood of ruthlessly winning any test of power.

Other than its frightening leftists into submission, the first stage of the takeover was characterized by brief outbreaks of anti-Semitism. Sporadic beatings of Jews by the SA, although not officially encouraged, were surely the implication of the vicious agitation. A successful boycott of Jewish stores was reported in April 1933 in the NS paper as a German triumph over Jewry. "Only the iron discipline of the party saved Jews from popular wrath", it said. Actually the SA had failed to stop patronage of Jewish stores. But boycotts became more subtle, and in five years' time were effective. The only other overt and mass attack on the defeated "enemies" came after the burning of the favorite NS meeting hall on May 1, 1934, which led to many arrests. After some denunciation of their treachery, everyone was released. The unpublished police report noted that the fire was the result of negligence, not the trumpeted "sabotage".[5]

Augsburg differed in the extent of local party power and in the intensity of the violence against socialists and Jews. Yet in any state, anyone with power continues the process of expansion or defense of his domain, against other domains or against the suppressed masses. There followed not only this defense of personal and local power but a difference in policy implementation occasioned by personal and local cir-

[5] *Tagebuch*, 3.5.34.

cumstance and the values of the holder of power. Such was clearly the case in Augsburg, beginning with Karl Wahl.

Gauleiter Wahl

The stereotype Gauleiter of the whip-carrying, heavy-heeled, brute has an obvious basis in fact. Such men did well in the brawling early history of the party. One had to be fanatic, and it helped to be physically tough. But otherwise Wahl does not fit the stereotype. He was ill at ease among the Streichers and Adolf Wagners. Unique among Gauleiters, after his three years in prison, Wahl openly condemned the crimes of the regime, with a defense of the good intentions of "stupid men like myself" who gave the NS loyalty.

A small man with a large prominent forehead and something of the clerk and hospital orderly remaining about him, Wahl had the softness of manner and speech regarded as "Swabian". Some of his early newspaper clippings contained threats of violence to his enemies; his most famous quote referred to the NS state as something to be protected, as a lioness would her cub; yet Wahl's manner was soft in private. The most frequent ingroup complaint was, "Karl was too good", to which he always answered, "How can one be too good?". All who knew him as a person agreed that he was humble and well-meaning. He was not brilliant, not really powerful, nor vicious. Wahl's major fault as a leader, other than his political stupidity, was an unwillingness to intervene with subordinates who needed disciplining. He was too socially insecure for that. In class-conscious Germany, where the *Doktor* was all important, Wahl was well aware that he lacked the necessary training for his office. From a poor family, he had been forced from school at an early age into a subordinate role. In the army-like classless society to be created by Hitler, all would be treated as equals because all were fellow Germans. Wahl was proudest of his office hours, during which anyone was invited to bring any complaint. He held "court" twice a week in Augsburg and scorned other Gauleiter who wasted their time hunting, "the mania of the newly great".

At Wahl's trial, that he could not be charged with committing any crime was due partly to his inactivity. A friendly critic saw him as phlegmatic, like so many other Swabians, sitting for hours in a tavern saying nothing. An admiring colleague thought an illness in 1936-37 had robbed Wahl of his earlier energy, leaving good-naturedness as his remaining predominant characteristic. Wahl became convinced that if he kept things quiet in Schwaben, he would avoid dangerous publicity. Most people regarded as typical his reaction on learning that subordinates had arrested a man for having criticized him—Wahl immediately ordered his release and sent the man a letter of apology.

His most publicized action in the early years was the campaign to remove poverty from the Danube marshlands. To the end, he remained a person with more sympathy for the little man, with whom he could identify and mingle comfortably. Yet despite his lower class predilection for greater social equality, he did not attack wealth nor seize it. He had little liking for the greedy party elite. Other than this mania for Hitler, which was permanent despite his clear postwar break with the NS movement, he was ordinarily a sensible cautious person. Not the kind of person to make any stir in national politics, rather one to be found sitting rather placidly in the back row, still he was very proud of having "conquered his Gau", and was determined to keep it free from outside interference if possible.

The Party versus the SA

After 1945 Wahl identified himself with an internal party opposition to the police state of radicals.[6] He pictured himself, and other idealists who had followed Hitler, betrayed by the clique around Hitler, notably Himmler and Bormann. Wahl claimed to have modified, where possible, the orders for arrests that came from Berlin. Hundreds of persons testified at his de-Nazification proceedings that he had done just that and had been highly critical of Hitler's police state. For the

[6] Karl Wahl, *Es ist ein deutsches Herz*, Augsburg, 1954, 54; or see his introductory statement in his de-Nazification trial.

police, he doubtless retained a sincere antipathy, but he had to learn to fear the SA; Ritter von Schoepf taught him how.

The first competitor for power was this SA commissar, given, in the NS fashion, "plenipotentiary powers" which conflicted with Wahl's own plenipotentiary powers. (His "von" was a title for military bravery, not from family; his relative poverty was evidenced by the charge that he had stolen an SA comrade's coat in 1932.[7]) Schoepf came from outside the Gau. After entering the SA in 1931, he served as an honored hero in various parts of northern Germany until he was sent to Augsburg in February 1932, where he was "heartily welcomed" by Wahl.[8] Schoepf's critics described him as a brutal arrogant man with whom it was impossible to talk. His semi-defenders suggest that it was primarily a drinking problem that made him difficult. Drunk or sober, he followed a policy of widespread arrests, implemented by sub-commissars sent to various sections of the Gau. He was quoted as saying, "Even Gauleiters can be arrested".[9]

Whether because of rivalry for power or his honest rejection of the violence that hovered around Schoepf, Wahl worked to get him dismissed. Wahl came to regard commissars as completely unnecessary, as much so as the concentration camps, since both commissars and people in the camps were no threat to the state. He complained to Wagner; and went a dozen times to Roehm trying to get Schoepf fired. Only after gaining Hitler's attention and being required to submit a written account of Schoepf's behavior, with the accent on the latter's drunkenness, did Wahl get rid of him in January 1934. Schoepf claimed he had been railroaded out of office, that the photograph of him "drunk" on a park bench was merely of a nap from overwork. Schoepf was arrested in late 1939 for remarks "hostile to the state" and given a two-months sentence.[10]

Another overblown SA leader arrived and was reported in the paper to be the "ideal comrade and leader". Wahl found

[7] BDC—Schoepf SA File.
[8] *Neue National Zeitung* (NNZ), 15.2.32.
[9] Aschka.
[10] BRP, Schwaben, 9.12.39.

him "too small for the position" and got him fired within six months. Schwaben's reports had protested the SA arrogance, noting the need for limits on the authority of the SA and even on the party itself.[11] In April 1934, 50 SA forced a mayor out by chanting "traitor" in front of his house.[12] Wahl regretted such interference in political affairs by party men who lacked ability and whose "previous failures or dubious pasts brought them public contempt".[13] He had stopped such an attack on Woolworth's.[14]

By the time the third SA leader in 18 months had arrived, Roehm had been killed. Wahl expressed his joy in a letter of congratulation to Hitler; his only fear was that Hitler had been bothered. "I am filled [Wahl said] with particular pride today that for two years I have been the object of an irreconcilable hatred by this SA leadership clique, now ended by the Fuehrer."[15] Wahl spoke for Schwaben; all but a few breathed easier with the SA out of the local picture.

The immediate gainers were party leaders, like Wahl, and the state officials. The eventual gainers were the SS, until then an adjunct of the SA in Augsburg and small in numbers, albeit a big nuisance. The SA report in March 1933[16] noted the SA struggle with the SS for control of the police between SA Schoepf and SS Loritz, the latter reported by everyone as being arrogant and hated in the city. If the SS were to get the police, the SA "would be very restless".[17] SS organizations were nearly nonexistent in Schwaben, but Augsburg had a unit "commanded" since 1933 by an SS police president. About six of the SS were the town rowdies, the subject of frequent critical police reports, and a problem to Wahl. Their half-suppressed hatred of civilized society, later harnessed for incredible barbarisms by Himmler during the war, was, in local situations, primarily a matter of barroom violence against anyone who annoyed them, including the SA and the police.

[11] *Ibid.*, 6.10.33 and 3.3.34.
[12] *Ibid.*, 17.4.34.
[13] *Ibid.*, 1.10.34.
[14] *Ibid.*, 4.6.34.
[15] NNZ, 2.7.34.
[16] Schambeck in BDC File on Malsen Ponickau.
[17] BRP, Schwaben, 5.1.34.

Like most partially tolerated petty criminals, these SS were well known to the police. Beating up helpless Jews or socialists was scarcely a matter on which the police could challenge them, but excesses led to a counterattack by party and police which kept the SS in Augsburg under restraint, if not in their own world of concentration camps and conquered lands. In late 1933 an Augsburg SS man shot down a tavern-keeper, only to be freed by the judge. Another threw a communist worker out of a tavern, which killed the worker. A braver judge found the accused guilty and sentenced him to seven months. In court, the SS, including Humann, the police president, created a disturbance throughout the trial. On the evening of the verdict the SS challenged the authority of the state more directly by gathering outside the judge's home to shout abuse, and in their enthusiasm fired shots through his window. They were arrested on May 20.[18]

Also in May, Wahl and Mayr had to intervene to stop SS brawls with soldiers and civilians. Wahl's report regretted that the police could not deal with SS-SA attacks on Catholic charity collectors.[19] He noted a general popular disapproval of such attacks on Jewish windows in late May, as well as the illegal signs saying Jews were not welcome.[20] Renewed attacks on Jewish windows should be stopped, Wahl wrote in August.[21] A window smearer, a party cell leader, was arrested in September and released after a warning.[22]

Wahl's support of the police in their effort to contain SS violence may not be as impressive as Augsburgers believe, but with the export of these rowdies, first to trial in Munich, then disappearance from the scene into obscure camps as guards, there were no more such disturbances. The state was supreme locally.

Just as Augsburg had for decades felt itself threatened by the more dynamic and powerful Munich, so Wahl felt threatened by his neighboring Gauleiter, Wagner, who was much closer to the national party geographically and ideologically.

[18] *Tagesbuch*, 20.5.34.
[19] BRP, Schwaben, 1.6.35.
[20] *Ibid.*
[21] *Ibid.*, 1.8.35.
[22] *Ibid.*, 1.10.35.

With the aspiration of absorbing small Schwaben and ending the soft policies of Wahl, Wagner offered Wahl a phony advancement as assistant to Epp, but Wahl scorned the offer; after all he had "conquered" Schwaben. Yet Wahl's Gau nearly disappeared on various occasions. The leader of the Save Schwaben movement—Mayor Merkt of Kempten—informed Mayor Stoeckle in August 1933 that Siebert was on the verge of dispensing with the small Gau.[23] Siebert was "too busy" to see Wahl and Merkt, August 18, but sent word that he had already signed the law on "simplification of the state", and it would have to run its course. Merkt would not give up. By November they got an audience with a Munich Beamter who informed them without explanation that the law had been "delayed".

In 1934 Reichsleiter Ley suggested that there were too many Gaue, useful perhaps during the days of fighting for power when local initiative helped, but not useful as administrative units. Wahl declined the suggestion, only to receive a note from Hitler informing him that his Gau was dissolved and had been absorbed into Wagner's. A call to Ley informed Wahl that the order had come from Hitler and that absolutely nothing could be done. Wahl announced he would go immediately to Berlin. Ley told him not to bother Hitler whose signature was clearly on the document. Wahl suggested that many things have signatures without the signer being aware of them, and asked Ley not to publish the news.

When Wahl reached Berlin he was informed by Ley's adjutant that Hitler was busy all day and could not receive him. Wahl simply sat in Hitler's outer office the entire day. Late in the evening Hitler appeared, expressed surprise at finding Wahl in Berlin and asked what he could do for him. He then told Wahl that he had merely approved a reduction of Gaue, without knowing which would be eliminated. When appealed to by an "old fighter", Hitler agreed to reverse the Ley decision, with one condition that it not be reversed if once made public, to avoid the impression of confusion or indecision. Unfortunately Ley had had the news already pub-

[23] ASA 104/0101.

lished in the party paper. Wahl did not give up. He went to see Hitler again, overcoming the resistance of Ley and Hess, and talked him into an unpleasant reversal, the limitation being simply that the order would be reversed, but that the reversal would not be published.[24] Hitler was always very pleasant, Wahl thought, and would have made far fewer mistakes were he not the prisoner of the clique around him.

Wilhelm Aschka, the local DAF leader, linked the affair to a group inside Schwaben that was trying to get rid of Wahl. If so, this is the only reported rebellion Wahl faced. Probably his tolerance of subordinates made acceptance of his nominal power easier than rebellion. Wahl's critics thought Schwaben was largely ignored. Hitler almost never visited the city, in contrast to Nuremberg; yet Augsburg was later among the few cities selected by Hitler for special building subsidies.

Another threat in 1935 was turned aside by Merkt and Wahl. Merkt asked Mayr to write and protest the plans for Bavaria. Wahl had gotten all of his Kreisleiter except Schneider to write. Wahl gave up on Schneider, so Mayr should use some listed arguments about why it would be a bad move. The Gau was saved from reform by Wahl's perseverance and Hitler's sentiment.

Wahl as District President

With the Gau saved from Munich, the question uppermost in the Bavarian state papers was how to integrate the party leaders into the government. An early solution, pleasing to the officials but not to the five proud Gauleiters, was to permit them to attend the cabinet meetings. This involved trips to Munich to sit in on meetings in which each would have little influence, countered by the greater belligerency of a neighboring Gauleiter or the greater factual knowledge of a high Beamter primed for the meeting. Another proposal would have left the party and state separated on the local level, with state officials merely implementing orders from above—which would have excluded the local princes from a

[24] Wahl, *Herz*, 59.

role in the state and created an independent bureaucracy of which they were justifiably afraid.

The solution "adopted" in mid-1934 was to make the Gauleiter simultaneously the district president. Wahl later expressed regret at this device and explained it as largely a matter of party treasurer stinginess, an unwillingness to pay Gauleiter from party funds. He also expressed later a strong reluctance for taking the position, not evident in the record. Years of financial stringency must have made the salary of a president seem most attractive.

Whether Wahl wanted to be president is moot, but not that he rarely acted as one. He was head of the Schwaben state in name only. Beamten are quite status-conscious; one belongs to a certain level of the bureaucracy and reaches the top, if at all, only by compliance with the prescribed procedure. To have been a president would have meant being a "higher Beamten", which Wahl, as a clerk, was not. Training as a jurist would have also have been necessary, which Wahl also did not have. It is no wonder that Wahl rarely entered his president's office—some guess less than five times in 11 years. The administration of the state was turned over to old Beamten, particularly a Dr. Schwaab, who, like most of his fellows, had joined the party very late. He testified after the war that Wahl never asked the Beamten either to be party members or behave as such, but simply to do their jobs honestly.[25]

In his first speech Wahl extended the hand of friendship to those officials who were loyal to the Fuehrer but undying enmity to those who were hoping for the fall of the NS. He also asked the officials to treat the common man with the same courtesy they treated the upper classes.[26] The NS newspaper (NNZ) carried a denunciation by Wahl of those officials who might still consider party men such as himself, as dumbheads, fools, or rowdies. The public bluster against his new servants was balanced by a private awe of his Beamten "betters". The second-ranking person to Schwaab—Kreisslmeyer—reputedly scolded the President Gauleiter in front of

[25] SK, Wahl, 323. [26] NAZ 2.5.34.

everyone with impunity. Some thought Wahl was afraid of Kreisslmeyer's sharp tongue, which was always scolding the party, even asking new NS Beamten, "How can you belong to such a criminal organization?"[27] Wahl conceded that Kreisslmeyer was a difficult person to deal with. (Because Wahl had not forced him into the party, he was judged fit to become district president by the occupation powers.)

The Gauleiter busied himself, instead, with talking to anyone who had a complaint, and with his party organization, to try to make it viable. Usually called in to settle arguments, Wahl seems otherwise to have had little direct impact on local policy decisions, although visitors to the Gau detected a more relaxed atmosphere. Yet Wahl "presided" over rabid Kreisleiters like the one in Memmingen, whom he would later recall as "a bit overeager", and apathetic Kreisleiters, later considered "a bit lazy". He gave them little trouble, since one element of his continuance in power was that he could keep the peace.

An example of the tolerated diversity was in the schools. Wahl's choice for district school leader was relatively incompetent and fanatic. Yet Wahl also supported a highly competent and nonconformist scholar in Augsburg, whom few other Gauleiters would have permitted as a teacher, much less school superintendent. Rural schools remained the domain of the church, inculcated mostly Catholicism, while urban schools were formally instilling Nazism and racism.

Another area for minor local discretion was in the treatment of the Jews. In 1933-34 the local party, sometimes with Wahl's signature, denounced the Jews and urged the NS to stop patronizing their stores. Wahl's criticism of Jews was mild for the times. He criticized any attacks on them. He seems to have taken no role in persecuting Jews nor any public role in stopping the persecution. The most interesting evidence linking him to post-1934 anti-Semitism was a letter of his adjutant complaining about the relative luxury of Jews living in Augsburg in 1941.[28] In some individual cases in Augsburg Jews or half-Jews were given extraordinary as-

[27] Reg. Dir. von Rebay.

[28] CGD, T 81, R 179.

sistance by Wahl. Several were kept in key positions; he claimed even to have kept a Jewish Kreisleiter in power throughout. Anti-Semitic pressures which continued and which led to the expulsion of most Jews seem to have been either inspired by "subordinates" whom he did not stop or who were directed by Himmler. Wahl's postwar position seems to be a sincere regret for what "Bormann and Himmler did" to the Jews.

Another area of local policy difference was Wahl's attitude toward the Catholic church. There are isolated references in the newspapers to Wahl's opposition to church criticism of Hitler, but in general he favored cooperation of church and state. He was raised a Protestant, his wife a Catholic. The children were Catholic. None of his family left the church, nor did Wahl. Members of his staff did, and one report is that he asked them to. Wahl denied that either he or Hitler ever made any such request. If Wahl intervened, it was to assist the church, as he did in individual cases. Yet pressure on the church in Swabia was only slightly less than elsewhere. Anyone could denounce a pastor to the Gestapo as hostile to the state or as a sexual deviant. A "normal" number were arrested, more than in Franken.

Most remarkable in Swabia was the close cooperation achieved by Wahl and the second in command of the diocese, Bishop Eberle. Citizens were amazed to see the two walking together deep in conversation, a sight unthinkable elsewhere. Wahl and Eberle were both mavericks within their own institutions. Patriot Eberle took the position that the church should cooperate where possible, and for a time urged Catholics to join the party to work from within. He seems to have gone far beyond the wishes of his superiors as in his famous effort—without authorization—to negotiate directly with Hitler.[29] He wrote in October 1937 to Hitler of his admiration for his great work—this despite the bitter campaign already waged by the party against the church, which had dissuaded most church leaders from any hope for Hitler. Eberle asked for a chance to present his ideas for coopera-

[29] BA R43II/155a.

tion of church and state to Hitler. He noted in closing that no one but Wahl knew of his plan.

Eberle got his interview with the admired Hitler. Thereafter he implemented his plan by writing to three cardinals and to Pacelli, reporting Hitler's "desire for peace with the church". One cardinal declined to answer; the second sent a note showing receipt of the letter. Eberle's own cardinal—Faulhaber—answered after a two-week delay, asking him for a conference which, Eberle reported to Hitler, was completely without result. Faulhaber was completely disinterested in the plan. Eberle had been informed that the Bavarian bishops had discussed his ideas, but was not told of their conclusions. In January 1938 Pacelli requested a report. Eberle answered that Hitler wanted peace, but that naturally the church must change its policy, and not trust "false information" from Catholic emigrés. Pacelli had not answered; he probably saw Eberle as a hopeless case. A letter from Eberle in April to other bishops was also without result. Like Wahl, he seems to have been the only one ready to compromise. The nature of his compromise concerned youth, with the state given the area of "youth training", the church that of "religious training". While Wahl the compromiser and Eberle the burning patriot were in such amicable conversation, priests were being arrested even in Schwaben and dying in concentration camps for having defended the church's claim to any loyalty from the youth.

The Gau vs. Reich

In a sense, Wahl was part of two different governments—the party with its high command of Hess and then Bormann, and the state with its command through the Bavarian government to Hitler or one of his ministers. Although Wahl could send in requests for action in local matters, along with highly critical reports, with some hope of influencing someone's opinion somewhere, the Gauleiter, as such, had no voice in central policy. Conferences called by Hitler were simply to inform the Gauleiters of a decision already taken. There was no provision for questions, much less discussion or suggestions.

Frequently the Gauleiter, so praised and honored by great titles, were informed of an important decision such as the invasion of Russia by reading of it in the newspapers. Of other major decisions, such as to liquidate the Jews, the Gauleiters were never officially informed. On inquiry Wahl was told either the Jews were being taken to labor camps in the east or that it was none of his business. Should a Gauleiter have discovered any part of the horrible truth, it would have been by chance, as with any other citizen.

Although nearly powerless in Berlin, Wahl was correct in a sense in stating that he was independent in his Gau: "It is a silly fairy tale that the Gauleiter did not have any freedom in operation, that they willingly obeyed in the most narrowminded way all of the orders from above. There was for each Gauleiter other than the general party line, from which he could deviate at any time, no definite paragraphs or party dogma, with which he must comply. His commands were in his own heart. . . . With the Kreisleiters the situation was the same; they also had a far-reaching freedom, which they could use according to the situation of each Kreis. . . .It is further a mistaken idea that the NSDAP operated only with orders from above. In seventeen long years I never gave a single order".[30] Yet Wahl is also correct in contradicting himself a few pages later in noting that there were many different groups other than his party organization at work in each Gau,[31] each responsible to some different state or party agency in Berlin, and not to the Gauleiter. The most notorious enclave in his Gau were the police. Originally they were subject to some local influence, but with Himmler's centralization of the police the Gauleiter might ask that someone be arrested or be released, but it was up to Himmler or a subordinate to give the permission.

The anarchy was such that Wahl could report that only once was he inspected to see whether he had complied with instructions from above: "no one would have dared to compel a Gauleiter". An inspector from Bormann came to see whether his orders to close the cloisters had been carried out.

[30] Wahl, *Herz*, 83. [31] *Ibid.*, 88.

Wahl knew the man well; they addressed each other as old friends, with *du*. They agreed that this was a "hobby horse" of Bormann's. Wahl concluded by saying that he would have to think about it, and that was the last he heard of it; no action was taken.[32]

Doubtless Wahl chose on occasion to implement an order vigorously, moderately, or not at all, assuming correctly that whatever he did, very few of those who issued the orders could get Hitler to throw him out, and even fewer would try, as long as he did not interfere with their operations. This meant, of course, that Wahl accepted the concentration camps and worse, with only protests to Hitler, who had replied that they were necessary for the time being; or Wahl could get some individual out of the crushing machinery.

This was a value judgment made by anyone who stayed in any position of authority and was subject to endless debate about which was worse—staying and trying to moderate, or leaving the field to the "radicals". Wahl and his DAF man, Aschka, rejected the wartime order from Berlin to close down the vital textile industry. Claiming that competitors were after Augsburg, they battled until the order was rescinded. Those Wahl helped bless him for it; those who know only of the terror he assisted by his presence naturally condemn him as an accomplice.

The important variable involved was the courage and determination of the Gauleiter to deviate, and the determination of Hitler, or someone with Hitler's support, notably Himmler or Bormann to gain compliance. When things were going well, no one rocked the boat, e.g., from 1934 to 1943; when things were clearly in need of some new policy, such as 1944-45, people began pushing each other to escape the disaster that no one could admit he saw coming.

Wahl in his naive confidence in Hitler's judgment "when properly advised", offered his advice. In June 1941 he sent his congratulations to Hitler for the war on Russia and suggested seriously that the party leaders were not really needed on the home front, where their presence weakened the party

[32] Wahl.

in the eyes of the public. Therefore they should be sent to the Russian front.[33] Bormann answered angrily that the party leaders were more necessary than ever before for the "education" of the people.

Wahl aroused more anger from Bormann for his abortive effort in 1943 to create his special "home guard".[34] Wahl's orders had included the police, who objected to their loss of free time through channels up to Himmler, who, in turn, had ordered them to ignore anyone else's orders. Yet Wahl persisted, arguing that Himmler had no right to give him orders; only Hitler could. In October Kaltenbrunner told Himmler that Wahl's Home Guards were armed, not under Himmler's command, and not with only party members, as Wahl had reported. Bormann informed Wahl that he was acting contrary to orders, that the party's position had changed in 1933; it was no longer against the state but with the state. A November SS report noted that Wahl was continuing despite Bormann's order to stop, bringing much confusion because loyal party members and police did not know whom to obey. Himmler joined in the denunciation, to which Wahl answered in December that Himmler did him a great injustice in accepting so false an interpretation. The denunciators should be arrested. Among the charges brought by Wahl was that the police who had not been properly (party) motivated were using this opportunity to further weaken the party vis-à-vis the state.[35]

In January 1944 the local SS raised the question of what to do about the one policeman who obeyed Wahl—should he be sent to the Russian front? He was 56, had a hernia, varicose veins, and wore glasses. Himmler compromised, sending the poor man to Alsace instead. After another denunciation of Wahl by the local SS, for his falsely claiming to have authorization that he refused to let anyone see, Wahl gave in (Jan. 24, 1944). Himmler wrote a conciliatory letter suggesting that they have a friendly chat, to which Wahl re-

[33] CGD T 81, R 179 F 8919ff.

[34] T 175, R 31, 21.9.43.

[35] BDC, Wahl, *Partei Kanzlei Korrespondenz.*

plied with pleasure. Later in the year the long-delayed appointment of Wahl in the SS was announced, although in an investigation in 1943 the observer had concluded that Wahl was undeserving since he showed no interest in SS affairs.[36]

The very end saw denunciations again from Bormann, in this case of Wahl's lack of support to the similar *Volksturm* militia. Wahl answered that he had made the same proposal two years before and Bormann had vetoed it.[37] Wahl performed a clearer service to his Gau by refusing to send 5,000 men to dig trenches because they were needed for war production at home;[38] Bormann cancelled the order, although any Gau could have provided a similar analysis of manpower needs.

Mayor Mayr

The banishment of the very capable mayor, Dr. Otto Bohl, in 1933 without fault except for his BVP connection, was done with more than the usual decency. When Mayr was made second mayor in April, Bohl wrote him that he trusted Mayr to serve Augsburg, at the same time, impressing on him the importance of law and local autonomy.[39] Bohl later testified that he had, contrary to NS wishes, gotten Mayr as second mayor instead of the radical Schneider. By June the NS pressure was such that Bohl had to resign. At this point Mayr advised Bohl when and where to hide to avoid the wave of arrests. Then he got his safe passage promised by local SS. Mayr had respectfully gotten him a safe, good-paying, unpolitical position at a city-operated resort hotel in another town. Bohl thought Mayr actually would have preferred for Bohl to remain mayor, and tried to keep him. Over the years, Mayr supported Bohl against the party, even to the welcoming of Jewish guests at the hotel.[40]

Mayr was not made mayor immediately, partly because he did not have the *Doktor*. He had taken extra evening

[36] T 81, R 179, F 8943 and T 175 R 31.
[37] BDC, Wahl File, *Partei Kanzlei Korrespondenz*, 19.2.45.
[38] T 81, R 179 F 8919.
[39] ASA 108/57, 3.4.33.
[40] Bohl in SK J. Mayr.

instruction to advance himself, but was not within sight of the usual university training for mayors. Instead, a Dr. Edmund Stoeckle was imported, partly as protégé of Siebert, partly because he had the requisite formal background and had been mayor of a smaller town, and partly because he was active in the SS with rightist activity back to Epp's Free Corps and the Kapp Putsch.

Stoeckle did not last long; he was "called to Berlin" in December 1934. Some blame his departure on Mayr's sharp elbows. Mayr answered that Stoeckle simply was never there. Lethmaier, the permanent fixture as mayoral assistant before, during, and after the NS period, thought Stoeckle had paid too little attention to party affairs. Interested only in sports, Stoeckle had not built a basis of party support. Others attributed Stoeckle's rapid fall to a romance with a singer, which led to his divorce and a second marriage. Wagner wrote Wahl that neither Mayr nor Kellner were legally qualified to replace him, that only Frick could make the exceptions; Frick quickly approved.[41]

Mayr's specialty, learned from Bohl, was finance; he made the misleading public claim that Augsburg had been saved from bankruptcy by his financial ability. His first pronouncement as mayor was in favor of a balanced budget and extra expenditures for social needs. His administration concentrated on money. Mayr rarely spoke, and then with speeches written by the local NS editor. He felt himself more secure among columns of figures. He was regarded, other than in the blatantly flattering newspapers, as a man of medium *Format*, who did his work industriously, with no particular political emphasis. "He simply took charge of the cash register".[42] His chief assistant—Max Lethmaier, a devout Catholic who did not join the party and yet served for 45 years at city hall—regarded Mayr as moderate and decent, his administration competent and honest but not brilliant.[43] Lethmaier knew of no corruption; some of the city council received some favoritism with city contracts, as before and since, but not if there were a major difference in price.

[41] ASA 105/03. [42] Aschka. [43] Lethmaier.

The major evidence of Mayr's moderation is his deep respect for two non-NS Beamten, Drs. Ott and Kleindienst. His keeping these two "blacks" in two crucial offices of the city was greatly criticized by his nominal superiors in Munich, notably Wagner, but Mayr defended them for years, including the threat to leave if they were forced out. Wahl backed him up—and that was that. No one has questioned Ott's non-NS status (his record was clean enough for him to be made acting mayor in 1945). Kleindienst, in the more exposed cultural department, made more concessions. Critics noted a picture of Hitler in his office and thought his *Heils* more frequent than necessary; but Kleindienst would not join the party.

Lethmaier reported that Mayr remained business-like, rarely bringing the party into city hall discussions. He did not operate on the "Fuehrer principle", but encouraged discussion and left his department heads their traditional autonomy. He depended heavily on jurists Ott and Kleindienst, and on NS jurists Steinhauser and Bobinger as city attorneys. At meetings he would admit, "I'm no lawyer, what do you think?" He accepted their judgment of the law as binding.[44] Mayr worked well together with Wahl, although he criticized the Gauleiter for lack of initiative in protecting or advancing Augsburg.

The second mayor—Kellner—had the reputation of being the city hall radical. In charge of the personnel office, he could frighten those on the lower levels into the party or into a silent corner, with sarcasm or, on occasion, attacks of rage. When he instructed department heads to collect for the party charity, he emphasized that no compulsion should be used, although he was "sure that every employee would see his patriotic duty".[45] Ninety-three percent of the Beamten did, compared to only 62% of the employees and 32% of the workers. Some viewed Kellner as "not so bad", hard-working, although of medium capacity and less than medium training despite efforts to improve himself. He also had the reputation of being the city hall Don Juan; the aura of scan-

[44] Steinhauser and Bobinger. [45] ASA 110/047.

dal about him was partially redeemed in the eyes of the community after the war, when his last mistress remained loyal to him through his various trials.

There were no mass firings for party reasons, except on the city council, which became largely extraneous, as the NS party hacks could not dominate Mayr with his authoritarian powers. A leader of the resistance, the lawyer Reisert defended Mayr after the war. Of 4,000 city employees, he found only one who had been released for political reasons.[46] Fourteen were temporarily released before Mayr became mayor. Of these, three were Jewish, the others apparently SPD; six were streetcar employees, and four were city lifeguards.[47] The lifeguards caused a lengthy controversy. One was charged with having said that a party member had lice. This angered Wahl who thought that this non-NS should also learn about the misery of the unemployed, as had the NS. It would do him good to suffer a bit before the city found him another job. (Frick got involved and wrote for a generous interpretation for the non-NS.) A Mayr order limited "automatic" firings to communists, yet Reisert showed that a communist released from Dachau was given city employment.

Kleindienst testified that only once was a NS candidate given preference and then for a position in the theater. When this party man failed artistically, Mayr fired him immediately and ordered Kleindienst to get a good *Intendant* whether party or nonparty. Neither the city librarian nor archivist were NS. The library retained its forbidden books, yet did not leave them in the catalog; anyone with a "reason" was permitted to use Jewish or Marxist works. The city policy of promotions gave definite preference to the "old fighters"; a total of 15 received promotions in 1937-39.[48] Yet these were to minor positions and the normal promotion referred only to technical skills and nearly completely ignored party status. The policy was that party members with the equal qualifications received priority.[49]

[46] F. Reisert in SK J. Mayr. [47] ASA 110/040.
[48] ASA 110/048.
[49] ASA 110/0300, 26.10.38; also Lethmaier's view.

Mayr forbade the distribution of *Der Stuermer* at city hall. When Goebbel's local office tried to peddle anti-Semitic pamphlets to city offices, each asked Mayr what to do. His answer was, "No need exists".[50] He seems to have abandoned party activity. His only party office was one for communal politics, which devoted its very occasional efforts simply to defending local autonomy and giving advice to area communities on how to avoid interference in their business.

Kellner complained in 1941 to the Municipal Organization about party interference, in particular the party claim that it could try any Beamter in a party court. It was an "impossible situation" if any party member could initiate party action against his superior and have even a mayor hauled in front of a party court.[51] The Schwaben government backed the party, but fortunately the Bavarian government took a more reasonable position. Kellner listed the party charges against the city administration: using its influence against party work and the party charity; discouraging listening to a Fuehrer speech; and many "discourtesies".

Mayr became increasingly unhappy with limitations on his independence as mayor.[52] Not only did he come to believe that the Reich ministries, though NS, lacked the good old Beamten skill and tradition, but that the Laender ministries could be abolished without loss. But worst was intervention by "party men who did not understand the problems". The order dividing the party and state responsibilities had been "ignored by the party". It had the right to watch to see that NS were put in public office, but their further "illegal interferences were becoming unbearable".

The Mayor and the Kreisleiter

A common practice in the early days of the "revolution" was to give the party leader the comparable state position. This solution was not taken in Augsburg, for several reasons, most of them concerning the personality of the Kreisleiter. Tall, ascetic Schneider was another of the bright and ambi-

[50] ASA 100/050, 29.11.39.
[51] ASA 126/03. [52] ASA 120/03, 11.10.44.

tious people prevented from higher careers by the social rigidities of the early twentieth century. His training as a practical engineer, an occupation which kept him out of military service in World War I to his later regret, sufficed to give him a middle class income but not the rank of an "Academician" nor the legal training usually expected of a mayor. Schneider, an excellent speaker, would have qualified in the parliamentary sense. He would have had the support of the lesser party members and the more radical, but Mayr had the support of the city Beamten, of whom he was one, and more importantly the support of another old city Beamter, Wahl, who felt less at ease with Schneider, the "fire-eater".

Schneider may well have preferred the position of first critic of the city, rather than the burden of the strange office. For a time he was on the city council in a sort of tribunal role, but his efforts to influence Mayr without Wahl's backing proved fruitless, and he soon gave up. Not a particularly social person, but an ascetic who disapproved of the drinking and rollicking stories of the veteran-like meetings of the "old fighters", Schneider remained an outsider. He regarded himself as a selfless person, fully committed to Hitler and Germany, and thought deriving personal advantage improper. He devoted himself therefore to party affairs, working days at his engineering job as before, and evenings on party business, with 30 ward leaders to supervise. He did not have these well in hand; evidence thereto was their conduct—taking advantage of their position in ways Schneider would not.

That Schneider was a fanatic Hitlerite is denied by none, nor that he remained one after the war. During their postwar imprisonment Wahl was shaken by Schneider's bland prediction that they would be back on top within three years. This lack of reality was expressed notably in 1933 by newspaper appeals for NS activity and expressions of anti-Semitism. To his credit, Schneider profited little from his power, and, seemingly, was not overly eager to throw persons in jail. The police chief "remembered" no denunciations from Schneider; the postwar trial found seven denunciations that had gone through Schneider's office, one concerning a 60-

year-old woman sentenced to three years for "disloyal" remarks. Although his anti-Semitism, learned, he said, from his former Catholic church, survived the war, there is no evidence of an overt act against any particular Jew. His trial could find no act of violence. Schneider's was the intellectual act, the assassination by words which lead to the worst kind.

He pressured people into the party, particularly those in the city's service, but apparently did not attempt to proselytize among his colleagues at his private job. One such, a communist, testified that Schneider had helped him keep his job and avoid arrest, that he had gotten another communist friend out of Buchenwald.[53] Four testified that Schneider had kept them out of concentration camps.

A major difficulty between the mayor and the Kreisleiter came with Mayr's effort to make the non-NS Dr. Ott city treasurer.[54] The mayor wished to avoid the 1935 law on local government, which required open competition for the position because he wanted Ott. Lethmaier reported in November 1936 the other way of filling the position, but this required the approval of Frick and the NS delegate (Schneider). Mayr delayed asking but Schneider reminded him in February 1937 that the position was unfilled, the work was piling up, and that the law should be followed. Mayr wrote Wahl to have Schneider approve Ott, reporting that he had tried many times to get Schneider to agree; nothing happened. Nine months later, Mayr appealed again to Schneider to change his mind. Schneider replied that he had looked at Ott's records "to avoid personal bias" and saw that the appointment was impossible. Such an office could only be given to a party member who was also *convinced* of national socialism. Mayr should suggest someone who was both, and not Ott. Mayr appealed to Wahl, agreeing that he might get an old party member for the job, but that the city would suffer financial damage. Wahl appealed to "dear party member Schneider". He pleaded that the city needed an expert, that Ott had been accepted by the party in the city government in

[53] SK, G. Schneider, 124.

[54] ASA 105/042.

1933, that his finance office was not particularly political. "It cannot be the task of the party to set rules for a NS mayor in the use of his closest co-workers", Wahl said. Two months later Mayr wrote Wahl that Schneider had still not replied; would he try again? After another seven months Mayr reported that the latest Wahl urging had been without effect. He suggested that Wahl use his special powers as "commissar for Hess". This was done in November 1938. But the matter was not settled, as Ott had still to prove himself and his wife Aryan, and the Interior Ministry wanted evidence that the rights of the party had been protected. Ott was listed a nonmember but without explanation. Over a year later, he was finally named treasurer. It is interesting that Ott, thus kept pure enough to be made the first postwar mayor was quickly fired by a United States military governor because he would not automatically fire any NS in the city's service.

The Party and the City's Money

The record of the city's contribution to the party is incomplete. Yet from 1935 to 1940 there were regular contributions from taxes.[55] These suggest a level of a thousand marks here for a Hitler Youth home, a thousand there to the SS. By 1937 there were several thousand annually for a project of Wahl's, a Gau leadership school. By 1939 a major contribution of 45,000 marks went to the NSV party charity. The peak contribution—72,500 marks in 1940—went to the Kreisleitung, the NSV, and the HJ; but by June 1940 the city informed the party that the subsidies would be stopped because of the war.

These colorless notations contrast with the acrimonious correspondence of the city with SA-SS to get them to pay their bills.[56] Bohl and Mayr tried to get the SA to pay the bills of their auxiliary police and the gas bills of Schoepf and Loritz. Loritz answered that the city would get nothing from him. Mayr wrote Schoepf that the city must have some check on the use of its cars, that Schoepf's men must have a signed statement on the reason for and length of city-car usage. Lo-

[55] ASA 108/4001.

[56] ASA 108/57.

ritz denied that any misuse was possible; Schoepf could not understand the complaints because his men were just "creating order", and only after the people had turned to him because "the Beamten responsible had completely failed". He could not divulge the reason and length of car usage for fear of "spying".[57]

After more lengthy correspondence about who paid SA-SS bills, the city decided that no cars, gas, or oil would go to the SA-SS. The "costs of the revolution" by August were 5,158.41 marks, mostly for rooms for the SA police. The streetcar office complained that a car given Loritz in April had not been returned, nor had a repair bill been paid.

The city declined a request by Schneider to cancel the 16.70 marks bill for the use of tools for a sport field or to reduce it to four marks; and Schneider did not pay. A new September total of costs jumped to 18,287.49 marks, but Stoeckle reversed the September policy, ordering that the city could provide gas and oil and minor repairs to the SS, the Gauleitung, and the police chief. Yet three days later the city council reversed Stoeckle—no more cars, gas, or repairs to the party, and immediately. The SS whined that Bohl had promised them a car without any costs; besides, they had no money.

A long-standing issue, concerning who paid the rent on the refugee-Jew Einstein's house used by the SA-SS police, came to a head in April 1934 when the city told the SS that it would no longer pay the rent, that the SS must deal with the owner's lawyer. The SS complained, "the city always makes difficulties for the SS . . . they were badly treated, the city was never cooperative". They would tell Himmler. The city's attorney, Steinhauser, replied that he would not be scolded this way as a city official. He was angry that Himmler would be dragged into it.[58] Stoeckle rejected an appeal from the SS to cancel a 50-mark debt, though the SS had no money. The city declined to assist in arranging vacations for the SS in Augsburg, although these SS were pointedly described as "disciplined".

In October 1934 the matter of Einstein's house was again

[57] *Ibid.*

[58] *Ibid.*

troublesome. The lawyer asked that the SS who had left the building please return the stolen furniture and pick up their dovecote. The lawyer complained further to the embarrassed city that 15 windows, five chairs, and two stools were broken; in addition, three chairs were missing and the SS had refused to unlock four rooms. The lawyer subsequently sent another long list of items still missing. Steinhauser wrote an angry letter to the SS lawyer who again said that the SS were unable to pay. Finally the city paid for the repairs.

Mayr and Hitler

Although Hitler had a fondness for Bavaria, especially Nuremberg, and had great sums of money at his disposal with which to rebuild cities in his own monumental image, he at first paid little attention to Augsburg. On one of his rare visits, Hitler was shown the city theater; he told Mayr that they must build a modern theater as quickly as possible. Mayr replied that the city did not have the money (at his trial, Mayr emphasized his concern for the poverty still in Augsburg). Hitler insisted on the theater, and said he would arrange for the money from Siebert, Goebbels, or Ley.

A Lammers File on the Augsburg Theater[59] begins with a report dated May 31, 1938 that Hitler had promised 1,000,000 marks plus an annual subsidy of 100,000. Mayr wrote an insistent letter the next month asking that Hitler put the promise in writing, which Hitler did. In 1937 Hitler inquired of Wahl whether there was a Gau headquarters house. Wahl noted the rumors that there might not even be a Gau for long. Hitler announced that Schwaben would remain and therefore Augsburg must look like "a Gau city". In four weeks Hitler was back with a huge plan for much more than the original suggestion; now they were to build an opera house costing 4,000,000 marks, plus the entire rebuilding of a main street with various party structures; the total cost would be 120,000,000 marks. Mayr worried about raising the money. The rebuilding was begun, but

[59] BA R 43 II/1243a.

was stopped by the war; the half-completed street ended suddenly amid massive traffic congestion.

Hitler met Mayr at the 1938 party convention in Nuremberg and asked how the theater was coming. On learning that little had been done, a violent argument began which shocked the bystanders and Wahl, who wished to avoid trouble. Wahl regarded Mayr's opposition as largely the cashier's concern with money. Rich Liebel in Nuremberg regarded it simply as poor Mayr's lack of imagination in squeezing money out of industrialists, and sent him some free advice. The result of this unusual argument of anyone with Hitler was that two days later Bormann called Wahl and told him that Mayr was to be fired immediately because of "insufficient initiative". Wahl appealed the order to Wagner and Bormann and nothing more was heard of it. Wahl noted that many orders could be ignored if one simply wrote back explaining why the order could not be carried out and then forgot it.

In a letter remarkable for its obvious lack of gratitude, Mayr wrote in 1939 that the theater costs would be higher than estimated. Would Hitler add a million marks to help? In seven weeks came the answer that Hitler would. In October Mayr wrote again, saying that the costs were 386,000 marks more than estimated; would Hitler give that? Again Hitler would. After two years with the army Mayr returned to write that by oversight the annual 100,000 subsidy had not been paid. Hitler had promised him one for 10 years, so how about it? Don't forget 1939 and 1940! In less than two weeks Hitler came through and the subsidy was continued through the war, until November 1944.

The Mayor and the Augsburg Jews

Bernhard Bezen, an Augsburg Jew saved from destruction by the fact that he had an Aryan wife, wrote of his people's tragedy in city discrimination against the Jews dating back to medieval times. They had been permitted briefly to live in the city and then banished and allowed only to trade within the city for one day and at a high fee.[60] Under Napoleon the

[60] Bernhard Bezen, *Die Juden in Augsburg*, Augsburg, 1954.

Bavarian royal government forced the jealous merchants to permit the Jews to live and trade more or less freely within the city. The high point of Jewish freedom came under the Weimar Republic, with a growth of the "Israelite Community" to 1,250 members. Formal discrimination seemed to have disappeared and there were no local difficulties until 1933.

Even then, "action" was mostly boycott. Jews owned some of the best stores in the city, including a large department store feared commercially by NS small businessmen. The efforts to pressure citizens to stop patronizing Jewish stores was only partially successful. Angry NS reports told of the ignorant masses, poorly controlled officials, even party members, who continued to patronize Jewish stores. The Jews faced some petty legal difficulties but no real interference from the city.

In his inaugural speech to the city council in 1933, Mayr called for the end of "Jewish influence". The party newspaper periodically attacked the Jews, quoting such people as Martin Luther and Benjamin Franklin. The city merely forbade the Jews to swim in the public pools.[61]

Mayr's chauffeur testified to Mayr's confused concern for his city: "In the first years after the revolution signs appeared on the entry streets to the city saying, 'Jews not wanted here', one of which we saw during a trip to the city. Herr Mayr became very excited and described this as a great mischief and nonsense. Herr Mayr had me stop the car, took the sign and destroyed it. This happened a couple of times again on the drive. As we drove on Herr Mayr and I discussed the matter and decided to find and destroy all of the signs in Augsburg that very night, which was then done".[62] Yet Mayr had one of his public attacks of anti-Semitism in November 1936 when he forbade four Jewish doctors to practice with city-insured patients.[63]

One of the issues with the party was the city's acceptance until 1938 of a large contract with the Jewish firm, Kleofass

[61] NNZ, 20.7.35.

[62] Simon Miller, SK J. Mayr.

[63] BRP, Schwaben, 6.12.36.

and Knapp. Knapp wrote after the war that the city was decent until the party pressure became too large and Berlin pressure forced the Aryanization of the firm in 1938. Most of the wealthy Jews gave up before then, sold their businesses at a loss, and emigrated. Although there were countless insults, loss of jobs, and rare cases of physical violence against individual Jews, Augsburg was fairly calm.

The turning point was the night of November 9. Locally it was the SA who were involved, reputedly only one truckful—not Wahl, Mayr, or even Schneider, all of whom were quoted as denouncing the action. The fire department did intervene and prevent the synagogue from being burned down, although much of the interior was destroyed. Wahl's reports, usually critical of violence, were noticeably silent on this violence, though some presidents elsewhere in Bavaria were highly critical.[64]

This violence perpetrated by a small number, the majority since claiming to have deplored it, led to a more rapid emigration, although for a time more Jews emigrated, particularly from Franken. Representative of the increased public-private discrimination was the difficulty of the Jews in finding stores to serve them. Mayr reported in late 1941 that certain stores had to be set aside as those in which Jews could buy.[65] The wearing of the Jewish badge had created a problem, as Jews were easily identifiable for discrimination.[66] Mayr wrote to various economic organizations asking what to do; some replies thought it insulting for a German to be asked to serve a Jew. The city's order was for the Jews to be permitted to buy early in the morning when business was light. This rule had to be modified for those Jewish women whose working hours prevented them from using the early hours. The relative reasonableness of this modification contrasted with the city's lack of consideration for nonworkers with special problems.

Before the mass deportations of 1942 a Gestapo report

[64] BRP reports of early December 1938.
[65] BRP, Schwaben, 8.10.41.
[66] ASA 225/03022.

from Augsburg complained[67] that the Jews were still living in better-than-average conditions; the rents paid indicated that they had above-average apartments and still owned 18 houses. It suggested freeing the apartments to help solve the housing problem and sending the Jews to barracks. But the city officials saw no way to do so. Another possibility was to send them to a village where Jews had already gathered and they could somehow be crowded in. Their life was "too comfortable" and their "freedom little curtailed". Later reports, other than mentioning the transfer of Jews to the east in 1942, ignore their fate except for one interesting notation: "A widely spread rumor about the fate of the Jews sent east caused among the easily frightened citizens fear about revenge measures of our enemies in an unfavorable end to the war".[68]

In the next two years, pressured by Himmler's SS, the Jews were crowded into a few buildings and then sent away; the only survivors, like Bezen or Baruch Rupin, were saved by their wives' "race". In the last months of the war Rupin was sent to Theresienstadt, thus escaping Auschwitz and last-minute execution when the commander was guaranteed a safe passage by the Red Cross if he refused the Berlin order. Of the 1,250 Jews 650 emigrated in time; 600 were sent to concentration camps, of which barely five percent survived.

Neither the local state nor the party in Augsburg participated in these deportations. Almost everyone with any influence had helped some Jew to survive. The best remembered case was Piechler, the director of the Augsburg Conservatory, a half-Jew of great talent. On one occasion, Mayr hid him, then sent him out of town so the SS could not find him; Mayr told them he did not know where Piechler was. Retained by Mayr as director, Piechler testified that in 1938 an order came from Berlin to dismiss him, which Mayr refused: "As Goebbels then in a personal letter to Mayr threatened that my case would be solved by the Gestapo if I were not released, Mayr told me that I must remain at my position

[67] T 81, R 179, F 2880ff.

[68] BRP, Schwaben, 10.10.42.

and he assumed all responsibility. When there was anonymous denunciation against me Mayr helped and called police chief Starck immediately to get the arrest stopped. Finally in 1944 I had to be released, but the city was not responsible. I was then employed by the railroad. On December 12, 1944, I received an order from the Gestapo to report to a camp (Theresienstadt) as 'mixed race, Grade 1'. I avoided the order by fleeing to a farmer. My wife went to Mayr who gave her an assurance in writing that I had nothing to fear. Mayr suggested that I go to Gessertshausen so that I would be closer and he could protect me. He also gave me the advice to find various quarters, so that I could move quickly in case of need. This he did in cooperation with Wahl".[69]

There was also the case of Otto Mayer, one of the top men in the largest city industry, who had a Jewish wife; he had left Nuremberg because the party insisted that he divorce his wife. There was pressure to remove him from his leading industrial position. He insisted on staying at his job despite the hatred shown him, because, he said, "I am a German". DAF leader Aschka assumed responsibility for his loyalty. Mayer was given a medal in October 1944 for an outstanding contribution. On Wahl's suggestion his wife had gone to Switzerland to safety, with Mayer permitted to visit her as he wished. In 1945 the Gestapo, assuming sabotage, attempted to arrest him. At 63 he was to join a work *kommando*, but Wahl saved him. He was told not to report. Wahl telegraphed Bormann and nothing more was heard of it.[70] Only the Americans arrested Mayer, for several months, as a business leader.

Alfons Reisert, the brother of the resistance leader, testified for Mayr and his assistance to his Jewish wife.[71] On the basis of Gestapo information, he credited Mayr with saving her and the children. Mayr had also called to warn him while his brother, Franz, was on trial as an accomplice in the 1944 assassination attempt on Hitler.

[69] Piechler in SK J. Mayr.

[70] Mayer in SK Wahl.

[71] F. Reisert, SK J. Mayr.

The Scholar in the Schools

In any modern society the schools are the center of the state's endeavor. In a totalitarian state the need for control through the schools is even more vital, for if the system is to develop permanent strength, it must come from a school-bred fanaticism. Relative to other school systems, the Augsburg teachers were less exposed to fanatical pressures from above, albeit any fellow teacher, student or parent could still denounce any thoughtless, i.e., honest, word. The schools for the first two years remained under an old conservative, but then followed a bright young man with good party credentials, one of the relatively few officials who waged a deliberate and idealistic counterpolicy to that ordered from above.

This was surely one of the ablest persons in the city, so able that he could implement personal policies despite the exposed position of the schools. The judgment of his de-Nazification court reads like the highly flattering claim of a defense attorney. It accepts his contention that he not only passively resisted the methods of the NS, but actively resisted from early in the regime: "The accused had the confidence of opponents to the party; non-NS he assisted in innumerable cases, brought numerous anti-Nazi literary pieces to exhibition, furthered religious and Christian lectures, gave artists otherwise ignored by the party a forum in Augsburg, got property seized by the state back to its owners, drove on behalf of Bishop Meiser directly to Wagner to effect his release and to impress on him the effects of the obvious power politics. He conducted his office in the sense of resistance to the *Weltanschauung* of the party . . . to provide positions for open opponents of the regime . . . to protect the persecuted . . . to help the racially persecuted . . . to oppose the party youth organizations. The accused successfully hindered the creation of party schools . . . the efforts of the party to control the public and private kindergarten and children-homes . . . to keep the party women's organization with little influence, to nullify the efforts of the DAF and of the SS recruiters in the schools, the rejection of tendentious books, the representative of *Der Stuermer*, and the bestowing of scholarships on a non-party basis. The accused ordered the crucifixes to be kept in the schools, secured the continuance of religious instruction, retained the nun-taught grade schools, gathered forbidden religious books to provide for the continued supply . . . maintained close contact with the resistance movement of the church leader Bogner . . . distributed anti-fascist literature and propagandized against the Nazis in secret speeches . . . became a center of the resistance."[72]

This remarkable statement in such a trial is unique among all of the trials I studied. It may be exaggerated in tone, and surely in implication. The scholar obviously could not make an island of truth in a sea of lies. A few fanatic teachers, free to blatantly preach love of Hitler and hate of Jews, could undo the work of a larger number of reasonable men, if they existed, trying to moderate by more subtle means.

The scholar was clearly an idealist, both in his early work for the party and in his later work against the party. As a student he had joined the army in 1914 because "the Fatherland was in danger", and received a medal for exceptional bravery in battle. He was thrilled by the unity called forth by the common struggle, the unity of the jealous provinces who began to think as one nation, and the various classes which in the trenches fought as equals. To re-create this unity he joined the NS in 1931. This ideal of patriotism and equality, i.e. national socialism, motivated many middle class idealists, some of whom were later corrupted or became fanatics, others of whom joined the opposition to the party, more prone to opposition than the nonidealist who either joined the party late or not at all.

The disillusioning of this dream in National Socialism might well have taken much longer had he not been attacked by Streicher's paper as a "half-Jew". Soon after his appointment, but before its finalization by the Bavarian government (which took about six years), the question of his parentage

[72] The denazification papers, Augsburg, Amtsgericht.

was debated between Augsburg and Berlin. His appointment was the work of Mayr who had to battle the criticism of many in the party who did not trust the intellectual despite his "old fighter" status. No sooner had Mayr gotten him in than Rosenberg and Streicher tried to get him out. The facts were that his mother had named a Jew at the time of his birth as his father; legally, probably biologically, his father was as she stated. As in many other cases under the insane Nazi practice, the child, to save himself, had to maintain that the mother had committed adultery, that an Aryan had fathered him outside the law. The questioning of the mother was prevented by her suicide, for which some have blamed her son. Without, then, any direct evidence, this case had to depend on indirect "evidence", on "experts" who studied his features and decided whether they were "Jewish". After years of inquiry, the committee decided he did not "look Jewish". This incredible party intrusion into one's private family remains properly a private concern, yet it likely played an important role in his break with the party. It is further evidence, along with the Piechler case, of the ambivalent racial feelings of Mayr and Wahl, at least toward those they knew.

The scholar's technique of playing both ends against the middle was aided by his good party status as well as by the "Fuehrer principle" supposed to be used in the new order. His powers as school superintendent were nearly dictatorial. Backed by Mayr, he need consult with no peer or underling to explain a decision. Outsiders were discouraged from interfering in his affairs, because "authority" must be respected. Opponents were outmatched if they met him in debate. He took care to explain his policies at every invitation from a party group, thus showing his humble "willingness to cooperate". When the Gestapo called, his technique was to delay action, saying: "Why don't you send the file over here for me to study?" An official had so much to do and there was so much confusion that he usually would forget the matter. Another technique was to have any critic "put it in writing", which often left it undone. Above all, one had to listen to people, "let them talk themselves out", and appear conciliatory. The city lawyer noted how business-like and quietly the scholar defended his actions; they were always so well prepared that opponents were baffled. Only Streicher's "shot from Nuremberg" placed him in jeopardy in a dramatic meeting in city hall in his absence. Mayr, Kellner, and Steinhauser successfully defended him.[73]

He lost his position only under the occupation, when he was interned from July 1945 to November 1947, the American commandant giving him a good reference at his de-Nazification trial in 1948, at which scores of witnesses of the best credentials told of his years of opposition, with no evidence introduced against him. He was permitted to teach but not to supervise.

The City and the Police

The centralization of the Reich was most effective in propaganda and police. Yet local influence on the police was high during the early chaotic (prebureaucratic) days. Then the SA commanders could arrest people at will, although, once delivered to Dachau, the prisoner needed some nonlocal help to get out. Personal contacts with the local police and the local party could start or stop arrests and could often bring releases.

There were two police presidents, neither of whom were very active other than in arresting the helpless. Baron von Humann, an army officer from Hanover, had married into minor estates on the fringe of Augsburg and become active in the local SS in 1932. He became police chief in 1933. Contrary to newspaper reports of him as a man of great political wisdom, Humann was without police experience; he left the actual administration to his chief (non-NS) Beamter.[74] This effective commander was Captain Trillich, a conservative who tried to remain nonpolitical. Trillich was transferred to Munich in 1938 because of party pressure, and then to Epp's staff. He was hired and fired more abruptly in 1945 by the occupation authorities than by the NS.

[73] Steinhauser.

[74] Alois Mayer.

Humann continued the life of a baron, spending much of his time hunting and drinking, until his transfer. His relations with his small SS unit were strained, although he tried to gain their confidence as a drinking comrade. Yet the baron and his subordinates had little in common socially, and he exercised little control over their excesses. In one shooting incident in a bar, the NS city attorney had to pull his pistol to get the SS shooters to leave; Humann's police were fearful of SS wrath.[75] Starck, Humann's successor, thought a president had to remain aloof from the rank and file SS to gain their respect, instead of trying like Humann to "be one of the boys".

Starck, appointed in March 1936, was a short pudgy army officer who had entered the Bavarian police after World War I. Involved in a police plot to support the Hitler Putsch in 1923, he lost his position, surviving rather marginally as a seller of advertising, as adjutant to Epp, and in the SS. He remained with the SS in 1933 instead of immediately reentering police service. His SS file for 1934-35 shows that he desperately needed a job, but Himmler did not know how to use him.[76] Starck's modicum of success in the SS was due partly to his having been a military instructor of Himmler in 1917-18.

Starck's career might have ended before he came to Augsburg. He was charged with adultery by an SS court, which decided to take no action because Starck said he did not know the woman was married, that he was "happily married" and a "worthy NS".[77] This private affair helps explain why Starck made himself relatively inconspicuous as a police chief, playing almost no role in either police, SS, or city politics. It also gives credence to the Augsburg estimate of him as one who was too interested in "the good life", particularly hunting, to help the SS or the party. The SS report in 1937 said Starck had not entered the SS office nor attended any SS function.[78]

[75] Steinhauser.

[76] BDC, W. Starck SS File.

[77] SK 553s; BDC, Wilhelm Starck, *Akten des Obersten Parteigerichts.*

[78] SK Starck, 156s.

In 1944 a party leader complained to the party that Starck wasted too much time hunting. Starck replied that he had shot 21 deer in one month and had delivered over 500 pounds of meat to the market, which fed 65 families. This he thought better than "sitting around and complaining".[79] In 1942 he had to face the charge that he was a hoarder. His SS file indicates that his correspondence with Himmler was largely in search of more subsidy money, although declining to contribute to SS charities or any SS activity. It also shows a concern for his being properly honored at party functions and in the party newspaper. An SS trial dealt with charges of minor misuse of funds.

Starck claimed as Beamter to have created more respect for law to the local SS and party. After the arrest of an honored NS, Wahl called to inquire about the grounds, and learned the charge was incest. On mention of the man's party medals, Starck allegedly said, "He used to have medals". Trillich reported the 1938 Starck order to arrest two SS men for murder. Following an NS complaint Starck pounded a fist on the table and said, "I don't recognize party members, only people who break the law and they go to court".[80] He claimed to have moderated orders to his subordinates concerning entry to the party and exit from the Catholic church by displaying the order but not enforcing it. Starck "knew of no brutality" in his command; but he "knew" of astounding U.S. brutality toward prisoners, even toward its own soldiers. Reisert thought the Augsburg police in general behaved so well that he would have defended them in their postwar trials, this though he had barely escaped death from the Gestapo, that his nine-year-old son had been arrested for laughing during an NS flag-raising.[81]

One city file has survived, showing evidence of the city's effort to frustrate Himmler's drive to centralize the police, using the urban pressure group, the "German Municipal Organization" (DGT).[82] To counter Himmler's effort to control all police, the mayors met together in September 1938 and

[79] BDC Starck SS File.

[80] Trillich in SK Starck, 201.

[81] F. Reisert.

[82] ASA 200/01.

presented long lists of "police" which the city should retain, such as "construction police" (inspectors). One argument was: lacking any police, the city would have no one at the city hall to halt the jeers at weddings when the ages of bride and groom were so different or when the bride was clearly pregnant. The Augsburg police, caught between Himmler and the city, outlined their problems, observing that if Himmler won, the police could lose their streetcar passes and free theater tickets.

By 1940 the DGT, under Fiehler, took some initiative by protesting the law to take all the police, and trying to get it delayed until after the war. He raised the proper question: "When are police simply administrators and when are they police?" Starck agreed with the city that he did not have the personnel, the jurists, or even the room for all the assigned police jobs. He reported to Himmler that the implementation was impossible, along with his shock that the Munich police had already ordered implementation by taking over the "fishing police", "fire police", and "trades police". The DGT mobilized opposition—five cities in Bavaria, including Augsburg, reported that the ordered changes could not be made. It then reported failure; over its protests, the city of Nuremberg had been ordered to turn over all officials heretofore working as "police". The DGT advised the mayors to save what they could and noted that since many Beamten were only partly involved in such "police" duties they should not be given to the police.

Wagner used his position to urge compliance. He reported that Fiehler's Munich had made the shift without extra personnel. Starck calculated to Mayr that he would need at least a dozen officials to do these extra jobs and requested the files on the officials who had been working in these fields. Mayr appealed to the DGT, recalling that Fiehler had promised an effort to get postponement.

There was no response, except that Starck asked for six to eight rooms no later than April 1. Mayr replied at length and with heat, that the city had no extra personnel, that all the cities were against this change, and that Fiehler was trying to get it reversed. The change was contrary to the NS principle of "unity of administration" and to the NS Municipal Code. Mayr's solution was that those officials involved in security would be "police", and those involved in city codes would be "administrators". "Trade police" and "water police" could not leave city service because they administered city laws; these police were largely technicians: "Of particular importance is the attitude of the population. Whether correctly or incorrectly the people have the attitude that whatever is connected with the police is something one must avoid, because in the background is always the spectre of the denunciation, the pursuit by the city attorney and the courts."[83] The people felt closer to the city officials. Enforcement would be easier to the city because "everyone wants to avoid having anything to do with the police". The city had no rooms nor officials to give the police.

Mayr wrote any agency which might help, but his only answer was a brief note from Starck asking where the extra rooms would be. Mayr replied that their letters must have crossed, that he had asked Starck to give up a police building which showed how desperate the city was for space. Starck then referred to a Himmler circular, "which should remove any question about the change", and asked that two of his men be allowed to inspect the price control offices.

The efforts of the DGT finally bore fruit when Frick, observing the difficulties of space and personnel, reversed the process and ordered that all offices remain with the mayors, except price control office. Retreat came with Starck's limiting his request for "reports" on price control on which the police would take action. Mayr replied that his officials would have to take any action on the spot, to which Starck humbly replied that they should keep the police "informed".

Starck occupied himself in private and official ways without attracting attention until the very last days of the war, when he fled the city. Just east of Augsburg his small SS unit happened on a man who was arguing publicly that resistance

[83] *Ibid.*

to the Americans should stop. On the grounds that he had shot at an officer, the man was executed at Starck's order after a short hearing. One should be grateful that Starck's pleasant life had not been earlier interrupted. This was Starck's only provable "act of violence"; it extended his postwar internment.

Gold, the Gestapo Beamter

Police Beamter Hugo Gold, who became Augsburg Gestapo chief, presents a study in Beamten attitudes. Although Gold had musclemen as underlings, he was more the scribbler.[84] Originally from a regional village, he had learned the saddler's trade but had joined the army in 1913. After the war he wanted to reenter his trade but found no work. A friend told him of the opening of a job with the police which Gold joined in 1919. Progress was slow and sure, though his savings were wiped out by the inflation. In 1923 he advanced to the "criminal police" and by 1933 had risen by caution and diligence to a minor but secure Beamten position. His first political activity was entering the party in 1933. His wife's brother was a leading NS in Augsburg, who regarded Gold as "incapable of ever understanding national socialism."[85]

In 1933 a rapid turnover occurred in the Augsburg political police with the firing of the incumbent chief. His successor, an old NS, used some SA and SS but was soon recognized as incompetent. Another NS tried and failed to control the political police. In July 1933 Gold the Beamter was given the promotion with the right to dismiss the unfit. Like many other little Beamter concerned with promotion, Gold thus moved into the forefront of political persecution without any real political convictions or any real capacity for political police work. His family remained staunchly Catholic; his wife was "always at church". The family made frequent contributions to the church, including clothing for the nuns. His daughter attended a Catholic girls' school. Gold reportedly

[84] SK Hugo Gold, Munich. [85] *Ibid.*, 103.

went with his daughter every Sunday to church,[86] but to gain his promotion left the church in 1938.

Witnesses at Gold's postwar trial testified to his public brutality, his beating or condoning beatings when others of his staff were present. Brutality seems largely to have been directed against socialists and communists. He was less eager to act against the Catholic church. A former Himmler spy for Augsburg testified that Gold's superiors thought his Gestapo office was filled with pro-church people. Other witnesses testified that when they were able to see Gold alone in his office, in interviews frequently arranged by Wahl, Gold was very pleasant and helpful. He was helpful to a doctor trying to save a Jewish wife. In another case he saved the witness's life by removing evidence from the file.[87] An attorney for the politically persecuted testified that he had had frequent conferences with Gold, who had given him information on the case, which was definitely forbidden.[88]

Augsburg police and public sentiment regarded Gold and most of the Gestapo as ambitious men who saw a shift to the political police as a means of rapid promotion. There were a minority of Beamten who would beat prisoners, preferably foreign laborers. Most of the local Gestapo were ineffective spies, dependent on private denunciations for the scrap of evidence requisite for Dachau. Perhaps because of his supposed softness toward Catholics, Gold was transferred to Protestant Halle, where, no longer chief, he had trouble making friendships with his fellow Gestapo men and was soon transferred again, this time to Italy. The postwar court, taking notice that he had been totally bombed out and had already served 38 months, sentenced him to only 18 months.

Arrest and Survival: Franz Reisert

Dr. Franz Reisert, a brilliant attorney, represents a middle class opponent of the regime, one able on occasion to outwit the state and survive. From a devout Catholic and strong scholarly background, he had attempted in 1933 to convince von Papen of the folly of trusting Hitler. The only alternative

[86] *Ibid.*, 61. [87] *Ibid.*, 72. [88] *Ibid.*, 137.

to him after 1933 was to use his knowledge of the law to help save those who fell victim to the police machine. This he frequently did with success.

His courtroom technique was to pretend a stance on NS values and use them against the prosecution, then to argue passionately and emotionally. In one wartime case, to save a French worker and the German girl with whom he supposedly had illegal and death-deserving sexual relations, Reisert won with a medical report that supported the girl's claim that she was still virgin. In another case, a man was given a one-year sentence as a black market operator for having traded meat for tobacco. By noting that the man with bad teeth was unable to chew meat and had therefore traded his ration, Reisert confused the case, got a delay and finally an acquittal. His failures, usually in defenses of foreigners, meant quick and senseless executions. The Frenchman got six months.

The out-of-court technique was to cultivate the friendship of the judges. Although Reisert graphically documented the horrors of Nazi injustice,[89] he concluded that the majority of the judges were well motivated. The few beasts in their number—e.g., Freisler in Berlin and Rothaug in Nuremberg—were usually shunned by their fellows. To get quicker action, special courts with these willing judges were established, which became death traps. Other judges tried to show mercy, but mercy was dangerous to the accused, because the Gestapo was known to rearrest persons given a light sentence by the courts and arbitrarily shoot them. (Hitler, in a famous case from a news account of a light sentence, had ordered a death penalty.) Judges frequently gave fairly stiff sentences simply to prevent rearrest.

Although Reisert's wife was always with him in court, because one could never be sure he would leave the court a free man, he could have continued playing cat and mouse with the police and the courts had he not stepped over the line from passive to active resistance in 1942 when he joined

[89] F. Reisert, "Die deutsche Justiz unter dem Nationalsocialismus", unpub. manuscript.

a resistance group in Munich, the "Moltke circle". The leaders were executed following the July 20 attempt on Hitler; Reisert was arrested in September 1944 and appeared before the infamous Freisler in January 1945, along with von Moltke, Gerstenmaier, Fugger, Sperr, and Delp. Four were sentenced to decapitation. Gerstenmaier, one of the top Bonn statesmen, and Reisert escaped execution by feigning a nearly incredible naiveté. Reisert was given a five-year sentence. He credited his salvation, at a time when even a minor infraction or criticism brought death, to the intercession of Wahl and perhaps a pleading letter from Reisert's wife.

The Nerdinger Case

Among the socialist youth a variety of small resistance groups survived, disintegrated, and revived. One of these was the group associated with Bebo Wager of Augsburg.[90] Wager's closest confidant was the worker, later artist and brilliant director of the *Werkkunstschule* in Augsburg, Eugen Nerdinger. The group's courageous activity—which began with "romantic" counterpropaganda, information on rearmament brought to socialist agents in Switzerland and Czechoslovakia, and ended with wartime sabotage—belongs in a study of the "resistance". What is of interest in this context of the German state is the near miracle that Nerdinger survived.

The small group was destroyed in 1942; survivors guess from some betrayal within, a puzzle which still gnaws. After the first bombing of Augsburg, on the assumption perhaps of someone's spying to guide the bombers, Wager was arrested in April. Plans of the group and a small cache of weapons were found in his home; he attempted suicide and failed. Nerdinger and most of the others were arrested in May. Nerdinger was kept in solitary confinement in an Augsburg prison until December. On occasion he was able to see from his small window his wife and young son on the street far below. While in prison he made connections with a Catholic resistance group which worked to save him. Upon his release

[90] Annelore Leber, *Das Gewissen Entscheidet*, Berlin, 1960, 49-53.

Nerdinger was ordered to a "punishment company" about to be sent to nearly certain death in Russia. In January 1943 he was startled to be taken from this doomed outfit by an unknown lieutenant, who appeared with official orders which said that Nerdinger had been assigned to him as his chauffeur, although Nerdinger had never driven an auto. The Catholic group had somehow had orders issued which were obeyed despite his resistance record.

The Catholics in the army then had him assigned to a replacement depot at which the commander worked hand in hand with the bishop's secretary. He was transferred from one company being sent to the front to the next company being prepared, until June when the protecting commander was removed by the Gestapo.

The Catholic group continued to take care of him. Somehow they got him released in six hours from the army and had him assigned to the chairman of the Messerschmitt Airplane Company as an engraver. Despite the suspicions of the NS factory steward, Nerdinger remained "in hiding". His file was top secret, hidden in the personal safe of the manager. His activity, decreed necessary to the war effort, was to make playing cards with original designs for the managers, who were living a sweet life of massive black-marketeering largely outside the law. With little else to give as presents, the potentates needed artists to make their gifts, such as wood carvings. As Nerdinger put it, "They needed artists and they needed women". The Messerschmitt factory was frequently denounced by the NS as being close to sabotaging the war effort, but Wahl so effectively protected the owner that investigations were headed off. Messerschmitt responded by finding a job for Wahl after his prison release in 1948.

In 1944 Nerdinger's friends were tried, quickly found guilty despite Reisert's efforts, and executed in August. Again Nerdinger was luckier. Reisert, whose help was arranged by the bishop, got the sentence down to three and a half years. Reisert's argument was that what Nerdinger had done had been long ago, that it showed his strength of character not immediately to have switched from socialism to NS, that he was then married, had become a changed man and settled down to a bourgeois life. Luckily, the judge was hard-of-hearing and mistook the name "Fried" for "Frieb", Nerdinger's friend already found guilty. His bosses at Messerschmitt, however, kept postponing his arrest until it was forgotten in the confusion of the fall. They even forced the NS steward to sign a document which stated that Nerdinger's work was necessary to the war effort. After the July *attentat* attempt, his protectors became cautious and distanced themselves, but nothing happened, perhaps because the daughter of the steward had been a fellow student of Nerdinger's.

The Last Act: Illegal Surrender

With each community taken by the advancing Allied armies from the west, a drama of great local significance was played—that between Augsburgers who saw the futility of resistance and the centrally controlled party, military, or SS who at least pretended a determination to carry out Hitler's orders to defend to the last man and until the city was flattened. As a result of these hundreds of secret struggles, some communities were further ravaged by artillery and more people were killed. Augsburg was among those spared worse destruction in scenes of conflict, which demonstrated how local officials could defeat central orders.

Mayr was watched by his city, which desperately wanted a release from the hopeless war, and by spies from Berlin who had shot other mayors who disobeyed Hitler's orders. On April 20, 1945 Wahl was sent by the city to try to gain a surrender of Bavaria. But neither the crushed Epp nor the commanding general could be convinced of the necessity to give up. Any surrender had to come locally, but how? The *Volksturm*, the old men and the boys, could either be sacrificed by sending them to the front or kept, as was done in Augsburg, "to guard installations", in fact against NS fanatics bent on demolishing them. Wahl also rejected the order to raise another 5,000 men, and, with the cooperation of the factory managers, prevented the party from releasing men for the defense. Very few barricades were made and all were kept outside town to avoid a reason for further bombing. Mayr's orders were to give out no weapons under any circumstances.

The city soon recognized Mayr's good intentions, but its gossip placed him in greater danger. A Berlin emissary reportedly tried to arrest him on April 23, but Wahl prevented it. Three police came from Munich to arrest him during the night of 24-25, but Mayr was forewarned and could not be found. He made contact with the underground leader, Lang, who advised caution and offered him an armed troop for defense and a hiding place in the home for the blind.

On the 25th Mayr received the order to call out the *Volksturm*. Of the available 25 battalions he called up only five. He left orders with the commanders of each battalion, that they were to be ready to disband the group on his orders and to get their men home quickly and into civilian clothes—which they did on April 27. Bridges were protected from demolition by the army. Mayr had the explosives removed from each and placed under guard, but the salvation of the bridges was complicated by the frequent changes of command on the disintegrating front. In these few days he had to get an order for demolition cancelled five different times. On the 25th he got the promise of their not being destroyed if there were sufficient barricading and defense that the bridges could not be crossed within 24 hours. This was "accomplished" with a few hastily acquired railroad cars, but the barrier was scarcely effective.

The difficult task was to effect the surrender of the city to the Americans. At the command post there came the awaited call from the Americans just to the west at 5 p.m. on April 27. Mayr feared that Berlin was trying to trick him, and asked with whom he was talking. The reply was not clear, so Mayr said that they should talk with the military commander Fehn. The American insisted on talking to "Mayr" and his fears of a trap increased. He got five minutes in which to talk to Fehn, who refused to answer the call. When the Americans called again, Mayr asked that the "terror attacks" on the city not be started again. When the American objected to the "terror" appellation, Mayr was convinced. The voice stated, "The Americans know exactly whom to shoot at and you now know who the guilty one is".

When Wahl called stating that he could not reach Fehn, Mayr suggested bringing all the top people, including church leaders and Lang, to the bunker. Fehn, to Mayr's surprise, accepted the invitation to come to the bunker at 11 p.m. Mayr then tried to reestablish contact with the Americans but was told it was impossible. Lang promised to make an effort through his channels but doubted he could get through in time. Mayr was informed that the people were individually raising the white flag, and he ordered that no one stop them.

During the night, efforts to convince Fehn proved fruitless. Hope of contact increased when the artillery bombardment stopped. As a precaution Mayr had two councilmen remove the weapons of Fehn and his staff. The order went to the west end of the city to remove barricades and to raise white flags. Suddenly Mayr was told that two American representatives had arrived. His joy turned to disappointment when it became clear that the two had mistakenly entered the city to take charge of prisoner camps, thinking it already in American hands.

In the early morning hours of April 28, the awaited call came, asking for Mayr. He was told that a general was coming to speak to him. The general threatened to turn the city into ashes. Mayr told him that Fehn as military commander alone had the authority. Mayr begged Fehn then to think of the good people of Augsburg and to make the necessary decision. As Fehn was about to say no into the phone, Mayr interrupted the connection by pressing down the receiver hook. Expecting a quick reestablishment of the connection, Mayr told Kellner to take Fehn into the next room and carry on a loud conversation. As soon as Fehn was out of harm's way, the phone rang again. It was the general, who asked whether he was still speaking to the commander. Mayr said that he was. The general repeated his terms for immediate surrender. Mayr said that since he had too few troops under his command he had no choice but to accept. Mayr told the general how the command post could be found. The general answered, "I thank you. I'll be there soon". Fehn, surprised when the Americans arrived, tried to straighten out the mistake by talking to the general, but Mayr persuaded the Americans to ignore him. The city, already in ruins, was saved from further destruction.

Mayr was taken prisoner and confined for three years. He was a salesman until a fatal heart attack in 1957. Wahl spent even longer in prison, largely because he was willing and able to testify as a prosecution witness. He returned to the obscurity of a clerk. Schneider, after his three years internment, returned convinced of American, not NS brutality, again engineer, again a believer. None of the Augsburg leadership was further bothered by the city, or honored; they were ignored. The first "party member" to run for mayor (1964) from the Catholic party, although sincerely repentant, was soundly defeated by a "Prussian" socialist.

7 FRIEDBERG

FROM the myriad of Swabian small towns available for analysis Friedberg in Bavaria was selected because of the apparent abundance of microfilm documentation available and its advantageous position near Augsburg. This nearly random selection brought mildly surprising results: Friedberg appears to have been in constant turmoil during the interwar years, then subsided into the constant boredom of the war. There is no way to prove that it is typical, although it was likely more so than Eichstaett. But one cannot predict with precision the power struggle in any community, even in Hitler's Germany.

Friedberg, with a population of about 6,000 was slightly smaller than Eichstaett. It was not so isolated and had no significant nonparty, nonstate focus as did Eichstaett's bishopric. It was less rural. It was, in fact, partly a suburb of Augsburg five miles distant beyond the Lech River. It was partly a trade center for peasants to the east. But more significantly, it was the county seat, with a long individual history as an enemy of Augsburg. Its border location between Swabia and Bavaria meant that Friedberg was torn between its former rural Bavarianism and its creeping industrial Swabianism. It was transferred for convenience to Wahl's party Gau in 1933. Only a few years later Wahl got it transferred politically to Swabia from Wagner's Munich district. (This NS decision was reversed in 1945, but was then restored as the only logical solution.) Friedberg's orientation had to be Augsburg, although for centuries it was the Bavarian outpost defending itself against the aggressive city state. Economic necessity conquered ethnic differences and history.

The rest of the county, except for two smaller towns of 3,000 each, consisted of 40 villages. The population was solid Catholic; very few Protestants lived in Friedberg itself. Until the very end of the war, practically no Jews lived there. Before 1933 the town was solidly BVP, with only a token presence of the socialists and even fewer communists. This homogeneity is reflected in the placid quality of the town. The only fight was among the NS leadership, most of whom were alien, Augsburg-urban-oriented.

The NS made very slow progress within the town and even less in a countryside under Catholic control. Its measure of success could be traced perhaps to the local sport club, the Turnverein, which served for many of the lower middle class as a patriotic entrée to the party. The local Turnverein, since the time of Father Jahn a center for middle class nationalism, was the introduction to community action and politics for two of the top three—Kreisleiter Wilhelm Miller and SA leader Karl Boehm.

The third man, the most important early NS, was the teacher Pius Haeusler who gave the party an aura of respectability and a remembered symbol of the idealism of the early party, much abused by later power struggles. As teacher of the last class in the local school, the eighth grade, he had a wide acquaintance with the town. As president of the local gardening association and the society for bee-keeping, he was highly respected. He was active in the church choir until he volunteered for the army (though an older man) and died in Russia. This, plus the fact that he severed his connection with the party when its more malevolent aspirations became known, helps explain the continuing affection for his memory.

The dominant personality in the 1932-37 party was Wilhelm Miller who came from an old Friedberg family. His father was local postmaster for years, which made his name well-known through the county. As head of the Turnverein, Miller gained election to the city council in 1930, with no political affiliation or conceptions except perhaps to defend the interests of the Beamten and a position as a construction engineer with the Reich railway in Augsburg. As was so often true of the local party leaders, who were technically but not politically educated, Miller came to marvel at the simple NS, men like himself, yet men who were able to speak so convincingly. He joined the party in 1931 after hearing one of the very few NS mayors, Dr. Siebert from Lindau, later Min. Pres. of Bavaria. In lieu of properly qualified opposition, Miller was made city leader four weeks after joining the party. Others were fearful of losing their local jobs if they became too active in the party. For a time he was also deputy Kreisleiter under Boehm, the most radical of local leaders and the one in poorest postwar repute. With Boehm's frequent absence as a traveling soap salesman, the work fell more to Miller, whose personality was not such to take orders in any event. By the spring of 1932—with less than a year of party membership—he became the Kreisleiter. Miller's local power was basically through default, a lack of serious contenders. With a missionary-like zeal, great confidence and energy, he busied himself about the county, albeit without a car. He either borrowed Boehm's car or an unemployed worker's motorcycle.

Although notable success did not come at the polls, Miller, taking advantage of many social contacts, began to build up the county party which had hardly existed before and which was still only in its infancy in 1933. He lacked financial means and important sympathizers; the police were unsympathetic. His talking points in city politics were nonideological: (1) the need for younger men, less conservative and more willing to help the depressed city; and (2) the needed appointment of a fulltime mayor to look after Friedberg (the latter was one of Miller's major goals). Ideology mattered little to the peasants. Miller's greatest concern was to avoid offending their religious sensibilities. On occasion he had to stop imported speakers from criticizing the church because the criticism brought cries of anger and protest from the rural audience. His personal promises that nothing would be done to impinge on their religion temporarily eased but did not end their suspicion.

Yet the party had scarcely begun in the county when Hitler became Chancellor. The revolution sifted down to Friedberg when Schoepf appointed Boehm Special Commissar.[1] Friedberg, with its semi-urban orientation, had only 24 party members; there were scarcely 20 other members in the entire county. Miller's big problem in 1933 was to create a basis for operation in the countryside, where the Kreisleiter had to approve the mayors. Where could he find reliable people? Miller visited each of the 44 BVP village councils to sound them out. According to his report, his technique was to observe their discussion, making note of possible leaders, urging on a younger man where possible, and if the village had a party member who was not too low in repute, urging his appointment. The process was for him to make recommendations to the Landrat. In a few cases the non-NS Landrat objected and they compromised. Between one-half and two-thirds of the former mayors were kept in office, a fairly common pattern for the area. Most of these were voted back into office after 1945, which proved to Miller that he had made the proper choice. It also indicates that there was relatively little choice. The particular accomplishment Miller and his wife recalled with a missionary-like glow was the begging of bread, butter, and sausage which they made into sandwiches for the unemployed poor. The political memories were less happy.

Small town politics moved slowly on a first-name basis, as with the reorganization of the Friedberg city council. The party did not have to be as careful as in the villages, because there were enough party members to fill the council. First, a majority of NS was forced on the council, though the party had no majority of the votes. Then the non-NS councilmen and mayor were voted out. The mayor's office was left open until June, when the newspaper reported the election of Hans Hack, an outsider chosen by a committee of Miller, Haeusler, and Fritz Loew.[2] The announcement gloried in the report that Hack at 15 had been "the youngest German soldier in the war", had won the Iron Cross First Class, and

[1] NAZ, 5.4.33.
[2] NAZ, 5.6.33.

had promised to devote the most attention to the welfare of the workers.

The only arrests in the town in late spring were on orders from Munich that members of the county board be arrested; Boehm as SA commissar was in charge of the arrests. As with most arrests among either the middle class or the peasants in the county, this was handled familiarly. People were told to come to Friedberg, where they would be put into "protective custody" and nothing would happen to them. They were locked up in the town's largest tavern, where meals were brought to them and they spent two days playing cards.

The only other noteworthy demonstration of the state's power to arrest followed the burning of the major NS meeting hall in Augsburg in May 1934, which the party interpreted as sabotage. With Miller absent, Boehm took the occasion to arrest socialists and communists. Perhaps 100 were arrested and put in the same tavern. Finance Beamter Brehm, a deputy to Miller, who ran a comfortable middle-aged SA reserve unit, considered the arrest unnecessary, and claimed responsibility for the humane treatment of the persons arrested. Wives were permitted to visit, which added greatly to the general tumult. Hack and Miller, returning later the same day, were upset at the pandemonium and the arrested were quickly released.

Perhaps the lack of any real anti-communist sentiment explains the small number of arrests for any period of time, probably less than a half dozen. A school comrade of Miller was one of the few, and one whom he got released. Miller also used the fact that his sister was a good friend of the wife of a Dachau commandant to get the brother-in-law of his railroad boss released.

Kreisleiter vs. Mayor

In NS Germany conflict was common everywhere. It was hidden where possible from public view, but the bitterness of the battle in 1934-37 between the party leader and his choice for mayor was known to the entire town.[3] What likely

[3] GSA, Epp File 119. See also BDC, Hans Hack.

began as a personality difference between two stubborn people blossomed into a long battle that cost both men their jobs and ravaged the local party. Most of the early idealistic leaders left the field to opportunistic newcomers.

Miller, an inarticulate character, felt a strong attraction to fluent speakers. He was therefore attracted to Hans Hack, a relatively little known young man from the Rhineland, who had been active for the last year or so in Schwaben as Gau speaker. With his smooth charming personality he quickly became popular in Friedberg. There seems to have been no ideological difference between the two; neither man was concerned with ideas. What started the controversy was Hack's frequent absences from the office, his excuse being that he was busy elsewhere as a party speaker. He left the running of city hall to Dollriess, the chief Beamter, and never took administration seriously. Gauleiter Wahl had warned Miller when he asked for Hack that he had little interest in "sitting still", but Miller had been determined. Miller admitted later that he and his group were "inexperienced children in politics". When he chose Hack, he had not observed how Hack cleverly avoided answering certain questions after his speeches. He had also been unduly impressed as an "old soldier" with Hack's display of the Iron Cross First Class.

The blow-up came quickly. After a few months Miller told Hack at a city council meeting that his speaking at every "rabbit breeders society" had to stop. An argument flared which came very close to blows. Hack was immediately fired as deputy county leader but not as mayor, which Miller much regretted, because Hack then "turned the town against him". Soon thereafter two members of the Miller faction at a national party Tag accidentally learned from SA men from Hack's earlier home in the Rhineland that Hack had been much more active as a communist than Friedberg had imagined, although a speech about Hack's conversion from communism after a trip to Russia in the twenties had been Miller's favorite speech. The SA said they would love to get their hands on Hack for all of the "crimes" he had committed against the NS while a communist.

Other charges were brought against Hack and became part of the case, which went to the Highest Party Court.[4] Hack was accused of party disloyalty for having refused the discipline to his Kreisleiter. He was charged with incompetence and even embezzlement when he had his salary continued at an earlier level, despite orders to cut it, which profited him 2,646.34 marks. In early 1934 he had borrowed an auto and talked the council into paying for its operation; he used the car mostly for "party work". Hack "misused" funds accumulated for charitable purposes in an amount of about 2,400 marks, although he claimed these were also put to party use.

On one of Miller's many visits to Wahl to get him to make a decision, Wahl raised the question of whether Hack really had the Iron Cross First Class. Miller made a special trip to Berlin to check the official records and learned that Hack's name was not listed. This new charge added an argument to the case, but eventually muddied the waters; for Hack produced witnesses to testify that he had indeed been granted the decoration at the very end of the war but that it had not been properly recorded.

Hack then attacked Miller with charges that he was trying to get the job for a relative. Miller was a "dictator" and the people were so afraid of him that Hack must stay in Friedberg to protect them from the Kreisleiter. Substance is given to Hack's case by the support of the highly respected Haeusler. He and Miller became bitter enemies, partly about Hack, but also after Haeusler's objection to Miller's "roughness". During 1935-36 someone repeatedly threw rocks through Miller's windows; he blamed Haeusler.

By December 1935 after two years of charge and countercharge, Wahl finally fired Hack as mayor. Another debate immediately began about whether he should be paid the pension legally required. Although he had been active as mayor for only a short time, the city was obligated to pay him a pension, which rankled Friedberg taxpayers. For years they

[4] Hofmann communication, 27.7.37.

had had no mayor to pay; suddenly through NS bungling they had two.

Hack's successor, the controversial Franz Xavier Schambeck, was appointed commissar-mayor in April 1936. But the Hack forces refused to concede defeat. The city council meeting of January 1937 was devoted largely to a denunciation by Schambeck of the "stink-makers", the complainers, the "know-it-alls"—in other words, the Hack forces. Schambeck praised his men, who were largely new and opportunistic party men. He reported that progress had been made despite the "not quite rosy situation" he had found on assuming office.

At the party trial Hack widened his attack, blaming the trouble on the "evil" B. who had misled the "mentally ill" Miller. B. had tax difficulties and had overdrawn his savings account. He had his "concubine" given a job, from which another had been fired on trumped up charges of syphilis. L., the close friend of B. and a close Schambeck supporter, had gotten city contracts, although his bid was nearly twice that of the others. Hack expressed his anger at Boehm, whose debts he had often paid, but who had yet joined the Miller faction. Five friends of Hack had been summarily thrown out of the party because they had supported him; they had written Hess to inform him that Miller was "the most hated man in Friedberg".[5] Schambeck had tried to arrest more of Hack's friends in Friedberg, but the Gestapo refused.

Hack even criticized Gauleiter Wahl, who had eventually allied himself with Miller. "Wahl was warm only when he spoke of Hitler", but otherwise he was "unsure of himself"; his insecurity showed itself in his reliance on "educated subordinates whenever he had to confront someone with authority". Wahl was shaky ideologically. When Hack fired a man for having helped a Jew, Wahl rewarded the man with a high party post.[6]

To defend himself against the charges of financial irregularities, Hack observed that he had lived on his wife's inheritance until he was 33. He had not been able to buy himself any

[5] BDC, Hans Hack File. [6] *Ibid.*, 333.

new clothing while mayor, although he neither drank nor smoked. And he was deeply in debt.

Throughout the trial record, Miller's unusual behavior received some of the attention. He and his son continued to refer publicly to Haeusler as a *Schweinhund*. When a Hitler Youth leader ordered the son to stop, son and father refused, and Miller threatened to hit the Hitler Youth leader.[7] One of the oldest NS in Friedberg testified that Miller was "the most feared man in Friedberg", that he had indeed tried to get his relatives into city jobs. Other witnesses blamed it all on Miller, "the terror of the county".[8] Hack accused Boehm of having arrested anyone he disliked or anyone who criticized his "singular family situation".

A handwriting expert added to the "evidence" against Hack by testifying that the handwriting showed him to be "somewhat singular, overly convinced of himself, a not quite upright, very strongly erotic and sexually motivated character, who wishes to appear to be more than he is".[9]

Amid such dirty wash, the verdict of the court was obvious: Hack had violated party discipline. Whether his mutiny had just cause was ignored. In late June a delegation of Friedbergers traveled to Munich to get Epp to intervene, announcing that 90% of the town backed Hack. If Epp did not see fit to put Hack back in office, would he please appoint anyone else but Schambeck? As expected, Epp supported Wahl, who was forced to go along with Schambeck.

Later in 1937 the situation in Friedberg caused new alarm.[10] The report of Muendler, Wahl's deputy, to Epp, stated: "The conditions in Friedberg have taken such grotesque forms that they cannot long be tolerated". Hack must go, for he took every chance to say he was illegally removed and had protested to Hess and Hitler. He had some support in the party, but only from those willing to attack party discipline in "the most vulgar way". A case in point was the incident at a festival beer tent in July 1937, which Muendler reported as a deliberate provocation by Hack "to make the

[7] *Ibid.*, 458. [8] *Ibid.*, II, 207. [9] *Ibid.*, 341.

[10] Epp File 119, Muendler to Epp, 22.7.37.

already miserable conditions in Friedberg even worse". He referred to Schambeck's letter of July 20, wherein the mayor thought only the lucky coincidence that he had not been present had prevented anyone from being killed. Schambeck described Hack's entry to the popular gathering as most insulting: "He came in SA uniform, with his entire group of adherents, consisting of oath-breaking city councilmen, persons thrown out of the party, convicts, and naturally also Haeusler. . . . A completely evil person climbed on the stage, called through the microphone in the tent, which encompassed about 2,000 persons, amid the shouts and screams of the masses, that 'the most beloved' mayor Hack and his wife were with them again, and he then screamed into the microphone that as in the Bible so with Hack, 'one should not have any other gods', *i.e.*, Schambeck. Amid shouts of 'hurrah', the Hohenfriedberger March was played in honor of Mayor Hack. After this there was loud applause and many climbed on the benches and tables and screamed and whistled. The chant began, 'We want to see our mayor' ".

Schambeck, obviously shaken by this vote of "no confidence", noted that the majority in attendance were not from Friedberg, but Augsburg, that the "decent" Friedbergers wanted to have nothing to do with this mob, and that there were also shouts of *Pfui* against Hack. After two more hours of drinking, Hack left the tent with "no one paying him any attention". Schambeck's reaction was to call in more police rather than to appear at the tent the next day himself; this gave more substance to claims that the people of Friedberg preferred Hack. Yet Hack, "the beloved", faded away and disappeared after a last complaint in January 1938 that he was still forbidden to speak publicly.[11]

The three-year struggle with Hack not only cost Miller something of his mental balance, but also his job as Kreisleiter. In such an impasse Wahl decided to fire Miller once Hack was safely disposed of. By November 1937 Wahl had decided that Friedberg county, with only 20,000 people, did not merit its own party organization. It was amalgamated

[11] BDC, Hans Hack, Oberstes Partei Gericht, 452.

with Augsburg county. New Kreisleiter Kellner (also Augsburg vice-mayor) was not highly regarded by the few Friedbergers who met him; he was too remote to exercise more than a vague impersonal restraint. Party activity, if any, was transferred to Augsburg. With so much hatred created in the county organization, a local party existed in name only. As an organization it played no further role in either the city or the county government.

Miller's regime, born of his exuberant zeal and energy, died from his exuberant goal of domination. Even in his later career as a railroad Beamter he found that his party service did not bring him the advantages he desired. The loss of both sons in the war, one shot by the Germans for disobedience, brought a mental collapse until many years after the war.

The Schambeck Case

From the time Schambeck entered into the Miller-Hack battle until he was driven about on the hood of an American jeep like a hunting trophy in 1945, he had a difficult mayoralty. In some ways he seemed the typical Prussian militarist, the party fanatic terrorizing the community; but his career, debated through years of imprisonment and de-Nazification trials, is a puzzle which scarcely fits a stereotype.

What was most obvious to the town was his extreme contrast to Hack—Schambeck was always there and he worked hard. Although he came daily from Augsburg, he was the first one at the city hall every morning punctually at 7. He then had the staff line up in military fashion in the courtyard for a roll call. Those who had party uniforms were expected to wear them. Persons who entered his office were to follow the proper social forms, including a resounding Heil Hitler. Schambeck patrolled the streets daily to observe whether all was in order. While Hack charmed the city into support by lolling about the streets, Schambeck frightened it by marching through.

Schambeck's background was typical for an NS, one of frustration in social acceptance.[12] His father was a police

[12] SK, F. X. Schambeck, 1948-1951.

sergeant. Entering a secondary school for the Augsburg bourgeois, Schambeck had to quit after the first year. His further education came in a military school whose kind of behavior thereafter stamped him. A lieutenant during World War I, he had married a French-speaking Lorrainer, a woman who was "driven out by the French" after the war and who never quite felt at home in Germany, speaking only a broken German. Although the mayor's wife, she was not socially accepted and remained at home. The son became a truck-driver, the daughter a seamstress.

Schambeck's failure, of which Friedbergers were well aware, was his bankruptcy in the lumber business in the twenties—many thought from his own mismanagement. He survived until 1933 in semi-genteel poverty and obscurity. He had no interest in politics; the hunt had been more exciting. After joining the NS in 1931, he was asked in July 1932 to do office work for the SA for a few hours a day. Rapid promotion came in 1932 as his superiors involved themselves in a mutiny against the SA leader for having embezzled SA funds. With so many vacancies, Schambeck was given high position in the rapidly expanding SA just as Hitler assumed power in 1933. All of a sudden he had power to use against a hostile world.

The role Schambeck played during the early vicious days of the Augsburg SA is disputed. He was associated with units which made widescale arrests of suspected "traitors". He claimed simply to have been in charge of the office. Office work was indeed what he liked best, but he is unlikely to have had no knowledge of the brutality as he claimed. He acted as a kind of office manager, or chief-of-staff, for the SA commissar, Ritter von Schoepf, whom Schambeck described as an alcoholic. Although Schoepf's wife pleaded with Schambeck, he said, to be patient with her nervously sick husband, an obscure controversy ensued and Schoepf banished Schambeck in September 1933 from his native Augsburg, which brought on financial loss.

In the first of several party trials, Schambeck was charged with "swine-like behavior" in a tavern while stationed at

Landshut.[13] This also involved frequent riding of horses and the damaging of crops, but primarily drunkenness, particularly one evening when he allegedly got fresh with a married woman and after a night of drinking bothered the peasants early in the morning, demanding milk and insisting that a farm laborer pay him due respect. Schambeck's defense conceded that he had had too much to drink, but that he loved horses and nothing had really happened. Anyway, he had apologized. His SA accuser himself had been "too drunk to lead his outfit at Nuremberg". Schambeck was saved by a general amnesty for acts committed before June 30, 1934, but a friend who had promised to help Schambeck get started again in the SA was executed with Roehm.

In November 1934 a new commander permitted Schambeck to return to Augsburg, but life was still bitter for the SA man. Because of the Roehm affair he had to attend a special indoctrination school in Munich, an experience which produced a permanent antipathy toward the powers in the party. Older than most of his fellow students, he felt himself out of place. He thought himself spied upon as a result of his conflict with Schoepf, and disliked the life of a pupil, believing that only those who flattered the instructor were accepted.[14] He refused to participate in the more strenuous marches and games. The theoretical instruction, based on *Mein Kampf*, was beyond Schambeck. He lacked the answers; on one occasion he wrote only a minuscule page and a half. His complaints were reported, he thought, and this made life even more difficult for him. He threatened to quit the SA rather than go through the course again.

On practical and military matters he thought he had done well. On one occasion he had worked, he testified, until 2:30 in the morning on a problem, while his roommates had gone into town to amuse themselves, yet not he but another was given the commendation. He soon noticed that his hard work was not rewarded, but that having the proper party connections was what counted. He failed the course, a permanent

[13] BDC, SA File on F. X. Schambeck, 27.8.34.
[14] Schambeck in SK, F. X. Schambeck, 48ff.

scar on his party ego, and was asked to leave. (Schambeck's immediate superior in the Augsburg SA was also required to take the course, and also failed; he, too, joined the SS.) After long delays, contrary to orders to fire him immediately, Schambeck was thrown out of the SA office with no apparent future in the party. On April 13 he was suddenly called without any foreknowledge and told to report to Friedberg as mayor. He was installed the same night, whereupon several of the councilmen immediately resigned.

This precipitous appointment represented the desperate Miller, who begged Wahl to do something to end the Hack crisis. Wahl told Miller that Schambeck had "his weaknesses", but that he was the best then available. "I have no one better now, I beg you to take him."[15] Miller took him in hopes of driving Hack out. While Miller and Hack battled all the way up the hierarchy to Munich and Berlin, Schambeck tried to hang on with practically no local support.

He found the situation in city hall "terrible"; the officials had lacked restraint under the non-NS Dollriess and were in need of a firm hand. He put them back to work on time and put an end to the alleged constant sausage-eating and beer-drinking during office hours. He recalled that a very large number of the Beamten, particularly the higher variety, were basically lazy, that it was to him a great joy to get them to work, because his position was that the Beamten were there for the people and not the reverse, as they believed and behaved. Two men were immediately fired as potential troublemakers, which is nearly the extent of firings. By doggedly trying to master the job he maintained himself into the summer of 1937 when Wahl apparently decided to start all over again and call in an SS man; the SS by this time seemed to support Hack and oppose Schambeck. In September 1937 Schambeck received a letter from Kreisleiter Kellner that he had already been transferred to a party position in Munich. Schambeck got the decision reversed, strangely, with the support of Friedbergers.

The city council was given the choice of either keeping

[15] Brehm.

Schambeck or calling in an SS man. With such an alternative they voted overwhelmingly to keep Schambeck, despite his unpopularity, perhaps fearing another housecleaning, this time by Himmler's bullies. With such unexpected support Schambeck was officially installed as mayor in September 1937. The town resigned itself to its sergeant-like mayor. The party merely tried to get him to behave less like one and more like a mayor. Schambeck defended his roughness on the basis of the "mess" left by Hack.[16] He had to restore law and order.

How oppressive his tenure was is debatable. He was gruff as one expects a tyrant to be. He was publicly at least a fanatical Nazi, threatening persons with dire punishment if they did not conform. The first city council meeting was unfortunate. Schambeck, aware of their opposition, told the councilmen that they could easily end up in Dachau if they did not follow his orders.[17] He seems to have had only a very few citizens arrested, and no councilmen, perhaps because he wished to avoid the impression of causing popular unrest. Two of his opponents he assisted in being called to military service during the war.

Public opinion polls did not exist, but a letter to Epp in 1939 described Schambeck as Friedberg's "misfortune and shame", a "bankrupted lumber merchant, who had sought his last salvation in the party". The letter quoted Schambeck: "If the Friedbergers will not love me, they will fear me". The writer of the letter thought Friedberg neither loved nor feared him; Friedberg simply hated him. Friedberg complained about the city council which was blind to his financial waste, including 10,000 marks for a mayor's garden, which Schambeck needed since he was afraid to leave his house.[18]

Those who knew Schambeck as a colleague, including his deputy mayor (elected mayor repeatedly after the war), thought, although Schambeck treated the citizens as a sergeant treated troops, he behaved decently with the city coun-

[16] GSA, Muendler report to Epp, 22.7.37, Epp file 119.
[17] Hans Brehm in SK, F. X. Schambeck, 3f.
[18] GSA, Epp File 119.

cil, that he would listen quietly to the debate and accept suggestions gracefully before making a decision, that his goals were order and honesty in government, and that he came in time to understand his job.[19] The city council reported pleasure not only with his energy but his willingness to keep them informed of events, as Hack had not.[20]

His conduct toward the Catholic school was such that pastor and nuns gave him partial credit at his trial for having protected them from harm. A June 1937 Munich summary noted that Friedberg was the only town not to have turned to the NS-desired "community school" instead of the Catholic school.[21] The church remained relatively undisturbed; nuns and crucifixes were unbothered contrary to Wagner orders. He described the nuns as his best teachers and gave permission for baptisms in the hospital, which was also contrary to orders.[22]

During the war Schambeck was reported as being decent to the prisoners assigned to Friedberg. The French were permitted to live in private homes. The pastor testified that Schambeck knew that he was hiding an escaped Russian prisoner for three months, but winked at it. A number of Jews were transferred from Augsburg to Friedberg late in the war to avoid the bombings. They said at his trial that they were treated decently by Schambeck, not even required to wear the "Jewish star", a major concession.

At his trial Schambeck claimed that his hostile treatment by the party had determined him to give it only lip service. Therefore the party had had to pay for any city rooms used for meetings; he had participated in no party or SA activity, excusing himself as too busy with city business. Although he was active in getting employees to contribute to the party charities, he refused to release city employees for party work. Persons were not fired from city employment because they were not party men; those he released were party members.

[19] Hohenbleicher.
[20] GSA, Muendler to Epp, 22.7.37, Epp File 119.
[21] BRP, Munich, 19.6.37.
[22] Kaplan Scherer in SK, Schambeck, 31.

His most severe critic, whom he released, he said, was a daughter of a Hack supporter and known as one who denounced the nonparty, and always insisted on a Heil Hitler. He assumed she was the one posting the anti-Schambeck signs about town.

Schambeck claimed never to have spoken for the party as mayor. In 1942 he received a direct order from the SA to speak once a month to the local group. He simply burned the order. After repeated reminders, he told them that the order was lost, but that one who was found lacking in party ideology in 1935 should not be asked to speak. The SA did throw him out of their organization, but the charge was black marketing.

Schambeck, who demanded military discipline from subordinates, was on trial repeatedly for disobedience, charged with violations of the rationing laws.[23] His defense was that he had in 1936 arranged that the garbage of the city hospital be given to the Catholic sisters to feed their pigs. In return they had sent him in gratitude "a few pounds" of sausages from each slaughtering; he had taken the meat "so as not to insult them". The SA court did not accept the mayor's story and expelled him, observing that he had been punished by the civil court with 150 marks or 15 days in jail. They protested the mildness of Wahl's party court, which had not prosecuted under the rigorous rationing laws. In the SA's opinion, Schambeck was a disgrace to the SA and should never be a mayor.

During the years 1937 to 1945 Schambeck, the superficially obedient, kept the town quiet. The machinery of city government moved without particular imagination or enthusiasm, leaving behind some minor public works and the lowering of the city debt. The relative skepticism among Friedbergers is reflected in a series of candid police reports, which show a general lack of obedience to state and party leaders.[24] (The problems of the party and state in the villages of the county is treated in the next chapter.)

Something of the relationship between leaders and led is

[23] BDC, Schambeck SA File. [24] CGD, T 580, R 100.

evident in the final surrender of the city. The city took the law into its own hands; the women of the city tore down the barricades on the west edge of the city toward Augsburg because these might provoke the Americans into further bombardment. Schambeck, unable to disobey openly, failed somehow to prevent the popular action. The proud ex-lieutenant was ridden through the town on the hood of an army jeep. This was followed by a 32-month imprisonment and inconclusive trials that lasted until 1951. He lived in poverty and obscurity until his death.

8 THE VILLAGES

ONE of the great undiscovered continents in historical research is the history of villages, the communities which more than any other have encompassed the whole of life of the vast majority of peoples who have ever lived and probably those still living. These relatively small groups of humans governed each other for thousands of years in a fairly constant fashion, which suggests both the most democratic of governments and the most restrictive. Villages have traditionally solved their local problems, largely centered on problems of land usage, by more or less democratic group action through an elected chief or head. This democracy has made possible, on the other hand, the small-townish kind of dictatorial social control, the control of the gossipy housewives, whose sharp tongues kept almost everyone in line.

The relationship of the villages with outside, formal "government" has been the peasant problem that was least satisfactorily solved, in the judgment of villagers. Farmers have had little interest in kings and their wars, and in the decisions of kings, now presidents, who have had as little understanding of their peasants. The ritual of central government commanding and peasant avoiding of clear obedience or disobedience has been one of the great unplumbed rituals of history. The often frantic efforts of kings to collect taxes or men from thousands of villages testifies primarily to the skill of peasants in failing to understand the complex world which tries to intervene in their stable and well-ordered lives. (Tax avoidance is a classic peasant achievement testifying to the success of their disguise of ignorance.)

Except to one who has read the records, e.g., district reports as found in the Geheim Staats Archiv in Munich, the truth is self-evident that the peasants loyally obeyed the Fuehrer. Although peasants can differ, Bavarian peasants seem to have been among the first nonleftists to have reservations about the new government in Berlin. These peasants were predominately conservative; some of them assumed the Nazis to be backward looking, like themselves, and not radical. They shared the strong NS antipathy to socialism, which seemed to endanger those two things peasants hold dearest—the church and ownership of the land—but they came to discover that National Socialists could disturb their lands and their church.

Much of the peasants' suspicion of Hitler's Berlin was a continuation of their traditional suspicion of any central government. The peasant did not want to be bothered by any external government. If he could grow and sell his crops, the world was in order. But the NS wanted more. In a limited sense, the NS was a 20th-century urban movement trying to bring the peasant into an integrated modern world, with the standard 1930s devices to coordinate farm production and control prices. In another sense, the NS was a 19th-century romantic movement that dreamed of re-creating a Germanic yeomanry—Darré's notion of *Blut und Boden*—which involved an intervention into the peasant's pattern of life to maintain, or possibly rebuild, a type of preindustrial society the peasant no longer found profitable. Central policy, therefore, involved not only the urban goals of absolute loyalty to the state, as evidenced by a party-dominated behavior, but the goals of maximum delivery of food at the lowest prices, and the somewhat contradictory reorganization of society to provide a preindustrial yeomanry. Effecting these policies required the cooperation of Landrat, Kreisleiter, mayors, and hordes of "ignorant beasts of farm labor".

Friedberg County: Landrat and Mayors

The Friedberg villages of Kreisleiter Miller showed a remarkable stability and continuity of Catholic influence in contrast to the party turmoil in Friedberg. The Kreis's state authority was represented by the Beamten Landrat, whom the villages much preferred to the more aggressive party men.

Schmidt, the first NS Landrat and an old Beamter, who

was sent in 1933 to Friedberg, was regarded as an official with decency and courage, able to defend some state prerogatives against Kreisleiter Miller. His Beamten remained the same, avoiding the attention of one or two suspicious NS, and avoiding change, trouble, unnecessary work, and responsibility. His successor was Fuerst who was in office from October 1936 to May 1945. Previously in Franken, Fuerst had been sent to Friedberg as punishment for an inability to please the demanding Streicher. He was praised by his former non-NS assistant, K. Hefele, as a capable administrator, correct in every way, respected by all who dealt with him. Although Fuerst joined the party in 1937, he was regarded as no more than a nominal party member. He exerted no party pressure on subordinates. He ignored party orders that officials whose positions exposed them to state pressure were to be active in the party. His subordinates saw him as their shield against the party. He did not permit party propaganda or announcements to be attached to office boards or walls. Possessing no uniform, he appeared as an obvious outsider at any party functions he had to attend. With the possible exception of Schambeck, who was NS and could have used his influence with the Gauleitung, Fuerst had excellent relations with all of the various mayors in the county. Schambeck's reports of any derelictions forced Fuerst into an outer conformity in contrast to an inner lack of compliance, in Hefele's opinion. She concluded her high praise of Fuerst with the mention of his arrest and death in December 1945 in a U.S. internee camp, where he had spent months in the open without proper medical care.

Although Fuerst theoretically had the power to modify village practices he bothered the villages as little as possible, merely consulting with the mayors, as was done before 1933, on practical matters of mutual concern. Mayor Haas remembered Fuerst's first visit to his village; Fuerst bluntly announced that he "had not come to snoop". His only advice was to maintain good relations with the pastors and to be fair to the villagers. Fuerst had backed Haas against the party, helping him to avoid such party phenomena as the SA, SS, even the Hitler Youth. All of his meetings with the mayors were business-like, with no reference to party politics. At one such meeting in September 1939 a party representative predicted early victory. After the party man left, Fuerst quietly advised the mayors to expect a long war; "the enemy has weapons, too", he said. Fuerst's ultimate honesty was in his insistence on living on his ration food allotment, particularly commendable for a person subject to bribery with gifts of food.

Village relations with the government were confined to the five or six meetings a year with Fuerst, a yearly inspection of the village buildings, streets and air raid programs. Government otherwise meant food rationing (rather meaningless to peasants) and the draft. The party representative was supposed to check the peasants' census of livestock, but he signed without looking. The quotas for grain delivery were kept down by reporting more "roads" than existed and extra "waste land".

Fragmentary reports from Fuerst to Munich suggest a resigned attitude toward passive disobedience by the peasants. Peasants were rejecting state orders and nothing could be done.[1] Fuerst, reacting to the effort in 1941 by Interior Minister Wagner to get crosses out of the schools noted his personal disapproval of the order and the popular opposition. The peasants' reaction to the state order to transfer the popular Corpus Christi celebration from a workday to a Sunday was not to hold the cherished procession on the weekday as compliance with the order, but also not to work.[2] Also contrary to state desires, the lesser holiday of Ascension was celebrated by both peasants and city people; the reaction of the peasants was "They can do what they want, we will still celebrate our holidays".[3] Fuerst reported that the holiday was observed everywhere and the order banning them simply further lowered morale. A new reason to celebrate was found in 1942: the 25th anniversary of Pope Pius's dedication as

[1] CGD, T 175, Roll 430, F 9560ff.
[2] Ibid., 9778. [3] *Ibid.*, 9799.

bishop. One report noted nothing out of the ordinary; attendance at the church service was 100%, as always.[4]

Efforts to get tighter controls of the 1,300 foreign workers in the county proved fruitless. In each case, the mayor, including NS Schambeck, vouched for the Russian workers, otherwise disciplined. The Landrat agreed and instructed the police not to require any reports.[5]

Village Derching

Another defender of Fuerst was Florian Kastl, the postwar mayor of Derching, who began his tenure in office in 1933.[6] When requested by Miller at the death of the mayor to take the job, he acceded rather than permit the bringing in of an outsider. His frequent inclination to resign was almost successful in 1937-38 when Kastl was ordered to join the party. As was the common practice, his consultation with the village priest convinced him to stay in office.

Through the 12 years Derching remained largely Bavarian Catholic despite a fanatical teacher who tried to break through. Only about a dozen in the village ever joined the party. The first priest had been denounced in 1933 for opposition and left in fear of the teacher. His successor, a brother of the Augsburg bishop, urged caution; he also urged some to join the party to bring a good influence to it.

Although it was forbidden to collect money for any purpose other than the NS charity, every year the village sent a collection to an Augsburg cloister. A critical priest, Max Mayr, was sent to Dachau; the village remembered him with a package every week.

The usual village story of teacher versus priest and town ensued, with the teacher so angry at frustrations that he eventually asked to be transferred. As elsewhere, the NS teacher and representative of the state had to play the organ for the Sunday services. An HJ organized by the teacher rarely met, and then out of town. The effort to organize a non-Catholic, i.e. community school, in Derching in 1937-38 was frustrated; only one vote was cast for it in the entire village. The mayor

[4] *Ibid.*, 9560. [5] *Ibid.*, 9764. [6] SK, Florian Kastl.

had stood up at the village meeting and announced, "We won't do it; we won't give up our rights".

The SA functioned scarcely at all, a few wandering off to a larger neighboring village, which had a unit. The only flags displayed were the colors of Bavaria, the blue and white.

In addition to the normal religious recalcitrance of the village, Derching did not implement two other peacetime economic policies of the Reich government, the first of farm consolidations to eliminate the scattered strips which attracted little interest until after the war. The Darré policy of *Blut und Boden* was avoided by the mayor on the advice of Fuerst by simply taking in two brothers as "joint owners" so that he did not qualify. The 1964 Landrat, Florian Kastl's brother, thought Darré's policy was ignored in the entire county.[7]

Wartime controls were easily avoided. With the cooperation of the mayors and the likely knowledge of the Landrat, private slaughterings were of several animals instead of the one reported; one reason was the need to feed foreign workers properly. The meat was conserved in cans hidden in the ground. Foreigners were treated as human beings, as near members of the family contrary to government pleadings for racial unity and purity.

Village Laimering

Georg Haas, mayor of Laimering from 1936 to 1964, became mayor and a member of the party for the same reasons as his friend Kastl. The military government investigation concluded that he had done so to prevent a real Nazi from assuming power, and that he had used his position to prevent such things as the HJ.[8] He had the support of a teacher, Kneissl, an army veteran who opposed the NS movement even though Kneissl's wife denounced him to Kreisleiter Miller. Kneissl and Haas jointly protected the pastor, warning him of Gestapo visits and answering Gestapo questions in his favor. Kneissl, the village teacher since 1927, took great pride in the fact that Laimering remained Catholic "to its bones". Pastor Muesmann, in Laimering, for 23 years,

[7] Landrat Fabian Kastl.

[8] SK, Georg Haas.

regarded Haas as the best mayor in the area. Well he should, for Haas was always in the church processions forbidden by the party and always sang in the choir.

The de-Nazification court accepted Haas's statement that he had attended NS meetings only twice in 12 years, and that none of his children were in the party youth organization. Two SA men active before they came to Laimering never wore uniforms nor attended meetings thereafter. The triumvirate saw to it that party schooling was ineffective. The county propaganda leader was thrown out of the village and did not return. Only two party members were in the village—which was the legal minimum—one as mayor and one as peasant leader. There were no arrests in the village.[9]

Village Warmisried

The Swabian village of Warmisried is nearly typical enough to be worthy of consideration; yet it had a priest and mayor who made it different enough to merit special reference.

Located in the southern corner of Schwaben, it literally nestles in the foothills of the Alps. It is somewhat remote, although a major highway is within five kilometers. It has existed for centuries among rolling hills made productive by the toughness and determination of its people. It is solidly Catholic and solidly Swabian, which means that its image is one of a friendly, generous people, yet sceptical and sensible. For centuries it tended to regard all outsiders with suspicion, even those strange Bavarians living just beyond the next range of hills. Its population is about 500, nearly all farmers.

This combination has meant that Warmisried has voted Catholic and peasant, the BVP before 1933 and the Christian Social party since 1945. The other more radical (Weimar) peasant group, the *Bauernbund*, took advantage of peasant discontent with inflation and depression and led some peasants to vote for change, but just a few here.[10]

Its leading political personality from 1930 to the mid-1960s was Johann Huber, a peasant of moderate land-holdings and limited education, yet he had a superior shrewdness.

[9] *Ibid.*

[10] SK, Johann Huber.

Huber was a man with a natural feel for dealing with people, settling grievances of the less reasonable villagers, and yet stubborn enough to defend his village from outside pressures. Huber was elected to the village council in 1924. These eight members, plus the mayor, had been elected to run the village for as long as anyone can remember; even under the Kaiser this council was regularly elected every five years. With the death of the previous mayor in 1931, a new election pushed an unwilling Huber into office. His name was not even on the list of candidates, as he thought himself "not big enough" for the job. The year before, Andreas Rampp had come to Warmisried as their priest. Rampp was a large, intelligent, powerful man, able and willing to save his flock from any godless philosophy such as the Nazi one.

With the devout Huber as mayor and the strong Rampp as priest, Warmisried found itself in the midst of the fateful elections of 1930-33. The Bauernbund enticed a maximum of 30 votes away from the BVP to the NS in 1932. This aroused the combative instincts of Rampp who as the only educated resident acted as the village spokesman. In every campaign the NS from outside were met by the powerful priest. Huber recalled how Rampp, his hero, baffled every NS speaker sent from the Gau with his sharp questions and answers. He recalled how the younger people cheered at every victory their priest scored over the imported speakers. In a remarkable tribute to Rampp's control over the village, the NS vote in Warmisried dropped from 30 in 1932 to 12 in March 1933.

There were almost no party members in the village before 1933, and a small number joined after the Nazi's seizure of power. Their party activity was limited to the paying of dues. Huber could recall no more than three or four meetings during the entire 12 years. The SA had several members, some attracted by the uniform, but that attraction was temporary for most. No local unit existed; a small number were associated with the unit of a neighboring village.

Like nearly all mayors in Bavaria, Huber was loyally BVP. Not too eager to be "in politics" under the best of circumstances, he was requested by Rampp in 1933 to remain as mayor. (This is a remarkable feature of Catholic villages: the priest often made the decision about who would join the party and therewith remain in control of the village.) Rampp told Huber that if he did not join the party it would put in a real Nazi, in this case a man doubly repugnant because he had been a communist until 1932.

The local NS and SA leader was the owner-operator of the bakery. He seems to have been virtually the only fanatical NS in the village. Huber regarded him as basically a harmless fellow, but one who returned from peptalks with the Kreisleiter full of unreasonableness—for example, ordering party members to have nothing to do with the priest. To the NS's frustration, Huber and Rampp remained the closest of partners. The baker party-leader continued to attend services for a time, then, obedient to party desires, stayed away. He secretly attended Easter services, but outside the village to avoid detection.

The other potential opposition to the priestly dominance was the teacher—the typical village anti-clerical situation. The school's compulsory religion instruction of five hours weekly was assigned to the priest for all students for the eight years of the school. Despite instructions from above to the contrary, the teacher was forced by the community into the traditional role of church choir director and organist.

The power of the priest vis-à-vis the state teacher was demonstrated in the attempted plebiscite to change from a confessional school to a community school. Although the sudden election was supposed to have been kept secret from Rampp, he learned of it and set out to organize the parents on the morning of the election. The NS peasant leader assigned the task confronted the parents and discovered that the parents were following the pastor completely. He had no choice but to resign; at the pastor's suggestion, no replacement was named. From the beginning, when the peasants had beaten up SA men and an imported speaker, it was risky for party leaders to appear. The county school leader declined to visit the village after a threat that his neck would be broken if he dared return.

The village lacked other normal appurtenances of the Nazi state. The HJ, as such, did not exist except as a weak auxiliary of the next village. The county leader had to request time for the HJ at the church service, since only at church could all of the youth be gotten together. The Catholic youth organization continued in operation for boys over 16, and, contrary to all instructions from outside, met once a month. The mayor saw to it that there was no NS women's organization. There was no party sponsored function, even on the cherished party holidays of January 30, May 1, or November 9, not even the harvest-thanksgiving or any gathering for the party charity, the most harmless of party functions. Party flags were not displayed.

Rampp, in secure control, was impatient with church leadership for its caution. When Pope Pius expressed disapproval of the NS state "with burning care", the attempt to prevent its circulation was easily foiled. The speech was mimeographed in Augsburg and distributed via auto; each pastor was given two copies with the orders to read it to the congregation and all but one priest in the area read it.

Police who might enter the village world to check on Rampp's sermons were easily recognizable. Of such dangers Rampp was warned by the Kreisleiter and even the local party leader. The showdown came when the teacher, perhaps envious of the priest's power, perhaps to obtain a better position, betrayed the priest. In 1938 in three sharp Rampp sermons against the party, the teacher-organist took stenographic notes of the sermons. The Gestapo appeared, searched the pastor's rooms and found nothing. Dangerous materials were hidden under the church floor and never found. Yet they arrested Rampp for interrogation at a jail in the area.[11]

By Sunday the news of the pastor's arrest had spread. A priest-friend of Rampp's went to the mayor's house and asked for his help. The mayor told him to draw up whatever state-

[11] BRP Schwaben, 2.9.38.

ment he thought would help and the mayor would sign it. This he did although the statement was not quite truthful, i.e., that Rampp had never criticized the NS. The mayor noticed that even the police who arrested Rampp were unenthusiastic about the job. Rampp thought himself well treated by the prison staff although he was kept in solitary confinement. He was allowed to work in a garden; he could read anything he liked; he was even permitted a light to read by. The prison director came each evening at ten to turn out the light personally and to wish him a "good night". The prison also supplied him with Schnapps and wine for Holy water.

The imprisonment lasted four months, at the end of which Rampp must either be released or sent to Dachau. Had the village not stood solidly behind Rampp, he would have been sent to Dachau. Only two persons in the entire village could be found to testify against him—the teacher and the baker party-leader. The mayor's testimony was crucial. The Gestapo came from Munich in mid-November and interrogated many people over a two-day period. At Huber's interview he was treated quite kindly by the Gestapo who showed him his signed letter and had him verify it. Then came the question of what Rampp had said on the Sunday in question. Huber knew precisely how Rampp had criticized the party but told the Gestapo he had heard nothing like that recorded by the teacher. Why not? It had been a warm day and he had perhaps dozed off. Despite Gestapo entreaties to support the teacher's statement, no one other than the party-leader, who had not been a witness, would criticize the pastor's loyalty. Rampp was released after a polite hearing, at which he was assisted by the state's attorney. Rampp's subsequent transfer to the bishop's staff had been planned before ahead of time; under the circumstances it seemed best to keep him in a less exposed position in the diocesan finance office, but he remained close to *his* village, for 30 years driving there during his vacations.

The village took its own kind of revenge on the baker party-leader who had so endangered the priest. From the time of the priest's arrest practically no villager bought anything from the bakery. The baker was forced out of business in short order and forced to leave the village. In a way, this was unfortunate for Mayor Huber, for he inherited the job of party leader. The Kreisleiter appeared to find a replacement for the baker leader. The council wanted Huber to assume both jobs, although the Kreisleiter would have preferred anyone else. After two hours of fruitless pressure on the council, the Kreisleiter gave in and made Huber the acting party leader for the village, for no other party member would take the job.

The two successor priests were more careful. Kees, the 1964 pastor, remembered that Huber had asked him in 1943 not to disturb the peace and quiet; since there was almost no Naziism left in the village to expunge, there was no purpose in attracting the Gestapo again. Village opposition was along traditional lines, as for example, the reports of livestock holdings. Inasmuch as they were forced to turn over a quota of their livestock, the peasants systematically reported only a fraction of their true holdings; it was impossible for the mighty state to discover the truth.

The war, greeted with no enthusiasm, cost the village 30 dead out of the 100 called to service. Other than wartime economic exactions, which were partially avoided, the major change was the importation of foreign laborers to do the work. The law was quite explicit: there was to be no fraternization with "inferior" foreigners and only the minimal provision for their needs. The state reports constantly show its frustration with the peasants who treated the foreigners as their equals. Such was clearly the case in Warmisried. There were some 15 to 20 Serb prisoners and Polish civil workers. The prisoners slept in the council house with one guard; the workers lived with the peasants. Among the various forbidden amenities, the mayor saved them cigarettes which they "returned" to him after the war. They ate together at the same table as members of the family and went to church together. They were permitted in the local tavern and to the showing of movies. On occasion, the movie house was three-fourths filled with Poles. They were paid about what Germans would have been paid. Had they been badly treated, the Poles would have arranged a transfer to other villages, as all peasants were eager for their help.

One Jew, who fled a neighboring town, was able to live out the war by working in the local sawmill. Like the foreigners, he testified after the war that he had been given friendly aid beyond the call of duty by Huber. He described Huber's activity as a sabotage of Gestapo measures.[12]

That which was most explicitly forbidden was the contact of foreign workers with German females, left alone by the exodus of men for the front. Cases were highly publicized of Poles elsewhere being executed for having "defiled Aryan women". Yet such romances even in the small village were numerous and well known to the mayor who could list the number of children resulting from such forbidden international relations. Of course, no one was reported to the police. No police existed for the village and those outside were reluctant to intervene without the mayor's support.

Although Huber was able to avoid serious incursions on his and the priestly domain by the NS, he had less success with the Americans. When the first American officers appeared in May 1945, they asked the new priest, Kees, who had given Huber full backing as a non-Nazi and decent person. He was retained in office. However, the Counter-Intelligence Corps arrived in June to arrest him because he was nominally the village party-leader.

During the early days of his arrest Huber observed a certain inhumanity in the treatment of prisoners—e.g., the standing at attention for hours with hands behind head, during which many fell and could not be helped. A few prisoners were beaten. Six months later his wife learned of his whereabouts. Life became better, with a package a week from his village. The worst was the imprisonment without any trial, only one questioning and that lasting but a minute or so. That he had been the local party leader, in name at least, simply meant an "automatic" arrest.

Over two years passed. Finally because of the energetic

[12] SK Johann Huber.

intercessions of Pastor Rampp, a trial was arranged by the end of November 1947. The court placed him in the lowest category of "guilt", even lower than that requested by his defense counsel, one for which the punishment would have been at most a small fine, not the two and a half years already served in prison.

On his return the villagers wished to elect him mayor once again, partly perhaps because they recognized that because of him no one else in the village was arrested. He avoided politics in the first election in 1948 but was made mayor again in 1952 and has been reelected each time since.

The Villages as Seen by the Government

Each village could provide variations on the theme. For generalizations we have the state's monthly reports which reflect the situation much as described in postwar trials and interviews.

Although Bavarian peasants were outwardly loyal to the state, rising to a kind of revolt only when their church was attacked, the NS reports regarded them as an unconquered land. The swing of many of them to the NS fold in 1933 represented primarily an economic protest. (A district report in January 1933 regarded even the communists as a great danger because of their appeal to the peasants, appearing at auctions as their friends.)[13] The reports noted that the swing to the NS was strongest among the poor peasants; those with debts or back taxes admitted that this was why they supported Hitler.[14]

From the beginning, the peasants were alienated by the changes in governmental personnel; they preferred the known conservative Catholics to the unknown NS.[15] The peasants resisted changing their mayors; "a rather large percentage of the old mayors have been voted in again".[16] Where the Kreisleiter did not accept the peasants' choice there was "unrest".[17] One area reported popular "unrest" when an SA

[13] GSA BRP, Munich, 2.1.33.
[14] Munich, 4.3.33.
[15] Schwaben, 22.3.33.
[16] Schwaben, 6.5.33.
[17] Munich, 19.5.33.

unit attacked a Jewish firm.[18] SA attacks on the police were unpopular, as were the arrests of the Catholic party leaders who had resigned anyway.[19] Most of the arrested were released in a few days.

The Franken reports thought it would take years to persuade BVP voters to switch to National Socialism. "Some areas of the region are as yet absolutely untouched by the ideas of Hitler" it said.[20] The difficulty with the many villages was increased because they were so poor that they did not even read newspapers. Many did not even have a radio in the village. In one area the report noted 97 such villages, where the only NS in the village were those serving on the new village council. Of these new members "so many changed colors so fast, one cannot be sure what they think".[21] A peasant rejection of the Darré changes in the inheritance law was reported.[22] The leaders of the peasants, the clergy, were increasingly reported as in "passive opposition"; Franken noted that though "they are quiet and avoiding trouble, they never express sympathy with the new regime".[23]

The reports from Schwaben showed a particular concern that public (peasant) opinion was unfavorable: "There is dominant in broad peasant circles a dull quiet, a noticeably stronger reserve . . . than before. One is cautious and as silent as possible in trying to avoid any deeper probing into various questions. . . . In this 'capsulising' [*Abkapselung*] is shown a serious loss of confidence and a serious danger. . . . It is most apparent in those communities where persons on the basis of their previous party work pushed their way into jobs for which they were not qualified".[24] One form of peasant dissatisfaction was the nightly attack on NS monuments, for example, a tree dedicated as the "Hitler oak". Reports were dismayed that the Hitler oak had been sawed down during the night.[25]

[18] Franken, 6.4.33.
[19] Munich, 4.7.33; Schwaben, 6.7.33.
[20] Franken, 19.7.33.
[21] Schwaben, 3.8.33.
[22] Schwaben 21.10.33 and 8.8.34.
[23] Franken, 19.1.34.
[24] Schwaben, 4.5.34.
[25] Schwaben, 18.6.34.

Franken lamented that "one cannot get the peasants to talk".[26] Regensburg also reported the population extremely reserved, very distrustful and cautious, that the Goebbels campaign against "complainers" had backfired with its crude criticism of the church and Beamten.[27] The population preferred that Hitler would "clean up his own party instead". Catholic priests were clearly not National Socialist. The poor peasants with debts were happy with the NS policies, but they were not the desirable peasants.

The impact of the law of 1935 on local government which in theory made appointments from above instead of elections from within, brought few changes. In one community an unpopular mayor was forced to leave town by the united action of the Catholic women's organization which boycotted his store, reducing his gross profit for one day to five marks.[28] Pressures on the church had less success in the countryside. In one case the party leader tried to limit collection for the Catholic charity—in the cities mobs of HJ forced the police to forbid the collection—but in the rural case every person wore the *Caritas* button and NS organizations collecting received almost nothing.[29]

Another case of violence was the boring through of a large May Pole on which a swastika had been placed, so that it had to be sawed down. A note was left with a favorite Nazi boast: "And yet we have won".[30] More important was the reading of a forbidden bishopric message in 3,000 churches in June 1935.[31] Where the peasants stood in the party versus church struggle was indicated in the report that the peasants in some communities gave more to a forbidden collection for the Capuchin priests than they did for the NS sponsored charity. In one church service the priest criticized the *Der Stuermer* display cases, Streicher's pornographic attacks on Jews and Catholics. Thus aroused, the peasants attacked party functionaries and wanted to tear down the box. An old

[26] Franken, 9.8.34.

[27] Regensburg, August 1934.

[28] Munich, 11.11.35.

[29] *Ibid.*, Bav. Political Police Report, June 1936.

[30] *Ibid.*

[31] *Ibid.*, July 1936.

lady finally tore it down and was arrested. Rocks were thrown through the window of the party functionary who had erected the display case.[32]

Reports of the removal of holy pictures from the schools in one area of northern Germany and the Bavarian effort to close church-operated schools alienated opinion. In one community a mass meeting to save the nuns was told by the Landrat that it was hopeless, that they should not resist the law. Yet they tried at the Bavarian Education Ministry and failed.[33] In another area mayors helped priests tear down offensive HJ propaganda. The police were aware of the peasant violations of the rationing laws and that they kept many more animals than reported. In one case a peasant was discovered to have seven extra animals.[34] But arrests were rare.

In January 1937 there was more violence. In one village the NS demonstrated at night in front of the pastor's house for having attacked the mayor for having fired the nuns without informing his town council. Fifty followers of the priest marched to the county headquarters, where the Kreisleiter was surrounded by angry men. Eight of these were arrested for a few days. The church authorities refused to transfer the pastor.[35] In another village, angry at the removal of the sisters, the NS teacher aroused the village further by insulting the morning school prayer and implying that the crosses would be removed. The state recommended that the teacher be transferred.[36] In mid-1937 there was a wave of angry criticism and popular anger against the mayors who approved the school reform, the creation of "community schools" with a weakening of the Catholic domination.[37] The Goebbels attack on the priests as moral criminals and smugglers convinced very few peasants.[38]

The pressure against church holidays brought increased celebration among the peasants. The forbidden All Saints Day was reported celebrated everywhere outside the large

[32] Schwaben, 6.11.36.
[33] Schwaben, 6.1.37.
[34] *Ibid.*
[35] Schwaben, 7.2.37.
[36] *Ibid.*
[37] Munich, 19.6.37.
[38] Franken, 8.7.37.

cities. One official report strongly urged that the authorities respect these traditional holidays.[39] Peasants were also bitter about the high cost of labor, up from five marks a week in 1935 to seven or eight in 1937.[40] Compulsory labor for all youth soon provided a cheaper labor supply and eased peasant complaints.

In mid-1938 a report stated that a clear majority of adult peasants were behind their priests, although one could detect in the cities a reduction in the number of marchers and watchers of processions.[41] What these peasants thought important was indicated by the fact that village recruits for the army did not know who ruled in Bavaria, had not heard of the war heroes Hindenburg and Ludendorff, could not distinguish on a map between the Danube and the Vistula, could not find the industrial Ruhr area—but every peasant knew the Pope's name and where he lived.[42] The power of the priest was further obvious in the report of the priest who told a women's congregation that "your men will soon be at war; you'd better have them come to confession". The women left the church crying.[43] He was imprisoned for his accurate prophecy and five peasants who came to plead for his release were arrested briefly for their "fresh behavior".[44]

Of the negative popular reaction to the NS violence against the Jews in November 1938, the reports emphasize that of the peasants.[45] They tended to sympathize with the Jews! As criticism of the Jewish action continued, the report noted that only "church-influenced people" were still against anti-Semitic action.[46]

The party's effort to hinder missionary work in Germany was reported to be unsuccessful. The peasants were still strongly loyal to their faith.[47] Franken reported that the Catholics were still against the NS and their power among the peasants was evident in numerous incidents: heavy at-

[39] Schwaben, 7.12.37.
[40] Munich, 10.1.38.
[41] Regensburg, 7.7.38.
[42] Schwaben, 6.8.38.
[43] Schwaben, 2.9.38.
[44] Schwaben, 7.12.38.
[45] Regensburg, 8.12.38, Munich, 10.12.38.
[46] Munich, 9.1.39.
[47] Munich, 10.12.38.

tendance for the church celebrations; no display of swastika flags; sermons that denounced the NS policy of sterilization of "the unfit"; denunciation of the SS publication; the organization of Catholic youth on the successful Protestant example; the ringing of bells loud and long to welcome back prisoners released from NS "protective custody".[48]

Loyalty is indicated by money; a report complained that the church was still collecting inside the church building. "There is scarcely a church service at which a collection for some purpose is not taken, and as the population feels about things now, they give generously, while the party charities have to fight to get their pennies".[49] The people streamed to church on holidays, as before. "The antagonism of all sections of the peasantry has not ended; instead it has increased. In sharper tones all local reports describe the increased 'bitterness', 'resignation', 'the dull discontent', 'the listlessness', of the peasantry".[50] Some of this was economic. The high cost of help—up to 18-20 marks a week—overworked the wives. There were heavy taxes, "which had scraped out the tax ability of the peasants almost to the ground". There were increased party dues, the low price of wheat vis-à-vis the high price of flour. "The peasants know no other way out but to reduce their animal holdings and the areas of cultivation."[51] There were troubles getting machines, cement, and transportation for fertilizers. Schwaben reported a catastrophic lack of farm labor, in one area four applicants for 200 positions. The rural mayors had abandoned their usual reserved silence and demanded some action.

The increasing danger of war was noted as a further depressant of everyone's morale, as during the Austrian *Anschluss,* until it was evident war would not result. Enthusiasm for the Sudeten acquisition was completely overshadowed by the fear of war. The March 1939 seizure of Czechoslovakia increased the fear of war for which there was "little support".[52] This was particularly true of the peasants. A great task re-

[48] Franken, 7.1.39.
[49] Munich, 9.1.39.
[50] Regensburg, 9.1.39.
[51] *Ibid.*
[52] Wuerzburg, 9.3.39.

mained for the party in those villages where no flags were displayed although they had been ordered to celebrate.[53] When the war came, all reports agree that it was greeted with none of the 1914 enthusiasm.

The shortage of farm labor was a reason for army deferment or discharge. One area reported that 30 of the 70 men in the army had immediately applied for a discharge.[54] Franken emphasized the lack of peasant enthusiasm or understanding for the war. Many of the appeals for a discharge were unjustified because there were other members of the same family at work in the cities who would not come home to help; the peasants had tried to reject Polish workers in order to keep the labor emergency and get their men home.[55] Another dodge was to get married, frequently soldiers marrying women 12 to 15 years older than themselves. A rural pastor was arrested for stating that Germany's enemies would win the war because they were more pious.[56]

In May 1940 a peasant party-leader stated, "Morale is now so bad that the expression 'catastrophic' would be an understatement".[57] The effort to weaken the propaganda impact of the highly valued Corpus Christi processions, by prohibiting the processions on workdays, caused "great unhappiness". The order was interpreted as meaning no procession *outside* the church, so the procession was held inside. Some workers refused to work on the holiday. Teachers were under great pressure not to hold school; in one county 23 schools cancelled classes.[58] A priest was arrested for simply saying that people could take an example from the pious Poles who knelt at evening prayers.[59]

The victory over France brought a quick change in attitudes, as peace was commonly assumed to be near. Yet one report noted that some churches did not ring the victory bells as ordered, adding that rural soldiers were dominated by such churches.[60] A pastor was quoted as criticizing German sol-

[53] *Ibid.*
[54] Munich, 10.2.40.
[55] Franken, 7.4.40.
[56] Schwaben, 7.5.40.
[57] Franken, 8.5.40.
[58] Franken, 6.6.40.
[59] Schwaben, 10.6.40.
[60] Munich, 9.7.40.

diers and praising those of the English and French.[61] The reports criticize the toleration of the church toward the prisoners of war; a priest was arrested for refusing to segregate Poles during the service and praising the Poles as better than Germans.[62] Peasant women's "kindnesses" toward Polish prisoners in the absence of German young men constituted a serious problem which even the death penalty for those detected did not solve, nor the earlier device of having the unlucky girl parade with hair shaved off and a sign saying, "I am a Polish whore".

Evacuations from the cities, first of children then of adults, angered the peasants, as in January 1941 when Hamburg children caused problems in rural Bavaria, singing the song, "We don't want to be Christians because Jesus was a Jewish swine".[63] Rich city women displaying their city wealth and city laziness was another object of peasant discontent.

The failure of the universally expected attack on England to take place brought the decline of morale again; by the spring of 1941 "fantastic rumors" of an attack on Russia were abroad; the author regretted that "the source of these malicious rumors could not be found."[64] Better strategists than Hitler, the people warned him through these reports that the vital matter was to defeat Britain before U.S. help could be important, that therefore war with Russia was unthinkable.[65] The peasants were also worried about reports that they were to be sent to settle the new lands of the east.[66]

A police report noted that the clergy was planning a massive campaign to regain youth, which was "barely within the limits of the permissible", and that both Protestant and Catholic were equally negative toward the NS.[67] The government's reports abounded with complaints of immorality among young girls with soldiers; yet when a priest urged girls not to appear immediately on the arms of newly arrived soldiers, he was warned by the police. The public did not believe the

[61] Franken, 7.8.40.
[62] Schwaben, 8.8.40.
[63] Munich, 10.2.41.
[64] Schwaben, 8.5.40.
[65] Wuerzburg, 12.5.41.
[66] Munich, 10.5.41.
[67] *Ibid.*

official story of Hess's flight and were quick to note and be saddened by Hitler's phrase "next year we will have even better weapons", which meant the war would continue at least that long.[68] Official reports made increasing reference to a disbelief in the official line; no one seemed to take seriously its version of Russia's having attacked Germany. Passive resistance to the order forbidding Corpus Christi processions showed a greater participation than before; even some factories were stopped. Rural counties participating 85 to 100%. Contrary to the law, church flags were displayed on houses.[69]

During the violence against the crucifix decree, peasant women were often on the march. One case involved 50 women demonstrating in their mayor's yard for the release of their arrested priest. They threatened to stop their work and their food deliveries.[70] Near mob violence after a church service against the NS teacher and the party leader included an "old fighter" and a HJ leader who helped lead the mob. In another town the party leader had his fruit trees and grapevines torn down as a protest.[71] The HJ in another rural county embarrassed party leaders by not appearing as ordered; only seven out of 30 showed up, the rest playing or watching football.

Difficulties with peasants taking the wrong attitude toward POWs fill the reports—e.g., that the public was angry at the hanging of a Pole for having had sex relations with a German woman, who after all was also guilty.[72] The population could not see why the prisoners should be treated as inferiors. One Landrat expressed the belief that the guards must be more energetic in stopping the civilians from throwing food and cigarettes to the POWs.[73]

Optimism for an early peace disappeared during the fall and winter of 1941. The U.S. entry into the war and the bombings added to the gloom. The church went up and the

[68] Munich, 10.6.41.

[69] Franken, 8.7.41, Schwaben, 8.7.41, Wuerzburg, 11.7.41.

[70] Wuerzburg, 13.8.41.

[71] Wuerzburg, 10.9.41.

[72] Munich, 10.11.41.

[73] *Ibid.*

party went down: "One Landrat reported that the churches are ever fuller and the party meetings ever emptier; for the NS dedication of the youth on March 22 almost no one appeared except the designated and dedicated party members, not even the parents."[74] A Landrat reported that nearly all of the youth attended the church, "while they remained distant from the Hitler Youth meetings on the same day."[75]

Peasant resistance was noticeable in the decline of reported animal production, in one area one-fourth less than the previous year. During one check a peasant was discovered to have left unreported 14 swine. When controllers came to check, the peasants were angry that the controllers were not at the front with the peasants' sons.[76]

Through 1942 complaints continued about kindnesses to POWs. Large number of French prisoners ran away, aided by peasants who gave them civilian clothes.[77] The Poles were reported most difficult, talking about the farms they would seize when the Germans were defeated. The trouble was that "the peasants treated them as equals to German workers and simply would not change their ways".[78] Some of the regretted decency toward farm laborers may have been common sense. One county with 45,000 residents, mostly women, had 4,000 foreign workers from 16 nations. For their control were only 14 police, none under the age of 40.[79] One peasant woman had said, "I am the one who is the prisoner".

Contrary to the state policy of making Slavs into second-class humans, the peasants regarded them as better workers than the "Aryan" French, though the Russians had become less eager to work since paid only one-third of their wages; the rest was sequestered by the state. The peasants were unhappy at this because their workers could not buy the necessary clothing and the peasants no longer had extra clothing to give them. A Landrat emphasized that the workers should be given their absolute necessities before they arrived.[80] The

[74] Schwaben, 10.4.42.
[75] Wuerzburg, 9.6.42.
[76] Schwaben, 10.4.42.
[77] Schwaben, 9.5.42.
[78] Schwaben, 8.6.42.
[79] Munich, 9.2.42.
[80] Schwaben, 11.8.42.

authorities suggested occasionally the permission to "can" foreign workers who caused problems, or to send the Poles to north Germany as the south German Catholics were too easygoing. One peasant couple was arrested for letting prisoners call them "father and mother" and having their pictures taken with them.[81]

A much expanded skepticism and cynicism about the war is reported in 1943, as was increased resistance particularly in the farm areas to Waffen SS recruitment. The parents were strongly opposed to their sons volunteering.[82] The story of the Katyn massacres, blamed by Goebbels on the Russians, increased fears. Rumors of what the Germans were doing to the Jews and the Russians led to worry that the Germans could suffer similarly in defeat.[83] A rural Landrat thought it significant that there had been a massive revival of Christian "Greet God" greeting and that Heil Hitler had become a "rarity".[84] Christianity, with a stronger grip on reality than the NS, had won back whatever peasants had been tempted by economic prosperity and military victory.

The villages were too homogeneous, too suspicious of any outside world, too loyal to its faith to accept an alien conformism.

[81] Regensburg, 10.2.43.
[82] Regensburg, 10.3.43.
[83] Schwaben, 10.10.42 and 10.5.43.
[84] Schwaben, 10.6.43.

9 A STATEMENT OF CONCLUSION

ANY historian who returns from the past and claims to have discovered all of its secrets should be immediately suspected of not telling the truth, or all of it. Any semicertainty about "what happened" must perforce refer to a very small part of the past—what A wrote or said to B at Moment X. Even these simplicities can be challenged. More importantly, such simple repetitions of who said what constitutes but one facet of what happened, even to A and B, not to mention the countless others. Although history emphasizes who *said* what (what can be documented), the past is also who *did* what. With Rankean documentary history this is often ignored.

With so much controversy about Adolf Hitler, the figure on center stage on whom so much light has been played from all sides for 40 years, there should be real skepticism about anyone's being certain what the millions of persons in his historical shadow thought, said, or did, either the relative few who shared to some extent in his power over others, or the tens of millions whose major goal was simply to retain some power over their own lives. Even those who lived in 1933-45 Germany could not know "what happened" except to themselves, because nearly everyone was forced to lie, more than most men must lie, and the public domain of the news was at its seldom best, a half-truth.

The description in this book of what happened to these specific individuals in these specific times and places is as true a description as I could create. Yet like any other description of past or present it is only a partial view of the truth, to complement other partial views. These are but a few of the many realities. Of greater significance and less certainty would be any conclusions to be drawn from the described episodes, as well as from many others omitted. What does the sound and fury of these sections of NS society signify?

The endless human pushing and pulling for reasons of endless human pettiness and principle would evidence, at least, the omnipresence of "the human factor". There is no robot to be found in these pages, but a variety of humans, each much more complex in action and motivation than a historical account bound by some rules of evidence could hope to recapture. Perhaps only novels, free to invent incidents, words, and thoughts, can recapture the individual reality. The novelist's approach is particularly attractive for the NS world where the best known reality made all fiction seem pale by comparison. Yet this recounting of the relatively normal, local, individual and group life which also existed under Hitler should provide a checkpoint.

The abnormal worlds of the concentration camps were semi-robotical. Yet even they developed remarkable internal power relationships, with the stronger prisoners creating a brutal aristocracy. Perhaps thousands of near-robots existed in the extermination camps. Perhaps a different "breed" existed there; the SS usually absorbed and indoctrinated men inclined to be brutish or fanatical from communities, often glad to be rid of them. Yet it is quite possible that normal people, even normal non-Germans who found themselves after years of hate-propaganda in such an SS society, would have behaved according to similar principles—conform where absolutely necessary, stay out of trouble where possible, and leave the dirty work to someone else.

The difference in the normal bureaucratic machinery that operated the traditional society and that which operated the concentration camp was partly due to the differences in the humans who somehow found their way into each situation. (Less sensitive persons were more likely to join the SS.) Yet some of the difference resulted from the enormous pressure of environment. People adapt to environment. If a man lives among murderers, he comes to accept the fact of killing and some men under social pressure became killers, much as those in a normal environment would be under pressure to peaceful behavior.

Perhaps most importantly, this evidence should suggest the compartmentalization of modern life, not only within the mind of each fragmented individual, but among thousands of groups. This fragmentation was furthered by the prevention of mass media communication. People were deliberately kept from contact with others and with reality. The world of the civil administrator remained fairly normal, almost traditional, at the same time another kind of world, as at Auschwitz, existed almost side by side, but nearly without contact between the two.

The worst element is that an individual, well-adjusted in one of the worlds, could be ordered to the other and adjust there as well. As suggested in the Weiss play, *The Investigation*, killers and killed were simply performing their assigned roles.

Diversion by Hitler

To begin to understand the origins of the horror one can return to the questions posed in the introduction, first to what extent was Hitler's total power limited by Hitler himself? The image of Hitler projected on the NS propaganda screen obviously was of a man of superhuman determination for good. With the evil that followed, one naturally assumes that he was a man of superhuman determination for evil. The devil-theory requires that he has to be a perfect devil; but what is perfection?

Hitler was purposefully kept on the fringe of this study, to compensate for the many other studies in which he attracts the spotlight and the rest of the world is kept in the shadows. This does not mean that further study of his personality is not one key to understanding the history of his times. Nor does this shift in emphasis deny Hitler's central role; it merely reminds us of what Hitler told Rauschning: he did not operate in a vacuum; there were millions of others involved. One reality cannot be understood without the other.

The bits of evidence accumulated strongly suggest that

Hitler was never as sure of himself and his position as both his enemies and friends thought. He was a man playing in a game of chance, a German roulette, that most men would not join if they could and in which the stakes shook even Hitler. Particularly his early days in power, until the Roehm murder and the death of Hindenburg, give evidence of real fears of opposition and then real surprise that the opposition had melted away. This was not unlike his later surprise when his foreign opposition melted away at Munich. Like most common men, he overestimated the ability of his "superiors". When he himself was the "superior", he avoided meetings with subordinates who might question a decision, or he flooded them with monologue to prevent their raising any objection. This is a sign of weakness, not strength.

Hitler could on occasion be decisive, as he wished to appear to the world in an exaggerated stance of manly decision in newsreels and radio speeches. His fits of screaming rage were genuinely frightening; even Himmler feared execution until the very end. But the emotional rage could be followed by another emotional fit, one more ambivalent, "forgiving" people he knew or people he needed. What is striking is the rarity of finding a clear decision by Hitler, or of finding him involved in the actions of his government at all. He was shielded by bureaucrats like Lammers who ascended to Mount Sinai and returned with 10 pious commandments. What Hitler actually did in internal administration is hard to discern, although he set, or agreed to, the broad lines of policy—ending unemployment; rearmament; and some form of persecution of the Jews. Otherwise, he concerned himself, so far as possible, with what interested him: art and war. Much of the rest of internal policy, like Himmler's police state, seems to have arisen largely from Himmler's or some other subordinate's ambitions which Hitler accepted.

Hitler is found at the end of a long argument among these subordinates, after what would appear an unnecessary delay, finally deciding, or more surprising, *not* deciding in disputes crying for some judgment. The suspicion is strong that Hitler avoided the really difficult decisions and acted only when forced to and then not from a long-considered specific plan, but from simple prejudices and the inspiration of the moment. Possibly he was overrun by circumstance. Precise plans, as against romantic dreams, may have been the concern of his more methodical subordinates, and possibly of more inventive historians who "discovered" them.

This view of Hitler—the man who does not decide—would help explain the eternal confusion of the men working for him, a literal anthill of aspiring and fearing people trying to please the "great one" or escape his wrath or to avoid notice altogether, and never quite sure how—i.e., to know what he wanted them to do after they had said Heil Hitler. The bloody battles which never ceased among the powerful could have been minimized by a forceful commander, but Hitler rarely tried.

Perhaps it was a Hapsburg-like divide and conquer, to keep the wolves at his heels quarreling among themselves. Perhaps it was, as he stated, the survival of the fittest. By not deciding, Hitler would let "nature" decide; the strongest would win and Hitler would recognize the superiority of the survivor. But real strength was being able to acquire, or pretend to, Hitler's support. The power process was circular. Hitler supported people who had "succeeded" precisely because he had supported them. Perhaps Hitler was afraid of gaining enemies among those close to him; for that reason he would scold but rarely punish. But he seemed sentimental as well as ruthless. He carried many an incompetent old comrade with him long after a pragmatic chief would have dismissed him. So both the fit and the unfit survived.

Not only can one wonder about Hitler's tactics in dealing with his subordinates, but one can wonder what he really wanted, other than personal power, German power, and an end to a supposed Jewish power in Germany. One cannot merely quote his writings or speeches, which are full of contradictions (e.g., peace and the recovery of Germany's frontiers). The listener could hear what he preferred to believe. Some of Hitler's followers are still convinced, despite massive evidence to the contrary, that Hitler really wanted peace. What of his policy toward the Catholic and Protestant churches? Many still believe it was not Hitler but the evil Bormann who conspired against Christianity. Hitler can be quoted to prove nearly anything.

A man's motivation is the natural stuff for centuries of debate about "the great men". In this book I must defer a decision about Hitler's precise motivation and leave the matter open for further research. Suffice it to say here, his contemporaries did not know what he wanted in most of the decisions they made, nor exactly what tactics he wanted them to use to attain whatever was desired. Battles were therefore all battles of principle. Each leader had his own, each leader said that these were Hitler's principles, and each leader was possibly correct. Hitler was surrounded by a maze of contradictions, as were his followers. For all of the supposed simplicity of the party line, recited in flowing and oh-so-trite phrases ad nauseam in the propaganda, when it had to be applied to the daily decisions that make up political life, it evaporated. (Patriotism, however emotionally satisfying, is irrelevant to most human problems.) The residue was a romantic, albeit to the young, compelling, image of The Fighter, but fighting whom and for what? The war gave an answer, but the war itself was an immense stupidity.

Diversion by the Party

The image of the NS party is that of fanatic multitudes with but one will—to serve Hitler to their last breath. Unquestionably some of these party men believed in Hitler almost as a god, but it is a long step between belief and action. Even the undoubted Christian God could rarely get His followers to do His will. Hitler did scarcely better. He had his Gestapo—assuming they would follow his commands; otherwise, other secret police could presumably arrest the first secret police since they were bitter rivals. But the Gestapo was rarely used against anyone of status, the party powerful, or any of the powerful of state, army, or industry, although Hitler had few illusions that these men were really committed to him.

The Limits of Hitler's Power

The party powerful were loyal, but they were also ambitious men; otherwise they would not have been the fighters in the 1920s, when there was real opposition to be conquered. They were habitual malcontents, and the habit had a hard time dying. Frantic fighting persisted within party ranks and deluged party courts with denunciations. The oldest and highest of the party were misfits in Weimar Germany; they remained misfits in the Germany they created. The greatest of the misfits were the local satraps, the Gauleiter. None of them would have permitted himself the thought that he was disloyal to Hitler. Disloyalty, i.e. righteous resistance, was always toward "those other people" about Hitler "who had misled him" and whom the Gauleiter must sweep aside. This is the key myth of the absolutist society—the father figure at the top is good, but he is surrounded by evil advisers who keep him from the truth and from the people. His dependence on intermediaries means that the dictator can be honestly resisted by the loyal because they have loyalty to only one man.

In their loyalty to Hitler and his principles, the Gauleiter openly resisted his government, continuously, and, toward the end, so successfully that the government of Berlin was turned over to them. At least that was what Hitler ordered done (like most of his orders, this one was partially obeyed). The local leaders were a rebellious lot, albeit always for Hitler, they said. With rare exceptions, they were left in their jobs no matter what they did or failed to do. Hitler rarely bucked or offended them. They had little really to fear, except that he would ignore their desires as they ignored the desires of his administrators.

Not only the Gauleiter but the top Reich leaders were less than robots. Assuming for the moment that Hess's flight to England was an insane disobedience, it is remarkable that the deputy to Hitler, the symbol of unthinking loyalty, disobeyed him to counter a major foreign policy and did so publicly. His successor, Bormann, became the most hated man in Germany, pursuing his personal goal of power and cutting off the party faithful as much as possible from the Fuehrer.

Under Bormann the party became much less the beerhall crowd going wild during an emotional Hitler speech than the lifeless bureaucracy they abhorred. Hitler had disappeared, like his known enemies, behind barbed wire, locked away even from the party which became primarily the machine of personal advancement, as operated by Bormann.

The party, if ever united, became permanently divided in 1933. Those on the inside were largely for a cessation of "revolution". These few select ones were given the top jobs; the rest were left largely without reward. Until Roehm's fall in 1934 the insiders were afraid that the outsiders would drive the sinners out of the temple. The government was not thrown open to the party, as such, but to the favored few who, as usual, became loyal to the government that busied and paid them and not to the party, which did neither. The wealth of the country remained as remote as before for most party members, as much a monopoly of the old rich—excluding, of course, the scapegoat Jews. Any internal radicalism, except against Jews and leftist enemies, was squelched. The revolution ignored its children; it was the price of conservative support.

The new-style party man crept in, more educated, more middle class, not the fighter but the schemer, not the person with dreams of social change but dreams of personal advance for which party membership was useful. These men were rightly suspect to the "old fighters"; they claimed in 1945 half-truthfully that they had never "believed", but had been compelled "to go along". Whether old *or* new, the party man's policy diversion was everywhere subtle and petty, but it was everywhere.

Diversion by the State

This was my original research problem—the original and incorrect assumption that Hitler and the party presented one united will to which the state and/or the army, as a part of it, would be the factor of diversion. The history of the army's lack of resistance, its planned resistance and slaughtered resistance, is well known. It was the kind of opposition traditional history would expect: disagreement, a resort to weapons from which the victor survived. July 20, 1944 was only the visible, i.e. violent, part of the iceberg of resistance to the party within the armed forces of a more bureaucratic kind; the best example was the bureaucratic head of Counter Intelligence, Admiral Canaris. Although military resistance was deliberately left out of this study, it should be noted in answer to those who sniff at the failure of the plotters that the German army did more as resistance than any army in any comparable state organized on modern lines. They did it in a time of war; it was treasonable; it opened the country to hate-filled enemies, which made open disloyalty a most difficult decision.

There may appear in these pages to be the constant contradiction of the assertion that resistance is impossible and the constant recitation of a type of resistance. This paradox arises from the broad meaning of the word—e.g. someone who expressed doubt about victory in 1944 was resisting, in fact, sufficiently so to be executed as an enemy of the state.

The apex of effective resistance is the seizure of the state. In Germany this failed. Next is the diversion of a major policy: preventing war in 1939 or preventing the slaughter of the Jews—this, too, failed. Less difficult was the diversion of policy, such as the centralizing policy or the anti-Christian policy; this largely succeeded, because it operated as "loyal opposition". The central thesis is that *open* resistance to the state is impracticable to most people most of the time. The resistance to the seizure of crosses in villages was the closest to open resistance, but it was selective resistance to an action that was not clearly state policy. Neither Hitler nor the "law" had dictated the seizure of crosses. This selective resistance was more practicable: group values had been attacked and the village group was united. It occurred also in time of war when Hitler wanted unity, and among the isolated peasants whom the government then had to conciliate.

The civil servant, although unarmed, had a special opportunity to "resist" the dictator's policy in a semi-practicable manner in such a society—but only if he stayed in office.

One could leave the country or leave government service and thereby remain "pure"; but one would also remain powerless. One could stay to fight, but there were many risks.

This staying behind to fight from within was a motive of some of the civil servants. Yet other than local village mayors who were not typical Beamten, only a small percentage of Beamten collaborated simply in order to resist. This was the logical way to oppose Hitler, but relatively few men then, in Germany, and probably relatively few men in any society, felt strongly enough about policy to fight against their society from within.

Many of those who remained within the state had ambivalent feelings. They simultaneously approved and disapproved different policies, the balance shifting with circumstance, but they did make some effort to modify any irrational orders they disapproved. It was a disappointment not to find more Beamten with the will and intelligence to effectively resist. Yet there is a human multi-causality for their apparent inhumanity to man: Hitler had assumed power legally, or almost so. He was recognized by important Germans like Hindenburg. Hitler was recognized by foreign states; even the Pope at first chose to "deal" with him. Hitler did plan good deeds as well as bad; he ended unemployment, or, as any German man in the street would think first, "Hitler built the Autobahn".

Most patriotic Germans agreed with Hitler's original foreign policy, especially reversing the Treaty of Versailles. No one likes to be defeated; no one likes to lose territory and honor. The war of 1914-18 was a long, miserable, senseless, incredibly costly war for Germany. The country in 1933 was still sick from the frustrations of that war. Opposing the accepted national aspirations as Hitler stated them would be near treason; the few real resistance fighters hesitate even now to suggest that they really did something to bring the Nazi defeat, because this seems to most also the German defeat. The horrible dilemma was: to oppose Hitler was a kind of betrayal of one's country.

That few directly disobeyed orders from superiors resulted

from a human cowardice, but this should also be seen in the context of only a few officials receiving orders that involved moral qualms. The great bulk of the officials did what they had done before—carried the mail, drove a streetcar, collected the taxes. Few, as a part of their duties, had the opportunity to make a moral decision to resist. During the war, so much of daily life was involved with the state—rationing, foreign laborers, the truth about the war—that moral decisions were greatly expanded and disobedience multiplied. Some drove trains that serviced Auschwitz; but they were only doing "their job". In a highly specialized world, killing is a specialty of the few.

Further to be noted was the tradition of the German civil service which was trained in loyalty to the state, even a state one did not believe in. For that reason, the bureaucracy, although more loyal to the Kaiser, served Weimar democracy. There was some disloyalty to Weimar, but less than that to Hitler. Ordinarily one would have to accept this desirability of civil servant neutrality, but in the case of the NS the result of normal wartime loyalty went so far that neutrality of the civil service becomes absurd in retrospect. No one could have foreseen the indirect results of their passivity. One protected one's own small world, but this no longer sufficed. The fragmentation of power meant that elsewhere, at Dachau and later Auschwitz, the most horrible crimes were being committed by other parts of the machine.

Despite the caution of its members, the over-all impact of the state inside Germany was to restrain and modify the wishes of Hitler and the party. They were successful in 1933-34 in saving the state from the incursion of the SA, who doubtless would have preferred to replace state and army with SA men as the true carriers of "the revolution". The sheer survival of the state was an important victory for the conservatives, with whom the Beamten were nearly synonymous. The party simply did not have enough able men to dislodge the conservatives from the state or to break Hitler's dependence on them. Instead, it forced many Beamten to join the party or took advantage of their opportunism when they asked to join. The state, whether run by old or new party members, was committed to slower and more rational procedures. Where rapid folly was decreed, the command and power went to the SS.

First and foremost, the bureaucracy preserved itself and almost all of its members, contrary to the wishes of the radicals. Relatively little was changed in the procedures for selection, retention, or dismissal of civil servants. Since almost no leftists were in the state's service, the exceptions to the ability of the bureaucrat to save his own were the Jews. Even there, the Beamten law was only partially brushed aside in dismissing the small number of Jews; they received their pensions until 1939.

Although the party and Hitler protested the habits of the bureaucrats—that they were impolite and brusque with citizens, overly slowed down by legalism, "red tape", and precedent—relatively little was changed. There was much talk of great reforms, even when forbidden, but bureaucracy got worse, not better. The descriptions by Bormann and Hitler of the state machine after 10 years of NS rule show their enormous frustration with the balky bureaucrat.

An amazing fact is that the war brought double or triple the amount of work, accomplished by many fewer bureaucrats, including many untrained women brought in as replacements. One cannot escape the conclusion, from this as well as postwar observation of the Beamten, that the German bureaucracy, while highly trained in law, intelligent and persistent, was not efficient. Hours remained fairly comfortable; the pace was leisurely; procedures were slow. Reflecting, perhaps, its aristocratic origins, an aristocrat nonchalance about work carried over into the officialdom, it remained a privileged class based on education.

The bureaucrat's major weapon of defense was the "mystery" of his work—the more mystery, the more authority. He obviously required many years of specialized study in the complexities of law and a doctor's degree to accomplish it. One marvels at high school dropout Hitler who ran the entire show; and one should not overlook the fact that the party versus state struggle had elements of a democratic (popular) effort against the aristocrat. The more technical the operation, the more secure the official. Army bureaucrats dealt constantly with military secrets, e.g. the amount of soap or beans sent here or there, and one dared not divulge these secrets even to the party. The Finance Ministry, a good example, with its endless stream of figures and calculations, baffled the party member and absorbed the rare party man who tried to enter its world.

Technical ministries easily built protective walls about themselves. Those ministries which dealt in social matters, those about which any citizen can form an opinion, had more difficulty hiding. Suffering the most was the school Beamter, since he worked in public with some students and some parents listening for a slip from the simple party line. Justice was also simple and public. Judges tried to avoid the limelight; luckily most of their cases were nonpolitical, but the few that interested the party attracted a dangerous publicity and even a Hitler intervention in order to pervert justice. The judges and the teachers, watched from above and below, were the officials most frequently guilty of a "cowardly" conformity.

A part of the Nazi ideology assisted the bureaucrat trying to avoid publicity; the Fuehrer principle meant that one should obey one's superior, i.e. bureaucrat, and not the party. Hitler reinforced this by ordering that everyone mind his own business, that no official tell any more about his work than absolutely necessary. The official could hide behind this shield of official secrecy and run his own show if he had brains and courage.

The success of the bureaucracy had reverse effects on the party, in furthering its own bureaucratization until it became practically a copy of the state it paralleled. Being this shadow state was not enough; therefore, the second NS reaction to the bureaucracy was the creation of a third competing "state", the SS. The SS bureaucracy, highly indoctrinated and somewhat carefully selected, became the key police power. It was not loyal to the competing party organization, as such, although its leader, Himmler, pursued at least one party objective—the end of Jews in Germany. In a dialectic process in reverse, it combined bureaucratic impersonality with party fanaticism.

Should one accept as valid the foregoing picture of the NS state as one of constant confusion and conflict, one could logically wonder why such a state crushed every attempt at revolt and submerged most of Europe until a world coalition of power finally destroyed it. Why did not so much inefficiency temper the absolutism more seriously?

One explanation is the impotence of the individual before any modern state and the difficulty of combination into any secret organization to match the power of any official organization. Organization equals power. Even poor organization has more power than no organization. Secret police maintain a vacuum. Organization also requires motivation. Patriotism is the strongest motivation and that was Hitler's refuge.

One might also suggest that government, with the possible exception of a communist state at the peak of its idealism, carefully selects the areas on which it can effectively focus its power. There are the commanding heights—the police, the press, the army. By maintaining a control of some sort over these high places, a state survives. It merely prevents a combination against itself. Survival is not so difficult to ruthless men.

The massing of armies to attack other states is more of a challenge. Yet in fragmented Europe, like fragmented modern society, a combination against Hitler was not achieved. Hitler attacked the weak, one by one. Only the victory over France occurred against a comparable foe, but one obviously divided and undetermined. He did not defeat the smaller but united England.

War demands genuine sacrifices from the population, which should create resistance, but in time of war the phenomenon of nationalism provides the power. Patriotism provides men for the army, while tax money provides men for the factories. States survived long before there was much nationalism or money, probably for the reason that inertia keeps a state going in almost every case; defeat in war is one of the few openings for change. People otherwise prefer to avoid contact with government; contact means trouble. They mind their own business and hope the government will do the same.

Hitler's power indicates that governments derive their powers neither from the active consent of the governed nor from the skill and unity of the governors. Effective government may not be the logical process suitable to textbook explanation. It may have been precisely Hitler's administrative irrationality, the proliferation of machineries, the party-state relationship, that increased the manipulative powers of Hitler. The fatal assumption of the Beamten may have been that government, to be powerful, must be rational. Some irrationality may help. (The irrationality of the defeated Germans has obscured the irrationality of the victors.)

The Varied Motivation of Diversion

Ideological

Ideology played a surprising role. The most effective diversion of policy came from those whose ideology seemed closest to National Socialism. The few democrats and many socialists were largely recognizable by their previous activity, and were eliminated from positions of authority. Persons with the opportunity to influence policy were perforce those best described as "national", i.e. middle class, with evident patriotism and medals to prove it. The 1933 coalition of the Right included these non-NS; contrary to wishes of the radical party, these bourgeoisie stuck their noses under the tent for good. If it could be demonstrated that one had not been politically active for a Weimar party, it was not difficult to simulate a National Socialist stance and share in the spoils of power.

Among the middle class patriots were relatively few who had strong convictions for democracy, for the wisdom of the masses. From their point of view, the masses had been unwise enough to vote Hitler into power. The masses, in turn, could accuse the nationalists with having provided the extra support in 1933 to make a majority coalition. A "liberal" philosophy was more important to the middle class—their rights as individuals, Locke's "life, liberty, and property". The apparent intrusions on middle class life were not truly totalitarian. In particular, their property was respected. Life for most people continued much as it had before 1939. Tyranny, I think, is more easily ignored than Americans suppose.

Even in a mature democracy like the United States, only a tiny minority participate politically. In a representative democracy, many merely cheer or boo; most merely complain privately. The minority's opportunity "to participate" in Germany was hardly missed.

NS restraint primarily meant censorship, which bothered primarily the relatively few writers. The sports page remained. The selective consumer could buy foreign newspapers, the sale of which markedly increased because NS papers were dull. More Germans listened to foreign broadcasts, even when forbidden, than ever have in the U.S. Most men were able to avoid the time-wasting meetings and parades.

Otherwise, the state, until the war, made few demands on adults, except for public silence. Privately one could tell jokes and complain. Children were more exposed to society's demands, but this is true wherever there is a compulsory education. Hitler deliberately avoided asking too much. The postwar evidence of horrible excesses of the NS outside Germany came as a double surprise to many Germans who had observed the compromises Hitler found necessary with them.

With others kept silent, the conservatives were the significant competitors. With an emphasis on the authoritarian state, as they visualized the Hohenzollern, some saw in Hitler the savior of Germanic law and order. It was this group, strong in the civil service and in army, that gave a near-voluntary and often enthusiastic service to Hitler, particularly during the early years. It was also this group that became disillusioned, some at first because of the SA violence.

So Roehm was destroyed to appease them. Yet disorder, Dachau, and disillusion continued. Unreason and the extreme demands of the new order disillusioned many "National" allies. It was this group of men—Schacht, Popitz, and Goerdeler in the civil service; Beck, Canaris, and Stauffenberg in the military, who became the most effective divertors of the NS state.

That they were allies meant conservatives occupied important positions, which they could usually keep undisturbed if they made the formal obeisance of joining the party, a very simple step. Hitler denounced them, but he kept them. This conservative opposition could be considered an antidemocratic opposition, inasmuch as they wished the impartial authority of the law to be reasserted to curb the irrational popular will of the NS masses. Yet it could also be considered a liberal opposition, since it wanted the law to protect the individual against lawless NS behavior.

Diversion of policy for reasons of humanitarian feelings doubtless occurred despite the immense organized inhumanity of the SS. Himmler complained that every German, even every Nazi, had a friend who was a "good Jew" and who was obviously innocent. If one believed them all, he thought, no Jew could be touched. Humane feelings did not suffice because of the important distinction in the feeling leaders and followers had for persons they knew personally and the general feelinglessness for persons unknown. After 1938 the worst inhumanity to the Jews and to foreigners was shifted out of the country, as far from public knowledge as possible.

Important also was the difference between private and public action. One had to do good in secret. A mayor who publicly banned Jewish doctors from city service could also privately save the life of a Jewish friend and thereby risk his own.

The pressure of massive propaganda—which separated the Jews into "something different", aided by the Jewish tradition of being different, plus the fear of being personally attacked if one expressed sympathy for the Jews—gradually wore down humane feelings. Fear broke down communication. Yet as late as the night of November 9, 1938, there was widespread sympathy for Jews, officially reported and regretted. It is significant that this is the last anti-Jewish violence attempted or permitted within German communities. Formerly pogroms occurred publicly. After 1938 violence occurred secretly. When the Jews were pushed "out of sight" and then "out of town", they drifted "out of mind".

During the war the urge for self-survival and the constant death at home and abroad wore down further the ability to feel for anyone. In a mass society, where human contact is fragile at best, with a mass *noncommunication* maintained by the state, war is a very effective dehumanizer. One is not really aware of the mass killing, whether done by bombs or gas chambers; anyway, "enemies" must be killed. Therefore, there was the paradox of an apparently normal society existing side by side with an Auschwitz.

The Diversion from Egoism

Selfishness by far outweighed in importance the policy diversion derived from principle, which should not be surprising. Self-survival, not only physically but psychologically and socially, has to be the individual's normal concern. With the exception of the Jews, the only definite group from whose banishment the party could not be dissuaded, most individuals were able to save themselves and some of their position. Some leftist leaders and religious leaders were sent to concentration camps, as warnings to the rest, the terror implicit in the entire regime; yet workers and businessmen, other than publishers of newspapers, were left remarkably undisturbed. The promises of reform, e.g. the destruction of the department stores to save the small businessman, were in practice ignored, a fact that embittered the party idealist.

Although the ideal was NS sacrifice of the person to the state, among the powerful, personal ambition flourished more than before. Idealism for self-sacrifice existed, particularly among the innocent young, but the conduct of party and nonparty alike represents a blossoming of egoism. Those with party credentials could implement personal desires more than the Weimar elite had, because public criticism was practically forbidden and because almost any egoism could be cloaked behind one of the party's confused goals. The one impediment to ego-satisfaction was the counterambition of someone else with party credentials equally good, a kind of constant check and balance which worked within the country, though it failed elsewhere. The result was the division of domination into thousands of little empires of ambitious men, domains that were largely unchecked by law, that had been replaced by Hitler's will, which was largely a mirage.

The intensity of the power struggle should dissuade anyone who would take seriously the picture of cheering colleagues united in self-sacrificing loyalty to the Fuehrer. In every fanatical leader there is also an egotist, which should indicate the limited meaning of loyalty in a dictatorial state. Hitler had to delegate power, and as soon as power was delegated it could be used and resisted selfishly. One need only read the complaints of party leaders to the active party courts against another party "comrade". Not infrequently the supreme NS insult had to be used: "He is worse than a Jew!" A pseudo-peace existed when the jurisdictions were fairly well defined and superiors let inferiors run their own local shows; local leaders, in turn, were generous in their granting of rights to their subordinates, i.e. peace by decentralization. But pressure from above was usually met by counterpressure from below. Eternal vigilance was the price of power.

The party leader typically was a much frustrated person, someone who had been unable to make the desired social advance in face of the traditional tight class structure. This type in America would likely have had the opportunity to become a "self-made man". Doors had been shut in the prewar semi-modern society which postwar violence would try to burst open. Actually most of these doors remained firmly shut. The party man, unless among the minority closest to Hitler, made little advance; he remained socially inferior, thus the drive for more success by the nation.

The unceasing quarreling was encouraged by the lack of effective control from above, with Hitler constantly lamenting but rarely acting to halt the interparty struggles; perhaps he enjoyed the scrambling and scratching on the ladder beneath him. Mounting hate and frustration were then channeled to "enemies," then concentrated on the most helpless enemies, the Jews.

Local loyalties remained strong; linked to such personality conflicts, they blossomed primarily within the party elite. The Gauleiter thought they wanted a strong Reich, i.e. centralism, but they soon discovered that centralism meant an increase in state power and a decline in their own. To save their own domains they persuaded Hitler to reverse the process to demolish the various provinces begun in 1933. The machinery of government, so far as it worked at all in such matters after 1939, was working to destroy itself, ordering the return of its embryonic powers achieved in the first years back to local authorities. Centralism was found not only to offend the powerful but to be inefficient; the central government was unable to maintain effective administration, with the possible exception of the SS police administration. Localist Gauleiter had a keen hate for centralist Himmler.

Local administration experienced relatively little intervention from central authorities; the many orders, streaming down from a multitude of authorities, seemed largely irrelevant or petty, and were ignored. It would seem unlikely that anyone could have obeyed all the orders from so many conflicting agencies, and in such profusion and complexity. The attitude, however, seems to have been to take note of the orders if they helped or if someone was watching, but otherwise do what one wanted. Inspections to check on implementation seem rare. The party was not well enough informed. The secret police were baffled and rebuffed by the complex state administration. Since only bureaucrat superiors could be sure what was intended, the bureaucrat superior had to verify policy implementation. Some did, but most did not, unless it were something fairly obvious, because they were busy, lazy, or indifferent. As officials, they remained largely in their offices and contented themselves with the paper world found there instead of the real world outside.

The Beamten in the national government existed largely outside politics. Their loyalty was to the civil service, where group protection could be outweighed only by self-advancement. They lived in large cities where political life was formal and noninvolving. The civil servants living in the smallest communities, the villages, i.e. the mayors, had a primary loyalty to the village. If the village were united, and the most compelling uniting factors would be economic interest and religion, the mayor was frequently compelled by this group into a strong but camouflaged anti-central policy. Between the anonymity of the Reich civil servant and the total group involvement of the village mayor flourished a wide spectrum of environments. In general, the smaller the community the more the administrator was dependent on local public opinion. Large city administrators were nearly as anonymous as those of the central government and permitted therefore the code of the Beamten, for better or worse.

Small towns seem to have been the ideal place for conflict. It was there that neither the community nor the trained civil service, as such, could exist apart from the other. The town, unlike the village, needed government, and the local government, unlike the central government, needed the support of the group because they literally lived together. It was therefore in the small towns that the extremism or counter-extremism could find expression, extremism in the personal brutality toward the Jews, who could be viciously squeezed out by a combination of state pressure and small town prejudice. There was no big-city anonymity either for the Jew to escape persecution or for the non-anti-Semite to escape the role of passive or active persecutor.

Furthermore, the small town was diverse enough for battles involving people to take place. On the one hand, the individual could not hide in numbers, as in the big city; on the other, he could influence policy implementation by entering into the small-town cliques. If the small town was dominated by radicals, the life of the Jew, or possibly leftist, became a hell (e.g. Guenzenhausen). If it was dominated by religion (Eichstaett), the church clique could resist fairly successfully, as villages could, central restrictions on local religious expression. Much depended on the personalities involved.

The Significance of Loyal Disobedience

Despite the awesome tribute of Auschwitz to unrestrained power over helpless minorities, it is clear that a uniformity of belief and desire did not exist in Nazi Germany, even within the party. Most people can be fooled some of the time but rarely when the lie hurts them or theirs. Most people disagreed in small ways, mostly for self-defense. This disagreement could not find public expression, as possibly it could in the open state, but it could find expression in the private actions of millions of people in millions of daily decisions diverting from the Fuehrer's wish for a total commitment to him.

This is the only resistance that is feasible in terms of self-survival in a totalitarian state. Saying "I am opposed" is too easily brought to the notice of the secret police. Yet by disobeying while saying "I am loyal", one can both survive and still effect the minor changes that make one's own existence and perhaps that of a few others more livable. Persons with authority, within a state or party, by loyally disobeying can bring about a different drift in policy than can the official line. If nothing else, one passively drags one's feet, a reason why Germany was at its slowest in 1939-42 in preparing for total war.

The further assumption here is that an unrealistic state policy, such as total control or world conquest, will eventually encounter reality and be countered. If this reality is denied by the head of state kept remote from the facts by his ideology and advisers, it will be experienced by his subordinates who will have to compromise the leader's fantasy with reality. This awareness of reality will remain within the administrative machinery, and as new men rise to the top who are aware, at least in memory, of the difficulties of policy implementation, they will attempt gradual changes in the name of orthodoxy, which taken altogether and in their entirety, will effect a revolutionary or reactionary change. (From the standpoint of Weberian theory this would be the bureaucratization or rationalization of a society with the passing of the man of charisma.) Such indeed seems to be the process taking place, slowly to be sure, in the post-Stalin communist world, as reality causes a change in ideology, in fact at least, if only later in theory.

This process did not save the world from Hitler's war and the downward swirl of destruction. That this would have happened in Germany, *if* there had not been the war is impossible to say; with Hitler alive war was likely but not certain. There was a "settling down", at least until 1938. Anti-Semitic action was legalized, restrained by law, which seemed preferable at the time. The process that ended in Auschwitz is not a straight line that could be predicted, no matter what hindsight says. Instead, it was a confused on and off, pushed and pulled by personality and circumstance. The final radicalism, begun almost by accident in 1938, at the earliest, was finally decided only in 1941.

This wavering of policy between reason and unreason dulled the general awareness. The pendulum should swing back reasonable men hoped. One expected the conservatives to balance the radicals, as the conservatives had done until 1938. Even Jewish leaders assumed that the wave of hate would ebb as had those of the past, but hate, like war, had become institutionalized. Yet conservative Christians, the majority, were able to save themselves as the majority.

The obvious failure of the conservative forces was that they did not prevent the war and did not save the Jews. The law saved some; hiding saved some. Relatively few tried to do either, too many were affected by the war-born hatred, of which anti-Semitism was the most evil product. Secondly, in the diversion of this policy the organizational drag did not suffice, because an ad hoc counterorganization—the SS—provided its unique service of death. Yet while elements of the state machinery, but more particularly the new SS machinery killed, state machinery elsewhere acted as a brake on killing.

The deep irony of history of this period is that conservatives doubtlessly tried to use the state to brake party excesses, and often succeeded. By so doing they kept the machinery going, often by ignoring the irrational commands. What would have happened had they not kept the state in operation but had by obeying fully, by leaving or by obviously sabotaging, permitted the state-machine's collapse which Hitler's fully implemented policies would likely have produced?

Would this collapse have been preferable? In retrospect, anything would have been preferable to the destruction of Germany and the Jews, not to mention the disaster to the rest of Europe. But who could have imagined the horrors of 1942-45? Not even a Hitler or Himmler had foreseen what they would do.

Granting the opposition sincerity of its motives to save and not to destroy, by their conservatism they saved the machinery which was then used to destroy lives in an incredible fashion. The question was Hamlet-like: to stay or not to stay. By staying, by serving and waiting, they and their world experienced the slings of a truly outrageous fortune.

Bibliography

Note: the Bibliography is arranged by chapter.

CHAPTERS 1 AND 2

Document Collections:

National Archives, Washington, Microfilms of Captured German Documents

Bundesarchiv, Coblenz, particularly the Lammers File, "R 43II" and Finance Ministry, "R 2"

HauptArchiv, former Prussian Secret Archives, Berlin, particularly the Pfundtner "Schriftgut" File 320

Institut fuer Zeitgeschichte, Munich

Berlin Document Center

Trial Records:

International Military Tribunal, Trial of German War Criminals, London, 1947, particularly the record of Wilhelm Frick

Trials of War Criminals before the Nuremberg Military Tribunals, Volumes XII, XIII, XV, trials of Stuckart, Meissner, Lammers, Krosigk, Darré

MEMOIRS:

Dietrich, Dr. Otto. *Zwoelf Jahre mit Hitler*, Munich, 1955

Frank, Dr. Hans. *Im Angesicht des Galgens*, Munich, 1953

Gisevius, Hans. *To the Bitter End*, London, 1948

Hassell, Ulrich von. *The Von Hassell Diaries*, London, 1948

Hitler's Secret Conversations, 1941-44, New York, 1953

The Kersten Memoirs. New York, 1957

Krosigk, Lutz Graf Schwerin von. *Es Geschah in Deutschland*, Tuebingen, 1951.

Meissner, Otto. *Staatsekretaer unter Ebert, Hindenburg, Hitler*, Hamburg, 1950

Weizsaecker, Ernst von. *Memoirs*, Chicago, 1951

Interviews:

Buelow, Prof. Dr. Staatssekretaer Bundes Justizministerium

Fiehler, Reichleiter for Communal Questions

Florian, H. H. former Gauleiter in Duesseldorf

Fauser, Dr. Ministerial Dirigent in Bundes Finanzministerium

Globke, Dr. Hans. Staatssekretaer Bundes Staatskanzlei

von Grolman, General of Police, former adjutant to Frick
Jobst, Dr. Heinz, former assistant to Fiehler, in communal government
Kahlenberg, Dr. Bundesarchiv specialist on Finance Ministry
Lex, Ritter von. President of German Red Cross
Matzerath, Dr. Researcher for Berlin Forschungsstelle fuer Kommunale Politik
Vollert, Ernst. Ministerial Director, Interior Ministry

Monographs:

Aronson, Shlomo. *Heydrich und die Anfaenge des SD und der Gestapo*, diss., Berlin University, 1966
Borch, Herbert von. *Obrigkeit und Widerstand*, Tuebingen, 1954
Bracher, Karl, Wolfgang Sauer, Gerhard Schulz. *Die Nationalsozialistische Machtergreifung*, Cologne, 1960
Bramsted, Ernest K. *Goebbels and National Socialist Propaganda, 1925-1945*, Lansing, 1965
Broszat, Martin. *Nationalsozialistische Polenpolitik*, Stuttgart, 1961
Buchheim, Hans. *S.S. und Polizei im NS Staat*, Duisdorf, 1964
Buchheit, Gert. *Soldatentum und Rebellion*, Rastatt, 1961
Davidson, Eugene. *The Trial of the Germans*, New York, 1966
Dror, Dr. Yehezkel. *Beamtenpolitik of the Third Reich*, Harvard Graduate School of Public Administration, available at the *Institut fuer Zeitgeschichte*
Facius, Friedrich. *Wirtschaft und Staat*, Schriften des Bundesarchivs, Coblenz, 1959
Gisevius, Hans. *Adolf Hitler*, Munich, 1963
Heiber, Helmut. *Adolf Hitler*, Berlin, 1960
———. *Josef Goebbels*, Berlin, 1962
Heiden, Konrad. *A History of National Socialism*, New York, 1935
———. *Der Fuehrer*, Boston, 1944
Hilberg, Raul. *The Destruction of the European Jews*, Chicago, 1961
Hofer, Walter. *Die Diktatur Hitlers*, Konstanz, 1960
Jacob, Herbert. *German Administration Since Bismarck*, New Haven, 1963
Leber, Annelore. *Das Gewissen Entscheidet*, Berlin, 1960
Lewy, Guenter. *The Catholic Church and Nazi Germany*, New York, 1964
Neesse, Gottfried. *Staatsdienst und Staatsschicksal*, Hamburg, 1955

Nyomarkay, Joseph. *Charisma and Factionalism in the Nazi Party*, Minneapolis, 1967

O'Neill, Robert J. *The German Army and the Nazi Party*, London, 1966

Petwaidic, Walter. *Die Autoritaere Anarchie*, Hamburg, 1946

Pollock, James K. *The Government of Greater Germany*, New York, 1940

Rauschning, Hermann. *The Voice of Destruction*, New York, 1940

Schaefer, Wolfgang. *NSDAP, Entwicklung und Struktur*, Hanover, 1957

Schoenbaum, David. *Hitler's Social Revolution*, New York, 1966

Schweitzer, Arthur. *Big Business in the Third Reich*, Bloomington, 1964

Seabury, Paul. *The Wilhelmstrasse*, Berkeley, 1954

Staff, Ilse. *Justiz im Dritten Reich*, Frankfurt, 1964

Stuckart, Wilhelm and Hans Globke. *Kommentare zur der Rassengesetzgebung*, Berlin, 1936

Uhlig, Heinrich. *Die Warenhaeuser im Dritten Reich*, Cologne, 1956

Waite, Robert. *Hitler and Nazi Germany*, New York, 1965

Articles:

Baum, Walter. "Die Reichsreform im Dritten Reich", *Viertelsjahresheft fuer Zeitgeschichte*, 1955, 36-55

Bunin, Frederic. "Bureaucracy and National Socialism", *Merton Reader in Bureaucracy*, Glencoe, 1952

Heiber, Helmut. "Zur Justiz im Dritten Reich, Der Fall Elias", *Vierteljahresheft fuer Zeitgeschichte*, 1955, 275-96

Kielmansegg, Peter Graf. "Die Militaerische Politische Tragweite der Hossbach Besprechung", *Vierteljahresheft fuer Zeitgeschichte*, 1960

Koehl, Robert. "Feudal Aspects of National Socialism", *American Political Science Review*, LIV, December 1960, 921-33

Loesener, Bernard. "Das Reichministerium des Innern und die Judengesetzgebung", *Viertelsjahresheft fuer Zeitgeschichte*, 1961, 264-310

Neufeldt, Hans. "Entstehung und Organisation des Hauptamtes Ordnungspolizei", in *Zur Geschichte der Ordnungpolizei*, Bundesarchiv, 1960

Plum, Gunther. "Staatspolizei und innere Verwaltung", *Vierteljahresheft fuer Zeitgeschichte*, 1965, 191-224

Schramm, Percy. "Adolf Hitler, Anatomie eines Diktators", *Der Spiegel*, 1964

Vialon, Friedrich. "Die Stellung des Finanzministers", *Vierteljahresheft fuer Zeitgeschichte*, 1954

CHAPTER 3

Documents:

BSA *Bayerisches Staats Archiv*: Munich
Bayerisches Innen Ministerium: 71469—74158
Bayerisches Finanz Ministerium: 66814—66950
Sonderablagen, 1451-1891

GSA *Bayerisches Geheim Staatsarchiv*, Munich
Epp Files 6-196
MA 105246—105798
Sitzung des Ministerrats 1933-39
Berichte der Regierung Praesidenten 1933-43

BA Bundesarchiv:
R 43II/Lammers file, particularly "*Bayern*—1311-1321".
R 2 Reich, *Finanz Ministerium*, 10860-10897

CGD Captured German Documents: Alexandria
T 580, Roll 339-340, excellent, chronologically organized Epp File
T 81, Roll 184 and 185
T 175, Roll 467

IZG *Institut fuer Zeitgeschichte*

ASA *Augsburg Stadt Archiv*

Berlin Document Center:
Files on: Dr. Ernst Boepple
Franz Epp
Paul Giesler
Hans Georg Hofmann
Max Koeglmaier
Dr. Ludwig Siebert
Adolf Wagner

Trials:

Dr. Ernst Boepple
Hans Dauser
Max Koeglmaier

Interviews:

Karl Fiehler, Oberbuergermeister, Munich; Chairman Deutsche Gemeinde Tagung

Dr. Hellmuth, Gauleiter Main-Franken
Dr. Benno Martin, Polizei Praesident, Nuremberg
Dr. Josef Mayer, Ministerial Director in Kulturministerium
Robert Scherer, Former cultural advisor to Wagner
Karl Wahl, Gauleiter, Schwaben

Letter:

Dr. Ottmar Kollman

Monographs:

Baumgaertner, Franz. *Bavaria*, Munich, 1963

Donohoe, James. *Hitler's Conservative Opponents in Bavaria, 1930-1945*, Leiden, 1961

Hueber, Heinrich. *Dokumente einer Christlichen Widerstandsbewegung*, Munich, 1948

Mitchell, Allan. *Revolution in Bavaria, 1918-19*, Princeton, 1965

Schwend, Karl. *Bayern Zwischen Monarchie und Diktatur*, Munich, 1954

Volk, Ludwig. *Der Bayerische Episkopat und der Nationalsozialismus, 1930-1934*, Mainz, 1965

Articles:

Gollwitzer, Heinz. "Bayern, 1918-33", *Vierteljahresheft fuer Zeitgeschichte*, 1955, 363-87

Landauer, Carl. "The Bavarian Problem in the Weimar Republic, 1918-1923", *Journal of Modern History*, XVI

Vogelsang, Thilo. "Das Verhaeltnis Bayerns zum Reich in den letzten Monaten der Weimarer Zeit", in *Bayern, Staat und Kirche, Land und Reich*, Munich, n.d.

Watt, D. C. "Die Bayerische Bemuehungen um die Ausweisung Hitlers, 1924", in *Vierteljahresheft fuer Zeitgeschichte*, 1958, 270-80

CHAPTER 4

Documents:

Nuernberg Stadt Archiv:
Geheime Sitzung des Stadtrats Nuernberg
Stadtchronik Nuernberg
Verwaltungsbericht der Stadt Nuernberg
Series DA/S, pp. 7-23

Bayerische Staats Archiv:
Bayerische Innen Ministerium
71719 Unruhe in Ober und Mittelfranken

71885 Nuernberg Polizei Direktion
71958 Nuernberg—Beschwerde gegen Beamten
73708 Anti Juden Demonstration in Guenzenhausen
72066 Nuernberg Polizei
72372 Nuernberg Polizei
Sonderablagen
1451 Personalakt Wilhelm Liebel
1451 Martin und Malsen-Ponickau
1615 Martin to Himmler 1936-38
1617 Martin Schriftwechsel
1730-37 Nuernberg-Akt über J. Streicher
1742-44 Nuernberg-Akt über Karl Holz
1884-91 *Der Stuermer* 1923-41
Bundesarchiv:
R 43/II 575, 575a—Liebel
IMT:
Trial of Julius Streicher, in Vols. v, vii, xviii
Document 1757 PS, Goering Commission, Vol. xxviii, 55-234
CGD:
T 81, Roll 57, Frames 60275ff Aryanization
T 175, Roll 123, Frames 8443ff—Telephone tapping
T 175, Roll 406, 8951ff SD report 1941—to Frame 9036
T 175, Roll 124, 9652-6 Martin-Himmler correspondence 1942
T 81, Roll 57, 0220 Aryanization
IZG:
NG 616—Aryanization
MA 328—Martin-Wolff correspondence 1942
NO 4773—Ohler—Russian PW's to Dachau
Bayerische Staatsarchiv-Nuernberg
Akten-Bezirksamt Weissenburg
A file of *Der Stuermer*

Books:

Stadtrat zu Nuernberg. *Schicksal juedischer Mitbuerger in Nuernberg, 1850-1945*

Daumiller, Oscar. *Gefuehrt im Schatten zweier Kriege*, Munich, 1961

Manuscripts:

Dr. Arndt Müller, "Juden in Nuernberg 1146-1966," Stadtarchiv Nuernberg

Dr. Anton Wegner. "Kurs Martin, Polizei einmal anders," 1946, Stadtarchiv Nuernberg

BDC Personal Files:

Karl Holz, 27.12.95
Willy Liebel, 31.8.97
Hans Lammers, 27.5.79
Dr. Benno Martin
Hans Guenther v. Obernitz, 5.5.95
Wilhelm Stegmann
Julius Streicher
Hans Zimmermann, 18.10.06
Erasmus Malsen-Ponickau, 5.6.95

Spruchkammer—SK:

Dr. Hans Dippold, 21.11.76
Dr. Benno Martin, 7 vols.
Hans Zimmermann

Interviews:

Dr. Heinz, Reg. Direktor in Ansbach, former Landrat Weissenburg
Dr. Hilger, Landrat Schongau, former Landrat Hilpolstein
Dr. Hans Kirsch, Reg. Direktor, Ansbach
Dr. Konrad Fries, Beamter Police Presidium and City
Dr. Rudolf Koetter, Editor of Fraenkische Kurier
Fritz Nadler, Nuremberg journalist
Dr. Hans Rollwagen, SPD mayor Bayreuth, former Nuremberg city council and police presidium
Dr. Schregele, former Reg. President, Ansbach
Dr. Schultheiss, Stadtarchivist, Nuremberg
Georg Wurdak, Police Major, journalist
Dr. Benno Martin, former Police President
Dr. Alexander Mayer, Nuremberg Industrialist

Letters:

Franz Haas, Buergermeister Nuremberg, 26.2.65
Dr. Benno Martin, 31.1.65

CHAPTER 5

Documents:

Personnel File, Dr. Walter Krauss, Stadt Archiv
Sitzungsprotokolle des Stadtrats, Stadt Archiv, Akten 113-121

Gestapo *Berichte*, CGD, T 81, Roll 184
Spruchkammer Akten—SK
Dr. Edgar Emmert
Gregor H.
Dr. Walter Krauss
Josef Kleber
Josef Maier
Hans Roesch
Berlin Document Center, files for:
Dr. Josef Baeuml
Dr. Max Foerderreuther
Dr. Edgar Emmert
Dr. Walter Krauss
Berichte der Regierungs Praesidenten, Franken, Munich
BSA, *Akten Innen Ministerium*, Munich

Newspapers:
Eichstaetter Volkszeitung
Eichstaetter Anzeiger

Journals:
Der Gerade Weg, Katholische Studenten, Munich, 1925-1932

Interviews:
Baeuml, Dr. Josef, *Landrat*, 1938-1943
Eger, Josef, *Amtmann*, Rathaus. 1933-1939
Emslander, Richard, *Brauereibesitzer*
Halbich, Anton, *Amtmann*, Landesgericht
Hutter, Dr. Hans, Buergermeister
Neubrand, R., *Jugendamt*, Eichstaett
Kraus, Johannes, *Domkapitular*
Dompraelat Kurzinger, Eichstaett bishopric
Kleber, Josef, *Amtmann*, Eichstaett
Maier, Josef, *Stadtkaemmerer*, Eichstaett
Domkapitular Rieder (Rindfleisch), Eichstaett
von Rebay, Reg. Direktor, Ansbach
Spiegl, Anni, Catholic youth leader, Eichstaett
Wittig, Alois, Journalist, *Volkszeitung*

Memoirs:
Kraus, Johannes. *Erinnerung aus meinem Leben*, unpub. manuscript in author's possession, Eichstaett.

Secondary Sources:

Bauch, Andreas. *Im Dienste von Glaube und Leben*, Eichstaett, 1959

Neumayr, Maximilian. *Pater Ingbert Naab*, Munich, 1947.

Steiner, Dr. Johannes. *Propheten Wider das Dritte Reich*, Munich, 1946.

James Donohoe. *Hitler's Conservative Opponents in Bavaria, 1930-1945*, Leiden, 1961.

CHAPTER 6

Bavarian State Archive Documents

Berichte der Regierungs Praesidenten, 1933-1943

Bundesarchiv—Reichkanzlei Documents

R43II/155a Eberle correspondence

RA43II/1243a, Augsburg Theater

Berlin Document Center

Karl Wahl File

Wilhelm Starck File

Matthias Kellner File

City Documents:

Akten der Staedtischen Verwaltungen—Stadtarchiv

Augsburg Stadtratsitzungen—Stadtarchiv

Tagebuch der Aussendienstpolizei, 1919-1945, Augsburg

Captured German Documents:

T 175 Roll 31

T 81 Roll 179

T 580 Roll 347-348

Newspapers:

Die Neue Augsburger Zeitung, 1933-1939

Die Neue National Zeitung, 1933-1939

Der Schwaebische Schulanzeiger, 1933-1940

Trial Records:

Volksgerichtshof Hauptverhandlung (9.10.11), January 1945, gegen Moltke, Gerstenmaier, Sperr, Reisert, Fugger, Delp

Spruchkammerakten—SK:

Aschka, Wilhelm, DAF

Brandl, Josef, Gestapo

Donner, Magda, Frauenschaft

Gold, Hugo, Gestapo
Kellner, Matthias, Kreisleiter
Mayr, Josef, Oberbuergermeister
Sewald, Josef, Editor, *NNZ*
Schneider, Gallus, Kreisleiter
Starck, Wilhelm, Polizeidirektor, a.D.
Utz, Dr. Maximilian, Police director, a.D.
Wahl, Karl, Gauleiter

Interviews:
Aschka, Wilhelm, DAF leader, 1933-1945
Baer, Fritz, Direktor Kriminalpolizei
Baur, Valentin, SPD leader, emigré
Bellot, Dr. Josef, Stadtbibliothekar
Beyschlag, Bernhard, SPD leader, resistance
Bobinger, Dr. Stadtreferent
Brenner, Wilhelm, Beamtenbund
Deffner, August, early SPD leader
Deininger, Dr. Heinz, Stadtarchivist
Drexler, Sylvester, journalist, *Augsburger Allgemeine*
Fueger, Friedrich, Verlagsdirektor, *Augsburger Allgemeine*
Hintermayr, Leo, journalist, *NNZ* and *Augsburger Allgemeine*
Haussner, Dr. Eugen, Vorstand Amtsgericht
Lappler, Max, former KPD leader
Lethmaier, Max, Vorstand Hauptamt, Rathaus
Mayer, Alois, Oberinspektor, Kriminalpolizei
Mueller, Dr. Klaus, Altoberbuergermeister
Nerdinger, Eugen, Resistance, Direktor *Werkkunst Schule*
Neubling, Dr. Eduard, Schulrat
Ott, Dr. Wilhelm, Stadtkaemmerer, 1919-1958
Pochman, Freiherr Fritz, Direktor Industrie und Handelskammer
Poehlman, Dr. H., Richter
Randler, Magdalena, Schuldirektor, a.D.
Reisert, Dr. Franz, Rechtsanwalt, Resistance
Rupin, Baruch, Jewish resident who survived
Schepp, August, Polizeidirektor
Schneider, Gallus, Kreisleiter
Seeman, Wilhelm, Regierungs Oberamtmann a.D.
Sewald, Josef, Editor, *NNZ*, 1933-1945
Seyboth, Gertrud, journalist, *NNZ* and *Augsburger Allgemeine*
Speckner, Georg, journalist, *Augsburger Allgemeine*

Starck, Wilhelm, Polizeidirektor, a.D.
Steinhauser, Dr. Paul, Stadtrat, a.D.
Trautner, Dr. Johann, Richter
Utz, Dr. Maximilian, Polizeidirektor a.D.
Vierback, Albert, Domprobst
Wahl, Karl, Regierungspraesident, a.D.
Westermeyer, Friedrich, Evangelischer Kirchenrat
Wismann, Heinrich, SPD Resistance, Stadtangestellter
Woeger, Franz, SPD, union official

Unpublished manuscript:

Reisert, Dr. Franz. "Die deutsche Justiz unter dem Nationalsozialismus".

Books:

Bezen, Bernhard. *Die Juden in Augsburg*, Augsburg, 1954
Wahl, Karl. *Es ist das deutsche Herz*, Augsburg, 1954
Zorn, Walter. *Augsburg*, Augsburg, 1955.

CHAPTER 7

GSA *Berichte der Regierungs Praesidenten*, Schwaben and Munich, 1933-1943
CGD, T 580, Roll 100—SD reports

Party Files:

The Hack Fall in the Epp File, 119, found in the Geheime Staats Archiv in Munich
Oberste Partei Gericht Bericht on Hans Hack, found in the Berlin Document Center, 2 vols.

BDC:

Hans Hack
Wilhelm Miller
F. X. Schambeck

Spruchkammerakten—SK

Karl Boehm, Friedberg SA Fuehrer
Hans Brehm, SA Reserve Commander
Hans Dollriess, chief official in mayor's office
Georg Haas, Buergermeister Laimering, Kreis Friedberg
Josef Hohenbleicher, Buergermeister Friedberg
Florian Kastl, Buergermeister Derching
Fritz Loew, Stadtrat, DAF Kreisobmann

Wilhelm Miller, Kreisleiter
Franz Xaver Schambeck, former Buergermeister Friedberg

Interviews:

Hans Brehm, former member of city government
Karoline Hefele, Administrative Assistant at Landratsamt, Friedberg, since 1929
J. Hohenbleicher, postwar mayor of Friedberg, legal advisor and second mayor to Schambeck
Fabian Kastl, postwar elected Landrat of Friedberg county, brother of Florian Kastl, Mayor of Derching
Hans Koppold, April 24, 1964, Director Stadtsparkasse, Friedberg
Fritz Loew, Owner of electrical shop, early party member and member of city council throughout
Wilhelm Miller, Kreisleiter 1932-1937
Georg Haas, Buergermeister Laimering

Newspapers:

Neue National Zeitung, Augsburg, 1933-1939
Neue Augsburger Zeitung, Augsburg, 1933-1939
Friedberg, Altbayern in Schwaben, Sonderausgabe der Zeitschrift Bayerland, Munich

CHAPTER 8

GSA *Berichte der Regeirungs Praesidenten*, 1933-1943, Munich
CGD T 175, R 430
Spruchkammer Akten—SK
Johann Huber, Warmisried
Georg Haas, Mayor Laimering, Kreis Friedberg
Florian Kastl, Mayor Derching, Kreis Friedberg
Wilhelm Miller, Kreisleiter, Friedberg

Interviews:

Huber, Johann, Mayor of Warmisried from 1931
Kees, Georg, priest for Warmisried
Rampp, Andreas, former priest for Warmisried
Brehm, Hans, Friedberg Beamter
Hefele, Karoline, Administrative Assistant, Landratsamt, Friedberg
Hohenbleicher, J., Mayor Friedberg
Kastl, Fabian, postwar Landrat Friedberg
Loew, Fritz, Friedberg Councilman
Miller, Wilhelm, Friedberg Kreisleiter

Index

Index